Writing Research Papers
Across the Curriculum

Fifth Edition

Susan M. Hubbuch

Lewis & Clark College

THOMSON
™
WADSWORTH

Australia   Canada   Mexico   Singapore   Spain   United Kingdom   United States

Writing Research Papers Across the Curriculum, Fifth Edition
Susan M. Hubbuch

Publisher: *Michael Rosenberg*
Acquisitions Editor: *Dickson Musslewhite*
Editorial Assistant: *Stephen Marsi*
Editorial Production Manager: *Michael Burggren*
Executive Marketing Manager: *Carrie Brandon*
Associate Marketing Manager: *Joe Piazza*
Permissions Editor: *Kiely Sexton*
Manufacturing Manager: *Marcia Locke*
Compositor: *Thompson Steele, Inc.*
Project Manager: *Thompson Steele, Inc.*
Cover Designer: *Corey, McPherson, Nash*
Printer: *QuebecorWorld Taunton*
Cover Image: *Wassily Kandinsky, "Yellow, Red, Blue", 1925.*
© 2004 Artists Rights Society (ARS), New York/ADAGP, Paris
Photo Credit: CNAC/MNAM/Dist. Réunion des Musées Nationaux/Art Resource, NY

Printed in the United States of America.
3 4 5 6 7 8 9 10 07 08 06

For more information contact Thomson Wadsworth, 25 Thomson Place, Boston, Massachusetts 02210 USA, or you can visit our Internet site at http://www.thomson.com

ISBN: 1-4130-0237-4
(Fifth Edition with InfoTrac® College Edition)

Library of Congress Control Number: 2004105202

Text credits begin on page xiv, which constitutes a continuation of this copyright page.

Contents

SECTION

3

Finding the Evidence
page 43

SECTION

4

Reading Critically and Taking Notes
page 89

SECTION

7

Polishing Your Final Draft
page 194

SECTION

8

Documenting Your Sources: The Basics
page 206

APPENDIX A

The MLA Style
page 256

APPENDIX B

The CMS Notes & Bibliography Style
page 277

APPENDIX C

The APA Style
page 304

APPENDIX D

Scientific Styles: The CMS Author-Date Style and Two Systems in the CSE Style
page 323

APPENDIX E

Interviews

page 362

Sample Student Papers

page 371

Preface

To Students

Since I pictured myself talking directly to you throughout this text as I take you, step by step, through the process of doing a research paper, here I need add only a few words about the way this book is set up.

It is very important for you to begin where I do, with the first two sections, because there I explain what a research paper is and show you how to set up your Researcher's Notebook. After that, it may occasionally be necessary for you to consult parts of this book in a different order from the one in which they are printed. But don't worry. The cross-references and the table of contents should make it very easy for you to find exactly what you need when you need it. As you will discover, the term "research paper" can mean different things to different instructors. Thus, in Sections 2 and 5, I explain three basic types of research papers—reports on studies and experiments, review of the literature papers, and critical papers. Similarly, since instructors in different departments prefer different methods of documenting sources, I include introductions to four styles of documentation standard in academia. But I have tucked this material out of your way in appendixes at the end of the book. Once you know which documentation style you will be using in a specific paper, you can treat the relevant appendix as a quick reference guide, learning how that system and style works, and determining how to document specific types of sources. Be aware, though, that these appendixes are not a substitute for formal style manuals or guides. Becoming comfortable with formal style manuals is, in fact, part of the process of learning how to do research papers, so in Section 8.C, I explain how these manuals are set up. Otherwise, in Section 8, I give you further information about documentation, information that your instructors and librarians may assume that you already have. Take a few minutes to skim through this section, and do your skimming early in the research process, when you are getting ready to start searching for sources. Notice, particularly, Section 8.D., "What You Need to Know About. . . ." Information here could prove particularly helpful in reading citations you gather in your searches, and thus in tracking down these sources.

The most important thing to me is that you feel secure and confident every step of the way and, to give you the confidence you need, I explain each step in the process and give you a variety of strategies to use to accomplish each step. Because my suggestions and strategies come from years of working with students, I know they work, but you may not be totally convinced until you see them work for you. At first you may distrust some of my advice or find some of the strategies awkward. It is difficult to do things in a new way, especially when you are under the pressure of deadlines and grades. And you may not fully experience the benefits of my suggestions until you've used them in several research projects. It is for this reason that I've designed this guide so that you can use it while you are doing a paper for art history and use it again next year when you are doing a paper for economics. Instead of thinking about this book as a text to sell immediately at the end of the semester, I'd suggest you look upon it as a reference book to keep on a shelf with your dictionary and other handbooks.

To Teachers

The initial impetus for this fifth edition came from the continuing advances in the digital revolution, particularly those changes it has brought to the researching aspects of doing research papers. As a consequence, although Section 3 is still titled "Finding the Evidence," little else remains in it from earlier editions. (I did keep the elaborated advice for doing interviews, but it has been moved into Appendix E.) The proliferation of sources in electronic formats has required the refining of forms for citing them appropriately, so my initial plans for this edition also included updating the relevant sections of the appendixes, where I introduce students to standard academic styles of documentation. But when I turned my attention to the back of the book, I realized that this new edition gave me the opportunity to make some further changes here which would strengthen and enhance the main objectives I have always had for this text. So . . . those familiar with the fourth edition will find that the core of *Writing Research Papers*—Sections 1, 2, 4, 5, and 6—is substantially and substantively the same, although I have done a bit of housekeeping, updating where necessary and cleaning out some clutter. In addition, a concerted effort has been made throughout to "lighten up" the appearance of the text in order to make it more visually appealing, and, I trust, easier for students to comprehend and to use. Making the text graphically more user friendly, and the need to catch up with the digital revolution, combined to produce major changes in Sections 3, 7, and 8, and the appendixes.

One of the most obvious changes is my transposition of the contents of Sections 7 and 8. My suggestions for polishing the final draft are now in Section 7. The substance here has not changed, although I have added more detailed advice and strategies for proofreading papers. In contrast, I have greatly expanded my general discussion of documentation, now in Section 8. In my mind, Section 8 is something of a linchpin. On the one hand, it looks back to and complements material I cover in Section 3. On the other, it looks forward to the appendixes, providing a more in-depth introduction to documentation and the particular styles that immediately follow. Before I comment further on these two sections, let me say a few more words about changes I have made in the appendixes.

Very briefly, my objective was to pare down information about specific documentation styles to bare essentials, and to present this information as cleanly and as graphically as possible. What, I asked myself, was the best way to answer the typical question of the research/writer: "How am I supposed to cite____ in the ____ style?" My solution has been to focus on a specific example of the most common types of sources, adding just enough commentary to explain the basics of each element of the citation. If and when this commentary is not sufficient, students are encouraged to turn back to Section 8.D, "What You Need to Know About . . . ." Creating subsection 8.D allowed me to further streamline the appendixes by moving here material that had been scattered through, and often repeated in, the four appendixes. Moreover, subsection 8.D. gave me the perfect place to address issues regarding authors, editors, titles and other aspects of citations that we assume—often erroneously—students already know. I have more to say about Section 8, but, before I do, let me point out a few more features of revised Appendixes A through D.

• Notice that each appendix opens with a brief explanation of the way that style works, reinforced by a graphic illustration.

• One type of source that I have chosen to foreground in this edition I call "Part of a Book." In this section of each appendix I explain and illustrate the appropriate form for a work published in an anthology or collection. My decision to highlight this type of source was prompted by the frequency with which students use such works, and the frequency with which they make mistakes in citing them! The more I used the fourth edition to show students how to cite such sources, the more I came to realize how "buried" this information was.

• In addition to the MLA, the APA, and the two systems of the Chicago style (here termed the CMS notes & bibliography style, and the CMS author-date style), I now cover the two scientific systems laid out in the 6th edition of *Scientific Style and Format: The CBE Manual for Authors, Editors, and Publishers.* Under the assumption that the Council of Biology Educators intends to change its name to the Council of Science Educators, I have used the acronym CSE for this style. The two systems of the CSE along with the CMS author-date style can be found in Appendix D: Scientific Styles.

Finally, I want to emphasize that these appendixes are designed to provide only an introduction to each of these styles, not to give exhaustive coverage. As I make clear in Section 1, *Writing Research Papers* is not intended to be a style manual, nor a guide to bibliographic instruction or information literacy. Which has meant that covering documentation and the research process—the contents of Sections 8 and 3—has always been problematic for me. Ironically, the rapidity with which the digital revolution is advancing has nicely resolved the issue. It seems pointless to go into detail about materials or functions that could be outdated by the time a student reads this text. Moreover, technical and particularized aspects of research are best left to the experts—a faculty member who knows the best resources in his or her discipline or field, and information specialists in the library whose job it is to help library clients use available resources. What we writing teachers can do—and what I have attempted to do in revising Sections 3 and 8—is to provide students with a solid foundation upon which they can build. One aspect of this foundation is basic knowledge and information that will enable them to understand the experts! Take, for example, the citation. The citation connects Sections 8 and 3 inasmuch as it is a central part of the documentation system a writer uses to acknowledge her debts to others; and inasmuch as it is, similarly, the central unit in bibliographic databases that writers use to search for sources in the early stages of a research project. Explaining common patterns in the way we represent information about texts should help students by dispelling some of the "mystery" and confusion that can cause them great consternation as they try to complete research projects.

The other aspect of this foundation that we can provide for students has been central to the aim of *Writing Research Papers* from its inception. It has to do with the mental posture or stance of the student researcher. It is expressed in the trope of the passive sponge versus the active detective. Thus Section 3 begins with three specific ways in which students must actively use their critical thinking faculties in the research process. One of the three aspects of the researcher's stance is being a critical consumer of information. Section 4.B.1 lays out strategies for assessing the quality of books and articles one has in hand. In this edition assessing sources is also covered earlier in the research process in my general commentary on authoritative sources (Section 3.B.2), and the strategies I encourage students to use to evaluate online sites and the material they find in them (Section 3.D).

While "active detective" seems a very apt analogy for the stance of the student engaged in a research project, to me it is an analogy not limited to this type of classroom assignment. To fully reap the fruits of higher education students must be more than passive sponges; they must continually exercise and thus develop their critical thinking faculties. In fact, much of the material in this text—from the advice I offer, to concrete strategies I recommend, to general information I provide—is material I use day in and day out in working with students on all sorts of written assignments for courses across the curriculum. Thus, in spite of the narrower focus implied by the title, I believe that *Writing Research Papers* gives students insights into the demands of academic writing in general and provides them with practical means for composing such papers. For these reasons I encourage teachers to put the emphasis on Sections 1, 2, 4, 5, 6, and 7, and to treat particulars of "research" as a necessary extension of the critical thinker's need to consider the available evidence before reaching conclusions.

Acknowledgments

So many people have contributed to the development of *Writing Research Papers* over the years that it is no longer possible to acknowledge them all by name. Nevertheless, I remain in their debt for the generosity and willingness with which they have given me the benefit of their expertise, their suggestions and criticism, and, above all, their encouragement and support. I owe the most to the students with whom I have worked in the Writing Center at Lewis & Clark. It is they who have given me insights into the various challenges and barriers individuals encounter in entering the world of academic research, and they who have, in turn, challenged me to find ways to make the research/writing process more intelligible. My efforts to clarify this process in the current edition were substantially aided by individuals who deserve special recognition. I owe a great debt to the information specialists who work on the reference desk of the Watzek Library at Lewis & Clark College—Dan Kelley, Elaine Hirsch, Joanna Haney, Betty Ann Smith, and Mark Dahl—for all they have taught me about electronic resources. A particular note of thanks goes to Elaine Heras, Associate Director, who had the patience to wade through my first stabs at revisions of Section 3, and who provided me with invaluable information (including appropriate terminology). I also want to take this opportunity to remember Johannah Sherrer, director of the Watzek Library from 1993 to 1998. She was instrumental in first bringing me and this text fully into the current information age. Our loss of her to cancer is still deeply felt by all of us who had the pleasure of working with her. My thanks also go to Mary Bricker, for giving me permission to reprint her fine paper on the ama and decompression sickness, and to Nick Joyce, for the efforts he made in revising his paper on the way that children relate to and categorize their peers. I also want to thank the two professors for whom these papers were originally written: Janet Davidson, Associate Professor of Psychology, and Kellar Autumn, Assistant Professor of Biology. Finally I owe a major debt to Mikal Sherman for his contributions on GMOs and the terminator gene in Section 5. This fifth edition of *Writing Research Papers* would not exist without the nudge of Dickson Musslewhite and the efforts of Michael Burggren at Wadsworth and Nancy Freihofer at Thompson Steele, Inc.

Copyright Acknowledgments

SECTION

1

What **Is** a Research Paper?

To many students, there is nothing more discouraging—or even frightening—than the words "you are required to do a research paper for this course." "Research paper" often conjures up a depressing picture of hours of frustration and mindless busywork. Not knowing where to begin or what to do, many students spend weeks fretting—and procrastinating. Finally, a few weeks—or perhaps a few days—before the paper is due, they force themselves to do a few Google searches, download a pile of material, perhaps check out a book or two from the library. Back at their desks, surrounded by an imposing pile of "stuff," they struggle to find a way to string all this information into some sort of paper that "flows."

- Have I just described some experiences you have had?

- Are you confused about how to go about doing a research paper?

- Are you discouraged by the grades you have received on research papers in the past?

- Are you tired of doing research papers that have not given you a sense of real personal accomplishment?

If your answer to any of these questions is yes, you should find this guide helpful. I have written it for anyone who feels frightened, confused, discouraged, or frustrated by research paper assignments—and for anyone looking for ways to make a research project a more intellectually challenging and personally satisfying experience.

1

A. How to Use This Guide

There is no magic formula for doing research and writing a paper using the research you have done. No two research projects that you do will be exactly alike. The subjects you investigate will vary, the purpose of the research will vary, the way you analyze your evidence will vary. The study you do of wild-eyed fruit flies for your biology class will differ from the study you do of F. Scott Fitzgerald's novels for your literature class; the study you do of group communication processes for your communications class will differ from the study you do of seventeenth-century Dutch portraiture for your art history class.

My purpose in writing this guide is to help you develop a clear sense of direction and purpose when you set out to do a research project, regardless of the subject matter and the field in which you are working. If you do not feel that you know what you are doing, if you do not feel that you are in control of the whole research process, you can feel frustrated, discouraged, "lost." Having a sense of direction and purpose is the best cure I know for any anxieties you may feel about doing a research paper. Developing your own purpose and direction for a research project is the best cure I know for the attitude that completing such assignments is just another tiresome and boring exercise one must go through in order to pass a course. If you expect to feel a real sense of accomplishment when you hand in a research paper, that paper will have to be your response to an intellectual challenge you have posed for yourself. I have written this book to show you how to make an assignment to write a research paper a personal quest for knowledge and understanding, and how, in the process of pursuing this quest, to avoid *unnecessary* expenditures of time and energy, *unnecessary* frustration.

This section of the guide is devoted to an explanation of the general purpose and nature of research projects. *Don't* skip over it. If you want to have a clear sense of direction, a sense of control, you must understand what you are doing when you do a research project. I emphasize the word *research* here because

> the secret of an effective research *paper* is the *research process*
> that precedes it.

The preparation you do at the beginning of the process can make all the difference between a paper that is really yours and a dull, pointless regurgitation of material that you download from the computer or find in the library. So you mustn't skip over this section of the guide, and you mustn't skip Section 2. But you should pause at the end of Section 2 and apply the techniques and suggestions I have laid out for you, using the actual research project you are doing for a class. Do not read over other sections in this guide until you are ready to begin those parts of your research project. Doing a research paper is a rather complex process. But the one thing I want to prevent is having you become overwhelmed by the project. Instead of having you give up because the process is too complex, I want you to have a sense of control through all its stages so that you can eventually produce a paper that gives you a real sense of personal accomplishment. For this reason, we will be using a problem-solving approach. Instead of tackling the major problem (writing a good research paper) in its entirety, we will break down that major problem into parts and tackle each part. This book is not a book *about* research papers; it is a *guide* to the *research process*.

Any technical information I have introduced (about library resources, documentation forms) I have tried to introduce in ways that allow you to use the information when and where you need it. However, this book is neither a style manual nor a technical guide to library and Internet resources. Many such texts are available for your use if you need them. My focus in this book is on you, the researcher, and those activities—especially those intellectual activities—you should be engaged in at various points in the research process.

B. Overview: What Is a Research Paper?

During the past few years I have worked with hundreds of students as they were doing research projects for history, communications, economics, biology, art history—for classes in almost every department on campus. One of the biggest problems that many of these students face is their notion of what research and research papers are; their notions can be very distorted and inaccurate.

Let's get things straight. A research paper is *not*

- a mindless regurgitation of everything you have read about a subject;

- the reiteration of an argument you have found in a book or article, with a few other sources thrown in here and there to show your teacher that you "covered" the subject.

A researcher is *not* a passive sponge. As a researcher, you are not going to absorb countless pieces of information that you will, when you write your paper, regurgitate for your instructor. If all you were supposed to do as a researcher was to reproduce what you read, wouldn't it be much easier to make copies of material you've found, staple them together, and give them to your instructor?

Actually, *you* are the most important element in your research paper. Your job is not simply to absorb information; your job is to digest information, to think about it, to determine what this information means to *you*. The paper you eventually write will focus on the thinking you have done about your subject.

> **A research paper is a report that an individual presents to others about the conclusions he or she has reached after investigating a subject and critically assessing the evidence he or she has gathered.**

If you are wondering what a research paper looks like, you need go no farther than the books and articles you will be reading on your topic. Writing and publishing "research papers" is an activity common among people we think of as experts. One secret to your success in doing your own research project is your recognition that books and articles are not records of "truth" or "facts." Fields such as history, economics, biology are not static bodies of knowledge in which everything to be known is known or in which everything that is considered to be known remains unquestioned. Quite the contrary. History, economics, biology, and other disciplines are best defined as groups of people working together to discover more about the object of their mutual interest and to explain the puzzles and problems that arise as they search for understanding. Historians, economists, biologists construct and reconstruct what they "know." Because members of a discipline work together, they spend a great deal of time talking to each other—exchanging information, telling each other about things they've uncovered, sharing their theories and views of a particular phenomenon, trying to convince each other that one way of interpreting certain evidence is superior to other interpretations. And a very common means they use to carry on these lively dialogues is to write books and articles for each other, the very books and articles you'll be reading. These published texts are really segments in a conversation that is still going on.

When an instructor asks you to do a research paper, he or she is inviting you to join one of the conversations in progress in his or her field. You shouldn't be intimidated by this fact. Your instructor realizes that there is a difference between you and experts in a field. Experts become experts through years of investigating and thinking about their subjects, through years of listening to and talking with their peers face to face, and by reading and writing. They have a sense of confidence that you may not feel right now. But this does not mean you have nothing to say. When an instructor asks you to do a research project, he or she is inviting you to experience what it feels like to be a professional. **Doing a research project not only gives you the chance to learn about the problems the experts are puzzling over, but in doing a research project properly *you will be doing the very same thing* the experts do.** Even if you aren't planning to major in the field in which you are taking a course, in doing a research paper you'll find out what the discipline is by thinking the way members of that field think. Doing a research paper allows you to strengthen the same skills that an expert uses when he or she sets out to investigate a subject. A research paper, then, is an invitation to sharpen your ability to think critically.

C. Learning, Thinking, and Research Papers

The major objective I have for the remainder of this introduction to research papers and the research process is to convince you that

> critical thinking—*your* critical thinking—lies at the heart of any
> research project.

Since the seventeenth century, in Western culture thinking critically has meant observing, questioning, investigating, analyzing, synthesizing. And the day-to-day work of historians, philosophers, musicologists, political scientists, biologists, economists, chemists, and members of other academic fields involves observing, questioning, investigating, analyzing, synthesizing.

Thus, when you set out to do a research project for one of your college courses, regardless of the department in which the course is taught, you are beginning a process of inquiry that will entail

- asking questions;

- gathering as much information as possible on the subject to find answers to those questions;

- carefully and systematically judging the meaning of the evidence gathered so that you are confident that the answer you have developed is a reasonable one.

To give you a better sense of what engaging in such inquiries will require, let's consider in more detail what thinking critically means for the faculty who teach college courses across the curriculum.

1. The evidence

A contractor cannot build a house without lumber, nails, pipes, electrical wiring—the physical materials of a building. Nor will she be able to build this house without plans that tell her what materials are needed and that give her a picture of how these materials should be put together. Similarly, human beings cannot construct ideas—conceptions of various parts of their world—without concrete facts from that world. Paradoxically, without a notion of the bigger picture, we don't know what we are looking for when we search for facts because this notion or idea of the phenomena tells us what constitutes a fact. Thus, both facts and ideas are forms of evidence that researchers seek and with which researchers work. S. I. Hayakawa can help us understand this connection better; as our framework for categories of evidence, let's use his classification of types of statements.[1]

a. Facts

Facts are pieces of information that can be observed and measured objectively, like

- the size and chemical composition of rocks found on the moon;

- the standardized test scores of specific students at a specific school in a given year;

- the number of images related to the sun in Shakespeare's *Richard II*.

---

[1]*Language in Thought and Action,* 4th ed. (New York: Harcourt Brace Jovanovich, 1978), 33–38.

b. Inferences

Inferences are statements "about the unknown made on the basis of the known."[2]

A conclusion drawn by an expert—for example, a statement that "playing action video games increases children's eye-hand coordination"—is an inference. The researcher cannot have studied the eye-hand coordination of *every* child (and adult) who has ever played an action video game. His or her statement—about *all* children who have played such games—is based on a study of *some* children who fall into this category. His or her conclusion is *not* a statement of truth; it is a *hypothesis* that may or may not be valid. Similarly, a statement like "Richard's fall and the usurpation of Bolingbroke emphasize between them the necessity of the political qualities for the successful exercise of kingship" is also an inference.[3] Observing certain elements of Shakespeare's *Richard II*, the critic Derek Traversi has reached this conclusion about the meaning of Shakespeare's play. It is not a statement about *the* meaning of the play, since the play contains many features that can be interpreted in a variety of ways, depending on the point of view of a particular critic. Traversi's statement is his inference of the meaning of a variety of elements he has observed in the play.

c. Judgments

Judgments are, in Hayakawa's words, "expressions of the writer's approval or disapproval of the occurrences, persons, or objects he is describing."[4]

Statements like "action video games are good for kids" or "*Daniel Deronda* is George Eliot's weakest novel" are judgments. They are statements about the writer's personal feelings about a subject.

Making inferences and judgments is the natural function of a human mind. Facts in and of themselves are meaningless. What difference does it make that the temperature outside is 23°F or that there are forty references to the sun in *Richard II*? Such facts simply "are" until a human mind operates on them and makes some type of meaning out of them. Reacting to the thermometer that reads 23°F, one person may say, "It's cold out there; I'd better wear my hat and gloves." Another person may say, "Perfect skiing weather." The fact—the temperature of the air—has been interpreted by each of these people to "mean" something according to the mental sets and needs of these two people.

2. Evaluating the evidence

In their quest for knowledge, researchers regularly use evidence that falls into Hayakawa's first two categories: facts and inferences. While researchers also

---

[2]Hayakawa, *Language in Thought and Action*, 35.
[3]Derek Traversi, "The Historical Pattern from *Richard II* to *Henry V*," in *Shakespeare, the Histories: A Collection of Critical Essays*, ed. Eugene M. Waith, Twentieth-Century Views (Englewood Cliffs, N.J.: Prentice-Hall, 1965), 105.
[4]*Language in Thought and Action*, 37.

regularly engage in evaluation, they try to avoid making statements that are based solely on their "personal feelings" about a subject. In academic circles, a field of study is called a discipline to alert us that, in that field, the subject under investigation is studied in a systematic, "disciplined" fashion. The history of modern disciplines has been the history of constructing knowledge about our world that attempts to circumvent the distortions of our senses and perceptions, that openly questions assumptions and presuppositions that may be nothing more than the idiosyncrasies of individuals' minds or the biases and prejudices of a culture. Members of disciplines have thus sought systematic, objective ways to uncover facts about their objects of study, and systematic, objective ways to examine and evaluate what these facts mean; and they articulate the meanings they arrive at in statements Hayakawa calls inferences so that these conclusions are open to further testing. These systematic, objective ways of uncovering facts and examining and evaluating their meaning are usually called methods or methodologies.

As various members of a field offer their findings and their inferences to their colleagues, dialogues are also going on about the implications of these findings. What do these findings suggest about what the subject is and how it works? They answer this question by forming a theory. Dialogues within disciplines tend to be lively because there are usually several theories under consideration, which spawn a number of different types of methodologies. This explains why, for example, you can find that Professor X approaches psychology in a way different from that of Professor Y, even though both are members of the same department at a college or university. In setting up studies in which rats learn how to negotiate a maze, Professor X is testing the behaviorist theory that our actions are conditioned by external rewards and punishments. Meanwhile, operating on the Freudian theory that our actions have their roots in the psychic dynamics of the id, ego, and superego, Professor Y analyzes the effectiveness of techniques of psychoanalysis. In each case, a theory of human behavior dictates the methods by which Professor X and Professor Y carry out their investigations.

So it goes in all the disciplines. A theory leads researchers to develop better methods of seeking the factual evidence the theory tells them they ought to find; analyses of the evidence thus gathered prompt them to form more inferences, which they then test by doing more studies. This continuous investigation often results in modifications of a theory, or even rejection of that theory. One of the most famous of these paradigm shifts occurred in physics at the beginning of this century, with the rejection of Newton's mechanical theory of the physical world in favor of Einstein's theory of relativity and quantum mechanics.

While all disciplines can be called disciplines because their members pursue knowledge in this systematic fashion, the methods or investigative procedures specific to certain disciplines can and will differ. Thus, the way an historian studies the development of labor unions can differ from the way a botanist studies peach trees, and both can differ from the way a cultural anthropologist studies traditional dances in Bali. Differences in the methodologies of each can be explained in part by obvious differences in those aspects of our world that each field has taken on as its object of study. But these differences are also the result of differences in the way that historians and biologists and cultural anthropologists have come to define valid and meaningful knowledge. As you take courses across the curriculum, you will become aware that a major dividing line separates the sciences and the humanities and often bisects the social sciences. This dividing line, created by critical differences in how one arrives at meaningful and valid knowledge, distinguishes the "hard" from the "soft" sciences.

The hard sciences—the pure and applied natural sciences and areas of the social sciences—are so called because they prefer empirical modes of testing, modes that rely on mathematical models and/or the use of instruments. Whenever you find yourself in a laboratory, collecting data by recording numbers produced by a piece of equipment or through some other precise means of weighing, measuring, or observing, you are engaged in testing procedures fundamental to hard science. You are seeing similar hard science procedures at work when your reading for a social science course includes a report on the results of a survey in which the quantifiable data gathered have been submitted to rigorous statistical analysis.

By contrast, the objectives of the humanities have led members of these fields to quite different methods of investigation and analysis. The humanities take as their subject of inquiry artifacts of conscious human construction: paintings, musical compositions, the work of architects and choreographers, and written texts that range from Plato's *Republic* to the poetry of Wordsworth to the *Bhagavad-Gita* to historical documents such as royal proclamations, nineteenth-century newspapers, or letters and diaries. In the humanities, meaningful knowledge about these artifacts is determined by "reading" them through the framework of an accepted mode of interpretation, a mode derived from a particular theory. The validity of such interpretations is tested and demonstrated, not in any quantifiable way but by using standards of logic.

3. Sources of evidence and types of research projects

While all researchers are involved in the quest for a greater understanding of that aspect of the world that is the object of study in their discipline, certain research projects take researchers closer to the phenomena or primary source of evidence than do others. Understanding the differences between primary and secondary *sources* will be useful to you as you read the published work of the experts, and understanding the differences between primary and secondary research *projects* should enable you to get a better sense of what's expected of you when instructors in various departments assign research papers. Primary and secondary research projects make different demands on researchers—in their use of the work of the experts, in the way they spend their researching time, and in the purpose and focus of the papers they produce.

A research project falls into the category of primary research when the *main focus* of the researcher's investigation is some actual manifestation of the discipline's primary source of evidence. The chemist who sets up an experiment in the lab to learn more about the properties of mercury is engaged in a primary research project, as is the anthropologist who spends months in a village in Java, observing the lives of the people and gathering information from them about their culture. A political scientist who studies the papers of a former president of the United States in an effort to understand the inner workings of his administration is engaged in a primary research project, as is the literary critic who travels around England seeking letters and personal papers of a well-known novelist and interviewing her friends and acquaintances to develop a greater understanding of her novels and creative process. Because the phenomena they study are consciously made human artifacts, members of the humanistic disciplines don't always need to leave home to pursue primary research. As long as the historian can obtain records of the Parliamentary debates on the Corn Laws, or the musicologist has facsimiles of the scores of Beethoven's sonatas, they can pursue their investigations of these primary sources in the comfort of their offices. Clearly, the bulk of time these experts spend on these projects is devoted to gathering facts from these primary sources; and, normally, when they sit down to write at the end of their investigations, their purpose is to report on what they've found—not only to share with their colleagues the factual data they've collected, but also to add the meanings they've made of these facts to the dialogue going on in the discipline. The specific form these reports on primary research take, of course, depends on the discipline of which they are members. However, since engaging in primary research is an important part of the work of all disciplines, and thus reporting on such work is a common form of communication among members, most disciplines have developed certain standards (and sometimes formats) for such reports. As we might expect, there are differences in primary research papers in the hard and soft sciences and, as you'll see in Sections 2 and 5, the hard sciences have a fairly distinctive format for such reports.

Published reports on primary research themselves become important sources for all members of a field. A person planning a primary research project relies on published investigations for several types of important information. A review of this work lets her know what members of the field think they have ascertained as knowledge, and what they still consider unknown or problematic. It gives form to her own investigation, telling her what kinds of facts still need to be uncovered, what inferences or hypotheses require further testing, what important questions still need to be asked. Further, from the procedures and techniques others used for collecting and analyzing data, she can derive sound methods for doing her own inquiry, assuring herself that her colleagues will judge her findings to be valid and meaningful.

As is the person engaged in a primary research project, the researcher who undertakes a secondary research project is also prompted by questions he has about the phenomena under study in his discipline. But, for evidence, he turns to the books and articles published by his colleagues. The evidence he seeks is not only the facts and data they've uncovered but also the inferences they've drawn to make sense of these data. He carefully scrutinizes the methods they've used to collect these facts, and her continually matches their inferences against the meanings he makes of these facts. From the evidence he assesses to be valid, he constructs a picture of the subject under investigation. In the paper he writes, he will present this picture in some detail. His objective is to convince his readers that his is the most logical interpretation of the knowledge currently available. His paper will be considered a secondary source of information on the subject, both because he stood at one remove from the primary source of date (the facts he uses were collected by others) and because, in reporting to us on what others did and have said, we readers are one remove from the published sources on which he relied.

Since experts in fields regularly do both secondary and primary research, they can certainly publish work that draws both on evidence they've gathered from direct study of the phenomena and on evidence they've taken from the investigations of others. Such a mixture is most frequently found in book-length studies, where an expert gives us the fruits of years of investigation, thought, and reflection.

As you are reading the work published by the experts over the next few weeks, you'll find it helpful to keep in mind how close the author of a book or article was to the primary source of evidence. Thus, if you want to form a better understanding of the Berbers of North Africa, the ethnography that Sally Smith wrote after living with the Berbers for six months will be more enlightening than John Doe's summary of Smith's work in a book about the peoples of North Africa. The ideal, of course, would be for you to gather information about the Berbers by going to North Africa yourself.

For undergraduates, such primary research isn't usually feasible, and for this reason most college instructors assign research projects in which, they assume, you'll be gathering most of your evidence from the published works of others. On the other hand, college instructors are eager to have their students get first-hand experience of the way members of their discipline work. Instructors in the hard sciences may well assign primary research projects when doing such research is feasible and when they judge students to have sufficient knowledge of disciplinary methodologies to do valid studies or experiments. Since primary sources in the humanistic disciplines are far more accessible, even introductory-level courses usually ask students to develop interpretations of paintings, musical pieces, works of literature, or the writings of philosophers. When you are asked to do a primary *research* project in one of these fields, however, you'll want to remember that the interpretation you develop of your subject is intended to be guided by and put into the context of the work the experts have done.

D. Summary

The preceding pages were intended to give you a general overview of what writing research papers across the curriculum entails. Lest you are feeling overwhelmed and perhaps intimidated—feelings this book is intended to alleviate, not create—let's return to the central theme of this section: thinking critically. It is the core of the two central messages I would like you to take away from this introduction to research papers.

The main purpose of the courses you take in history, biology, psychology, art, philosophy, chemistry, and other departments is to teach you how members of those disciplines seek and construct knowledge. In asking you to do research projects in their courses, your instructors expect you to apply what you are learning about the ways members of their particular field observe, question, investigate, analyze, synthesize—whether you use this knowledge to evaluate work published in books and articles or to set up your own primary research project. Since the specific methodologies you will use in any such a project are integral and specific to the field in which you are working, my ability to talk in any detail about particular modes of critical thinking is severely limited.

What I can do, in the pages that follow, is to remind you constantly that the success of each and every research project in which you engage **hinges on your willingness to think critically.** You will not be working the way the experts do unless you are constantly using your brain—questioning, searching, weighing, assessing, drawing inferences of your own, and critically examining the inferences of others. You are, of course, perfectly capable of this kind of critical inquiry. The problem may well be that your past experiences have taught you to think of researchers as passive sponges, mindlessly soaking up the ideas and facts of others, and then regurgitating them in a paper that is little more than a scissors-and-paste version of this reading. Because this is not the way real researchers behave, my objective in this book is to give you another role to play and, through a variety of suggestions and strategies, to show you how you can play that role successfully. The role is that of a detective because detective work comes closest to approximating what real researchers do.

Researchers set out to find a solution to an intellectual puzzle or mystery. Like good detectives, they are always asking questions, always alert to the possibility that the smallest piece of information may be a central clue. They look in the most unlikely places for evidence, always trying to put clues together to arrive at a satisfactory solution. Their work is not easy. They do run into dead ends. Clues are not handed to them on a silver platter. Researchers are constantly arranging and rearranging evidence until it falls into some meaningful pattern.

So before you begin a research project, you must think of yourself as a **detective.** The mystery is not going to solve itself. *You* must find and develop a solution. You will be in charge of this investigation. Your guiding purpose will be your need to know and to understand. The direction your research takes will come from the questions you ask, from decisions you make about where to search for evidence, from your critical assessment of the evidence you find.

There is, however, one major difference between you and Sherlock Holmes. Sherlock Holmes usually comes up with *the* correct solution to the mystery. But it is unlikely that you—or any researcher—will find *the* correct solution. As Milton says of truth, "Yet it is not impossible that she may have more shapes than one."

Your quest is not for *the* solution, *the* final truth. Your quest is for *a* solution, *an* answer that the evidence points to. Your evidence is going to point the way to your conclusion. The individual who seeks only the evidence that supports his or her original assumption and disregards the rest is not a researcher but a rationalizer, an ostrich burying his or her head into the sand.

Now that you understand the major purpose and aims of a researcher, where do you begin?

2

Where Do I Begin?

Students tend to assume that the first step in a research project is to do research, so they begin their projects by logging on to their computers, or heading for the library. I think it is safe to say that many students engage in such activities only when the deadline for the paper becomes too close to ignore any longer. To address the causes of such procrastination, but also for a variety of other very good reasons, I'm suggesting the research process begins in a very different place.

The successful research project begins in the mind of the researcher. The smart researcher starts with something he or she wants to understand better.

I must stop here to interject a warning that you have probably heard so many times that you are sick of hearing it. But I must repeat it:

You must begin your research project early.

The researcher needs *time to research*. Your search for facts and evidence will lead you into dead ends and into highways and byways that you cannot predict when you begin. You must give yourself plenty of time to find everything you need.

The researcher needs *time to think*. As you gather your evidence, you must think about it. You must mull over what you have discovered, push the facts this way and that, decide what further evidence you need. You will constantly be formulating ideas and discarding them.

One weekend is certainly not enough time; nor is one week, or even two. This is my advice:

- Set up a work schedule for yourself, working backward from the date on which the paper must be given to your instructor. In subsection I at the end of this section you will find a handy worksheet on which you can record these deadlines:

  - **Due date.**

  - **Date to begin polishing the final rough draft.** The amount of time you give yourself to copyedit the final rough draft and to proofread the polished copy will depend on how much time—if any—you need to allow for typing. It is imperative that you be realistic about your typing skills and speed because, once the text is typed, you must still have sufficient time to proofread carefully and make necessary changes. If someone else will be typing your final paper, you must be realistic about typists' schedules, and you need to allow enough time for you to proofread the typed copy *and* take it back for corrections.

  - **Date on which your first draft will be finished.** This date is dependent on the length and complexity of your paper and the amount of work you have to do for your other classes between this point and the due date. I'd suggest a date no later than two to two-and-a-half weeks before the due date, and you should allow yourself more time if the paper is going to be longer than ten pages.

  - **Date to begin your first rough draft.** This date is also the target date for having the major part of your research completed; for those of you doing studies or experiments, this is the date on which you will have all the necessary results and data in your hands. I'd suggest **no later than three weeks before the paper is due,** perhaps earlier if your paper is more than ten pages.

  - **Date to begin work on the research project: when the assignment is given!**

- Once you have set the deadlines above and developed your research strategies, you will be able to—and should—set deadlines for yourself for intermediate steps in the process. If you are doing a secondary research project, you should set deadlines for such things as gathering your first list of promising sources, having certain books and articles read, doing interviews, and the like. If you are doing a study or experiment, it is crucial for you to set a number of deadlines: when your research design will be complete; when you will put together your apparatus or find your subjects or pass out your questionnaires; when you will run the experiment or study itself; and so on.

- Plan to devote an hour or two *every day* to this project. If you follow the steps laid out in the first four sections of this book, working on this project in small units of time won't be that difficult.

If you space your work out over weeks and even months, rather than trying to cram it into a concentrated period of time, you allow your brain to do its work—and your brain is the secret to a good research project.

Before you begin to gather evidence, there are three major decisions you need to make:

- You must decide *which idea* (working hypothesis/thesis) you are going to test.

- You must decide *how* you are going to test that hypothesis/thesis.

- You must develop a research *strategy,* a plan of action for finding your facts and evidence.

A. Step 1: The Researcher's Notebook

I am going to urge you to begin every research project you undertake by setting up a Researcher's Notebook for that project. While the term *notebook* suggests a three-ring binder (which is the format I prefer), you should think of the Researcher's Notebook as a strategy that concretizes the control you want to have over the research process. It provides you with a central place to keep an ongoing record of the various activities in which you will be engaged, not the least of which will be the intellectual activities of thinking critically about your subject and assessing the evidence you gather. I am going to suggest that your Notebook have four major divisions, and I'll be referring to these divisions in the remainder of this book. But nothing about the Researcher's Notebook is set in stone. Divide your Notebook up the way I suggest, or create your own divisions. What's important is that you understand the purposes the Notebook serves. The first purpose—most obvious in the first two divisions—is comparable to that provided by personal planners. Here the Notebook becomes a central place where you will direct and plot out your investigation. The second purpose of the Researcher's Notebook—and its most important function—is found in the next two divisions. Here it is a journal of what is happening in your mind as you examine and digest the evidence and construct your own meaning of your subject.

Once you understand these purposes of the Notebook, you should choose a format that you find most comfortable and convenient. Your Notebook should be portable, so it is always at hand whenever and wherever you decide to work on your project. If you have a laptop, your Notebook could be comprised of files and folders in your word-processing program. Otherwise, I'd suggest a three-ring binder. Three-ring binders are portable, so you have them with you to jot down your thoughts between classes, or when a eureka moment occurs. They are also flexible. Sections can be made up of loose-leaf paper and print-outs or photocopied material. Sheets can be shifted around from one section to another, and new material added at any time. If you decide you need another section, all you have to do is add a divider.

1. The **Sources section** is simply a place *to keep a list* of books, articles, and other sources that have the potential for providing the evidence you need.

Here you will store the complete citations for books, journal articles, Web sites, and other promising sources you find in your searches of bibliographic databases and the Web (which I will cover in detail in Section 3). This is the place you will also copy out citations of promising sources that you find in the bibliographies and reference lists of sources as you read them. Here's where you'll record texts suggested by your instructor or other experts you consult. If you decide to do interviews, this is a good place to jot down the names, addresses, and phone numbers of people you want to interview; you should also note the dates of the interviews. You need to keep a record of full bibliographic information for promising books and articles because you won't always have time to locate them when you come across information about them. Keeping a list of potential sources in one place makes it less likely that you will forget about, or misplace essential information about, a book or article or document you want to review. When you are ready to locate these sources, you will be assured you have all the information you'll need to do so. The Sources section is a labor-saving device; it will save you unnecessary frustration, too.

2. The **Research Strategy section** contains *lists of things to do*. You may want to subdivide it into several sections. The first page of the Research Strategy division of your Notebook would be a good place to record your various deadlines (see subsection I). Another subdivision should be devoted to writing out the research questions suggested by your working hypothesis/thesis and various places to check in your quest to answer them (see subsection E). There are any number of ways you could lay out this subdivision: questions on the left-hand page, places to look for answers straight across on the right-hand page; questions separated by lines left blank so that you can fill in places to look for answers; questions in one color ink, places to look for answers in another.

   You should probably reserve another part of this division for a miscellaneous ongoing list of things you need to do. These are the types of items that might appear on such a list:

   • See if Reed College has a copy of Browning's book.

   • Make a list of books to request on interlibrary loan—and put in those requests!!!!

   • Ask Prof. Smith for names of people I could talk to at the Boys and Girls Society.

   • Find a color reproduction of *Afternoon on Grande Jatte*—check shadows.

   • Find out about Baha'i—some encyclopedia of religion?

   • Read Wilson's book Now!!!

3. The **Reading** section of your Notebook has two related functions that will become much clearer when you reach Section 4, "Reading Critically and

Taking Notes." In Section 4, I explain that in this Notebook you won't be recording the evidence you find; you'll have a separate system and a different location for that material. As you'll see, note taking involves something quite different from mindlessly copying material from your sources. The Reading section of your Notebook will provide you with a guarantee that you won't turn into a passive sponge at this crucial stage of the research process. In this section of your Notebook you'll be doing **Reading Logs** in which you will **freewrite**[1] about the reading you are doing *as* you study various books, articles, and other material. By asking and answering questions of the sources you are reading—the problem or puzzle the author is investigating, his/her analytical framework or investigative procedures, the way he/she interprets the facts—you will reassure yourself that you are reading actively and critically. Writing your way toward a solid comprehension of what each author is saying places you in a much better position not only to take accurate and appropriate notes on each of your sources but also to critically evaluate the work these authors have done. The writing you do in your **Reading Logs** will enable you to write a **summary** of each of your sources, and these summaries themselves will prove to be a highly valuable form of evidence. But I'll go into these issues in much more detail in Section 4, when you are ready to begin reading critically. In the meantime, as you are putting your Notebook together, consider the specific nature of your project. If it involves your own careful study of primary texts (poems, plays, pieces of music, paintings, films), you may want to add a section to the Notebook, one in which you will keep ongoing records of your responses to and thoughts about these pieces.

4. The **Working Hypothesis/Thesis section** of your Notebook is the most vital one. The rest of *Writing Research Papers* is premised on the assumption not only that you will keep this journal of your thinking but also that your work in this section—and in the Reading section—is your assurance that your own thinking will remain the core of this whole project. It is in this section that you should use the strategies laid out in the next three steps of the process. Once you have a working hypothesis/thesis and start testing it, you should return to this part of your Notebook every few days, writing to yourself about what you are thinking at each stage regarding the accuracy of your working hypothesis/thesis, whether it is the "right" answer to your initial research question. If your research project is going to change direction, it is here that you will make that discovery and here that you will

---

[1]Freewriting is a means of talking to yourself on paper, a means of recording what is happening in your mind as you are mulling over an idea. Freewriting is a very loose, unstructured mode of writing. One of its major advantages is that it gives you permission to record ambiguities and contradictions you see and/or feel, and to change your mind. When you freewrite, all your attention should be on what is happening in your head. Do not try to write elegant prose, and don't even worry about correctness (grammar, spelling, sentence structure); all you need to concern yourself with is putting enough down on paper so that you remember a week from now what you meant.

decide which new direction to take. If you decide that your original thesis is not "right," it is here that you will rewrite it to fit your current thinking. In this section of your Notebook you should talk to yourself, honestly and specifically, about whatever comes to your mind when you focus on the puzzle or mystery you've decided to "solve." Jot down any ideas that pop into your mind related to your topic. Write down any questions floating around in your head, no matter how silly or farfetched they may seem. Talk to yourself about confusions you are experiencing and tell yourself what you need to do to clear up these confusions. Use this section of your Notebook to carefully fit parts of the puzzle together.

There are no real rules for a journal of one's thinking—except that, when you write here, you need to be thinking. It would be a good idea frequently to devote a whole entry to your answers to these questions:

- What picture is emerging from the evidence I already have?

- How does it compare with my original hypothesis/thesis?

- What areas of the emerging picture are still fuzzy for me?

- What information do I need to make them clearer?

- Should I revise my working hypothesis/thesis?

- What *should* it say?

Here's a sample of what an entry made several weeks into the research process could look like:

> I came into this project convinced that an open classroom was the best environment for kids' learning. Now I'm not so sure. Ramirez, Wilhelm, and Kim all stress how important it is for children to have structure. So—what's the story? A completely free environment in which kids do what they feel like doing when they feel like doing it or a version of military school? There has got to be something in the middle. OK, let's start with structure. What does that mean? If I am understanding what I've been reading, these experts are saying that children need . . . what? (1) a sense of what is appropriate and inappropriate behavior, (2) they need to know what kinds of tasks they are expected to do and when they should hand them in, (3) they need to know how to go about doing these tasks. Do students need to sit in rows of desks facing the teacher, never talking unless asked a question by the teacher, to have these kinds of structure? NO. Children talking to each other doesn't have to be classified as inappropriate behavior. In fact, Hashimoto and DeMartino both say that kids learn best when they work in groups. But they do need to be told HOW to work in groups. There's the structure. I'm cooking. Let's go on with this.

I cannot emphasize too much how important it is for you to *use* your Researcher's Notebook constantly throughout the research process. If you want to break the "passive sponge" syndrome and take control of your research process, you must keep a *written* record of your own thinking. If you do not jot down ideas that pop into your head, you forget them. If you try to work out a complex idea in your head, you may soon become confused and overwhelmed. Write out these ideas; putting them down on paper will give you the chance to look at them and decide what is right and what is wrong. I've seen too many students get so befuddled by trying to work out their ideas just in their heads that they give up all hope of ever sorting out what they really think. Don't let this happen to you.

If you continually write in your Researcher's Notebook *as* you do your research, you will find that you are actually doing **THE** groundwork for your final paper. You are discovering what *you* want to say about your subject. When the time comes to start drafting your final paper, you will realize that an important part of the writing process has already occurred because you've been writing yourself into an understanding of the subject, and because you've been doing your thinking in writing.

Once you have set up your Researcher's Notebook, you are ready to start work on your research project.

B. Step 2: Deciding on the Research Question/Assumption That You Are Going to Test

As you take various courses in college, you will find that the conditions set up for your research projects will vary. In some classes your professors will give you a list of possible areas of investigation. In other classes the professor will outline the type of investigation you should undertake; she may, for example, tell you that your task is to design and carry out a study in which you observe some specific way in which people use nonverbal communication, or she may instruct you to focus on the connection between the rituals of a particular culture and the underlying values of that culture. In other classes the instructor will leave it up to you to choose both the area of investigation and the method of testing your hypothesis/thesis.

In some classes you will feel comfortable selecting a topic for your research because you are familiar with the material. In other classes you may be very ill equipped to choose a topic because you know very little about the course material.

In the next few pages I will provide some strategies for selecting your area of investigation because, as you may well have discovered firsthand, selecting a topic is a critically important part of the research process; it can make all the difference in the quality of the paper you eventually write. But you cannot afford to spend weeks making the decision; every minute you waste flitting from one possible topic to another is a minute you could have spent researching.

One way to take some of the fear and anxiety out of the need to commit yourself to a topic is to see your topic as a "point of departure" rather than an "end point." Many students are in the habit of selecting a topic on the basis of their perception of the amount of information available about the subject. Their thinking goes something like this: "I have to write a ten-page paper. Ten pages are a lot of pages to be filled. I'll write about computers because I know that there are lots of books and articles in the library on computers." Let's consider the basic problem with this line of reasoning. The student who is thinking this way is really saying to herself: "If I had to write a ten-page research paper for this class *today*, I would have a very difficult time filling up ten pages because I do not know much about the material." But every researcher feels this way. If I had to write my conclusions about a subject *before* I researched the subject, before I thought carefully about the subject, I would have a difficult time filling up ten pages. What students often forget is that between the time they choose a topic and the time they write the final paper, they will have gathered quite a bit of evidence about the topic, regardless of what the topic is, and they will have generated all kinds of ideas about the subject. If you do your research properly, more likely than not, when it comes time to write your paper, you will wish that you had more than ten pages to discuss your conclusions. All of us experience the anxiety of "How can I write this paper?" when we begin a research project. The best antidote is to get on with the actual business of selecting your focus and using a more reasonable criterion for making that choice.

I have already introduced the idea that this process is going to ask you to think critically, and I'll be elaborating much more on this point in the pages that follow. But the years of experience I've had working with students on research papers have alerted me to some far-reaching assumptions that students can make about what it means to be objective, fair, unbiased. To them, being "reasonable" seems to require that they have no views or feelings on the subject *at all*. In other words, some students seem to have concluded that a research paper, by definition, can be nothing more than a group of uncontestable, hard, cold facts ("facts" here include what other people think about the topic). Thus these students assume that, to carry out such projects, they must choose a subject in which they have little or no interest—or that their instructor has already chosen such a subject/topic for them. In the eyes of these students, the paper they are to write, by definition, is intended to be *dull, dry, boring*. There are multiple ironies in this line of thinking, but the most important one is that the mental posture of *real* people who do *real* research could not be more different. Actual researchers choose to investigate something because it interests them! They are driven by their curiosity, by their desire to learn, by their need to understand something better. And this is going to be your benchmark for this whole project:

What do I want to understand better?

You are going to use it throughout the coming weeks to test what you are learning and to determine the direction further research is going to take: am I understanding X better? What am I understanding that I didn't see before? What do I still need to understand?

If you want to produce a research paper that gives you a sense of personal satisfaction, you must begin the research process by selecting an area of investigation that has some *personal meaning* or *importance* to you. In considering your topic, think in these terms:

- What do *I* want to know more about?

- What am *I* personally interested in investigating in some depth?

- What subject is important enough to *me* that I need to spend time and energy learning more about it?

  What do I want to understand better?

If at this point you respond that nothing really grabs your interest or that you are too ignorant of the material to know what might interest you, here are some strategies you can use to overcome these obstacles. Do not put it off. Get out your Researcher's Notebook and start writing out your answers to these questions in the Working Hypothesis/Thesis section:

- Think about the reasons you had for taking this class.

  - What did I expect to learn in this course?

  - What did I assume the textbook or the teacher would say about the material?

  - What questions do I have now about the material?

  - What do I look forward to learning about?

  - Have any issues been raised in class that I want to pursue further?

- Have I had any contact with this subject before?

  - Is the subject related to material I've studied in other classes?

  - Have I read about this material in magazines or newspapers? What have I learned?

  - Have I heard anything about the subject on the radio or TV? What have I heard?

  - Has this subject come up in conversations I've had with others? What was said?

- Is the material in this course related in *any way* to subjects I already know quite a bit about? Don't neglect the obvious. If you are interested in popular music, and one subject covered in your course is baroque music, research in baroque music would deepen your understanding of music in general.

- Take out your textbook, your course syllabus, and, if your instructor has provided one, the list of topics for this paper. Look them over.

  - What particular subjects attract me?

  - What have I enjoyed learning about? What do I look forward to learning about?

- If, in the course you are taking, you are dealing directly with primary materials—art objects, pieces of music, poems and novels, or the writings of people important in the field (Darwin's *Origin of Species*, Machiavelli's *The Prince*)—go directly to these primary sources. Acquaint yourself with them.

- Do any of these works catch my interest?

- Would I like to see more paintings by one particular artist? Would I like to read more poems by one of the poets? Would I like to read one of the primary sources, like Darwin's *Origin*, more carefully than class time will allow?

Do not simply look over these questions. If you expect to find a topic for your research paper that truly interests you, you must write out your answers to these questions. The questions are here to give you a place to start exploring, to discover that area of the course's subject matter that you want to pursue further on your own. At this point it does not matter if you feel you don't know much about the subject that interests you. The important issue here is choosing an area of investigation about which you have some personal need or desire to increase your knowledge.

Choose something you have a personal need to understand better.

Without that personal involvement, the research process is probably going to be a dreadfully boring process that you will hate and resent. Without that personal involvement, you will never feel the curiosity and thirst for knowledge that drives the experienced researcher forward.

C. Step 3: Formulating Your Research Question/Assumption

Once you zero in on a subject or area that you want to know more about, the next step is stating your topic. Perhaps you are used to expressing research topics in noun phrases like "the causes of the Civil War" or "sun imagery in *Richard II*" or "the importance of nonverbal behavior in communication." Perhaps you've already discovered that such phrases aren't very helpful in giving you a clear sense of direction in your research. They map out an area in which you can gather information, but they don't express *your* personal, intellectual involvement or interest in the material.

From now on, therefore, I will not talk about "topics." We will reject the idea that research should be guided by nouns and noun phrases. Rather, I am going to encourage you to express your interests in full grammatical sentences. Specifically, from now on I will be talking about assumptions, research questions, and working hypotheses/theses.

The **research question** is the particular question you are asking about your subject. It focuses on what you want to understand better. Typically, when we ask questions such as these, the question arises from an assumption we have already made about the subject.

The **assumption** is either some view or opinion we find that we have about the subject, or it is the answer we think we will find before we have done any research. Either way, we call it an assumption because, as of now, we can't really make a good argument for this idea we have. The **working hypothesis/thesis** is still an assumption from your point of view, but it is an assumption you have about the subject refined into a statement that lends itself to testing. It does not matter at this point if you are fairly certain that your original assumption is way off base. It is what **you** know, or think you know. It is **yours.** Besides, you are turning this statement into a question.

The research and writing process from now on out will be guided by your research question and working hypothesis/thesis. They are mirror images of each other.

> Napoleon was the original architect of the bipolar world.

> Was Napoleon the original architect of the bipolar world?

These two sentences model the question-and-answer dialogue you'll be having with yourself and with the experts and sources you'll be reading, studying, thinking critically about.

In the Working Hypothesis/Thesis section of your Researcher's Notebook, write out your assumption and your research question. If you have more than one assumption, or more than one question, write them all out.

Here are some examples of assumptions and research questions.

ASSUMPTION

My girlfriend swears by Echinacea. She is convinced it helps her fight off all sorts of illnesses, and she wants me to start taking it.

In class we've talked about differences between males and females. From listening to my brother and his male friends and comparing their talks with the conversations I have with my girlfriends, I'd say there is even a difference in the ways males and females talk.

My cousin is having a terrible time finding a place he can afford in the city. And I sure have noticed all the fancy restaurants and expensive condos in a part of town that used to be nothing but ugly warehouses. We talked about gentrification in our econ class, and I'm thinking there is a connection between gentrification and the problems my cousin is running into.

RESEARCH QUESTION

Does Echinacea help fight off illness? What *is* it? What do Western doctors think about such herbal remedies and other forms of alternative medicine?

Is there a difference in the ways males and females talk? Do they use different vocabularies? Do they talk about different things?

Is there less affordable housing in Portland these days? Is it related to gentrification? If so, what is the connection?

ASSUMPTION

I just read the allegory of the cave section of Plato's *Republic* and it blew my mind! I mean, just like the *Matrix* films! I assume that the guy (guys?) who wrote this film had read Plato!

My prof says that Dickens' novels were published sections at a time over many months in magazines. That's probably why they are *so* long. I wonder if he wrote the whole novel first, or if he was still composing it after sections were published. If he wrote sections, I wonder how he kept the plots and characters straight. I'd imagine that an author who writes a novel as it is being published writes differently from one who writes a whole novel, then publishes it.

Yesterday in our international law class we got onto the topic of environmental issues that cross nation–state boundaries: industries in one country dumping pollutants into rivers that another country uses for drinking water; acid rain (U.S.–Canada); global warming. Evidently there is no international organization that has the power to establish and enforce international environmental policies. There ought to be!

I've been disgusted by what I've read in our U.S. politics class about Teapot Dome and other government scandals in the 20s. I've decided that Warren G. Harding must have been a terrible president.

I just saw a piece in the paper about the problem of disposing of old computers. Full of all sorts of toxic metals. And how many thousands and thousands of old computers are there in the U.S. today ?! We are going to have to figure out pretty soon how to dispose of them safely and economically.

RESEARCH QUESTION

Were these guys influenced by Plato? Did they just dream up this idea of alternate realities all on their own, or were they influenced by stuff they read? If they were influenced by stuff they read, what were some of the things they read? How did it influence them?

How did Dickens write his novels? The whole novel at once, or as it was being published? Did anybody else publish novels in magazines? Why? If Dickens wrote his novels as they were being published in parts, did he write differently from an author who composes the whole novel first, then publishes it?

Why isn't there an international organization to establish and enforce environmental policies? Aren't environmental problems considered important enough? Does it have to do with issues of national sovereignty?

Why do I say that Warren G. Harding was a terrible president?

What are people/companies doing to develop safe and economical ways to dispose of computers? Exactly what makes these machines so dangerous in landfills? Why is it so hard to get rid of the problem? Economically, what might we do to encourage businesses to go this way? Are chemical engineers at all interested in "de-toxifying" these machines? I'd particularly like to use my knowledge of chemistry to get into the technical side of the issue.

In doing a research project for some classes, you may find that it is easy to come up with a list of assumptions/research questions that you'd like to pursue. But in other courses you may find that your sense of your ignorance of the subject matter stops you cold. You may find yourself saying, "How can I write my assumptions about what I will find when I know almost nothing about this material?" "Maybe I'd like to investigate the Crusades, but I'd be starting from scratch. I don't even know what the Crusades were." "I've heard this term *behaviorism* a few times, but what is it?" "Black holes sound intriguing. What are they?"

In those cases in which you find that your personal knowledge of a subject is so meager that all you can say is, "I'd like to know more about X, but what is X?" you will have to do some basic preliminary reading before you can formulate your assumption and research question.

There are two strategies you can use to find an assumption/research question on a subject about which you feel very ignorant:

- If you find yourself saying, "I'd like to know more about X, but what is X?" begin to educate yourself by reading material that is meant to be an introduction to the topic.

  - Read about X in your course textbook or any textbook that introduces the subject.

  - Read about X in a book that is designed to be an introduction to X.

  - Read about X in an encyclopedia. A specialized encyclopedia or dictionary may be more helpful than a general encyclopedia.

  I'll cover this issue in more detail in Section 3.B.3.

- Browse in the library. Go to the section of the library where recent issues of magazines, journals, and newspapers are displayed. In articles in these periodicals the experts are talking about what they consider the most interesting research questions and areas of investigation in their fields. Look for articles on issues or subjects you are studying in your course. You may want to look specifically for periodicals in the field that are authoritative but accessible. As you browse, you are looking for articles you want to read because they interest you. The article may suggest a research question you'd like to use as your research question, or the subject matter of the article could be a subject you'd like to investigate further.

But don't turn into a passive sponge now. Even as you are doing this preliminary reading, read critically. In your Researcher's Notebook, record questions that pop into your head. Write down assumptions that you are making about what you will find as you read further. **Be particularly alert to any associations you find yourself making between this material and knowledge you already have.**

Once you have your research question/assumption, you are ready for the next step, which is to refine your assumption into a working hypothesis/thesis.

D. Step 4: Formulating Your Working Hypothesis/Thesis

Remember that the whole research process—the activities you will be engaged in during the coming weeks—is a process of *testing* assumptions that you are making now. You are not committing yourself to proving your initial assumptions correct. Indeed, your attitude toward your current thinking should be quite the opposite. Instead of saying to yourself, "I already have the right answer," your stance needs to be, "How valid are my present views?"

Testing ideas—opening them up to systematic, objective analysis—is the key to research. In fact, the readers of your final paper will not be judging your work simply on the conclusion you finally draw. They will be far more concerned about the way you drew that conclusion; they will be far more interested in your testing procedures and the way you analyzed your evidence. As they read your paper, these are the questions they will be asking:

- Is this researcher actually testing the hypothesis he said he was testing?
- Has this researcher found and considered all the important evidence?
- Does this researcher's final conclusion rest upon legitimate, relevant data?
- Do I consider the reasoning in this paper to be logical, valid?

You are beginning this research project with assumptions you are making to assure yourself that your own thinking will be the heart of the process. If you don't start with your assumptions, you don't really have anything to critically analyze, assess, and examine. Your assumptions give you something concrete to test. At this stage you are going to turn your initial assumptions into one considered statement that answers your initial research question. **Think of this working hypothesis/thesis as a means to an end, not the end itself. It will act as a touchstone, giving you a model of *one* way to make sense of your subject.** If you phrase it properly, it will tell you the type of data/evidence you need to look for, and it will suggest a means you can use to assess and analyze the evidence you find. As you gather and assess the evidence, it is very possible that you will decide that your initial assumptions were not valid, but the working hypothesis/thesis will have led you to other, more informed and thus valid, ways of fitting the parts of the puzzle together into a meaningful picture.

The following three strategies will help you turn your assumptions into a working hypothesis/thesis. So take out your Researcher's Notebook, open it to the Working Hypothesis/Thesis section, and follow the procedures outlined in the next three steps.

1. Strategy 1: Discovering your assumptions about your area of investigation

If you have stated an assumption that you have made about your subject (and you should have already written out such an assumption, even if you think it is probably wrong), you do have some ideas about the subject. You may know that your ideas are very general. You may know that your ideas are probably wrong. You may know that you don't have any sound reasons for assuming what you have assumed. The issue here is not the correctness or validity of your ideas. The point is that you yourself must be aware of the thoughts and feelings you have about your subject, or thoughts and feelings that have influenced your thinking about your subject. Whether you are aware of these thoughts and feelings or not, they will influence your research and the way you look at your evidence. You will have more control of the research process if you put these thoughts and feelings down on paper, where you can take a long hard look at them.

I personally believe that it is impossible for human beings to be entirely objective, but there are gradations on the subjective/objective scale. We can strive to be objective, an effort that, to me, means opening ourselves to ways of looking at a subject that are not the ways we have been used to looking at a subject. In my own experiences as a student and researcher, I have found that one important step toward objectivity is having as clear a picture as possible of what my present point of view is. I need to know my *basic* assumptions and attitudes toward my subject. I need to know what I *want* to find when I research. Pulling these assumptions out of myself is not easy because they feel as much a part of me as the color of my eyes or my name.

To make yourself aware of your basic assumptions and attitudes toward your subject, do some freewriting. For this technique to work, you must be as honest with yourself as you can be. Try to record on paper things that seem so obvious that you feel they don't need to be said. As you do this freewriting in your Researcher's Notebook, be as personal, as concrete, and as specific as possible.

- Go back to your original reasons for selecting your assumption/research question. Why did you choose this assumption or question? What train of thought led you to this assumption?

- What associations do you have in your head when you think about your assumption? Do *not* discard ideas just because they don't seem related. Write down *everything* that pops into your mind.

- When you write down a statement, force yourself to question that statement. Ask yourself, "What do I mean by that?" "Why do I say that?" "How did I arrive at that idea?"

Here are three examples of freewriting in which writers explore assumptions and attitudes they have about their subjects:

> As I start this investigation of child care programs offered by businesses, I have to admit that I am very biased. I believe very strongly that women have a *right* to demand that companies provide such programs. To pretend that I'm totally objective just isn't going to work—but I have to come up with some kind of assumption that can at least be tested. Probably the first thing I'd better do is find out why I believe that women have a right to child care. OK. Let's start with the fact that more and more women are working. And let's assume that women will continue to have children. So—somebody has to take care of the kids! Who? Grandma? Househusbands? Baby-sitters? Day care? I assume

that most women are paying someone to look after their children. So where do businesses come in? Well, the businesses hire these women; they can't just turn around and say, "Having kids is your problem—we pay you—you can use your salary to pay for child care." Hmmm, why do I say that businesses can't say "It's not our problem"? I'll bet that's the attitude of a lot of companies. But it is my opinion that businesses ought not to be able to say that . . . here we go. Child care is a national problem . . . a general social problem . . . businesses have to take responsibility, become involved . . .

I decided to investigate performance-enhancing drugs because of Rick's heart attack. The doctors say his heart wasn't damaged, and he'll be OK, but twenty-two-year-old athletes are healthy! They don't have heart attacks! The doctors say definitely that the cause of the attack was ephedrine. That's why my assumption is that ephedrine is dangerous! The fact of the matter is that I don't really know much at all about ephedrine or steroids or the other stuff athletes take to make them bigger and stronger or whatever. I do know that plenty of the guys down at the gym are into this stuff, and I know that at least some of these drugs have been banned by various groups and organizations (the Olympics? NFL?). I'm assuming that these drugs have been banned because they aren't good for the athletes who are taking them. But this then raises the question: if they aren't good for the athlete, exactly how are they harmful? In what way (or ways) do they endanger the health of the athlete? But it suddenly occurs to me that there could be another reason they have been banned—is it that some organizations don't want certain individuals or teams to have an unfair "competitive advantage"? Which gets into the whole business of sports as competition, if not sports as a profit-making enterprise. No, I don't think I want to go there. Being pre-med, I'm a lot more interested in the health/science part of this topic. And, actually, now that I think of it, what really interests me is less of the downside (how the drug hurts a person) than the reason athletes take the drugs in the first place. How do these drugs work? What do they do to/for the person to make him a better athlete? Add strength? Make a person bigger? Add endurance? How? What's the physiology? I'm pretty sure I have enough bio, chem, and human anatomy under my belt at this point to understand the technical side of things. OK. I feel better. There are a lot of possibilities here. Definitely the first step is just to get some information about these drugs, and I can go from there. My first stab at a research question/hypothesis focused on ephedrine, but I'm thinking now that maybe I should first of all take a look at all kinds of these drugs to see what's out there. Are they all alike? Do they all do the same thing? How do they affect the body? I know that I will have to narrow down, but I want to see my choices first . . .

I took this psych course on learning because I assumed it would be good background for me to have when, in a couple of years, I start teaching second grade. My working hypothesis for this research paper is that learning disabilities are a major reason that kids have trouble learning to read. That assumption is based on the last chapter of the textbook we used in Teaching Reading last semester. I don't think we spent enough time on that topic, so this psych course gives me a great chance to get into the issue more. See, I think learning to read is maybe the most critical key to academic success. Yes, that is one of my assumptions. And so is the fact that one of my major goals as a teacher will be to make sure all my kids do learn how to read. So it makes sense for me to want to understand the reasons that some kids have so much trouble becoming good readers. Yes, I realize that there can be a lot of different reasons. We covered a number last semester. That's partly why I'm narrowing down to LDs. But from what I remember from that last chapter in the reading textbook, LD itself stands for lots of different things. So

where am I? What I'd like to do in this paper is to put together what I know about reading with what we are learning in this class about the brain and cognitive functions and
information-processing and so on. In other words, how is the brain functioning when
we read? Then LDs fit in here (I'm assuming!) because they represent "things" that
interfere in some way with the brain being able to make sense of print. Yes, I think this
is the assumption I am making . . .

Even if it seems to lead you off the track of your specific research question/
assumption, this exploration of your personal thoughts and feelings about your
area of investigation will help you in two important ways:

- You will know what your emotional reactions to your subject matter are,
  and you'll begin to see that some of your personal values and judgments
  have influenced the assumption you've made, even if you don't seem to have
  any personal feelings about your research assumption/question. Once you
  are aware of your own point of view, you are in a better position to open
  that point of view to critical analysis: Do I have any concrete, specific, logical reasons for my feelings and attitudes? Are they based on facts and evidence? Am I going to be able to look at this issue objectively?

- You may discover that the research question/assumption you started with is
  not really the research question/assumption you want to work with. As you
  freewrite, you may discover the real assumption you want to test. Do not
  worry about how narrow or specific the question seems. Look for the ques-
  tion/assumption that you want to pursue further.

I have encouraged you to choose a subject or an area of investigation in which
you have a personal investment. But, as I noted a moment ago, to carry out this
project successfully you are going to have to be aware of, and deal appropriately
with, your personal feelings. If the area of investigation you have chosen is one
that you have very strong feelings about, or one to which you respond very emotionally, I have two recommendations for you:

- Do a freewrite in which you fully and freely give expression to these feelings. Write what you would *really* like to say in your paper about the subject, and about your involvement with it.

- When you are done, have a conversation with yourself about whether this
  subject is a good one for you to take on for this research project. Ask yourself if there is an angle you could take, or a place where you could position
  yourself in relationship to the subject, that would allow you to assess the
  evidence you find in a reasonable, fairly neutral fashion.

2. Strategy 2: Turning judgmental statements into inferences

If you remember my discussion of facts, inferences, and judgments in Section 1,
you'll remember that a judgmental statement is a statement about a person's

approval or disapproval of something. Judgmental statements don't lend themselves very easily to testing. Here are judgmental statements:

> Abortion is wrong.

> The Industrial Revolution hurt the common worker.

> You should take lots of vitamin C.

> Warren G. Harding was a terrible president.

> Funding grassroots programs is the best use of development aid to Third World countries.

> *Citizen Kane* is a great movie.

> Urban planning in our metropolitan areas is more critical than ever.

You can begin to turn such judgmental statements into inferences, into statements that lend themselves to testing, by underlining judgmental or evaluative words or phrases and then writing down what these judgmental or evaluative words mean to you.

JUDGMENTAL STATEMENT

> You <u>should take</u> lots of vitamin C.

When I say "should take," I mean:

> Vitamin C is a necessary component of a healthy diet.

> *or*

> Large doses of vitamin C allow the body to resist colds and flu.

JUDGMENTAL STATEMENT

> Warren G. Harding was a <u>terrible</u> president.

When I say "terrible," I mean:

> Warren G. Harding exhibited few leadership qualities, qualities that all presidents are expected to have.

> *or*

> Warren G. Harding put together an administration of men who were irresponsible and corrupt.

> *or*

> The way Warren G. Harding was chosen as the Republican candidate in 1920 shows the weaknesses of the nominating process.

JUDGMENTAL STATEMENT

> Funding grassroots programs is the <u>best</u> use of development aid to Third World countries.

When I say "best, " I mean:

> When foreign aid allocations are designated for specific grassroots programs, the odds are increased that the money will get into the hands of the people rather than being diverted into the bank accounts of corrupt bureaucrats or greedy leaders.

or

> Grassroots development programs avoid cultural imperialism by enabling the inhabitants of a region to determine their needs and what type of improvements in their area would best meet those needs.

or

> Grassroots development programs can empower women in Third World countries.

JUDGMENTAL STATEMENT

> *Citizen Kane* is a <u>great</u> movie.

When I say "great," I mean:

> Film critics and aficionados have consistently ranked *Citizen Kane* one of the best films ever made in the United States.

or

> *Citizen Kane* perfectly illustrates Orson Welles' dramatic and innovative cinematography.

or

> *Citizen Kane* has an absorbing plot and very convincing performances, especially by Joseph Cotten and Orson Welles.

JUDGMENTAL STATEMENT

> Urban planning in our metropolitan areas is <u>more critical than ever</u>.

When I say "more critical than ever," I mean:

> Unregulated gentrification in inner cities is making affordable housing harder and harder to find.

or

> The continued development of outlying bedroom communities is environmentally unsound for various reasons: for example, it destroys the ecosystems of the land that is developed; it decreases the amount of land available for agricultural purposes; and it encourages increases in the use of automobiles, which in turn increases air pollution and the carbon dioxide levels that contribute to global warming.

or

> To form a real community, people must live in areas where shops, workplaces, churches, homes, places for cultural and other leisure activities are close together.

When you underline and explain the judgmental words in your own assumptions, you may come up with two or three statements, as I have done. Note that each of these statements is a separate assumption with its own focal point and direction. In the last example, the first statement points to a study that will focus on the socioeconomic status of inhabitants of the city. The second statement focuses on the effects of suburbs on the natural environment. The third statement reflects an interest in the concept of "community." Obviously, each statement would point me in a different research direction. If you come up with several statements, you should give some thought to whether you want to pursue all these lines of inquiry. Each of the statements in the last example would be broad enough for a research project.

3. Strategy 3: Defining your terms

Defining key terms in your statement is yet another means you can use to turn your assumption into a working hypothesis/thesis. Like the other two strategies, defining your terms is a way to clarify your idea for yourself.

In defining your terms, do not, at first, use a dictionary. What you are attempting to do here is discover what *you* meant by those words.

> Grassroots development programs avoid cultural imperialism by enabling the inhabitants of a region to determine their needs and what type of improvements in their area would best meet those needs.
>
> What do I mean by "grassroots development programs"? By grassroots development programs I mean . . .
>
> What do I mean by "cultural imperialism"? By cultural imperialism I mean . . .
>
> What do I mean by "enabling the inhabitants"? By enabling the inhabitants I mean . . .
>
> What do I mean by "improvements"? By improvements I mean . . .

After you define all key terms in your own words, you may want to check your definitions against the definitions in a dictionary. Does the word *cultural imperialism* mean what you thought it meant? Is *cultural imperialism* the term you want? Your working hypothesis/thesis must say what you want it to say. The words on the page must reflect what you have in your head. Don't change your ideas; just find the right words for what you want to say.

These three strategies are designed to help you come up with a statement that is precise, that says directly and clearly what you want it to say. When you finish these exercises, you ought to have a statement that tells you what kind of evidence you need to look for, and that also tells you how you are going to go about assessing the information you find.

WORKING THESES

> I assume that Warren G. Harding can be used as a negative example of those leadership qualities that Americans expect of their presidents.

I assume that grassroots development programs avoid cultural imperialism by enabling the inhabitants of a region to determine their needs and what type of improvements in their area would best meet those needs.

I assume that Orson Welles' cinematography, as illustrated by *Citizen Kane*, was dramatic and innovative.

I assume that the continued development of outlying bedroom communities is environmentally unsound for three reasons: it destroys the ecosystems of the land that is developed; it decreases the amount of land available for agricultural purposes; and it encourages increases in the use of automobiles, which in turn increases air pollution and the carbon dioxide levels that contribute to global warming.

Looking over these examples, you may be thinking that they are too narrow and specific. "I couldn't," you may be saying to yourself as panic overtakes you, "write a ten-page paper on *that!*" This response would make sense if you were expected to complete the paper tonight. But, of course, the fact is that the paper is not due for weeks and weeks, and between now and the time you have to have a polished draft you are going to know much, much more about your subject than you do now. Moreover, this final paper is not going to be simply a laundry-list of facts. If you take the stance I'm encouraging you to take, you are going to have a much deeper understanding of your subject, and it is this understanding that will give shape and meaning to the draft. Developing arguments, explaining ideas to others in such a way that they understand you takes space. How many times have you seen "please explain" or "develop this idea" written in the margins of your essays?

The "I-can't-write-ten-pages-on-that" panic may also have its source in the assumption that you are committing yourself to this working hypothesis/thesis forever and always, that it is something you are obliged to *prove* is *right*. So I must remind you that neither of these assumptions is accurate. The working hypothesis/thesis is a *strategy*; it is a device, as you'll see in a moment, that grounds you, that is going to enable you to begin research right away. The working hypothesis/thesis replaces the amassing quantities of paper as your objective in the research part of the process. It provides you with a sense of direction by giving you a destination. But I am calling it a *working* hypothesis/thesis because its status is provisional and most definitely open to change. And you should assume that odds are great that it will change in some fashion as you learn more about your subject. Such change is natural, and you must be flexible enough to let it happen. If you are engaged in a secondary research project, or in a primary research project in the humanities, make these assumptions:

- If, as you research, you find the facts suggest that your working thesis was incorrect, you will rewrite it to fit the picture that the facts suggest. It is very possible you'll revise this thesis several times.

- It is also very possible that, as you research, you realize that your original working thesis is too broad to research thoroughly, or you may find that your interest shifts to a different angle of the subject. This often happens to researchers, and, again, they respond simply by revising their working thesis.

You should assume that your research may take you into areas that you cannot anticipate right now; you should assume that you are going to learn a great deal in the following weeks. And you aren't going to let this prospect of change panic you any more than the prospect of a narrow working thesis does. You are going to remain in control of this project at all times because you have a clear sense of direction, and that sense of direction is provided by the combination of the working thesis and research question, even though they may undergo transmutations between now and the time you begin your final draft. And underlying them is your touchstone:

> Am I understanding my chosen area of investigation better? If so, what understanding am I reaching? If not, what do I still need to know?

Of course, if you are still nervous that your working hypothesis/thesis is too narrow, by all means show it to your instructor. As a matter of fact, in subsection G, I recommend that you prepare a proposal of your research project for your instructor so that you can be reassured that you are heading in a profitable direction.

E. Step 5: Choosing Your Research Strategy—Research Questions

The working hypothesis/thesis allows you to operationalize the research process. What this means is that the working hypothesis/thesis tells you, specifically, what you need to know, what you need to find out. If you deconstruct your working hypothesis/thesis, you will be formulating a whole series of questions that will direct the first stages of your search for sources. In other words, instead of following the passive sponge approach of finding everything that has been written about X, you are going to let "what I need to know and understand about my assumption about X" direct you to sources that promise to have the information and material you need. The working hypothesis/thesis also has the added value of giving you a feel for further ways in which you may have to narrow your focus.

WORKING THESIS

> I assume that the continued development of outlying bedroom communities is environmentally unsound for three reasons: it destroys the ecosystems of the land that is developed; it decreases the amount of land available for agricultural purposes; and it encourages increases in the use of automobiles, which in turn increases air pollution and the carbon dioxide levels that contribute to global warming.

RESEARCH QUESTIONS

> • One central question that immediately arises is, am I going to be making huge generalizations about urban sprawl throughout the Western world, limit myself to the United

States, or limit myself further to specific cities? In order to really make my case, I'm obviously going to have to have some concrete examples in mind. So—I need to see if there are any case studies out there about the environmental impact of specific suburbs.

• Am I correct in assuming that metropolitan areas continue to build bedroom communities? All over the US? In some places and not others?

• I say "bedroom communities," but am I correct in assuming that all the building on the periphery of cities is for residential suburbs? Is this outlying land being developed in any other way or ways?

• What do I have in mind when I say this urban sprawl destroys ecosystems? What kind of ecosystems do I have in mind? Again, this points to my need to investigate some specific cities and areas. Exactly how does the building of houses and roads destroy ecosystems?

• I assume that bedroom communities take land away from agricultural use, and that this is a bad thing. Does the development of bedroom communities take land away from agricultural use? If this is true, is it necessarily a bad thing? What other purposes might this land be used for? Are these other purposes good? How am I going to be defining "good" and "bad" here?

• Do bedroom communities increase the use of automobiles? How and why?

• Do automobiles increase air pollution? Exactly how?

• Do I have this business about carbon dioxide contributing to global warming right? What are the specifics?

• What do the experts have to say about this general issue of urban sprawl and its environmental impact? Who are the experts? Environmentalists would be a good group to start with, but others? Urban planners?

And on and on as you find out what information is available and what others have to say.

F. A Few More Words about Research Projects and Testing

All researchers—regardless of the field in which they are working, regardless of the type of project in which they are engaged—are involved in a quest for knowledge and a deeper understanding of a subject. Their quests are characterized by attitudes of questioning and critical inquiry. Whatever answers or conclusions they eventually reach will be based on a solid foundation of evidence that they have submitted to rigorous analysis. However, as I noted in Section 1, the forms specific investigations take can and do differ. The way a researcher spends her researching time, the use she makes of the work of other experts, and the purpose and focus of the paper she writes when her research is complete are dependent on various factors. One such factor is the source or sources from which she collects the major portion of her evidence. Her activities will differ if she is engaged in a secondary or a primary research project. Moreover, the

activities of researchers engaged in primary research projects in the hard sciences
will differ from those of researchers doing primary research in the humanities.
These differences account for my references to working hypotheses *or* theses.

Before you proceed further with the project that you are now starting, you
need a clear sense of the type of research project in which you will be engaged.
Here I will describe three general types of research projects/papers frequently
assigned in college courses. Compare them to the assignment your instructor has
given you. If you have any questions or confusions regarding your instructor's
expectations, now's the time to talk with him or her. Knowing where your project fits within these broad categories of academic research will help you clarify
the purpose and direction of your research, thus strengthening your sense of
control of this process.

1. Studies and experiments

Primary research projects in the hard sciences—the pure and applied natural sciences and areas of the social sciences—are usually called experiments or studies.
The major focus of such projects is collecting data directly from the phenomena
under investigation in the discipline and empirically analyzing them. The intellectual energies of the researcher go into carefully designing the process through
which she'll reach this end. Normally, she'll begin by developing a research question and/or an hypothesis that can be tested empirically. To assure herself of the
validity of the results she'll report on in her final paper, she'll select a procedure
for collecting data that is used regularly by experts in the field, just as she'll use
an accepted quantitative or qualitative method for analyzing the data she obtains.

You are engaged in such a primary research project if you set up and carry
out an experiment in the lab. You are doing such a primary research project if
your focus is on gathering specific kinds of information from a select group of
people and analyzing that information with some mode of statistical analysis.
You are engaged in such a project if your objective is systematically observing a
specific group of people, animals, or plants. You should do such studies or
experiments only under the guidance of an instructor who is a member of the
field in which such studies or experiments are undertaken regularly, and only if
such an instructor has either assigned this type of project or is willing to give
you the assistance you will need.

The success of your project hinges both on your developing a sound hypothesis and also on your selecting the best methods for testing this hypothesis.
Experienced researchers rely on the work of other experts to help them with
both these tasks. Thus the early stages of your project will be spent learning
what experts have to say about your subject but, particularly, learning about
investigative procedures they've used. Your critical reading of these sources will
enable you to choose just the right wording for your hypothesis and to choose
the most important methods for testing it.

Since the heart of your project is designing and carrying out your experiment or study, and since such activities take time, you must set up reasonable

deadlines for this stage of the project. I urge you also to submit a proposal for this project, including your hypothesis and details about your research design, to your instructor early in the project, *before* you do the study or experiment. A seriously flawed study or experiment will produce worthless results. You may also want to turn to Section 5.B now and read more about the report you'll write when your project is complete.

2. A review or a review of the literature paper

Papers called reviews or reviews of the literature are common in all fields. A researcher who sets out to write such a paper is engaged in a secondary research project. His objective is to locate and study as much published material (literature) as he is able to acquire about a particular topic. In the paper he writes his purpose is to give his readers a clear overview of the conversation that is currently going on in the field about this topic.

If you are engaged in this type of project, your research time will be spent locating as much published work on your topic as you can. Your search will probably be limited to material published over the past ten, or even five, years; but, if you find an overwhelming number of sources, part of your intellectual energies will have to go into limiting the sources you'll have to study by somehow redefining the topic.

Your basic research question will be, "What are the basic trends and developments in the field's quest for knowledge about X?" Your working thesis will be your answer to this question. The object of your critical inquiry will be to make sense of these various studies by discerning and bringing into focus patterns you find in this work: patterns of investigative procedures, of the theories that drive them, and of the knowledge they produce. Clarifying these patterns will constitute the substance of the writing you do in the Working Hypothesis/Thesis section of your Notebook.

I talk more about this type of paper in Section 5.C. It would probably be helpful to read over this material now.

If you are not sure if your instructor wants the type of paper I've just described, check with him or her right away. It might be helpful to take this book along with you in case your instructor wants to see what I've had to say about such projects.

3. Critical papers

Whereas the two research projects I've just described are fairly narrow and standardized, a number of different types of projects can lead to a critical paper. This type of paper could be written by a researcher engaged in a secondary research project in any field. Such papers are normally the culmination of primary research projects undertaken in the "soft sciences" or humanities.

The central characteristic of critical papers is that they are arguments. The writer has chosen to look at her subject from a particular point of view, and her objective in the paper is to persuade us that hers is a logical and meaningful way to make sense of the subject. In the opening paragraph of such papers the writer presents her point of view in an assertion or claim or conclusion (usually called a thesis statement); she devotes the rest of the paper to explaining how and why she reached this conclusion. If the researcher was engaged in a secondary research project, the majority of evidence she uses in making her argument are facts collected by others as well as the inferences these experts have drawn about the meaning of such facts. If the researcher was engaged in a primary research project, her claim will be about the artifact she has been studying—a painting, a musical composition, a poem—and, as evidence, she will use facts she's uncovered in her systematic analysis of this object. Because, however, she's been engaged in a *research* project, she will also have investigated what others have had to say about this object and the way these experts have analyzed it. She will place her claim in the context of the work others have done; in addition to features of the object she's uncovered, she will use relevant facts and views of the experts in making her argument.

If the paper you will be writing for this research project is a critical paper, you will begin by formulating a working thesis. This working thesis is a claim or an assertion you would make about your topic now, before you've begun your investigation. But you are opening up this working thesis to question. In the coming weeks your objective is to test this assumption. Whatever claim or assertion you make about your subject in the paper you will write weeks from now, that claim must come from an objective, systematic examination of your subject. Not only must you gather as much evidence as you can—both facts and inferences drawn by various experts—but you must also critically assess this evidence. To do such assessments, you will need a **frame of analysis.** If you are engaged in a primary research project, not only the evidence you've gathered from others but also your primary source of evidence—a text, a musical composition, a painting—must be submitted to such objective, systematic analysis.

A frame of analysis is a methodology, different in kind but not in purpose from the investigative procedures the hard sciences use for collecting and assessing data. The frame of analysis you choose will be provided by a theory, a model, or an interpretive approach that is currently popular or generally accepted in the field in which you are working. For example, to determine whether a violent change in government in a particular country can rightfully be called a revolution, you need a model or theory of revolutions—Marx's, for example. If you are assessing the viability of recycling efforts, you will have to choose a method of defining and determining viability. If you are studying a work of literature or music or art, you will have to examine that work through the framework of an interpretive approach currently popular in the field. A well-established method of making meaning of works of art has been to classify them according to styles or eras (baroque, romantic, expressionist, impressionist). If your project focuses on reaching a deeper under-standing of paintings by Monet, you could, for example, examine them through the frame of definitions of impressionism and accepted characteristics of that style.

The search on which you are now embarking, therefore, will involve more than a search for facts. After all, as I noted in Section 1, phenomena in and of themselves are meaningless. Your quest is for a frame of analysis through which to make meaning of the facts you collect. This will require your paying close attention to the theories, models, or interpretive approaches used by various experts. Paying attention to the frames of analysis through which they've looked at your subject will enable you to understand how they've arrived at their con-clusions. It will also enable you to select that frame of analysis which, in your eyes, best explains the available facts, and which, thus, leads to a better under-standing of this subject.

I want to end this discussion of research and testing by putting the emphasis on testing and your critical thinking. I grow more and more convinced that the suc-cess or failure of a student research paper depends a great deal on the mental posture or stance that the researcher/writer takes in relationship to the subject she or he is investigating. In my mind, the ideal stance is the Aristotelian Golden Mean. It rests in the middle ground between total disinterest (which usually means "uninterested") and disengagement at one extreme, and complete immer-sion in emotions or ideology or values on the other. To put it in other terms, the motive of the researcher is neither to uncover some reality which is unassailably and absolutely true, nor is it to rationalize what she or he *wants* to be true. The testing that I have in mind is very different. *Testing* is a very different process from *rationalizing, justifying,* or *proving* (as the word is often used in debate). A person may be able to give several good reasons why marijuana should be decriminalized; but simply being able to give a few good reasons for (or against) a particular position does not necessarily mean that a person has carefully stud-ied all of the available facts, critically reviewed the various opinions of the experts, and developed a final conclusion from his or her critical thinking, based on those facts and opinions of the experts.

The ideal researcher goes through this critical evaluation quite simply because she wants to have good reasons for holding the opinion or view she has of the subject. She wants to know, at a conscious level, why she sees the subject as she does. She wants to be able to articulate these reasons to herself so she can decide if they really do make sense to her, and, when she finds a position that does make good sense to her, so that she can articulate her rea-soning to others. You will notice that the suggestions I've been giving in this section revolve around a pattern of questions and answers. Notice how similar it is to the pattern of discussions that your instructors encourage in class. This pattern of asking questions, developing your own answers for them, but questioning the answers you develop is what critical thinking is all about. You need to internalize it, which is what the Reading and the Working Hypothesis/ Thesis sections of your Researcher's Notebook are here to help you do. Regardless of the subject you are investigating and the method of testing you decide to use, you are beginning with a hypothesis/thesis that you are opening up to question. As objectively as possible, you are going to examine your assumption to determine how valid it is.

Because your goal is to develop your own conclusion, based on your critical assessment of the facts and the opinions of experts, you are obliged

- to find as much information as you can about your subject;

- to consider *all* of the evidence you find, even if it seems to be saying that your original hypothesis/thesis is incorrect;

- to select a sound method of testing, whether we are talking about the research design for a study or experiment, or a frame of analysis for a project that will result in a review or a critical paper.

G. A Research Proposal

Don't be surprised if your instructor, in the early stages of your project, asks you to hand in some kind of description of what you propose to research for your paper. Even if such a proposal isn't required, it would be a good idea to do one anyway. If you are doing a study or experiment, as I've noted, submitting such a proposal, which includes a complete description of your research design, will go a long way toward guaranteeing the success of your project.

In the real world, writing research proposals is fairly standard practice. Research usually costs money, and researchers have to convince the people with the money—government agencies, private foundations, corporations—that their particular projects are worth the investment. Your professor will probably have different reasons for wanting to know what you are planning to do. Asking for such a proposal is a convenient method of encouraging you to get an early start on a research paper. But handing in such a proposal can profit you in another way. Before you do too much work, your instructor can give you an expert's opinion, warning you about trouble you may encounter, giving you useful information about sources of evidence that you may not be aware of, or helping you to refine your sense of direction even further. There is no standard format for a proposal you would write for a classroom instructor. In deciding what you want to say, remember that your general purpose is to let your instructor know the problem on which you are working and the type of investigation you intend to pursue. You will want to inform your instructor about

- your general area of investigation (liberation theology, the function of enzymes) with a *short* narrative discussing how you became interested in this topic and/or how your investigation fits in with the material you are studying in this class;

• your initial research question and your working hypothesis/thesis, explicitly labeled as such;

• your general research strategy—what kinds of evidence you will be looking for and where you will be looking for it. Often instructors will ask you to include a bibliography. To respond to this request, you will need to have started the next stage of the process, which is covered in Section 3, "Finding the Evidence."

There are no rules about the length of proposals. Just remember that the better your instructor understands what you have in mind, the more help he or she can give you.

H. A Final Note

The solution or conclusion you are seeking is not tucked away in some book or article in the library. Researching is not a game of treasure hunt.

Your conclusion is just that—the conclusion or idea that *you* develop as you examine, analyze, and consider the evidence you discover. You are, as I will remind you constantly, a detective. Like a detective, you cannot know where your search will finally end. But you can, and must, constantly give *direction* to your search. For this reason your Researcher's Notebook is your most important tool.

As your experience as a researcher increases, you will learn that research projects, especially complex research projects, often take unexpected twists as they develop. The puzzle you intended to solve at the beginning of your search gradually changes shape and turns into a new puzzle as you learn more about the subject you are investigating. As a researcher, then, you must remain flexible and alert; you must be willing to change, but you must always know which path you are taking.

If you are doing a secondary research project or a primary research project in the humanities, once you have your working thesis and research questions, you are ready to begin looking for the evidence. You should now turn to the next section of this book.

The next section of this book is also very important for the researcher setting up a study or experiment. Although your final goal is to collect and analyze raw data directly from the source, you must first have a sound hypothesis and valid testing procedures. The work that others have done in your field is critical to you in developing the design of your study or experiment. The following section of this book, which offers strategies for locating published material, can help you discover what others in your field have done.

I. Planning Ahead: Developing a Work Schedule

Begin with the date on which the paper is due, and work backward.

DATE

STAGE IN THE PROCESS

Due date, the date on which you will give your paper to your instructor.

Begin polishing final rough draft (at least two days before due date; if rough draft needs to be typed, *add* a realistic amount of time for this task).

First rough draft complete (two to two-and-a-half weeks before the due date).

Date on which all essential evidence has been collected and you begin drafting your paper (at least three weeks before due date).

Date on which you being the research process by selecting an area of investigation, developing your research question, and starting your Researcher's Notebook (within a week of the time you receive the assignment).

Once you have set the deadlines above and you have developed your research strategies, you will be able to—and should—set deadlines for yourself for intermediate steps in the process. If you are doing a critical paper or review of the literature, you should set deadlines for such things as gathering your first list of sources, having certain books and articles read, doing interviews, and the like. If you are doing a study or experiment, it is crucial for you to set a number of deadlines: when your research design will be complete; when you will put together your apparatus or find your participants or pass out your questionnaires; when you will run the experiment or study itself; and so on.

SECTION

3

Finding the Evidence

A. The Researcher's Stance

Now that you have articulated your working hypothesis/thesis and you've written out the questions that derive from it, your next major step is to begin the search for the evidence that will enable you to answer these questions. Before you turn on your computer or head for the library, I'm going to urge you to look over this entire section.

In these pages I have two interrelated objectives. One is to provide you with **practical information** that will enable you to find the evidence you need for the paper you are currently working on. But I have a more general and more important objective. I want **to educate you about the stance that an active detective takes in doing research.** Not surprisingly, this stance is very different from that of the passive sponge. The passive sponge will enter a few words into a search engine, click on a few links, and when he decides he has enough material to fill up ten pages, he will declare the research process finished. In contrast, as a detective researcher you will be using your brain vigorously throughout this search for evidence. Here are the three ways in which you will be directly invested in the research process.

First of all, your quest will be constantly driven and determined by your personal sense of what you need to know.

In Section 2, I showed you how to move beyond thinking of topics in the traditional sense of nouns and noun phrases—sun imagery in *Richard II*, the importance of nonverbal behavior in communication. Now you have to move beyond thinking of research simply as the task of gathering mounds of material, whether these mounds are comprised of books and articles you find in the library, or material you find on the Internet. Taking this step will require breaking "out of the box" of thinking of research only in terms of the place where you do your searching (the shelves of a library, an Internet search engine) and/or only in terms of categories of sources (Web sites, books, articles).

In Step 5 in Section 2, I urged you to break your working hypothesis/thesis down into a series of more specific questions. It is these questions, and others that come up as you think and write in the Working Hypothesis/Thesis section of your Notebook, that are going to drive the research you do. In this section of your Notebook you should be constantly assessing what you feel confident that you know and understand, and what you feel you need to educate yourself about further. You should be constantly asking yourself about the nature and quality of the evidence you already have, and what more you need to look for. Turn such issues into questions, and let them be the impetus for the searches you do. If you focus on the kind of information or knowledge you have to acquire in order to develop a meaningful answer to your research question, then your quest will be for "sources" that promise to contain such information or knowledge.

> **Secondly, in this quest for the information and knowledge you need, you will constantly be using your problem-solving skills.**

Those nouns and noun phrases that I've warned you against in defining the focus of your research project are going to come into play when you start your search because they are a major feature of systems for storing and retrieving information. In order to find the evidence you need, you will be entering nouns and noun phrases into search boxes in the library catalog, bibliographic databases, Internet search engines. To decide what nouns or noun phrases will produce the material you need, you are going to have to use your problem-solving skills. To help you in this endeavor, I'll explain how nouns and noun phrases fit into the systems used by people who classify and catalog print material.

With these systems of classifying and categorizing materials comes a lot of technical vocabulary. I want to be sure you understand this vocabulary because it is going to make it much easier for you to understand and to communicate with your instructor, librarians, and your writing center staff. There is, in addition, another major benefit to having a good grasp of this vocabulary. As you near the end of this project, when your paper is almost done, you are going to document the evidence that you have used in your paper. **Documenting your evidence** will entail telling your readers, in a formalized way, where you found this evidence. The forms in which you give your readers information about your sources will closely resemble the forms that library catalogs and databases use to provide information about books, articles, and other stored material. They resemble each other because these two sets of forms are derived from the same basic underlying concepts. As I define various terms, I'll be educating you about these basic concepts, and I do so in the hope that this knowledge will make your search for evidence—and your documentation of this evidence in your paper—much more comprehensible. I cover the basics of documentation in Section 8. Think of this section, and Section 8, as companion chapters. You might even want to scan Section 8 now, just to get a feel for what I discuss there. Treat these sections as reference materials which you will consult whenever you need the specific information they cover.

But to return now to the issue of your problem-solving skills. They are going to help you, I'll repeat, determine exactly where you are going to look for evidence, and how you are going to conduct specific searches. But you are going to need these problem-solving skills, too, to cope productively with the whole research stage of this project. I point out later in this section that research is never as neat and straightforward as we would like it to be. In fact, if your research is to be truly successful, you must remain open and flexible. At the same time, as I have been stressing, you need to be pursuing a specific objective. To do both at once is asking you to walk a fairly tricky tightrope. To help you maintain your balance and a sense of control, in this section and in Section 4 I'll be giving you a lot of practical advice. It is all aimed at showing you where and how you can be methodical and organized in finding and storing evidence, thereby freeing up time and energy for solving the intellectual challenges you have taken on.

Finally, then, and most importantly, as you search for sources you will always be using your critical thinking faculties.

I have already pointed out that, to produce a truly successful paper—one that not only satisfies your instructor but one that, more importantly, fully satisfies you—you will have to critically evaluate the information you gather. In Section 4 I talk in more detail about methods of evaluating print sources. But you can—and should—also screen information and material you find *as* you find it. I talk extensively in subsection D about the need for, and strategies for, evaluating material you find online, and, in subsection B, I introduce you to criteria that academics use for assessing the authority of texts.

The nice thing about this active researcher stance I am encouraging you to adopt is that, above and beyond the immediate benefits you will reap, it will continue to pay dividends not only throughout your college years but well after graduation. The resources and the strategies to which I am going to introduce you are going to be of immense value to you whenever you need to do research, whether the research is a required part of your job or profession, or it is necessitated by an illness in your family, or it is motivated by your desire to get a good buy on a car. More importantly, you are going to look at whatever you find with a critical eye. No longer will you assume that, just because someone says it (or puts it into print, or posts it on the Web), it must be true! In becoming an active detective-researcher, you will become a **critical consumer of information.**

So here's an overview of what you will find in the upcoming pages:

B. Sources and Resources
    1. Sources: Where Do I Find What I Need to Know?
    2. Authoritative Sources
    3. Resources
C. The Research Process
    1. What to Expect and How to Manage
    2. Bibliographic "Filing" Systems
    3. Searching for Potential Sources
       a. Know Your Database
       b. Searches by Subject and Keyword
       c. What Your Search Will Produce
    4. Locating Print Sources
D. Evaluating Online Sources
E. Information to Record about Electronic Sources
F. Summary

B. Sources and Resources

1. Sources: Where do I find what I need to know?

If, as I encouraged you to do in the previous subsection, you focus on the kind of information or knowledge you must acquire in order to develop a meaningful answer to your general research question, then your quest will be for "sources" that promise to contain such information or material. Inevitably, some of the sources you use will be print materials such as books and articles; it is very possible that you will also find valuable material on the Internet. But, as I said a moment ago, I want you to start thinking "outside the box." When you think **source,** think of a person, a place, or a procedure that could give you the **kind and quality of information or material** you need in order to answer your questions.

To continue this discussion, let's return to two concepts I introduced in Section 1. The first, based on the work of S. I. Hayakawa, suggests that we can break evidence down into facts, inferences, and judgments or evaluations. In this search of yours, some of your questions have answers that are **uncontested facts** (What year was Marie Antoinette married? Where was Harry Truman born? What are the chemical components of table salt?). But equally important are **facts, inferences and/or evaluations** that have been developed by others. Because the authority and credibility of the source is important, you will be looking for the ideas and work of individuals you consider to be **experts.** Texts that contain such material are, to use the other concept I introduced in Section 1, **secondary materials.**

If you remember, I said that a **primary study** is one that revolves around evidence a researcher gathers directly from the source. If you want to know what dramatists in the eighteenth century thought about Shakespeare's plays, or how the church portrayed Eve and the Virgin Mary in the medieval period, then going directly to the source would mean finding documents on these topics written during the historical period in question. If you want to know how college students feel about the cost of education, then going directly to the source would mean posing this question to individuals who are currently enrolled in college. If you want to know how three-year-olds behave, going directly to the source would mean observing three-year-olds in a systematic way. By contrast, in a **secondary study** we rely on the observations, facts, results, and opinions that others have gathered and developed on the topic. If you want to know how college students feel about the cost of education, and you read studies in which the authors gathered information from college students on this topic, you are relying on **secondary sources.** Just as all members of academic fields do, you are going to make use of secondary sources. But thinking outside the box encourages you to remember that books and articles are not the only place to find the views of experts. It also encourages you to consider possible ways of gathering **primary evidence,** even though the study in which you are engaged does not fully focus on such evidence.

- If your working thesis involves a subject with which you have or can have personal contact, would it make sense for you to gather information about your personal experiences with this subject? If you are investigating the work of a composer, should you attend a concert in which her music is played or listen to CDs of her work? If you are doing research on advertising on television or in magazines, would it make sense for you to look at certain ads yourself, recording what you see and how the ads affect you? If your working thesis has to do with mass transit, would it be valuable for you to plan a few trips on various parts of your local mass transit system?

- If your working thesis involves institutions that still exist or work that is still being done, think about gathering information from people who are employed by such institutions or whose jobs involve the kind of work you are researching. If you are investigating a subject related to a government or private agency, perhaps you should contact that agency for relevant printed material. Maybe some well-chosen interviews with key people in an organization would tell you what you need to know. If you are researching a foreign country, have you thought about contacting one of its embassies or consulates for information?

- The term *expert* is a word we use to describe a person whom we consider to have valuable knowledge about a subject, but not all experts' opinions or views are published in books and academic journals. If your working thesis is about an academic subject, you might want to talk to the "experts" who teach this subject at your school or on a nearby campus. Officers in an organization can tell you a great deal about that organization. But also think about others who might be able to give you an "expert's view" of the subject you're investigating. Who knows the pros and cons of a computer software program better than a person who uses it every day? While an official who works for a mass transit system certainly has one view of that system, the people who ride the buses and subways every day also have knowledge and opinions about it that could be exactly the type of evidence you need.

The determination of who is an expert, we see, is a contextual one. Similarly, **primary** and **secondary** are not inherent characteristics of a text, but rather describe the point of view or interest of the person using it. The issue here—and it is directly related to becoming an active researcher—is determining your definition of a text: how you are going to "read" it, the kind of information you expect it to give you. Let us say that you are doing a paper on theories of evolution. In this study you would use Darwin's *Origin of Species* as a secondary source; that is, you treat Darwin as one expert on the topic, and use ideas you find in *Origin* as reflecting his evidence and/or conclusions. But, let's say, you decide to focus a research project on Darwin himself. You want to understand better his scientific methodology and thinking processes. From this perspective, *Origin*, *The Voyage of the Beagle,* and other works by Darwin become primary sources for you. You will look at them as direct evidence of the way that Darwin's mind worked when he dealt with scientific issues. You will study them to develop your own views about how he assessed evidence and came to his conclusions.

Let me tell you a story that might help you appreciate the distinction I want you to start making. A first-year student who was doing a paper on the Second Amendment to the Constitution came to see me for help in citing material he had found on a Web site. To obtain the information he needed to cite this source correctly, we accessed the site on my computer. One of the first things I noticed about this site was that it was sponsored by a militant "right to bear arms" group. If the student had been looking for interpretations of the Second Amendment by groups with this or similar ideologies or political agendas, I would have said that he had found an excellent primary source. Clearly the sponsors of this site could be considered experts in this ideological/political perspective; thus, their views of the Second Amendment would have been excellent evidence of the way that individuals with such ideological or political beliefs interpret this part of the Constitution. Unfortunately, the student hadn't looked at the information he took from the site this way. He was still, intellectually, in the passive sponge mode, simply amassing any and all material that popped up when he entered "Second Amendment" in the search engine. To him, all this material had equal status as knowledge, and as knowledge to be repeated rather than critically assessed.

In this initial consideration of sources, I've been encouraging you to think outside the box in determining where you might find the information and the knowledge that you need. This has raised issues of experts and the authority of sources. These issues are important ones.

> Becoming a critical consumer of any sort of information
> means being a critical evaluator of sources.

I will be returning to this issue several times. Later, in subsection D, I'm going to go into detail about evaluating online material. In Section 4.B.1, I will provide you with specific strategies for assessing the quality of print materials you've collected. But you can save yourself work and effort if, from the very beginning of your quest, you consider the authority of sources. Let's turn now to some general criteria that academics use in determining which sources they are willing to trust.

2. Authoritative sources

Our willingness to accept certain facts, ideas, or opinions ought to depend on our assessment of the validity and value of the source of these facts, ideas, or opinions. In other words, the faith we put in **what is said** has a great deal to do with **who says it.** If the subject is black holes, whose views do we trust more: those of an undergraduate taking Physics 101, or those of a Ph.D. who has published widely on the topic? Back in Ancient Greece, Aristotle suggested that our willingness to take someone's words or ideas seriously is based, in part, on our assessment of that person's character and credentials.

Determining who might be an authoritative primary source can often be easier for students than knowing how to assess secondary sources. Whose studies and arguments should you value? Where do you find secondary sources you can trust?

You will discover that, in academic circles, the answer to the first question, generally speaking, are individuals whose stance toward their subject matter is the very stance I have been encouraging you to take toward your own subject matter: that of the thoughtful person who carefully and critically weighs the available evidence and then draws logical conclusions. More specifically, when the subject matter is within their disciplines, academics assess the work of their peers by using disciplinary standards: is the problem or issue the author is investigating a significant one in the field? Has the author/researcher used an accepted and appropriate method in collecting and evaluating the evidence? Are the conclusions the author draws warranted? Are they consonant with the field's concept of meaningful knowledge? Moreover, all fields have individuals who, by virtue of the quality of the work they've done over a number of years, are granted special status by their peers. These are the experts' experts.

The answer to the second question is that finding such material is really not that difficult, but there are a few things you do need to know. Let's start with a **second definition of a source.** In the previous subsection I defined a source as a person, a place, or a procedure that could give you the kind and quality of information or material you need in order to answer your questions. But a **source can also be the person, organization, or commercial enterprise that makes certain information, or a particular text, available to the public.** For example, let's say you read an article by Sandra Findlay in the magazine *Communication Weekly.* If Ms. Findlay draws certain conclusions in this article, she is the source of those ideas. But we can also consider the publication *Communication Weekly* a source because it chose to publish the article by Ms. Findlay. Let's say that you find an essay by Harry Thorp on a Web site sponsored by The Organization for the Protection of Laboratory Rats. Again, Mr. Thorp is the source of ideas he sets forth in this essay, but the OPLR can also be considered a source because it chose to post this essay on its Web site, thus making it available to the public.

So, part of your assessment of the value and validity of sources of information can be made by paying attention to who has made, or is making, this material or information public. Making judgments based on publishers of books will be difficult for you if you are new to a field. But, generally speaking, you ought to feel comfortable trusting material published by university presses and professional organizations. If you continue to do research in a particular field, you will also notice that certain commercial publishing houses can be trusted to produce authoritative work.

Another initial indicator of the authority of a text might be its date of publication. I'm not suggesting that what is newest is by definition the best. However, in the early stages of your project, as you are educating yourself about your subject, you want a good sense of the conversation that experts in a field are currently having about your subject. The best place to look for this conversation is in recent issues of **scholarly journals,** and thus these journals will probably be the major source of authoritative secondary texts for your project. Journals are part of a more general category of sources called **periodicals.** If you consider its root, a "periodical" is a publication that is issued periodically or at regular, recurring intervals—once a quarter, once a month, once a week, daily. Magazines, journals, and newspapers are all periodicals. Essays in these periodicals are usually called **articles.**

In looking for authoritative periodical literature, you need to be aware that academics draw a pretty distinct line between popular periodicals and those that are considered scholarly (and hence authoritative). The distinction is based on the audience for which a periodical is published, which in turn affects who writes the material it publishes and the standards these writers must meet.

Popular periodicals are written for the general public. These are the newspapers and magazines you find at your local supermarket or bookstore. *Time, Newsweek, People,* the *Atlantic Monthly,* the *New York Times* fall into this category. Material from any of these publications could prove to be excellent primary material, but, if you are looking for trustworthy secondary sources, you are going to have to be careful. Some magazines and newspapers written for the general public have developed reputations for producing thoughtful and reliable material, and/or for publishing the work of people whom academics would consider experts. Among newspapers that fall into this category are the *New York Times,* the *Christian Science Monitor,* the *Wall Street Journal.* In the area of magazines, most academics respect the *Economist, Harper's,* the *Atlantic Monthly,* the *New Yorker, Science, Nature, American Scientist, Scientific American.*

There is one issue regarding the popular press that you should be aware of. If and when you run across a report in the popular press about a "recent study" (such studies tend to be about scientific issues, and particularly health-related issues), never rely on that report. Always track down the original source, the report written by the researchers who carried out the study. Comparing the original with the report in the popular press can be an interesting education in the way that even the most reputable popular periodicals can distort the measured voices of the scientific community in order to grab a headline.

Generally speaking, however, you should be actively seeking out **scholarly periodicals,** which are usually referred to as **journals.** Actually, many of these publications have the word "journal" as part of their title. You want to seek out articles published in these periodicals for two reasons:

- Material in current issues of scholarly journals will be much more up-to-date than material in books, simply because periodicals can be published more quickly than books. And, these days, material in online periodicals can reach the public even faster than that in print journals.

- In the eyes of your instructor, certain scholarly journals will be the most authoritative sources of **secondary literature.** (Another bit of lingo. Although the word "literature" may conjure up for you poems and plays and novels and other works of creative writing, the term is often used in academia, as I have just used it, to represent a body of printed or published texts. The word is generally modified—"secondary" literature—to indicate which body of texts the writer/speaker has in mind. Thus "secondary literature" is another way of saying "secondary sources," but it is the more common phrase.)

Academics consider the material published in scholarly journals as authoritative for several reasons:

- Typically, scholarly journals are published by professional organizations. Academics and others who are practicing scholars in a given academic field make up the membership of these organizations. In other words, the organizations are a formal instantiation of the community I talked about in Section 1.

- These journals are written for members of the disciplinary community, scholars and experts in the field.

- The individuals who write the material in these journals—the research reports, the essays, the reviews that make up the content of these journals—are also members of the disciplinary community, scholars and experts in the field.

- Most importantly, articles in most of these periodicals are refereed. Scholars and experts such as the faculty at your institution of higher education send manuscripts to journals to be considered for publication. The editors of journals (who are themselves practicing scholars in the field) screen the manuscripts. If they decide the content of a manuscript has merit, they send it to two or three colleagues who are considered to have particular expertise in the subject matter the author is writing about. The editor will usually not publish an article until and unless it meets the standards of these referees/reviewers.

The best place to look for articles published in scholarly journals is to use bibliographic databases, especially those that focus on literature in a particular discipline or field. I'll be going into more detail about these databases shortly.

Although scholarly journals contain the authoritative information you want, the fact that in them experts are talking to other experts may cause you some trouble, especially in the beginning of your research project. In Section 4.B.3, I'll have some suggestions for tackling articles in scholarly journals and other material that are highly technical or otherwise promise to be difficult reading. But there is another alternative. Most fields have what I call "authoritative but accessible" periodicals. The information in them is considered sound by scholars in the field, but, for the non-expert, their articles are easier to comprehend than those in more scholarly journals.

In this matter, your instructor is perhaps your best resource. Ask about authoritative journals in the field. If discussions of your subject tend to become technical and abstruse, inquire particularly about authoritative but accessible periodicals.

3. Resources

The Library as a Resource

By this point it is obvious that your library can—and should—play a major role in any research project you undertake. But what I have to say about libraries is going to make more sense if you think about a **library not so much as a building or a place, but rather as a resource.** It is a resource in the sense that it attempts to provide patrons like us with the books, the articles, the maps we want to locate. But it is more obviously a resource in the sense that it can provide us with means to negotiate the territory between our research questions and the information that will enable us to answer them. This is what this section is all about.

The desire to make materials more available to more people was the impetus, in the nineteenth century, to the erection of public libraries and many institutional libraries. Up through the twentieth century brick-and-mortar structures were necessary because most of the material libraries were making available to the public was printed on paper, and a building was necessary to house it. Even with the growth of the Internet and the proliferation of materials in electronic format, most written texts are still available only in paper versions.

So, your library will be a resource in providing various print materials. But it has much more to offer you than just the books and periodicals it houses on its shelves.

- It probably won't matter if your library doesn't own a book you want to read, or if it doesn't have a subscription to a particular newspaper. More periodical literature is being made available through **full-text databases,** which we'll be considering in more detail later. And, thanks to various networks that have been created among libraries, you have access to large portions of the collections of libraries across the country, regardless of where the building actually stands (see subsection C.4).

- Keep in mind, too, that libraries today also have collections of electronic material including audiotapes, videotapes, audio CDs, and DVDs. Check your library's collections not only for commercially-produced material, but also for tapes made on campus for instructional use. The latter would include radio and/or television programs, as well as concerts or lectures that have taken place on campus.

Reference Materials

In my experience, students tend to be least knowledgeable about one of the library's greatest resources—**reference works** or **reference materials.** Classic reference works include English dictionaries, thesauruses, general encyclopedias. If you think about the way such works are set up, and the way you use them, you have a good idea of what this whole category of sources/resources contains. A **reference work** is a text that we **refer to,** a source we consult to find some specific type of information, rather than a text that requires careful reading and study. Because reference materials are works that patrons consult, most libraries set aside an area of the building for them, a section that is, typically, close to the desks of reference librarians. And, to reassure patrons that these works are always readily available, most libraries don't allow them to be taken out of the building. These days, in addition to books on shelves, the reference areas of libraries are filling up with computer terminals where patrons can not only do searches of the library catalog, the Web, and bibliographic databases, but also browse through the electronic formats in which more and more reference works can be found.

Since I've been stressing the importance of using your research questions to guide your research process, let me approach reference materials from this perspective.

In many cases, at the outset of a research project students may need to educate themselves about a topic—that is, they may need a **general overview** or an **introduction** to it—whether that topic is a concept (socialism, existentialism, Freud's id), an event (the Pullman strike, Darwin's voyage on *The Beagle*), or the life or work of a person (Sarah Orne Jewett, Brahms). When and if you are in need of such an introduction or general overview, there are a couple of types of sources you could look for. One would be a book (perhaps a textbook) that is written to introduce readers to a particular subject. Try a keyword search of your library's catalog. Enter the word introduction and a word or phrase for the topic. If this strategy turns up nothing, ask a reference librarian for help, see if any of your friends have relevant textbooks, or visit a used bookstore. Another approach would be to look for a specialized dictionary or encyclopedia.

Specialized Dictionaries and Encyclopedias

As the term suggests, specialized dictionaries and encyclopedias are reference works that are much more focused than your general dictionary of the English language, or a general encyclopedia like the *Encyclopedia Britannica* or the *Encyclopedia Americana*. The focus is on a specific body of knowledge, typically one that corresponds to an academic discipline or field. There is also a category of dictionaries that cover the lives of notable people, living and dead. If you need some basic information about the life of a person, then look for a **biographical dictionary** (or a **biographical index**). In looking for other types of information, draw upon your experiences with general dictionaries and encyclopedias. If you want to find the meaning of a technical or specialized term, then a specialized dictionary would be an obvious place to look. If you want a quick overview of the gold rush of 1849, then an encyclopedia suggests itself. In these specialized reference works, however, the lines can blur. Words that may seem to be only technical terms could, in reality, turn out to be major concepts that could be covered in an encyclopedia; conversely, a specialized dictionary may do much more than simply define words. My point is that if your research questions suggest that you need some basic, general information about a subject, specialized dictionaries and encyclopedias would be excellent resources to look for.

To give you a sense of the wide array of such reference works currently available, I've included some eclectic lists in Figures 1, 2, and 3.

Biographical Dictionaries—General
American National Biography (full-text database)
American National Biography (online)
Biography.com (online)
Biographical Dictionary
Biography and Genealogy Master Index (database)
Chambers Biographical Dictionary
Current Biography
Who's Who
Wilson Biographies Plus Illustrated (full text)
World Biography Index
Biographical Dictionaries—Specialized
Artists from Latin American Cultures:
  A Biographical Dictionary
Baker's Biographical Dictionary of Musicians
Biographical Dictionary of Twentieth Century
  Philosophers
Native American Women: A Biographical
  Dictionary
The New Biographical Dictionary of Film

Figure 1

If you decide such sources could be helpful, here is some more information.

- To determine your library's holdings in these two categories of reference materials, look for works both in print and in electronic formats. You can do keyword searches in the library catalog using one of the terms I've just given you and a keyword for your topic or area of interest. So, if you want more information on the concept "socialism," try

  dictionary AND political science

  If reference materials in electronic format are not listed in the library's regular catalog, check the library's Web site, or ask a reference librarian for help.

An Eclectic List of Specialized Encyclopedias
Astronomy Encyclopedia
Concise Encyclopedia of Special Education
Encyclopedia Mythica (online)
Encyclopedia of African Nations and Civilizations
Encyclopedia of American Political History
Encyclopedia of Contemporary Japanese Culture
Encyclopedia of Crime and Punishment
Encyclopedia of the Enlightenment
Encyclopedia of Filmmakers
Encyclopedia of the Human Brain
Encyclopedia of the Human Genome
Encyclopedia of Postmodernism
Encyclopedia of Twentieth-Century African History
Firefly Encyclopedia of Insects and Spiders
The Louisiana Purchase: A Historical and Geographical Encyclopedia
The Malcolm X Encyclopedia
The Papacy: An Encyclopedia
Van Nostrand's Scientific Encyclopedia

Figure 3

- If and when you find print versions of these reference works, pay attention to the publication date. While some general information doesn't change, it is still best to use material that has been published or revised recently. If your topic is one in which knowledge is constantly undergoing revision, then your reference works must be current.

An Eclectic List of Specialized Dictionaries
Cinema: A Critical Dictionary: The Major Film Makers
Dictionary of Allusions
Dictionary of Art
Dictionary of Biblical Interpretation
Dictionary of Biotechnology and Genetic Engineering
Dictionary of Chemistry
Dictionary of Computer Science, Engineering, and Technology
A Dictionary of Literary Symbols
Dictionary of the Social Sciences
Historical Dictionary of Civil Wars in Africa
Historical Dictionary of Islam
History of Zionism: A Handbook and Dictionary
McGraw-Hill Dictionary of Scientific and Technical Terms
New Grove Dictionary of Music and Musicians
The Philosopher's Dictionary
Webster's New World Dictionary of Computer Terms

Figure 2

- Specialized dictionaries and encyclopedias are set up just like their general counterparts. So assume that entries in print text are expressed as key words or phrases—Pullman strike; Du Bois, W. E. B.—and that they are then placed in the volume or volumes in alphabetical order.

I had a hard time deciding if I should discuss these specialized encyclopedias and dictionaries here, or in the previous section on sources, because they can be used either as resources or as sources. I've just been talking about your using them to educate yourself, generally, about a topic, or to gather some commonly-accepted facts. In this sense, you are using the reference work as a resource, a place to find information that will function as a foundation for your reading of studies and analyses by scholars and experts in the field.

But many, if not most, specialized reference works can also be used as sources. They are usually published by reputable firms who hire specialists in the field to write the entries, and librarians in college and university libraries are careful to spend library money only on those works they consider to have authority. So you should feel confident that you can treat the information you find in them as authoritative and thus use it as valid evidence. This is particularly true of definitions of terms and words that have precise meanings for members of a particular field. *The Oxford English Dictionary* (usually called the OED) falls into the category of a highly authoritative source/resource, especially when in comes to the meanings that English words have had in years and centuries past. I should warn you, however, that college instructors usually don't look kindly on students' quoting definitions from ordinary English dictionaries, probably because the dictionary supposedly is telling us how most speakers of the language define the term. Certainly, if the word or phrase is a specialized one ("ego" in psychology, for example) or is fraught with meanings and connotations ("democracy"), and you are going to be hanging a great deal of your argument on this definition, you should most definitely head for an appropriate specialized dictionary or encyclopedia that you know is respected by people in the field or discipline.

If we can look upon these specialized dictionaries and encyclopedias as authoritative sources, then another way in which they could be particularly useful to you would be in **answering questions you have that require factual answers.** But always remember that there are facts, and there are facts. Specialized encyclopedias are good for uncontested facts, such as the dates of historical events, dates in the lives of notable people, perhaps the casualty figures for certain disasters. But when your questions require facts that could more aptly be called data or statistics, then check your library's reference section for another type of reference work: **almanacs, fact books,** or works with **statistics** in the title. The facts and data I have in mind here most definitely depend on their source for their reliability: unemployment rates in the United States over a period of years, percentages of ethnic minorities in particular cities and states, the number of people with HIV/AIDS in South Africa, data from one of the genome projects, and so on.

- To check out your library's holdings in this type of reference material, you could try a keyword search of the library catalog, using one of the terms I've just given alone, or with a keyword for your topic or area of interest:

statistics AND business

To keep their information as up-to-date as possible, publishers of fact books and current statistics are quickly moving to electronic formats. If electronic materials are not listed in the library's catalog, check the library's Web site, or ask a reference librarian.

- In fact, if one or more of your research questions requires these sorts of factual answers, I'd urge you to consult with your instructor and/or with a reference librarian. They are most likely to know which sources are going to have the most reliable data or statistics, and they can show you how to find them.

Finally, if your research strategy involves contacting businesses, corporations, organizations, a government or private agency, your reference librarians can help you here, too. They will show you where you can find lists of specific businesses, agencies, or organizations, as well as how to track down such information as addresses (street addresses and/or e-mail addresses), phone numbers, appropriate offices, perhaps even people you could contact.

ALERT!

If and when you take notes from any of the works or materials I've been talking about, whether in print or in electronic format, you must keep careful records of where you found this material so that you can document it appropriately in your paper. This applies both to the information you are gathering in an effort to educate yourself, as well as information you would consider to be evidence itself. I discuss this general issue in Section 4, beginning with subsection D.

If you access material using a computer, you are going to have to be especially careful to take down certain information about the source **at the time that you access this information.** See subsection E at the end of this section of the book; there's more about electronic sources in Section 8.D.6.

Bibliographic and Related Databases

There is another category of reference material that I especially want to focus on. It is a set of resources that scholars depend on heavily but one that, in my experience, many students know very little about. This set of resources are **bibliographic databases.** In their print versions they are called either **bibliographies** or **indexes.** A bibliography, as you know, is a list of books and articles, usually published at the end of a book or a paper. A bibliographic database is very similar. In an electronic format, it too is a list of works, a list of **citations** of works.

A **citation** contains information about a source, written in a particular format. Citations typically include the author of the text, the title of the text, and information about the text's publication, information that allows us to locate that text ourselves. The information in a citation is typically called **bibliographic information.** All this is pretty easy to remember if you notice that all these words derive from the Greek word for book, *biblion.*

Examples of citations:

Doe, John C. *A Study of Zebras.* New York: Wildlife Press, 2010.

Smith, Jane. "A Consideration of Violence on Television." *Mass Media Today* 45 (2011): 34–51.

This general family of databases is a family because all "members" provide citations of works—most generally periodical literature with a sprinkling of dissertations, books, and, more frequently now, electronic sources. They also share the objective of listing texts as soon as they are publicly available, so on most of these databases you can do a search for material that was published during the current month. But family members do differ. Some of these databases provide only citations of works. Others provide a citation and an **abstract** of the work, a summary of the content of the article or book. Some, usually called **full-text databases,** provide citations and the complete texts of all or some of the articles cited in the database.

In subsection C, when you are ready to begin your searches, I'll discuss these databases in more detail.

Here's what you need to know about this family of databases:

- Subject-specific bibliographic databases are going to be your best resource for current, authoritative secondary literature. Thus, using them must be part of your research strategy.

- While these various databases (those that include only citations, those that include abstracts, those that include full-texts) are online resources, you will not find any of them by doing an Internet search with a search engine such as Google or AltaVista. They are available **only to those who pay to subscribe to them,** and few individuals do so because they can be expensive. Libraries subscribe to them as a service for their patrons. So, you will have to look for these databases on the Web site of your library.

Librarians as a Resource

Finally, in my opinion the greatest resource that libraries provide are reference librarians. These people have the keys that unlock for us the wealth that the library's other resources contain. Today most librarians consider themselves information specialists, which tells us a great deal about the ways that they can help us library patrons (and I certainly include myself in the category of library patrons who lean heavily on the extensive knowledge and expertise of librarians). Reference librarians know about all sorts of resources, and not just the ones in their own libraries. They can tell you which bibliographic and full-text databases are most likely to have the sources you are searching for, and they know the tricks for doing productive and efficient searches of these databases. They know about Internet search engines, and often they can recommend trustworthy Web sites.

You should never feel shy about approaching a reference librarian. Their job is to help you find the information you need, no matter how simple or complex your question may be. They have excellent problem-solving skills and they love to use them. But, most importantly, reference librarians have become reference librarians because they love to help other people and to share what they know with them.

While you should never feel shy about asking a reference librarian a question, or asking a reference librarian for help in doing your searches, there are things you can do that will make it easier for librarians to be truly helpful to you. The advice I'm going to be offering you now is going to sound very familiar because it is part and parcel of the approach I'm taking to research throughout this entire book.

Before you seek the help of a librarian, you should have done your homework. This includes having set up your Researcher's Notebook, and gone through the various exercises I've laid out in Section 2. It also includes quickly reading over this whole section on finding the evidence, so that you have a basic grasp of the way libraries work, the terminology related to this work, and basic resources the library has to offer.

Librarians are most likely to provide you with the help you need if and when you can go to them with a **clearly defined question or agenda.**

- The question you ask may be directly about the subject you are investigating:

  Could you help me find current statistics on single-parent households in Texas?

- The question may be about library resources:

  Does the library have a full-text database of newspapers from small towns?

- The agenda may be to get assistance in doing a search of a bibliographic database.

  Could you show me how to find current articles on Joseph Conrad's *Heart of Darkness*?

Moreover, librarians are most likely to provide you with the help you need if and when you put your question or agenda in the context of **a clear, concise statement of your area of investigation and your research question.**

- For my Urban and Rural Politics class I'd like to do a study of my hometown, Galesburg. More specifically, I want to understand better how the town council goes about making decisions. Since the council holds weekly public meetings, I figure that information about what goes on in specific meetings would help me answer my big question. I'm assuming these meetings are covered by the *Galesburg Gazette*. Does the library have a database that would have copies of the *Gazette*?

- I'm taking Abnormal Psych. For my research project—which is, by the way, a review of the literature—I'm trying to find out what psychologists think about the link between violent behavior and genes. But I've never done research in psychology before, so I don't know where to begin looking for articles and books. Can you help me?

Your Instructor and Other Members of the Faculty as Resources

Finally, let me remind you that the instructor of the course for which you are doing this research project is an excellent resource, as are members of your school's faculty who specialize in the areas that your research covers.

However, in approaching any of these faculty members there are a couple of things you need to keep in mind. All the advice I just gave you about approaching librarians with specific questions and agendas holds true for consulting with faculty members. However, let me add two particular notes of caution:

- If the issue is your general ignorance of the subject or topic that your research question/working hypothesis revolves around, be careful what you ask of your instructor. I've had faculty members complain that students come to them asking for what amounts to the content of a complete course ("Tell me about nationalism"). You can certainly ask for specific help ("Could you give me the titles of two or three central works I should read about nationalism?"), but assume that you have to take responsibility for educating yourself. If your background in the area you are investigating is particularly limited, perhaps your conversation with your instructor should revolve around ways to reconceptualize your research question/working thesis so that they are built on ground that is more familiar to you.

- If and when you approach faculty who are not teaching the course for which you are doing this research project, be aware that they do not have any direct obligation to help you and thus that you could be perceived as imposing upon them. Much will depend on the size of your school and its culture. But I'm sure that most faculty will be happy to be of assistance if your requests are clearly stated, and if they can be accommodated with a minimum of time and effort on the part of the faculty member.

C. The Research Process

1. What to expect and how to manage

Why You Need to Start Early

Since I have put so much stress on starting early and planning ahead, let me explain why. Part of the answer lies in the mechanisms and logistics of research itself. But another, important part of the answer has to do with the intellectual dimension of the project. We researchers need to allow our brains to digest and mull over the material gathered and ask more questions that, in turn, may require more research. While we might like to think that, if we get ourselves organized enough, we can roar through a research project just as if we were on a straight, empty freeway in a high-powered car with the pedal to the metal, the reality is that the process more often resembles making one's way through a jungle. No matter how many maps we consult, and no matter how carefully we plan our paths through the territory, at times we will feel bogged down; the course will not always be smooth—nor will the path be straight.

Unfortunately, some of the time and energy you expend on your search will feel like tiresome busywork. Compiling lists of potential sources will take time; so may putting your hands on these sources. Unless you were born under a very lucky star, you will discover that an article that sounds very promising will have to be ordered through interlibrary loan, or that a book you really want to read is currently checked out. A person you want to interview is on vacation and won't be able to see you until two weeks from tomorrow. A month into your research you come across several sources that you really, really wish you had seen weeks ago. And, if you are carrying out a study or an experiment in the social or natural sciences, just ask your instructor how many things can potentially go wrong!

In addition to these typical problems in gathering evidence, there are also issues related to the way our minds work. Although I have encouraged you to have a clear destination in mind before you begin looking for your evidence, this direction can shift. As you educate yourself, you begin to realize that the original area of investigation is even larger and more complex than you originally thought, and you realize a specific section in this larger picture is what you really want to understand better. Or perhaps the evidence you find in pursuing your original research question suggests a more profitable line of inquiry. Or, as you research and read and write in the Working Hypothesis/Thesis part of your Notebook about your original research question, a picture of your answer starts to emerge, but to bring this picture into greater focus, you find yourself with a whole new set of questions. These various twists and turns are, in my experience, very natural. In fact, you could take them as a sign that you are doing this project the "right" way. They show us that the act of researching is really recursive. So you shouldn't assume that you will simply do one search, and the research phase of the project will be finished. Rather, assume that searches of various sorts will go on practically until the last stages of the writing process.

Finally, and most importantly, you need to allow plenty of time to carefully look over the material you find, digest the information, mull over the points of view of the experts, and put it all together into a coherent whole. Just as the research process is not straight and smooth, neither is the thinking process. Bringing the answer into focus usually feels more like a spiral. You circle around the central issue, and circle around again. Gradually, as you go through the process of refining your ideas, each circle brings you closer and closer, and the picture comes into greater and greater definition.

Since the logistics of research itself can be full of twists and turns, and since our minds need time to incubate material, to think through ideas, to ponder and reflect, you will have to start working well in advance of your deadlines to allow plenty of time for all this to happen.

On the other hand, I did promise you that I'd give you ways to cut down on needless time and frustration. Let's consider, then, how you might manage this process.

How to Manage the Research Process

You are going to be much more satisfied with the outcome of this entire process, and you are going to be much less stressed by it,

- if you recognize that research will require some mindless busywork and that snafus will occur; in other words, some time will be "wasted";

- if you get started sooner than later. Plan to begin your searches as soon as you have your specific research questions; give yourself plenty of time to search for potential sources and to put your hands on them;

- if you make the most of the time you do spend searching by using this section of my book to educate yourself about resources available to you and strategies for using these resources most efficiently;

- if you recognize that, throughout the process, you will have to call upon, and make use of, your problem-solving skills.

In the early stages of your research, think of your quest as having two levels:

- At the intellectual level, you need to develop a basic understanding of the subject or topic that your working hypothesis/thesis revolves around. To satisfy this need, you'll need to look for the types of materials that I described in subsection B.3 so that you will have the general overview you need.

- You will also have to start lining up promising sources that you will be reading carefully and assessing critically. We'll be talking more about the particulars of this process in a moment.

To this list you may want to add doing some searches online, but I'm going to suggest that you restrain yourself. Put these searches off until you have the knowledge you need to appropriately evaluate the material you find. More in subsection D.

Basic Strategies for Searches

Before we proceed, let me alert you to what you will, and will not, find in this section on searches.

What you will not find are specific instructions about how to do particular searches on specific databases or Internet search engines. I have various reasons for not going into such detail, not the least of which is the speed at which technology progresses. What I write today could well be ancient history by the time you read it. Moreover, I would point out that every database I've looked at has both advice for doing searches and/or a help feature. And let us not forget the librarians, who have kept up with technological changes.

All of these are good reasons for not getting into such detail, but my true, main reason brings me back to the promise I made at the beginning of this section on finding the evidence, the promise **to give you basic ways to conceptualize the research process and to give you basic skills.** If you master them, changes in technology won't faze you.

Good researching skills are, at heart, good problem-solving skills.

Good researching skills require us:

- to keep in mind, at all times, exactly what it is we are looking for. Good researchers, for example, resist being lulled into passivity by the first words they come up with to do a keyword search. They remember that the words are not ends in themselves, but the means to find evidence. If "teen" doesn't work, they try "adolescent." And if that doesn't elicit the literature they are seeking, they fall back on "children." What they always keep in mind is the underlying question about teen/adolescent/children that instigated the search in the first place.

- to be logical, to be flexible, to be patient. If plan A doesn't work, move on to plan B.

- to use our knowledge and understanding of reference materials and other resources to find those that promise to take us to our ends.

- to understand the basic systems used in library resources to store and access information.

Any reference work or database you might use to find material—be it an Internet search engine or a bibliographic database or an encyclopedia or a dictionary—has been set up according to some system. I want to start this section on searches by talking about cataloging systems because your searches for evidence are going to be much less frustrating and much more productive if you recognize:

- that the resources you are using are organized according to a system;

- and that, to use that resource most effectively, you need to understand the basics of the system.

2. Bibliographic "filing" systems

The issue is simple: storage and retrieval. When libraries became public institutions and their numbers and their holdings grew, librarians realized that they needed a system that would tell them what works they owned, and where to store or shelve specific works so that they, and their patrons, would know exactly where to find them. Moreover, if the system were standardized and used by all libraries, it would be easier for librarians to exchange information with each other about their collections, and it would be easier for library patrons to search for and find material in a number of different libraries.

The **Dewey Decimal System** was one such system. In most university and college libraries Dewey has been superseded by the **Library of Congress (LC) system.** The LC system determines exactly where a specific work—let's say a book—should be shelved by classifying it according to its **subject matter.** Subject matter is broken down into an elaborate system of categories and subcategories. Divisions and subdivisions in the LC system look like this:

   United States—History—Revolution, 1775-1783

   Astronomy—Mathematics—History

   Botany, Medical—China

This system of divisions and subdivisions of subject matter produces the **call number** of the book.

JK			PS	
2261	Bibby, John F., and L. Sandy		3515	Hemingway, Ernest.
.B493	Maisel.		.E37	*A Farewell to Arms*
2003	*Two Parties—Or More? The*		F3	
	American Party System			

The first letter in the top line of the call number designates a very general subject area. For example, works on political science are cataloged in J; works of imaginative literature (poems, plays, novels) as well as works on language are generally cataloged under P. The second letter in the top line (and often the numbers that follow in the second line) indicate a subdivision of the first category. Thus, books that focus generally on political science in the United States will probably be found under JK 1-9993. Works of and on American literature will be found in the PS section of the library. This is the storage part of the system.

   The retrieval part of the system is the catalog created of the library's holdings. In the old days when library catalogs were literally **card catalogs,** the catalog was comprised of 3-x-5-inch pasteboard cards stored in little drawers in wooden cabinets. To do searches, one had to open drawers and flip through cards. Depending on the size of the library's holdings, there could be thousands and thousands of such cards, and room after room of wooden cabinets, because there wasn't one catalog, but rather three. The three different catalogs contained the same information about the same works, but each focused on a different aspect of the classification system in order to let patrons do three different types of searches.

- In the **subject catalog,** the first lines on the card were the general subject category, followed by the relevant subcategories. Under that, you would have found the name of the author of the book, and the rest of the information about it.

- In the **title catalog,** the first line on the card was the title. Cards were arranged in alphabetical order, beginning with the first main word of the title (an initial article—*a, an, the*—was always disregarded).

- In the **author catalog,** the first line on the card was the name of the author, written in inverse order (last name first). Cards were alphabetized, first, according to the author's last name, then his or her first name, then middle initial, and so on. The system here was precisely the same system that is still used in print telephone directories.

We do not need to go into the numerous advantages we have now in being able to do searches of libraries' holdings electronically. But it can be very helpful to know that, although most of those wooden cabinets are now in basements, storage lockers, or antique stores, **the fundamentals of the old cataloging system are still very much alive.** Here's what I mean. The people who developed the Dewey and the LC cataloging systems

- thought about the works they classified and categorized in a particular way;

- decided that certain information about these works was important;

- represented this important information in a particular format.

Companies that produced print bibliographies and indexes followed the lead of these creators of library classification and cataloguing systems in designing their catalogs, and we can see many parts of this system still in play in electronic databases.

Here's what you need to know about it:

- The information that designers of these library classification and cataloging systems decided was important is the very same **bibliographic information** I introduced you to in subsection B.3 and directly affects **citations** of texts. Moreover, as I will point out in a moment, certain ways of representing this information have become conventions that are followed not only by librarians but also by anyone who deals with written texts, including authors of research papers!

- Because these categories were—and are still—used for storage and retrieval of texts, you will be using your knowledge of them in doing your searches for sources.

The pasteboard cards that used to make up the catalog of the library have been replaced by **electronic records** of the works in the library's collection. While the medium differs, the information in this record is very similar to that on the old cards. Moreover, the record of a work in one of the bibliographic databases I'll be discussing in more detail a little later is also based on these same basic principles and conventions. This **record** of a work, whether in the library catalog or a bibliographic database, is the basic unit of storage of this work. The record, in turn, is made up of a set of predetermined categories of information about the work. In the electronic database, these predetermined categories are called **fields.** You'll see these fields on the left of the screen when you open records in any of these databases.

A (Partial) Record of a Book in the Lewis & Clark College Library Catalog:

Author: Proulx, Lucille

Title: Strengthening emotional ties through parent-child-dyad art therapy: interventions with infants and preschoolers/ Lucille Proulx; forewords by Lee Tidmarsh and Joyce Canfield

Publisher: London; Philadelphia: Jessica Kingsley Publishers 2003

Subject: Art therapy for children
Family psychotherapy
Arts—Therapeutic use
Child development
Child psychiatry

A (Partial) Record from the PsycINFO Database:

Author: Balbemie, Robin

Title: Infant and toddler mental health: Models of clinical intervention with infants and their families

Source: Journal of Child Psychology & Psychiatry & Allied Disciplines. Vol 44(6) Sep 2003, 926. Blackwell Publishing, United Kingdom

Key Concepts: clinical intervention; infant mental health; toddler mental health; families

Subject Headings: • Early Intervention
• Family
• Infant Development
• Mental Health

Publication Type: Peer Reviewed Journal

What is important about **these fields** is quite simple:

- Records of works are created by catalogers entering the relevant information about a particular work into each field; this is the data in this database.

- When we want to retrieve records of works on these databases—when we want to find sources—we will do so by initiating searches through one or more of these fields.

When you do searches on the library catalog and in various databases, I want you to notice **the similarities in records.** You can see them in the partial records I've included here. Notice, for example, that there are **similarities in the fields that are deemed important** elements of the works being cataloged, and also notice **similarities in the way this information is represented in a specific field.** For example, prominent fields in both records will be **author** and **title**; they are given first. In the **author record,** the name of the first author of a work (if not all authors) is typically inverted. This format is the legacy both of the old card catalog and of printed lists of works, where the lists are organized in alphabetical order according to the last name of the first author. Notice, too, that the author and title are invariably followed by **information about the work's publication** (who published it, when, which edition this is, who is the translator and other information we need in order to find precisely this work). Again, the order in which this information is presented will be fairly standard from database to database, as will the conventions of representing certain types of information. This is perhaps most pronounced in the way databases give us information about periodicals. Although "keyword" has supplanted "subject" in prominence in search menus, subject categories still exist and, as we shall see in subsection C.3.b., can be a fruitful means to search for promising sources.

You are going to see these very same patterns repeated in **systems of documentation.** That is, you will see them in the **citations** of works in bibliographies and reference lists in the books and articles you read. These lists are part of the system that authors use to let readers know which sources they have made use of in their texts, and, for the same reason, you yourself are going to have to use a documentation system in completing your final paper. Since a central tenet of documentation is to give readers the information they need in order to locate sources for themselves, it should not be surprising that the form that authors use in giving information about sources in their texts closely resembles the form of citations in electronic databases. These similarities are the reason that I consider Section 8, where I discuss the basics of documentation systems, to be a companion to this section. In fact, in subsection D of Section 8 I go into more detail about certain elements of citations, elements that correspond to the fields in records in databases. If, as you collect citations from various databases, you have questions about information in any of these fields, check out the subdivisions of Section 8.D.

By this point I do hope that it is obvious that your search for sources will be a search for citations or records of particular texts, and that you will be searching for and retrieving these records in databases by entering a word or phrase in search boxes that, with the exception of "keyword," correspond to the fields in the record. Moreover, similarities in the way that bibliographic information is provided make it very easy to move among library catalogs, bibliographic and full-text databases, and citations you find when you read the sources you have located. I hope that you will also see the same patterns in the documentation style you will be using when it comes time to cite sources in your own paper.

Truly, it is all pretty simple once you can see the big picture!

3. Searching for potential sources

a. Know your database

You are now ready to focus your attention on finding those sources that are going to allow you to answer your research questions. In this initial search you should make a special effort to find appropriate secondary literature so you will know what scholars and experts in your subject have been doing and saying.
The databases you'll be using in this quest fall into two rough categories:

- databases that will **link you directly to the sources themselves** (full-text databases and hybrid databases that contain some complete texts; and Internet search engines that provide direct links to Web sites).

- databases that **provide you with citations** of books, articles, and other promising sources (bibliographic indexes and abstracted indexes).

Of these various resources, the one you are probably most familiar with is the **Internet search engine.** As I write, there are a number of such services available—Google, Yahoo, Ask Jeeves, AltaVista. No doubt by the time you read this, other such search engines will have been developed. Moreover, by the time you read this there will probably be more **metasearch engines** available, search engines that submit your keywords to a variety of more limited search engines.
The first thing, and the most important thing to remember, is this:

> Whether it is an Internet search engine, a library catalog, or a bibliographic index, no database contains records of everything!

Consciously or unconsciously, never assume that any one database you enter is going to contain all possible sources available on your topic.
Other important points to remember:

- Any search you do on an Internet search engine will necessarily be restricted, both in the sites the program scans and in the methods/terms it uses to conduct a search. The only records you will find on a given library catalog, full-text database, or bibliographic database are those records that have been entered by the people who create and maintain the database.

- It should follow, then, that smart researchers will educate themselves about contents of databases available to them for searches. General descriptions of Internet search engines and what they are designed to do are available. Similarly, for the various databases to which they subscribe, most libraries provide brief descriptions of the scope and nature of the literature that is indexed in each. Your best option, however, might be to discuss your project and research questions with a reference librarian. Have him or her suggest databases in your library most likely to contain the sources you are seeking.

And speaking of libraries . . .

> ## REMEMBER!
> - Access to the bibliographic and full-text databases I'm discussing in this section are available only to those who pay for subscriptions to them, which, in your case, probably means your school and/or a local library.
> - The databases available at specific libraries will vary.

So, go to the Web site of your library and check out the databases available to you—and, if they are limited, inquire about those at other libraries in your area. Keep in mind that the libraries most likely to have the fullest array of full-text and bibliographic databases are the libraries of institutions of higher education.

Clearly, to be most efficient in your search, you want to find those databases most likely to contain either (1) the **category of sources** you are seeking (newspaper articles, for example), or (2) sources that focus specifically on the **subject matter** of your investigation.

In the growing number of databases on the market, we can make another rough division.

There are **general or multidisciplinary databases**. These databases typically index both popular and scholarly works, and they also tend to cover a wide array of topics. As I write, some databases that fall into this category are:

Academic Search Premier

Expanded Academic ASAP

Article First

WorldCat (which focuses on books)

More importantly for your needs, there are **specialized or subject databases**. Content of certain of these databases is determined by an academic discipline or a specialized field, and the material they contain tends to fall more into the scholarly or authoritative category. I'll give you a few examples here, but you need to find out what your library has, and which of those databases best suits your needs.

ArtIndex

Biological and Agricultural Index

Business Dateline

MEDLINE (medicine)

Philosopher's Index

PsycINFO (psychology)

Here is more information that should prove helpful:

- Generally speaking, full-text databases will include only articles, usually those that have already been published in print periodicals. Typically, bibliographic databases also focus on periodical literature, although you may also find citations for some books, for dissertations, and perhaps some Web sites or electronic sources.

- Most databases are incredibly up-to-date. That is, they have records of material published almost up to the date you access them. But the literature they index goes back only so far in time. If you are specifically looking for "older" material, check the description of the index to see how far back its records go. If a database does not index the material you are seeking, talk to a librarian about print indexes.

- On the other side of the coin, there are companies that are creating databases of older material, some of it from the nineteenth century. Again, just for illustration:

  African American Newspapers: The 19th Century

  Art Index Retrospective

  AP Multimedia Archive

  Historical New York Times

  Poole's Plus—19th Century Masterfile

- Finally, there are databases that specialize in particular sorts of material, like Book Review Digest, or Mental Measurements Yearbook (which contains copies of standardized tests), or Papers First (which indexes papers presented at conferences around the world).

Once you've located some promising databases, you need to have efficient and effective strategies for searching them for promising sources.

b. Searches by subject and keyword

In the following weeks you are going to be returning to computer terminals time and again to do all sorts of searches, some quick and easy, some more extended and extensive.

Perhaps the most challenging of these searches—the ones that will require you to make the most creative use of your problem-solving skills—are the initial searches you do to get a feel for "what's out there." These are searches you do to discover, first of all, what sorts of sources are indexed on particular databases, and, at the same time, to get a sense of the current trends in scholarship regarding your chosen subject—what is it about this subject that interests the experts at this time?

The most fruitful places to do these searches will be on bibliographic and full-text databases, especially those in specialized subject areas.

Now—how to go about such searches.

There are more and less methodical ways to do searches. When I am working with students who are fairly ignorant of "what's out there," I find it helpful to do some really basic keyword searches first. By that I mean using obvious and general terms and phrases for the subject matter. You have to be careful with this strategy. You don't want a search that is going to call up thousands of records, just because it's wasteful of your time and that of the database. But I find a more general search useful because you can do a quick scan of the first twenty or thirty records, looking for patterns in topic and/or approach, as well as looking for specific texts that seem to directly address your research questions.

Then, when the picture of what's going on in the field starts to take shape— or, at least, when a picture starts to emerge from a particular database—you can switch tactics and do a more methodical search. You'll have to decide which strategies work best for you. What is *not* helpful or truly productive are haphazard efforts with no direction or purpose beyond a hope that something will "jump out at you."

Further Information

First of all, we have to make some important distinctions here in lingo. There is a difference between a **keyword search** and a **subject (or descriptor) search.**

When you enter a word or phrase into a **keyword** box, the program simply matches that set of letters against any comparable set of letters in any of the fields of any and all records. While keyword searches can be useful, they can also elicit records that have little or nothing to do with your subject.

In contrast, a **subject (or descriptor) search** falls into the category of methodical searches. If you look at a full record in a database you are using, you should see a **field called either subject or descriptor.** This field is comparable to those subject categories in the Library of Congress cataloging system. The compilers of the database have developed a set of particular words/terms/ phrases that they use to describe the contents of particular works. Clearly, then, one way to do a more methodical search is to find out the terms that the database uses for the kind of material you want to find, then do a subject or descriptor search using the term or terms.

If you look at the initial search screen of any database, you will see all sorts of features they offer you to help you restrict your search so that it elicits the kind of sources you want to read.

- Most databases provide mechanisms for doing either basic or limited/ advanced searches. The search screen, for example, may offer you various options for limiting your search (language, type of material, publisher, dates of publication, and the like). Or it offers you a set of search boxes, each of which you can limit to a particular field. Limiting the search makes sense. On the other hand, try various options just so you know you are not inadvertently cutting out some records of promising sources.

- If you want to do more methodical subject or keyword searches, look for a directory of the terms and/or phrases used in this database.

- Check the database to see if it supports phrase searches. If it does, when you enter more than one word in a search box—e.g., learning disability—the search results will include only those records in which those words appear together in that order.

- Notice that some databases have a box you can check if you want the search limited only to refereed journals! (Remember my discussion of this issue in the subsection on authoritative sources?)

Handy Tricks

In a way, we have come full circle. In my discussions of topics for your research, I've spent all sorts of time warning you not to use nouns and noun phrases. Now the key to your searches are nouns and noun phrases! And the particular words and phrases you enter into search boxes in theses databases will have everything to do with the success or failure of the search. Until computer programs are built with more fuzzy logic (and progress is being made here), they are going to be simple-minded in following your commands. They are going to scan the fields you ask them to scan with the letters you enter in the order you enter them. Typos and misspellings are going to negatively affect your searches, as will the "wrong" words. So one of your basic problem-solving strategies now needs to be thinking in terms of words, words, words.

- Before you get on the computer, make a list of words and phrases that seem to describe the sources you want to find. Technical terms can be particularly useful. For words, especially common words, that have various forms and synonyms, list the various terms: woman, women, girls, feminine, female.

- This trick is related to the last. In citations, words can have various grammatical forms (psychology, psychological, psychotherapy; drug, drugs, drug-related). If you want the database to recognize any and all of these variant forms, you can usually use the root of the word and an asterisk (called a wild card): psycho* or drug*. Be careful, though; if those letters in that order are common in many English words, the poor database may have a seizure trying to gather up all the matches!

- You can spread the net wide but still create reasonable parameters if you search with a phrase rather than a word, or if you use a couple of keywords rather than just one.

- I mentioned earlier that an obvious way to do a more methodical search is to use the database's standard subject terms or descriptors. In addition to using a database's directory to determine what those terms are, you can discover them by finding the record of a specific work that falls into the requisite category. There are a couple of other ways you could get to such a record. One would be the more general search I mentioned earlier. Another would be to do an author search for a person considered an expert in this particular subject. Or you could do a keyword search using the name of a person closely linked to your interests (if the person is really well known—let's say, Freud—you'd better limit such searches with other key terms or you'll get thousands of hits).

- And a final, central reminder. When a particular search produces no results—or material that doesn't fit the bill—active researchers do not assume that the material they are seeking doesn't exist. Rather, they question their own search strategies. Perhaps the search failed because what they are seeking isn't stored in this database. Even more likely is that the words they typed in are not the "right" words; the term or terms they used are not the terms used by the authors whose texts they are seeking. In short, most sophisticated researchers do not conclude that "nothing has been written on my topic" or "this information doesn't exist" until and unless they have done a systematic and exhaustive search, one that involves a number of databases and certainly some carefully thought-out search strategies.

Although my focus up to this point has been on bibliographic databases, many of the basic strategies I suggest here could also apply to searches of the Web, as long as you keep in mind the differences in the environments being searched. Searching in a database is like fishing in a pond that has been stocked with trout; searching on the Internet is much more akin to taking your gear up to a mountain stream. In the latter case, your fishing gear—and your skills in fishing—will count for something, but luck will still have a lot to do with your final catch.

c. What your search will produce

Regardless of the type of search that you do, a successful one will produce a list of potential sources. Typically, the basic results list will be truncated; the citations will include only title, author, and basic information about publication.

Depending on the company that produces it, and the database itself, the initial result page can give you a number of options. I'm listing some here so that you can look out for them, and, if they are available, you'll know what they can do for you.

- You can always see a **more detailed record** of any source. Such records provide complete information for each of the fields in the record. If the database provides it, the following information can be particularly helpful:

  - An **abstract** of the work. As I've already mentioned, these summaries of the content of the text, including the author's approach to the material, can help you decide if this text is one you want to read. On the other hand, abstracts can also be helpful in suggesting lines of inquiry you had not considered up to this point!

Note: In your final paper you should never give the impression that you have read an article or other work by making use of information you have found in an abstract. If and when you make use of information in an abstract, you must cite the abstract as the source of this information, which means including information about the database, since it is your ultimate source. See subsection D, where I talk more about the information you need to record about electronic sources.

- If the work is a collection of essays or articles, a more detailed record will typically list the authors and the titles of these essays or articles, allowing you to determine if one or more covers material of interest to you.

- Citations of articles published in magazines and journals will include the year of publication, the volume number (and perhaps the issue number), and the inclusive pages of the article. Some of these citations will be elliptical; that is, they will give the numbers without indicating what the numbers refer to. In order to locate the article, you will need all this information, and you will need to know which numbers are which. If you need help in figuring out the citation, turn to Section 8.D.5.

- Most databases have features that let you make note of the citations you want "to keep." In most databases I've seen, these are little boxes to the left of the citation. A click in the box puts it on your list.

- When your review of the results is finished, you will usually have several options regarding the list you have been compiling. One of these options is whether you want a brief record or a detailed record of your choices. I'd suggest the detailed record; it will reassure you that you have all the bibliographic information about the source that you may need. As far as getting this list out of the database and into your hands . . . you can print a hard copy, download it to the desktop (so you can save it on your hard drive or on a disk) or e-mail it to yourself. I'm going to suggest that, especially in your first round of searches, you opt for the electronic copies. Doing so cuts down on the amount of paper you accumulate. Later you can cull these electronic files, and then print whatever you want.

- Remember, though, that this information, no matter its format, needs to be filed right away in the Sources section of your Researcher's Notebook. You are going to need the information in these citations to locate the sources. In addition, complete database records can come in handy when its time to document sources in your final paper. They are available as a convenient back-up in those cases when the entries on your working bibliography turn out to be incomplete. Those of you using bibliographic software just need to be sure that you save this information in your program.

- Other features to look for:

  - An indication that the database provides a full text of the article in question.

  - An indication that your school's library (the one through which you have accessed this database) subscribes to the periodical in which an article has been published.

  - A link back to your school's library to do a search for the book that has been cited, or to do a search to see if your school's library has a subscription to that periodical.

ALERT!

If and when you decide to download a text from a full-text database, there is information you must record WHEN you do the download. Turn to subsection E for details.

---

4. Locating print sources

Locating Books

Your first step is to determine if your school's library owns a copy of a particular book. Using the citation you obtained from the database, you can do an author search, a title search, or a combined author/title search. Be careful about your typing; typos and/or spelling errors will lead to incorrect results.

If the citation you have is for **an essay or an article in a collection of works or an anthology,** be aware that this book is cataloged in (any) library under the title *of the collection* and under the name of the editor or author *of the collection.* So, if your citation reads:

> Doe, Jane. Dogs I have loved and lost. *Tributes to Our Pets.* Ed. Les Hall. Falls Church, VA: Petlovers United, 2010.

Then you will do a library search for either Les Hall or *Tributes to Our Pets.*

At times, searches you do will produce citations of **dissertations** in Dissertation Abstracts. Dissertation Abstracts is itself a database which contains summaries of the works graduate students have completed as part of their requirements for advanced degrees, normally the Ph.D. Finding abstracts of dissertations can be a mixed blessing. On the positive side, dissertations that have been produced in the last year or two represent truly cutting-edge work as far as the discipline or academic field is concerned. On the negative side, dissertations are technically unpublished material, and for this reason the dissertation itself (as opposed to the abstract) may be difficult, if not impossible, for you to obtain. If you have citations for dissertations, consult a reference librarian.

Some Tips

- If your initial search in your library catalog comes up blank, do a second search using a different field. In other words, you want to be very, very sure your library doesn't own the book before you go to your next option.
- If your library has the book, write down the complete call number next to the citation in the Sources section of your Researcher's Notebook.
- If the record in the library catalog indicates the book is checked out, put a hold on it. If the record in the library catalog indicates the book is available but you can't find it on the shelf, don't sit around waiting for it to appear. Make an inquiry at the reference desk.

If your search of the catalog indicates that **your library does not own a copy of the book,** you do have access to this book through another library. If you are not already acquainted with the arrangements your library has with other libraries in the area, and/or the library's procedures for **interlibrary loan,** ask a reference librarian right away. If the book has to be obtained through interlibrary loan, this process could take time (as, sometimes, weeks!). So, right now, you need a clear sense of how available the book is, and, if it may take a week or more to get to you, you want to start the process right away. To do an interlibrary loan request, you will need all the information in the citation you have. In addition, you may be asked where you found this citation! Be prepared!

Locating Articles in Journals or Magazines

Your first step is to determine if your school's library owns a copy of **the volume of the periodical** in which your article was printed. I say volume here because libraries subscribe and unsubscribe to periodicals. So do a search of the library catalog using the title of the journal or magazine (*Atlantic Monthly, Journal of Neuroscience*). If the search menu has a box for "periodicals" or "journal titles," enter the title there. If this search produces results, then check the record of holdings to see if your library has the volume you need, and where you will find that volume. Any volume number/year that is followed by a dash means that the library has all volumes and issues after this volume/year.

If your library has the volume you need:
- Write down the call number for the periodical next to the citation in the Sources section of your Researcher's Notebook. If there is no call number, your library shelves magazines and journals (together) in alphabetical order according to the first main word in the title.
- If the volumes are "on the shelf," take the citation with you when you go to find the article. If the article was published in the last year, look for the issue where your library keeps current periodicals. If the issue was published more than a year ago, look for it with **bound periodicals.** At the end of a volume year all the issues in that volume year are sewn together and put between hard covers so they look like a book; the volume number and sometimes the year are stamped on the spine of this book.

- If the periodical is a popular magazine, you will then need to look for the appropriate issue. If you have the month or the date of the issue you need, do your search for the article with this information. Otherwise, if all you have is the issue number, you'll have to go through the volume looking for table-of-content pages; issue numbers are next to volume numbers, usually in the upper left-hand corner.

- If the periodical is a scholarly one (if, for example, it has the word "journal" in its title), it may be paginated by volume (for more information on this topic, see Section 8.D.5). Right now, using the inclusive page numbers given on the citation, look for the page on which the article is supposed to begin. If your article is not on that page, follow the instructions above for popular magazines.

- If the volume you are seeking is fairly current and the catalog indicates that your library owns it, but you cannot find it (either with bound periodicals or in the current periodical section of the library), then check with a reference librarian. Periodicals can be unavailable for a few weeks when they are sent out to be bound.

- In some cases you may see the word "microfilm" or "microfiche" next to the volume you need. These terms indicate that the volume you are seeking is in a film-like format. Take down all the information written next to these words, and consult a reference librarian.

If your library does not have the volume you need, check with a reference librarian. He or she knows how to check to see if the library may have a copy of this article in a database. If not, she'll give you the procedure for initiating an interlibrary loan request. Such a request will bring you a photocopy of the article. As in the case of books, such requests take some time to process, so, again, get the request in the works right away. To do an interlibrary loan request, you will need all the information in the citation you found in the database. Be particularly careful in filling in the slots asking for the volume number, the issue number, and the page numbers. If you aren't sure you know which numbers are which, turn to Section 8.D.5. In addition to information about the article itself, you may be asked where you found this citation! Be prepared.

Locating Articles in Newspapers

Even if your library subscribes to a particular newspaper, the best place to look for a newspaper article is an electronic database, either a full-text database your library subscribes to, or, if the newspaper has a Web site available to the public, in its archives. Since newsprint is so flimsy and disintegrates quickly, print versions of newspapers are usually kept on the shelves for only a few weeks. At that point, the library either purchases microfilm versions of them, or the newspapers are no longer available. If you have any difficulty locating articles in newspapers, consult a reference librarian.

D. Evaluating Online Sources

If you were to do a bit of research in what college and university professors are saying about research papers, you'd see that high on their list of concerns is students' thoughtless, heavy reliance on material they find online. All of us have our "horror" stories illustrating what happens when passive sponges throw themselves into the ocean of the Internet. The old slogan of the passive sponge was, "If it's in print, it must be true." Today, it's " . . . but I found it on the Internet!" The problem here is not the medium, but the user. In your stance as a critical consumer of information, you will recognize that the "democratic" nature of the Internet simply increases your need to be vigilant; the democratic nature of the Internet makes it especially important for you to be discerning about what you are willing to trust and to accept when it comes to material you find on its sites and in material transmitted through it.

In this regard, I want to return to a central issue I raised in the discussion earlier of authoritative sources. Our judgment of material is affected by the means through which it reaches us. I talked about the authority that academics give to scholarly journals, in large part because the material in them has been reviewed by experts. Popular periodicals that gain the trust of discerning readers do so because of the high standards of their editorial staffs as well as of their reporters. On the other hand, anybody can create a Web site, or post material in areas of the Internet. And these individuals can include on this site anything they want. They can post facts and figures without indicating where they found this information; they can purposefully change or misrepresent facts and figures from reliable sources; they can simply make up facts and figures out of thin air. Unlike reputable publishers of print material, the Internet itself has no editors, no fact-checkers, no oversight body that regulates what appears there.

For this reason, here are my three basic recommendations regarding your use of public sites on the Internet. I exclude services your library subscribes to since the library staff has already evaluated the service or database, although I assume you will be evaluating whatever material you find in such databases.

RECOMMENDATIONS

- Do not turn to Internet sources until you have grounded your knowledge of your subject by reading authoritative print materials.

- When you do go online, have a clear sense of what you are looking for, and why you are looking for it there.

- Never download any material from an online source until and unless you've first critically evaluated both the site and the material.

I advise you to rely on print sources first because it is much easier for you to make initial judgments about their authority and reliability. Having this grounding will make it much easier for you to evaluate online material. Not only will you know the names of people who are considered experts in the field, but you will also know the names of other relevant people and organizations. You will have a general sense of what the experts are saying about your subject, and the types of facts and figures they are using. One of your major methods of critiquing what you find online will be to compare what you find on a particular Internet site with what you've found in print.

When I say that you should not go online unless and until you have a clear sense of what you are looking for—and why—I'm essentially discouraging you from doing scattershot keyword searches, especially those searches that have no other aim than amassing material. Instead, I am encouraging you to look at Internet sources through the lens of what I said about primary and secondary sources. In other words, before you do a search, you should know

- what kind of material you are looking for;

- why you are looking for that type of material;

- how you are going to "read" the material;

- what use you intend to make of it.

You will have met several of my criteria for evaluating material online before you even go online if:

- you are visiting a site recommended by your library or a librarian, your instructor, or a person you consider to be an authority on the topic;

- you are seeking the sites of particular groups—organizations, companies, governmental agencies—with a specific objective in mind. For example, you want to see what kind of statistics the World Health Organization is giving on cases of AIDS in sub-Saharan Africa. Or you want to see what certain companies say, if anything, about their hiring policies. Or you want to find sites created for and by people suffering from fibromyalgia to see what is being said on these sites about this medical condition.

Another step you can take before you even go online is to pay attention to the URL of the site (that's the address you use to access the site, typically starting with http://). If you know how to "read" parts of these addresses, they give you information about the site.

protocol	domain	top-level domain	directory path
http://	www.lclark	.edu/	cgi-bin/catalog2002.cgi?chin.dat.html

The people who register domains use the **top-level domain** as a general category. Here is what these abbreviations mean and the type of sponsor to which they are assigned:

Top-Level Domain	Type of Sponsor
.edu	institution of higher education
.com	for-profit business
.org	associations and organizations that advocate some cause, idea, issue
.gov	governmental entities in the U.S. (federal, state, local)
.net	institutions and organizations that played or still play a major role in the creation of the network we call the Internet
.mil	the military

Some new designations were added a few years ago. They include:

Top-Level Domain	Type of Sponsor
.info	for general use
.biz	for people in show business
.name	for individuals to use for personal home pages

This information will allow you to make some initial assumptions about the nature of the site you will find, but keep in mind that the categories are not hard and fast. Moreover, there are many areas of an .edu site that are not, ipso facto, scholarly and thus authoritative. To make this point, and to illustrate the reasons for the critical evaluations I'm advocating, let's consider two more students who visited me—yes, for help in citing Internet sources when their papers were ready to be handed in.

In one case, the student had used information about Islamic practices from an e-mail message that had been posted on the personal Web site of a student at an institution of higher education doing graduate work in computer science. In the other case, the student, whose paper was a thesis required for his undergraduate major, had based a central part of his argument on the definition of a term he quoted from a Web site. When we accessed that site, which also was part of the domain of an institution of higher education, it turned out to be the site of an introductory course in the discipline in which this student was writing his thesis. The definition he was using was a paraphrase of a definition of the term found in a textbook being used in the course. The site made this information very, very clear, along with the fact that the paraphrase was written by the student who created and maintained the site. Neither of these sources could demonstrate itself to have the type of credibility or authority the student writers should have been looking for in their sources. The really serious problem that these examples illustrate is that, when they first found this information, neither of these students even thought to question whose words they were reading, or who was providing this information.

Which leads me to reiterate the "rule" these students should have been following.

> Never download any material from an online source until and unless you've first critically evaluated both the site and the material.

And, in evaluating your online sources, these will be your criteria:

- Is evidence clearly documented and reliable? Are we told the sources of facts, statistics, quotations, and ideas of others? Are these sources authoritative?

- Do I consider this source authoritative for the purposes for which I intend to use it?

- Is this material current?

First, evaluate the site itself   Keep in mind the point I made earlier that one way to judge the authority of a text is to consider who published it. This is just as true of a Web site, whether we are talking about pages that are the direct responsibility of the sponsors of the site, or we are talking about essays, articles, or statistics that the sponsors have posted on the site. In the example I gave above about the e-mail regarding Islamic practices, it is very possible that the information in this e-mail was correct. My point here is that there was nothing about the sources of this information—either the sender of the e-mail message, or the sponsor of the site itself—that carried authority and thus there was nothing here to give a critical consumer of information a good reason to look upon this information as reliable evidence.

As the Internet matures, sponsors of sites, especially those sites whose purpose is to educate or to advocate, have come to recognize the importance of presenting their group or organization in a professional manner. They have come to realize that, if they want their agenda and materials to be taken seriously, they will have to provide visitors to the site with the kind of information and the kind of reassurances critical consumers of information expect.

These are questions you should ask about the site   Some Internet domains are very large, containing multiple sites created by different individuals or groups for different purposes. The domain of a large university would be an obvious case in point. The questions you are asking here should be directed to the specific site that you reached via a link, or the specific site where the material you are interested in is housed.

- Does the name of the sponsoring person, organization, or company appear prominently on all pages of the site?

- Do pages on the site have clearly marked links back to the main or home page?

- Are pages on the site dated with either a copyright date or a most recent update? Are the pages current?

- For whom has this site been designed? Who is its audience?
- On the main or home page:
  - Is there an "About Us" section, or some other place where the sponsor states the purpose of this site and/or the mission of the sponsoring organization or company?
  - Is there an easy way to contact the sponsors of this site?
  - Is there a date on this page (copyright or update)? Is it current?
  - Is there a clear directory that informs visitors about the content of the site and allows them to easily navigate the various pages?

If you do not find a link to the home or main page, and/or if it is difficult to ascertain who is responsible for this site, I suggest that you consider this fact itself a possible negative indicator. If you want to take the trouble to do so, you can probably find the main page by going to the URL, and, working from right to left, snipping off pieces of the directory path at the slash marks, dots, or other division markers. But the lack of links to the main page would tell me either that this site is not designed for the public at large (such would be the case, for example, of sites designed for students of a specific class) or that the sponsor of this site doesn't recognize or doesn't acknowledge the importance of information that critical Internet users deem important.

These are questions you should ask about the site sponsor
- Do I recognize this person or organization? Have I ever heard of this person or organization? What do I know about this person or organization from other sources? Does what I know about this person or organization indicate that it is a reliable source for *the type of information* I want to take from it?
- What does the purpose of the site or the mission of the organization tell me about the authority of material on this site? What do statements about its values tell me? If there are no statements of value, what can I infer?
- Look at the links this site provides to other Internet sites. Keeping in mind the adage that we can judge people by the company they keep, what do these links tell me about the values and objectives of the site's sponsor?

If you are satisfied that the site itself meets your criteria for reliability, authority, and currency, you are now going to apply the same criteria to the specific article, essay, or page that interests you.

These are questions you should ask about the material itself
- Is an author given for this essay or information? Is information provided about the author? What are the author's credentials for speaking on this topic? Do you recognize this author from other sources you've read? Has

this author published in authoritative print sources? (I discuss unsigned Internet pages in Section 8.D.6).

- Does the author of this page or essay document the sources of evidence he or she includes on this page? Are these citations complete; in other words, could you verify this information?

- Is this essay or article or page dated? Is the material current?

If and when you are satisfied that you can trust the material you have found, you want to be sure you record all the bibliographic information you will need in order to document this source *before* you leave the site. Turn to subsection E, and, for further discussion of electronic sources, see Section 8.D.6.

E. Information to Record about Electronic Sources

In Section 4.F, I recommend taking down full bibliographic information about each of your sources before you even look at it. In doing so, you are reassuring yourself that you have all the information you will need to document this material if you decide to use it in your final paper. Because of the evanescent nature of material online, this advice has to become a hard-and-fast rule. And I want to extend it to **any material you download from a computer,** including any articles you take from full-text databases. You will find more detailed discussion of electronic sources in Section 8.D.6. But I want to give you this advice here, at this early stage of the research process, because some bibliographic information you are going to need in order to document an electronic source correctly may be difficult to find if you do not make a record of it when you access the material. Besides, in order to get some of the information required for documentation you will have to check aspects of the material and its source (e.g., the site and its sponsor) that you ought to be looking at in order to evaluate the material. Requirements for documentation and assessment nicely complement and reinforce each other. So let me repeat:

It is critical that you **record full bibliographic information** about electronic sources **WHEN** you access the material or download it from the computer.

The specific information you will need to document electronic sources varies among document styles. So . . . here are your options:

EITHER

determine which documentation style you will be using in your final paper before you access any electronic sources so that you know exactly what information that documentation style requires. See Section 8.A through C.

OR

use the checklists I provide below.

Regardless of which alternative you choose, here are **some general tips:**

- All other things being equal, too much information is always going to be better than too little. If in doubt, record it.

- Requirements for full bibliographic information about electronic sources are really very similar to those for print sources: Who wrote it? What's the title? Who is responsible for making this material public? Where did you find it (or what information would you need to find it)?

- The two most important pieces of information you will need, and the easiest to forget to record, are (1) the URL of the page on which you find the material, and (2) the date on which you accessed it.

- My browser has a handy set of options that helps me remember to record some of the required information. They are in the print options part of the program, so if I print material straight from the Internet, my paper copy includes the date I printed this material (my access date), the title of the page, and the address (URL). Obviously, if your browser has such options, turn them on! But this feature will serve your needs only if you make a paper copy of the material when you access it.

- Have a system for recording the required information and keeping track of it. If you make a print copy of the material, be sure the first page contains **all** the bibliographic information you need; write in anything that is not already printed there. If you are storing this material in its original electronic format, you will have to develop a system for recording the required bibliographic information and storing it in such a manner that you can easily find it when you need it for documentation purposes. I talk more about getting organized in Section 4.D.

Here's the general kind of information you should record **WHEN** you access or download the material. If you download the text in print or electronic form, you'll notice that at least some of this information will be part of the text you download. These items are on the checklist just so you make sure you have them! If a piece of this information is not available, I advise you to record that fact, so you know you didn't just forget to look for it.

Checklist for Electronic Sources

Before you leave the **page** on which you found the material, double-check that you have:

- **The complete URL for that page.** As you know, your best bet is to electronically copy it and paste it with the rest of the record you are making. If the address is tremendously long and complicated:

  - for a regular Web or Internet site, also make a record of the links you used to reach this page from the search page, or from the main or domain page. You may be able to substitute the URL for the domain page and the links for the page's URL:

> http://www.hereweare.org/ Publications > Articles

- for a full-text database, you will probably need, at most, the address for the search page or (same thing) the address through the top-level domain and the first segment of the directory path (see above).

- The **author** of the material; if no author is given, make a note of that fact.

- The **title** of the material (or the name of the page if there is no title).

- The **date of the material itself,** if it has one. Otherwise, look for a date on the page (a copyright date, or the date the page was most recently updated); be sure to make a note of what type of date you are recording.

- **Publication information.** If the material is an electronic version of a print text, be sure you have all the information that is provided about the print text. If the text is an electronic publication (an e-book or an article published in an online journal or magazine), be sure you have all information about the electronic publication (if a periodical, for example, the volume, issue, number, date of publication).

If you are in a **full-text database (including online encyclopedias and other** reference works), you need to be sure you have three more pieces of information and you are done:

- The **complete name of the database** (e.g., Expanded Academic ASAP, Business Dateline, Newspaper Source, LexisNexis Academic).

- **The name of the service** or vendor or company that provides this database (e.g., EBSCO, OCLC, The Gale Group).

- **Today's date** (that is, the date you accessed this material).

- If you are using a database available only through subscription, the MLA documentation style will ask you to give the name of the subscriber, which will probably be the library through which you accessed the database. So, if you have accessed this database though a **library** other than your school's library, better write down the name of the library.

If you are **on a Web or Internet site,** go back to the **main or home page** of the site responsible for the material you have accessed. Be sure you have the following information:

- The formal **title of the site** (if it has one); underline it. If the site does not have a formal title, write down a description of its nature (e.g., home page of John Doe, a student at Moose U.).

- The full, formal **name of the sponsor** of the site (organization, company, individual). If you find no such information, be sure to make a record of this fact.

- In those cases where you are on the site of a scholarly project or a special collection of materials, look to see if this site has **an editor or editors.** If so, write down those names.

- **Today's date** (that is, the date you accessed this material).

Other Electronic Materials

The checklists above and your general understanding of the kind of information that academics expect you to provide about your sources should alert you to the information you will need to have about other types of electronic sources.

- If you are using material from a **CD-ROM disk,** follow the general guidelines for a database. Be sure you have the name of the company or vendor that provides this material, and the copyright date of the disk you used.

- For **online forums or discussion groups, newsgroups, material from list servers,** and the like, be sure you have the name of the author or the person responsible for the material, the subject line for the posting or message, the date of the message or posting, the name of the forum or discussion group if it has a formal name, and the URL.

F. Summary

You will be the ultimate judge, but if I have achieved what I set out to achieve in writing this section, you will now have a much clearer sense of the stance an active researcher takes when it is time "to do research." Because adopting this stance is such an important element in guaranteeing the success of the whole research project, it is worth reiterating its three defining characteristics.

- Any and all research that you as an active researcher do will be driven and directed by your personal need to know and to understand. Your ultimate goal is to make sense of your chosen intellectual puzzle, to form, in your mind, a picture that puts the available evidence together in a manner that is most coherent and most meaningful. To reach this goal, you need answers to questions, big and small, simple and complex. These questions will determine the "evidence" you need, and thus what it is you need to find.

- Since your quest is being driven by what you need to know and the questions you have, you will be constantly using your problem-solving skills in determining the most logical places to look for the evidence you need, and how to make the best use of resources available to you.

- Throughout the process your critical reasoning faculties will be working hard. They will have to be active because only you will know if and when material you find is answering, or is helping you to answer, the questions that are driving the research. Your critical reasoning faculties will have to be active because you will not automatically accept anything a search turns up as having legitimacy or validity or even significance. In fact, from the outset you will use your critical reasoning faculties to set up the searches most likely to produce sources you can trust as authoritative. You will take very seriously your role as a critical consumer of information. And you will be particularly conscientious in playing this role when you go online to search the Internet.

So—research is most definitely *not* a process of gathering piles of material until you are satisfied that you have "enough" to "fill" an X-page paper. You are letting go of the passive sponge approach because you trust me when I tell you that it is not going to produce the paper your instructor wants to read. You are letting go of the passive sponge approach mainly, though, because you are tired of working on papers that you consider dry, dull, and boring! In your new role of an active researcher-detective, you are going to experience moments of frustration, of self-doubt and trepidation, and probably more than a few moments of confusion. But you are going to recognize the positive nature of these moments; you will see them as signs of your intellectual growth!
Let me end with a few reminders and a little more advice:

- Not only will you think of any and all libraries available to you as resources, but you will take the time to educate yourself about the specific resources these libraries have to offer you, especially in the area of reference materials and databases created for researchers such as yourself.

- You will not be shy about asking reference librarians for assistance, but you won't turn into a passive sponge in doing so. You'll be prepared with a list of specific questions, along with to-the-point explanations of the general project that has instigated them. You won't be afraid to ask follow-up questions if and when the librarian gets into what is foreign territory for you. All in all, you will recognize that the two of you have a shared common goal— to enable you to find what you want to find—and you will take responsibility for your side of this communicative exchange.

- You will recognize that the "research" part of this project will not stop with your first search of bibliographic databases. As you read sources you will be checking their reference lists and bibliographies for more promising sources. You will be asking experts about potential sources. You will always be on the outlook for promising sources since you can run across them at unlikely times and in unlikely places.

- As you read the sources you collect and as you think about what the authors are saying, your research questions—and very likely your working thesis/ hypothesis—will change. With each shift in direction, new questions, and possibly even new areas of investigation, will open up.

When I first started teaching, the by-word on research papers was "research, then write." But people who pushed this agenda were ignoring a great deal, both about what goes on in the heads of experienced researchers before and as they research, and about the activities in which researchers engage through the process. Being truer to this actual experience, we are assuming that researching and thinking and writing are all interdependent and contemporaneous activities. And so you will assume that throughout the upcoming weeks you will keep returning to computer terminals to do various types of searches, from a quick check to see if your library has a book you need, to an effort to track down a particular document, to a more extensive search for sources that could educate you further about X or Y or Z.

With this in mind, let's now turn our attention to the issue of reading the sources you do find.

SECTION

4

Reading Critically and Taking Notes

If you have done a research project before, you are used to the idea that part of your time will be spent making lists of books, articles, and other materials and then gathering this material. But what then? What do you do after your desk is piled high with books and articles? This is the point in the process when many students are tempted to turn into passive sponges. From their sources, they copy sentence after sentence into notebooks. They have a wonderful time highlighting passages in yellow, pink, and green. For what purpose?

Notetaking is not the mindless activity of a passive sponge. It involves far more than copying phrases and sentences into your notes, or making paragraph-by-paragraph outlines of your reading.

To be a meaningful activity, notetaking must be the product of critically reading and studying your sources.

Researchers gather books and articles so they can learn about a subject by reading what others have said and done, and then by thinking about—synthesizing, analyzing—what they have read. In this section I'll be giving you strategies for taking notes—for keeping accurate records of the evidence you are gathering—but I'll be doing this is the context of your learning, thinking, and critical reading. This stage of the process has no point if you are not actively using your brain to make meaning of and from the work of others.

In this stage of the process, you will be keeping two categories of notes:

- In some systematic fashion, you will be recording the evidence you find.

- In your Researcher's Notebook, you will be recording your own thoughts about the evidence you are finding, the sense you are making of the material you are reading.

89

In the weeks that follow, you will turn regularly to the Working Hypothesis/Thesis section of your Notebook. As you continue to educate yourself about your subject and gather evidence, you will want to talk to yourself about the ways in which this knowledge and evidence is affecting your own picture of the subject. You will regularly ask yourself such questions as,

- Does my initial working hypothesis/thesis still seem "right"? If so, why is it right?

- If it is changing, how is it changing?

- If I were to answer my original research question right now, what would I say?

I'll remind you that, as investigation proceeds, researchers often change direction and focus, and you want to allow yourself this flexibility. If you find that there is a major question that interests you more than the research question with which you began, feel free to pursue it. Similarly, as your reading gives you a sense of what has been investigated, how thoroughly it has been investigated, and the parts of the puzzle that are still unknown, adjust your own inquiry accordingly. Unless you are writing a review of the literature paper, what you want to avoid is writing a paper that is nothing more than a recapitulation of what others have discovered.

At the same time that you work on the picture you are developing of the intellectual puzzle you are investigating, you'll need to keep a clean, easy-to-use record of the evidence you are accumulating. Beginning with subsection D, we'll consider in detail how you can keep a record of these two general categories of evidence:

- summaries of the sources you read: that is, the gists of the investigations and ideas of various experts;

- notes on specific information:

  - "building-block" evidence, facts or data such as dates, names and identities of people, definitions of terms, pieces of common knowledge, and so on;

  - specifics related to the points of view of the author of a source (the specific hypothesis tested, his/her precise conclusions, comments on particular matters, and the like).

The summaries you make of your sources will form a literal bridge between your record of the evidence and your Researcher's Notebook, since you'll be developing these summaries in the Reading section of your Notebook. Far more importantly, developing these summaries will allow you to determine what belongs in your record of the evidence and what belongs in the Working Hypothesis/Thesis section of your Notebook because you will be able to distinguish the ideas of others from your own thinking.

At this point you may be saying: "But you have just hit upon one of my basic problems. I can't always distinguish between my own ideas and those of my sources. I don't know very much about the subject I'm researching; that's why I'm doing the research. The experts, they're the ones who know. I have to depend on them."

All researchers, as I noted in Section 1, rely on the work done by others in the field. You, too, will need and want to use your sources. What you must avoid is having your sources use you. "Reading critically" has a prominent place in the title and content of this section because it reflects my experience that the secret of distinguishing your own thinking from that of the authors of your sources lies in reading your sources actively and critically. As the outline of this section indicates, you must first step back from your sources and develop a healthy relationship with them, and since forming that healthy relationship turns on strategies for active reading, let's consider them now.

A. Reading Actively and Critically: An Overview

Resisting the temptation to start taking notes immediately is not easy, especially since this mode of "reading" is often encouraged by the way various subjects are taught in high schools. If one assumes that a piece of prose is a conglomeration of facts and truths, it makes sense to skim pages for statements that seem important, highlighting these statements or copying them down as lists of things to memorize in order to pass tests. When students approach required reading for courses or sources for a research project in this manner, they should realize that they are acting like passive sponges. This manner of reading directly interferes with their comprehension of a book or article because it interferes with their ability to grasp what the author is doing and saying in his or her text. So it is important for us to consider what it means to read.

Reading has been defined in a number of ways. The definition that I prefer is Frank Smith's. Smith contends that reading is a very selective activity; we are "deliberately seeking just the information that we need. Need for what purpose? *To answer specific questions that we are asking.*"[1]

Do you notice that Smith's definition of reading is almost exactly the same definition I have been using for the research process? As researchers we are looking for information that we need. We are looking for answers to questions we have asked. We have gathered books and articles and other sources because we believe that they contain information that will help us answer our research questions, that will give us help in testing our working theses and give us the solid basis we need on which to draw conclusions.

---

[1] *Reading Without Nonsense* (New York and London: Teacher's College Press, 1979), 105.

The first important step toward active reading, then, is approaching each source with these questions:

- What do I expect to learn from this source?

- What do I need from this source?

- What are the questions for which I expect to find answers?

Sometimes the question a reader asks of a text is very specific and narrow:

- When was Julius Caesar assassinated?

- Where did the popes reside during the Babylonian Captivity?

- Who developed penicillin as a drug?

- What was the average price of bread in 1915?

When your question is this narrow and specific, you read by scanning a page, looking for a visual clue (like a particular number or a name) to obtain the answer you need. You are not concerned about what the author is saying about Julius Caesar, the Babylonian Captivity, or penicillin.

Scanning pages to find answers to questions is a perfectly natural and legitimate form of reading when your questions are highly specific and your objective is to find a discrete piece of information. You will be doing this type of reading in the course of this research project. But it is not the only kind of reading you'll be doing, nor is it an appropriate approach to most of the books and articles you will be studying.

Except for the special cases of almanacs, compilations of statistics, and other reference works, the books and articles you have gathered are *not* collections of facts. Indeed, resisting the temptation to approach these sources as conglomerations of facts and truths to be mined for the discrete pieces of information they contain is critical if you are going to read them productively. These books and articles are *interpretations* of evidence, interpretations that have been formulated by human beings. You can constantly remind yourself that what you are reading is the thinking of other human beings if you get into the habit of referring to your sources by using the names of their authors: Valdez says . . . , Jones looks at . . . , The way Greenberg and Yamada see it. . . .

Now Valdez, Jones, Greenberg, Yamada, and the authors of your sources obviously believe in the validity of their perceptions of their subjects, and they've written these books and articles to persuade you to see the subject as they do. For your part, you certainly want to *understand how and why each of these authors sees the subject* as he or she does; but you want to resist *mindlessly falling into his or her pattern of thinking.* You can resist unconsciously adopting the thinking of others as your own by keeping a respectful distance from each author. And you'll be able to gain this distance by considering what each author has to say in the context of what that author is doing: here she is telling me about the problem she wants to unravel; here she is giving me her hypothesis; here she's explaining to me how she went about examining the evidence; and here she is summarizing the conclusions she has drawn. You will, in short, **be looking at your sources as other human being's constructions of meaning.** After you've read a number of books and articles in this manner, you will see for yourself that there is no central "truth" for you to find. Not all experts interpret the evidence in the same way; not all experts use the same evidence. If you think in these terms, you should see for yourself that the authors of your sources are carrying on a conversation about the best way to understand this subject.

You are perfectly capable of joining this conversation. You are perfectly capable of thinking. You are perfectly capable of formulating a point of view. You have already taken a major step in this direction by beginning this research project with your own working hypothesis/thesis. Now you need to have confidence in yourself. You want to listen to what the experts have to say; you want to understand their points of view. But take the attitude of the little boy in "The Emperor's New Clothes": Never mind what others see; what do *you see?* What matters most is *what makes sense to you.*

"What makes sense to you" brings us to the heart of the distinction between your own ideas and those of others. The authors you are reading present you with what they see as good reasons for thinking the way they do. You may accept, reject, or qualify all or part of what they say, but you need *good reasons* for doing so. You will know that you are thinking for yourself when you can explain to yourself *how* and *why* one way of looking at your subject makes more sense than another. It doesn't matter if your thinking is similar to that of the experts (in all likelihood it will be); what matters is that you yourself have found a way to make the evidence mean something.

The working hypothesis/thesis you have developed in your Researcher's Notebook reflected your initial perception or point of view of your subject. The process of testing this working hypothesis/thesis will require your discovering the perceptions or points of view of others, particularly those regarded as experts. Thus, you will approach your sources with this central, broad question: **How and why did this author reach the conclusions he or she did?** Obviously, you won't be able to answer this question by focusing on a sentence here or there, or studying only one or two paragraphs. Rather, looking at each text as a coherent whole, you will have to read with the purpose of following the author's line of thought from beginning to end. Moreover, you will be far more apt to grasp what the author's words mean if you read these words through the framework of what you've decided the author is doing in that text.

The various suggestions and strategies I provide in subsections B and C are designed to keep you at a respectful, healthy distance from your sources so that you can understand them as coherent wholes, so that you will always be aware of what is yours, what is theirs, and so that, when you judge the views of certain authors to be logical and convincing, you consciously choose to agree with them.

B. Previewing Your Sources

Before you are ready to settle down to the reading of specific sources, you'll want to do some preliminary reconnoitering. Such reconnoitering is the first step toward reading a book or an article actively and critically, as we'll see in subsection C. However, before you even get to the reading stage, you'll want to weed out those sources that aren't worth reading, and to decide what you should read first. A preliminary reconnoitering will let you make these initial decisions.

For each of the books and articles you've located, take about five or ten minutes to check out the following features. You are looking for clues and hints which, when added together, will give you a general sense of where the author is coming from, and where he or she will be going in the body of the text.

For **books**, consider

- the title and subtitle;

- any blurbs by reviewers, or summaries of the content on covers or dust jackets;

- whatever information you can uncover about the author's interests and credentials (education, previous and current professions, the job he/she now has, and so on);

- the date of publication;

- publisher.

Then skim

- the preface;

- the table of contents;

- the introductory and concluding chapters.

For **articles**, consider

- the periodical in which it was published. What does its title tell you about the kinds of articles you'd expect to be published here? What do you know, or what would you guess, about the interests of people who regularly read this periodical?

- the specific title and subtitle of the article;

- the abstract, if one is included (it will be directly under the title);

- whatever information you are given about the author(s);

- the date of publication.

Then skim

- the section headed "Introduction," or the first couple of paragraphs;

- the section headed "Conclusions," "Discussion," or the last page or so of the piece;

- all headings and subheadings.

After you've gathered what information you can, put it together in a very quick, rough freewrite in which you guess or make predictions about what the author will be saying in the body of the text.

The first use you'll make of this information is to assess the quality of your sources, and decide what you should read first.

1. Determining the quality of your sources

Before you expend time and energy reading a source, it would be wise to assess its worth. The value of a source, of course, is dependent on many factors, not the least of which is what the reader wants from that source. As I pointed out in Section 3, you are going to read a text in one way if you are approaching it as a primary text, and in a very different way if you are looking at it as a secondary source. An instructor of physics looking for a textbook for the introductory course she'll be teaching in the spring would never consider a textbook published in 1948. Yet, if she is investigating the way physics was presented to college students in 1948, she'd consider this same textbook a highly valuable source of information. So, when you pick up a source, your first two questions will be:

- What is the copyright date of the text? When was it *originally* published?

- What do I want from this source? What do I expect to learn in reading it?

Even if the project in which you are currently engaged is going to focus on primary texts or data, you will still need to get into the secondary literature; you need a sense of the conversation that members of a field or discipline are having about your subject. I trust that, in Section 3, I brought home to you the idea that just because some material is public—or has been published—does not automatically mean that it has authority. You also need to realize that a text does not automatically have authority just because it has certain academic credentials. Conversations among scholars and experts change over time. Theories and methodologies that dominated a field twenty years ago could be considered out of date, or even unacceptable, by experts currently investigating your topic. Thus, evaluating sources depends on having some knowledge of the conversation that is currently going on in a field about your subject. If your general knowledge of a field is limited, judging the worth of certain sources before you have had a chance to do much reading and studying will be somewhat limited. On the other hand, the reading and studying you will be doing over the coming weeks is going to give you a much clearer sense of what, currently, is "in" and what is "out." So assume that assessing sources is an ongoing process. It is very possible that several weeks from now you will decide that a work you first deemed valuable is less credible than you originally thought. Such reassessments are a natural part of the research process. In the meantime, you have to have some place to start. In your efforts now to assess the quality of your sources, here are some factors you can consider:

- Pay close attention to the publication dates of sources whose purpose is to present evidence about your subject and/or interpretations of that evidence. Generally speaking, you'll want to focus on works published in the past ten years or so. In the social and natural sciences, particularly, you should be cautious of work published more than ten or fifteen years ago unless you have good reason to believe this scholarship is still considered authoritative.

- In addition to considering a work's publication date, you can also assess the specific credentials of the author and the source of the publication. As I indicated in Section 3, in academic circles articles published in scholarly journals and in respected newspapers will be considered more authoritative than articles published in sources aimed at the general public. Thus, for example, information about some scientific study will carry more weight if you take if from an article in a scholarly journal than from a newspaper clipping or a news magazine or, perhaps, a TV program. If the source is a book, its contents may have more authority if it was published by a university press than if it comes out of a "trade" publishing house (this may be particularly true of paperback books).

   Clearly, in higher education more credibility is given to work that is produced by academics for academics, and this carries over to the credentials of authors. If the topic of a work is an academic subject, authors who have advanced degrees and/or who are members of faculties of colleges and universities may be considered to have more authority to speak on your subject than those without such credentials. Of course, the credibility and authority of the authors of sources are ultimately and finally determined by the type of information you are seeking. If, for example, you are exploring the way Congress actually works, then the views and experiences of those who have served in Congress or who have worked on Capitol Hill should be some of the best evidence you can find on this matter.

- As you do your reading, you will notice that the work of certain authors is mentioned frequently. These references are clues that such material is considered important by members of the field, regardless of when it was originally published. You should plan to locate and study both specific works that are frequently cited, and other works written by authors whose names come up often.

- It is important that you not confuse the quality of a source with how "hard" or "easy" you find it to read. Unfortunately, some very valuable sources can prove difficult reading for you because the author is deeply immersed in the discipline's conversation, talking to other experts who are well versed in matters about which you may know very little. Don't reject such material now; in subsection B.3, I give you advice for dealing with it.

- If you have questions or are confused about the quality of certain sources, don't hesitate to consult your instructor. Often instructors who assign research papers ask students to submit bibliographies of sources they are discovering through their searches so that the instructor—who is knowledgeable about the conversations going on in a field—can warn students not to trust certain sources, or can alert them to important works they may not yet have discovered. If you are offered this opportunity, make the most of it by submitting lists of sources you've come across, even if you haven't as yet had the chance to read them.

2. Deciding what to read first

Making this decision is not always easy, but here are a few guidelines:

- Choose the material that is written as introductory material or material for nonexperts (look at the prefaces to books; here the author usually states his purpose and the audience for whom he is writing).

- If the focus of your working thesis is a primary source—a painting or paintings, a poem, a piece of music, a "classic" work like Machiavelli's *The Prince* or Darwin's *Origin*—study this primary source yourself and record your own reactions before you begin your research. Obviously you will have to come back to this source and study it several times in light of the evidence you collect.

- Choose the material that seems directly aimed at your working thesis/hypothesis and research questions.

- If you are already aware that certain people are considered *the* experts in the field, or if you know that Dr. X's theory is the most influential one in the field, read the work of these people first.

- If a source is a collection of essays or a book-length study, you will want to decide if you should read the whole work, or if only specific essays, chapters, or sections are relevant to your investigation. To make such decisions, look carefully at the table of contents. You can also use the index (if the text has one); look for key words that correspond to or are related to key words in your research questions and working hypothesis/thesis.

- Put aside more technical material that promises to be difficult to read (then read over the next subsection).

3. Coping with difficult material

As fields of study become more and more specialized and as more and more complex and sophisticated methods of testing become popular, research in many fields becomes more and more difficult for novices to read and interpret. If you come across articles and books written for experts in the field, you may find them very hard going; the vocabulary may sound like gibberish to you, and you will probably sense that the author is assuming you have knowledge that you, in fact, do not have.

Whenever possible, you should try to read this material, but you will have to use your common sense. You are having trouble reading the material because it was written for experts.

- Do not attempt to read the material until you have spent some time educating yourself about the subject. Go back to textbooks, introductory works, specialized encyclopedias, and accessible but authoritative periodicals before you try to tackle this material.

- The active reading strategies I provide in subsection C should prove especially helpful for this type of material. Your first objective is to gain as clear a sense as you are able of what the author is doing, and the basic approach he or she takes toward the subject.

- If the source seems to be one that contains information or insights that you will want to include in your collection of evidence, you'll have to be sure you have a good handle on what the author is saying. Go back to the critical parts of the text, read slowly and carefully, and talk to yourself in the Reading section of your Notebook about your understanding of the author's meaning.

- In this regard, it will help to isolate key terms (words or phrases) that are clearly important. Look up these terms in a textbook or specialized dictionary. Write out the terms and their definitions on cards. Try to understand the concepts they represent. When you come back to this source, have the cards at hand so that you can refer to them *as* you read.

- Often, putting some distance between yourself and the work will do the trick. If you become frustrated and discouraged in your initial efforts to comprehend a source, put it aside and plan to come back to it in a few days. Yet another reason for giving yourself plenty of time for this phase of the research project!

- Whatever you do, do not take notes on anything you don't understand. If you decide to take down some of the author's statements in the author's words, your notes should always include your interpretation of the author's meaning.

C. Reading to Understand What an Author Is Doing and Saying

Having previewed your sources and decided which you are going to read, the time has come to do that reading. Get out your Researcher's Notebook, and be sure you have lots of paper in the section where you are keeping your Reading

Logs. On the following pages I offer a number of strategies and suggestion to enhance your comprehension of these sources by helping you to approach them as coherent wholes. All these strategies and suggestions are designed to enable you to maintain a healthy distance from your sources: to listen attentively and respectfully to what each author has to say, to put mental energy into understanding how and why each sees the subject as he or she does, but always to recognize that each author's point of view is one of many possible points of view and the fact that this work has been published does not give it the status of truth. While the details of these texts—specific facts and particulars of the argument or study—are certainly vital parts of the text, reading actively encourages you to see these details in the context of, and subordinate to, the work as a whole. The "test" of your reading will not be how many of these details you remember, but rather how well you can reconstruct the overall picture.

Approaching these texts as an active reader begins with the previewing I outlined in the introduction to subsection B. Specialists in reading comprehension tell us that when we approach a text with a set of expectations about what we'll find there, our reading comprehension increases, even though our expectations may be general—and, perhaps, not always on target. Forming expectations activates our brains, opening up areas of knowledge and previous experience that will function as a framework through which we will filter the sentences and paragraphs we read, thus enabling us to make meaning of this language. For these reasons, it is important to preview all the books and articles you've collected and, even if you've decided to read only a chapter or a segment of a book, it is important to preview that book as a whole. After all, the author considered this chapter or segment to be part of a larger pattern of ideas; unless you have a sense of this larger pattern, you won't fully grasp the meanings the author intended an isolated segment or chapter to carry.

The first two strategies I'll be giving you consist of a series of questions you can ask yourself about each text you read. Because the content or substance of what the author has to say becomes fully comprehensible only in light of what he or she was attempting to do in a text, you should first answer the questions about what the author is doing as a means of orienting yourself to the author's area of investigation, the question or problem she posed for herself, the way she decided to carry out her investigation. It should then be much easier to answer those questions focusing on what the author has to say about the subject, the insights and conclusions she reached, and the line of thinking and analysis that led her to these conclusions.

Subsection 3 contains a series of suggestions about ways to use these questions and the answers you develop. Having you write is central to this process for a couple of reasons. The most important is that articulating, in your own words, what you hear and see the author doing and saying reinforces the fact that comprehension requires mental and intellectual exertion. Writing about what you've read guarantees that you are exercising your brain's meaning-making faculties. In addition, the writing you do in order to comprehend your sources is leading you toward summaries of each of your sources, summaries which, as I explain in subsection G, will become an important type of evidence you'll be using to form your final answer to your major research question. As with any set of strategies and suggestions, these are offered as possible ways to read more effectively and efficiently, as possible means to increase your understanding of the books and articles you've collected. It's up to you to decide which of these heuristics will be helpful to you and to determine how you want to use them, to decide how they best mesh with your own learning style.

1. Questions to ask about what an author is doing

Since grasping what the author is doing provides an important framework for understanding what the author is saying, answer the first general set of questions first. You will note that the more specific questions about what the author is doing sometimes require some background in the academic discipline in which and for which the author is writing. When you are doing a research paper for a class in a particular discipline, especially an upper-division course, these are important questions to consider. If you are writing your paper for an introductory-level class in a department or a composition class, answer the questions as well as you are able, but don't become too worried if you aren't able to provide full answers.

You'll find it helpful to refer to the freewrite you wrote when you previewed a source (subsection B) since you will already have considered some of the issues raised by these questions.

General Questions

- What is the author's main area of investigation? What field is she working in, and what part of the field is she focusing on? What main body of information/facts is she examining?

- What question has the author asked herself about this material, or what problems does she see in the way the material has been previously interpreted or examined? What, explicitly, does the author say about the problem she is addressing, questions she is asking?

- What is the author's basic approach to the subject? Answering this question involves considering the theories and/or methodologies she accepts or rejects, as well as the basic manner in which she systematically examines the facts.

More Specific Questions

- What do you know about the author? What is her area of expertise? Do you know anything about other work she has done?

- What, specifically and concretely, is the subject matter of this text? What exactly is the author looking at? How much "territory" does the author cover? What *type* of evidence is the author examining?

- What does the author tell you about where she stands in relation to other experts/theories/approaches in the field? What does she say about her agreement/disagreement with other people's work? theories?

- Consider the general approach or methods the author uses in examining the evidence. What does the author tell you about these matters? What do you know about this approach, method?

- What are some of the author's assumptions or premises? This question may be hard to answer, but try. Make a list of the general ideas this author seems to accept as "true" or "given" so that she simply alludes to them rather than explaining them.

- Using what you know about this subject (from class lectures, other reading, other sources of information), where does the author stand? Can you place her ideas in any specific school or approach? In looking for answers to these questions, pay attention to the author's technical vocabulary and/or explicit references to specific theories or experts.

- What does the "site of publication" of this work tell you about what the author is doing? If your source is a journal article, consider the title of the journal and what you can determine about the particular interests of its readers. If it is in a collection of essays, what does the title of the collection and the preface suggest about why the essay you are reading has been included in this collection?

Using the answers you have given to these questions, write a paragraph summarizing what this author is doing in this text.

2. Questions to ask about what an author is saying

Once you have reached some understanding of what the author is doing in a text, you have a context for understanding what the author is saying.

General Questions

- What major conclusion or conclusions has the author drawn? If he is making an argument, what is his thesis? What has he decided the facts mean?

- How did the author arrive at this conclusion or thesis? What is the general outline of his argument, or what specific procedures did he follow?

Strategies for Answering These Questions

- Putting the text aside and drawing upon what you remember, what topic does the author spend most of his time talking about? Why? Summarize in one or two sentences the general point he wants to make about this topic.

- In your own words, write out the author's *central* and *specific* conclusion in *one* sentence. If the work is a critical analysis, write out the author's main, specific thesis. If the work is a study or experiment, rephrase the hypothesis in terms of the results the author found after analyzing the data ("Results indicate that gasoline consisting of 10% ethanol does not significantly decrease the amount of carbon dioxide emitted from car exhausts").

- Consider the general pattern of organization of this work. How is the book or article laid out? What does the author talk about and where does he talk about it? How does the order in which the author raises his points fit with his main conclusion? If the work is a study or an experiment, write a short paragraph, in your own words, explaining why the procedures the author used are a logical test of the hypothesis.

- From memory, write a short paragraph encapsulating the author's *main* line of reasoning; ignore details and concentrate on central points. Now, read over what you've written. Can you see the logic in this progression of thinking? If not, write another version, making these logical connections.

3. Writing to comprehend what you are reading

As I noted earlier in this section, the act of highlighting sentences or taking notes the first time you read a text distracts you from the activity of comprehending the text as a coherent whole and encourages you to see it as a collection of specific details to memorize. For these reasons,

- I urge you to put your pen or highlighter away when you read. This advice is especially important for your first serious reading of a text. Read from beginning to end with the purpose of following the author's line of thinking.

- when you pick up your pen or sit down at the computer, it is not for the purpose of making notes of specific pieces of information. That comes later. Now you'll be writing to capture the picture you are constructing of the overall shape and meaning of the text.

You should plan to read each text twice, doing a freewrite after the first reading in the Reading section of your Notebook. You could try looking over the questions in the previous two subsections before you read, or after your first reading. A good test of your comprehension of the text would be answering the questions about what the author is doing and saying after your first reading, and then reading the text again. If, in some fashion, you read once, write from memory about the meaning you've constructed of the text, and then read again, I think you'll find that the second reading goes very quickly and you'll be surprised at how much sense the text now makes to you.

Some Further Suggestions

- Do as many freewrites as needed to solidify for yourself the gist of each particular text. With each you will be clarifying your understanding of the text and moving toward a paragraph (or, at most, a page) which captures the heart of this author's picture of the subject. If you use the questions in subsections 1 and 2, *write out* your answers to the questions you use. Answering these questions should be particularly helpful in making sense of sources that, on your first reading, were difficult or confusing. Especially in your initial freewrites, don't worry about being "organized." Remember that freewriting itself is a prod to memory and meaning-making, and, *as* you write, you should find yourself remembering more and seeing more and more connections. Finally, you should certainly write down any reactions you've had, either to what the author was doing or saying, or to your own experience in reading.

- I recommend—strongly—that you put the source aside when you write, and do your freewriting without referring to it—especially in the initial stages of making sense of the text. Writing from memory, using your own words, establishes that all-important distance you need from the text. Failure to establish this distance from a text is the primary cause of plagiarism in the notetaking phase of a research project.

  Plagiarism is a scary word, and students who become obsessed with it, ironically, tend to miss the very lessons they need to learn about the "causes" of plagiarism and thus about "solutions" to the problem. Let me reassure you that this entire book is dedicated to keeping you from falling into serious traps of plagiarism, which essentially means passing off someone else's ideas or words as your own. I discuss plagiarism in some detail in Section 6, and if you are concerned about the problem, I invite you to read Section 6.A now. More germane to the notetaking phase of research is my discussion of illegitimate paraphrasing, which I explain and illustrate in Section 6.B.3. Such illegitimate paraphrasing comes, essentially, from passively giving yourself over to the specific line of thinking of the author. The author's language—the words he uses, the sentences and paragraphs he writes, and the order in which he has written them—together embody the meaning he has constructed of the subject. The closer you stay to his language, the more you are pulled into thinking as he does. Your objective is to construct the meaning *you've made* of what the author is doing and saying, so it makes sense to use your own language to do so. A couple of these exercises in relying on your memory should satisfactorily give you a sense of the difference between the author's actual construction of meaning and the construction you make of his meaning; when you turn back to the text, you should be able to discriminate between your own language and that of the author. All of these activities should be sufficient to keep illegitimate paraphrases out of the summaries you write for your record of the evidence. And I'll remind you of these points when we come to recording specific pieces of information regarding the author's views (see subsection H.2).

- Finally, now's the time to grapple with texts or parts of texts that still confuse you or that you feel you still don't understand. It is especially important for you to do this intellectual grappling with those sources that you know will play an important part in your final paper. For these exercises you will want to have the text in front of you, but, again, carry out the process of making sense of this material by talking to yourself in your own language.

EXAMPLE

Latour's ideas on power are really hard to understand. I've got to see if I really am grasping what he's talking about. It sounds like he's arguing that if you have power you really don't HAVE power. You have power when other people do what you want them to do. Let's see . . . if my boss tells me to move these crates over to the loading dock, he has power because *I* moved the crates. *I* could refuse to move the crates, or I could ignore what he tells me to do—then we could say he has no power. That I can see. But I still think of somebody like my boss as HAVING power. Let's go back to what "power" means. Latour is saying that power = exertion, something/someone DOING something. Me, moving or not moving the crates. So Latour is saying that if the whole crew moves crates like the boss wants, the power = the crates being moved. The boss doesn't have power because he didn't move one crate himself, although he was the source of the crates being moved. OK. Let's say that is what Latour means. So what? Why is Latour defining power this way?

4. Critiquing your sources

By reading actively you are also reading critically because you are developing an understanding of what the author is saying to you. Another part of critical reading involves doing an assessment of the author's ideas and approach to the subject. There are two ways you could go about doing these critiques (which should also be written out in the Reading Log section of your Researcher's Notebook). One would be to ask the following questions:

- Did you find the author's argument, procedure convincing? Why? Why not?

- Did the author's final conclusion follow logically from his/her main points? If you see a problem here, what is it?

- Consider points/generalizations within the argument. Does the evidence or facts warrant such generalizations? If not, what's the problem?

- Did you accept the author's main premises and assumptions? If not, which are unacceptable to you? How does your rejection of one or more premises affect your response to what the author has done and said?

- Are you aware of anything (facts, procedures, theories) that the author failed to take into account?

Doing such evaluations can be difficult if you are still educating yourself about the subject. As I suggested in the opening pages of this section, you might find such critiques easier to do by writing about the dialogues the experts are having about a subject. After you've read several sources, write to yourself about points on which they agree or disagree, or about the different approaches they are taking to the same subject. In writing out these dialogues, use the names of the authors to remind yourself, once again, that this printed material is a record of a conversation that is going on among human beings.

EXAMPLE

I'm discovering that the issue preoccupying experts investigating violence on TV isn't so much the effects of violent programs on kids. I've looked at only a few of these studies (Clark &Clark, Valdez & Johnson, Martinelli), but all of these experts agree that a steady diet of violence encourages kids to be physically aggressive and to become callous about the harm violent acts do to people. In their review of such studies carried out in the last 10–15 years, Yamada & O'Neal report that this is basically the conclusion reached by most researchers investigating this matter.

What I'm finding is that researchers are turning their attention now to the violence on "reality" programs like "Cops" and on news programs because the amount of violence shown on these types of programs is increasing (evidence in that article which reported on a study by some media watchdog group—which? Check Notes!). What accounts for this increase? Bernstein & Larson answer: "crime sells." Interviews with news directors at local network stations in New York, LA, Chicago. Bernstein & Larson point out that these TV people assume that "news" means homicides, nasty car accidents, & other such stories in which people are threatened or hurt or killed. B & L conclude that the viewing public are passive victims of this journalistic philosophy. But I think Rodgers would take issue with B & L's conclusion that we are victims. Her study indicates that we ask for such violence. After showing her subjects 2 versions of a nightly newscast, one that featured stories with lots of gore & violent crimes or criminals, and one that didn't, a large majority of her subjects rated the "violent" newscast more "interesting" and "informative." Rodgers concludes that we WANT violence, we ENJOY it. I don't know if it's appropriate to bring Murray into this conversation—he's writing about evening "entertainment" programming, not news—but his argument is that there is lots of violence on these programs because Americans want action in the TV they view for "entertainment" and the easiest way to provide such action is to have bad guys threaten and chase and hurt good guys and vice versa.

My evidence says there is still a lot of violence on TV. But how should we interpret this fact? We could accept Rodgers' and Murray's conclusions that Americans enjoy violence, that we ask for it, but even if this is true, why do we enjoy it? Might not B & L answer that we want it because that's what the TV industry (and movies) have given us?

Those interviews with the news directors clearly indicate that decisions about what appears on TV are driven by ratings, yet ratings would seem to reflect what we want to see since they simply record the number of people watching. Would experts who've studied kids' viewing habits say that TV forms our "taste," so if we see a lot of violence on TV when we are young, that's what we LEARN to want and expect? Hmm. I should look again at the assumptions and conclusions of those authors who studied the effects of TV violence on kids—and also read Murray again.

D. Keeping Track of the Evidence: An Overview

Up to this point I have dissuaded you from taking notes on your sources, mainly to help you avoid the trap of simply transcribing huge chunks of these sources. On the other hand, you are gathering and reading these sources in order to find evidence, so let's now turn our attention to this matter. Evidence, I'll remind you, falls into two main categories:

- summaries of the sources you read; that is, the gists of the contents.

- notes on specific information, which breaks down into two more categories:

  - "building-block" evidence, facts or data such as dates, names and identities of people, definitions of terms, pieces of generally-accepted knowledge, and so on.

  - specifics related to the point of view of the author of a source (the specific hypothesis tested, his/her precise conclusions, comments on particular matters, and the like).

I'll go into more detail about each of these points in subsections G and H, but, first, gathering evidence raises the issue of what to do with it, which forces you to confront, once again, the need to be organized. Creating a Researcher's Notebook is one major step you've taken. Now you need another organizing system to handle the evidence you are now starting to accumulate. To illustrate the problems you want to avoid, let's consider the following scenarios. Perhaps one or two may seem familiar.

- As you are composing your paper, you recall a piece of evidence that would wonderfully illustrate a point you want to make. You spend twenty minutes digging through the piles of paper on your desk (bookcase, floor) looking for the article that contains this evidence. You manage to find it, but you realize that you failed to write down the line of thinking that this piece of evidence would illustrate, so, evidence now in hand, you cannot remember the point you wanted to make with it.

- Because you have recorded your evidence as notes on pages in a spiral-bound notebook, you must read over *all* your notes each time you need a particular type of evidence, or you are searching for a quotation you remember recording.

- You have a quotation that would perfectly illustrate and support a point you are making in your draft, but you can't use it because you failed to write down the source where you found it.

Anyone who has written a research paper has had these, and similar, experiences. They may not be unusual, but they are highly frustrating, and they can waste hours of precious time. More importantly, though, spending time searching for evidence distracts us from the central business at hand, which is putting the evidence together—in our minds, and then in a draft—to form a meaningful picture of the puzzle.

The scenarios I just gave alert us to the needs we researchers have:

- to record specific evidence we take from our sources in such a manner that (a) we can quickly and easily find a fact or quotation when we need it, (b) we can trust that what we have recorded is accurate, and (c) we know the source of each of these pieces of evidence;

- to be able to sort (and re-sort) our evidence into various different categories as one means of making sense of the intellectual puzzle;

- once we have a solid outline of the draft of our paper, to gather relevant evidence together so that it is quickly and easily plugged into appropriate places in the paper;

- to be assured that we have complete bibliographic information about every source we have looked at so that, if we choose to use it in the paper, we can appropriately document any and all evidence we want to take from it.

If you think about it, these needs are very similar to those of libraries and companies that create indexes and databases: to create systems for storing information in such a way that you can quickly and easily access it when you need it. And some of the suggestions that I have for you are going to resemble systems that I discussed in Section 3.

I am going to urge you, right now, before those piles of paper start to accumulate, to develop an organizing system for handling the evidence. My experience—both with my own research, and in working with student researchers—is that this system requires four interrelated parts:

1. The creation of a filing system (paper, electronic, or both) for all the copies of sources you have in your possession (e.g., photocopies of parts of books, photocopies of articles from periodicals, digital material you have downloaded from a database, digital material you have downloaded from a Web site).

2. A system of recording specific items of evidence (from now on we'll call these notes) so that the individual notes are easy to manipulate, allowing you to look at your subject from multiple perspectives by sorting items of evidence according to various criteria, and, later in the process, allowing you to sort items of evidence according to points on your outline.

3. A centralized record of complete bibliographic information on each source you have looked at.

4. A foolproof system in which the first three parts of the system are coordinated with each other.

Perhaps the most problematic requirement here is the second. One reason that note cards were so popular in the old days is that they perfectly fit the criteria of our second requirement. The cards (still available on the market) are sturdy pieces of paper of uniform size that fit easily in the hand—just like playing cards. On the other hand, doing notes on paper cards requires a lot copying by hand—from source to note, from note to draft.

There are citation management software or bibliographic software programs on the market that could fill at least some of the needs I have listed here. A database software program might also work. Or you might be able to meet requirement 2 with your word-processing program if your computer's operating system allows you to save files in folders, and if the Save feature of the program allows you to enter keywords and/or subjects for the file. If you have these capabilities, you could create files that would be the equivalent of note cards because you could shuffle them from folder to folder just the way you would create different piles with paper notes, and you could do searches with keywords or subjects to find files/notes on a given topic. Finally, of course, there is always the option of paper cards.

No matter what system you choose for keeping a record of the evidence, design it

- so that you can readily sort and review items of evidence using a variety of categories;

- so that you can readily access specific items of evidence when you need them;

- so that you are assured you have all the necessary bibliographic information you need about the source of each item of evidence in your collection.

Whatever system of record-keeping you decide on, *now* is the time to develop it.

E. Creating Files and a Cataloging System

Here I want to say more about the first requirement in this organizing system, the creation of a filing system (paper, electronic, or both) for copies of sources. This system is for photocopies you have made of parts of books, anything you have downloaded from the computer (either onto paper or onto your hard drive), articles you have gotten through interlibrary loan or that you photocopied yourself, material given to you by an agency or a company—in short, any material that you physically collect in this research process.

The objective here, to put it negatively, is to protect yourself from being overwhelmed by piles of "stuff," whether paper or electronic, and thus to minimize the amount of time you spend trying to find something in these piles. To put it positively, the objective is to create a system that will enable you to put your hands on something, whether a piece of evidence or a source in your possession, quickly and easily.

Let's start with paper.

If you do not own a filing cabinet already, consider purchasing one. If you are not ready for the real thing, at the very least invest in one or more of those cardboard boxes that accommodate hanging file folders. Invest also in some hanging files, some file folders, and labels for those folders.

As paper comes into your hands (you photocopy something, or print something from the computer) you are going to be in the habit of following these steps:

- Staple sets of pages together (in the right order, of course).

- Make sure that *complete* bibliographic information about the source is recorded on the front sheet of the set of pages.

- Make sure this source is recorded in your working bibliography (see subsection F). The information you record in the working bibliography and on the pages themselves will be the same. In both cases, take down as much information as possible. Too much is always better than too little.

- Place these sheets of paper in a manila file folder with an appropriate label, and immediately put it in its proper place in your filing cabinet/box.

What you write on the labels you attach to file folders and where you place these folders in your filing cabinet depend on the cataloging system you develop. And this cataloging system would be one that you could (and probably should) use for storing your notes as well as storing these copies of sources. My years of collecting copies of sources tell me that the most useful system for creating individual files is to use the last name of the author of the source, and a shortened version of the title. You would then file this folder alphabetically according to the author's last name. In this system your individual files directly correspond to entries on your working bibliography (subsection F) and summaries of your sources (subsection G), thus coordinating them.

But you will probably want to organize these individual files—just as you will want to organize your specific notes—into categories of some sort. The specific categories you choose should be suggested by your subject matter, your approach to your material, your research questions. Moreover, you can modify your cataloging system as your research progresses. After all, it is easy enough to create new labels for hanging files and easy enough to move file folders from one hanging file to another! And, believe it or not, such re-cataloging is really part of the intellectual part of the process, a kinetic means of making sense of what you are finding!

For material you accumulate and store electronically (e-mails sent to you, material from a Web site, or articles you download from a database), follow this same procedure by creating appropriate folders and naming files according to your system. But there is a task you'll have to add for sources you keep in digital form. In Section 3.E., I outline information you will need to record about these sources *when* you download them. Since you can't "write" on these copies, you will probably have to create a companion word-processing file for each in which you will record the necessary bibliographic information. Whatever expedient you hit upon, just be sure you are very aware of the information you are going to have to have if you expect to use such a source in your final paper.

As far as taking notes is concerned, it seems a waste of time and energy to make separate notes on material that you have in your possession. If you have a paper copy, it is easier to highlight relevant passages or otherwise mark up the document the way you normally take notes in your textbooks. My solution is to make separate notes in which I remind myself about what I have in my files, and to store these reference notes with my notes from other sources (subsection H).

> For Allen Jones's view of the causes of racism, see my copy of *The Plague of Racism*, p. 42.

> I have complete statistics on mortgage rates for the past 15 years. See my file from *Business Statistics*.

> Great quote illustrating the way that fans of *Matrix* see deep meanings in it. In computer folder for fans, file name Alex.

Some further advice:

- Please, please, please do not write in library books or other print material that does not belong to you! It is easy enough to mark relevant passages with removable adhesive notes, and you can write any comments you might have on them. If you find that you really *have to* scribble on certain pages, make a photocopy and do your scribbling there.

- Don't carry this research project around on your back. It is not good for your spine, and you don't want to hear my stories about the senior theses that have been lost when the backpack was misplaced, when the car was broken into, or the laptop was dropped by airport security. Plan to keep the bulk of "material manifestations" of this project safely in your room or your study. For transporting materials to your room, invest in a plastic portfolio or any comparable conveyance that keeps paper organized and unrumpled. And get into the habit of filing this material right away when you get home.

- The same advice goes for electronic files. Be sure you have multiple copies in various places (on your hard drive, on a couple of disks, on a server if you have space on one, in an e-mail attachment you send to yourself). And don't forget to update your back-ups whenever you work on files.

F. Creating a Working Bibliography

When I am engaged in research, the first thing I do when I pick up a source—a book, an article, an essay in a collection—is to make a complete record of the bibliographic information about that source. I urge you to follow my example. If you are not using a bibliographic software program, now, before you turn your attention to the content of your sources, create a working bibliography in which you will make a record of each of the sources you consult as you consult it. The most efficient bibliography would be one in a computer file, but if you prefer to work with pen and paper, add a Working Bibliography section to your Researcher's Notebook, write on one side of the page only, and follow the advice I provide here.

I trained myself to record this information before I even looked at the content of the source because I wanted the reassurance that, if and when I made use of any material from this source in a paper I was writing, I would have the information I needed to cite it. There are several other excellent reasons for keeping an ongoing list of sources as you pick them up. One is that, when you take notes, you won't have to write out complete bibliographic information about the source in each note you take. Another is that a working bibliography makes it easy for you to locate sources again if and when you decide you want to study them further, or need more information from them. And, last but certainly not least, a working bibliography can save you time and effort when the deadline for the paper looms. Your working bibliography can quickly be transformed into the list of sources at the end of your polished paper.

The amount of time such transformation takes will depend, in large part, upon the specific form in which you record information about your sources. The time this transformation takes will be much shorter if you record this information in the documentation style you'll be using in the final draft of your paper. Very simply, a **documentation style** is a formal and standardized method a writer uses to give complete information about the sources he or she used in a paper. In this book I cover this issue of documentation at two levels:

- In Section 8, as its title clearly indicates, I introduce you to fundamentals of documentation, both by giving you basic information about document systems and styles and the way they work, and by giving you advice and strategies for documenting your own paper.

- In Appendixes A through D, I provide detailed information about six document styles commonly used in academia.

If you agree that it makes sense to record information about your sources in the style you will be using in the final draft of your paper, here are the steps I suggest you take.

Right now, follow these steps to determine the style you'll be using and to get a feel for it.

- Read Section 8.A, "Choosing a Documentation Style."

- Confirm with your instructor the style you will use in your final draft.

- Locate a manual or guide that contains particulars about this style. If I cover the style in one of the appendixes, the appendix will work nicely as an introductory guide; at the end of the appendix I have a sample of the final list, so you can see, generally, what your final list will look like.

- Read Sections 8.B. and 8.C.

During the upcoming weeks, these are the steps you'll take as you find various sources (and in your working bibliography you need to include any and all sources you consulted to educate yourself generally about your subject or topic).

- When you pick up a source, use Section 8 and/or the style manual to determine the category (or type) into which the source falls.

- Locate the proper form for this type of source in the manual.

- Following the form, record the bibliographic information about your source in your working bibliography.

- Format entries as hanging indents; see Section 8.E.2.

Here's some more information and advice:

- In those cases when you aren't sure about the proper form for a particular source, create an entry using these two principles:

  - Call upon your understanding of the premises of all documentation systems and the basic way your documentation style works; see Section 8.B.2.

  - Take down as much bibliographic information as possible about the source; too much is always better than too little.

- When you enter information about a source into your working bibliography, be *very, very* careful about recording the **bibliographic information correctly.** That is, be sure you spell the author's name correctly, be sure you copy down the names of multiple authors in the order in which they appear on the title page, be sure to take down the title exactly as it appears in the original, and so forth. From now on out, you will be assuming that the information you record in this bibliography is correct, so you need to be sure it *is* correct.

- Be *very* careful to record *all* necessary information about material you download from a computer; see Section 3.E.

- At the end of the entry, write yourself a note about the location of this source. If you have a copy, write "In my files under XXXX." If it has a call number (a book from the library or a print reference work), enter the call number. If you found this book at a library other than your school library, add the name of the library. If you need to take a look at the source again, this information will make it easy to put your hands on it.

- In some documentation styles the final list of sources at the end of the paper includes only the works that the author actually cites in the body of the paper (called reference lists, or lists of works cited). However, enter **all** the sources you look at in this working bibliography. Until your paper is finished, you aren't going to know which sources you will use. Besides, it will be easy enough to delete any entries you need to when you are putting together your final list.

G. Writing Summaries (with a Few Words about Annotated Bibliographies)

As indicated in subsection D, you should plan to write summaries of each of your sources to include in your record of evidence. In addition to doing summaries of the books and articles you are reading, it would be wise also to write such summaries of nonprint sources; following the suggestions I give here, you can capture the gist of an interview, a film you've seen, ads you've analyzed.

These summaries are really the most important notes you can make. They will help you in several ways:

- They are some of your most valuable evidence. They pull together the general conclusions and approaches of experts who have done research on your subject. In most cases in your final paper you will be referring only to this summary information.

- As your research progresses and the direction of your search becomes more focused, you will realize that certain works are more important to you than others. Your summaries will tell you which works you should go back to and study more carefully.

- If, as your research progresses, you find that you need more specific information about a particular topic, your summaries will tell you where you can find this specific information.

- Writing these summaries will prevent you from wasting your time recopying massive amounts of a book or an article into notes. They will keep you from becoming a passive sponge. The act of writing these summaries is an act of digesting your reading, of pulling out the most important parts of the work and getting them into your head, which is where the information needs to be if you are going to think about it.

If you've used the active reading strategies outlined in subsection C, you have already done most of the difficult intellectual work that writing summaries requires. Your next task is to capture the meaning you've made of each of these sources in a tight paragraph. This is a final distillation or abstract of the work as a whole, a statement that reflects the core of what the author has done and the main conclusions he or she has reached, and for this reason you will probably want to integrate the major point the author has made within the context of what he or she was doing. In writing this final version of your summary, you could use a technique Linda Flower calls "nutshell and teach."[2] Pretend that you are on a television show. The moderator turns to you and says, "We're running out of time. In a minute or two could you give us the essence of this author's work?" In addition to boiling down the work to its core, you will probably want to make a note of any particular aspects of the source that could be helpful to you later in your research. For example, if the author gives extensive statistics that you know you'll want to make use of, jot down this information, or make a note of the way you might use this source in putting together your puzzle. I've included some samples of summaries at the end of this subsection to give you a clearer picture of what you are trying to accomplish.

Here are a few more issues to consider as you write. As the exercises on active reading have emphasized, summaries should be in your own words. After you have a draft, double-check it against the source to be sure particulars are correct (the number of subjects in a study, dates, technical terminology, and the like). If you find yourself using language that is close to the language of the author, quote the author directly, enclosing his or her words in quotation marks. Let me point out, though, that such quotations should be restricted to basic terminology the author uses throughout the work. Otherwise, you are getting into specific pieces of information, which should be recorded separately. Guidelines are given in subsection H.2.

Last, but certainly not least, these summaries must include sufficient information about the source itself so you know to which work this summary belongs. If you are keeping a working bibliography, the names of the author(s) and a short title of the work on the summary should be sufficient to take you to the correct entry on the bibliography. If you aren't keeping such a bibliography, you will have to include full bibliographic information about the source with the summary.

Normally your summaries will be written in an informal style since you are writing notes for yourself to jog your memory. However, sometimes instructors ask students to submit an annotated bibliography. An annotated bibliography is nothing more than a bibliography or reference list that includes summaries of each of the works on the list. If you are preparing an annotated bibliography, give the full citation of each source in the documentation style you will be using in your final paper. Following the citation will be your summary of that source, written in a more formal style since you are now writing for an audience. Here are samples of informal summaries and entries in an annotated bibliography.

---

[2]*Problem-Solving Strategies for Writing,* 3rd ed. (San Diego: Harcourt Brace Jovanovich, 1989), 116–17.

SAMPLE INFORMAL SUMMARIES

To Smith, the major conflict between the North and the South was the very different perceptions of slavery each region had, and these different perceptions, in his view, made war inevitable. To the North, a moral issue; to the South, an economic necessity. Bulk of the book devoted to supporting these contentions with documents from the 1850s—newspapers, tracts, etc. Discussion of the South includes lots of details of the kind of work slaves performed. Good statistics on number of slaves in each Southern state, 1850–1860 (pp. 250–75).

Schmidt and Hashimoto were testing the general hypothesis that results of polls on social/political issues shape public opinion on those issues (if I learn from a poll that 75% of Americans favor capital punishment, I'll decide that capital punishment is a good thing). 100 subjects—college students—half male, half female. Asked views on 3 issues before and after showing them results of polls. Then did follow-up interviews on half the subjects. Results: The only statistically significant finding was that subjects were more likely to change their views when a large majority (80% +) of poll respondents took a particular position. Interviews indicate that polls most likely to change people's minds if (1) person didn't know much about the issue, (2) person has no strong personal views on the issue. My questions: Are college students appropriate subjects for this study? How representative are they of the "American public"? How much does an individual's level of education affect the behavior being studied here?

Review of 1st exhibit of impressionists by French critic, published in Paris newspaper in 1874. Written as a little story in which reviewer and an Academy painter comment on paintings as they walk around the exhibit. Most comments VERY sarcastic. Message = these paintings are worthless. Could use to illustrate how "avant-garde" impressionism was—and differences in Academy, impressionist "standards."

Edwards' biography of Waller includes in-depth analyses of each of her novels, tying each novel to events in her life (actual people, places & her psychological state of mind). Basically psychoanalytic approach. Can use for biographical information and his interpretation of *The Harvest*. To him, it reflects her joy in fulfilling her "nurturing instincts" (rearing her young children, farming). Compare with feminist readings of these novels?

Murphy & Nolan studied the effects of temperature on the germination of sugar pine seeds. Looked at oxygen uptake, ATP levels, moisture content of seeds imbibed at 5°C and 25°C. Results: seeds wouldn't germinate at temperatures above 17°C. Murphy & Nolan suggest reason is the effects of high temperatures on membrane properties.

SAMPLE ENTRIES FROM A FORMAL ANNOTATED BIBLIOGRAPHY

Kessler, Lauren. *Stubborn Twig: Three Generations in the Life of a Japanese American Family.* New York: Random House, 1993.

Based on extensive interviews with certain family members and primary materials they provided her, Lauren Kessler paints a vivid and moving chronicle of the Yasui family that begins when Masuo Yasui, a recent immigrant from Japan, steps off the train in Hood River, Oregon, in 1908. Although the book is divided into three major sections, one for each of the three generations, the major portion of the narrative is devoted to the experiences of Masuo and his eight children. The story line resembles that of a classic Greek

tragedy as we watch Masuo's rise as a prosperous, respected businessman and community leader, and the major reversals in the family's fortunes brought about by Executive
Order 9066 (1942). By giving us everyday details of Masuo's four-year detention as a
suspected spy for the Japanese government, the experiences of his wife and younger children in internment camps in California, and the fleeing of his older children to cities
outside the West Coast "military zone," Kessler makes very real for us the financial losses
and personal degradations this action by the U.S. government forced on citizens whose
only crime was their ethnic heritage. In following the histories of two of Masuo's sons—
Min, a lawyer, who fights for legal redress, and Chop, the only member of the family to
return to Hood River, who attempts to put this episode of his life behind him—Kessler
gives us insights into the way Japanese Americans have dealt with this major trauma.

Collins, J. Fuji. "Biracial Japanese American Identity: An Evolving Process." *Cultural
    Diversity and Ethnic Minority Psychology* 6 (2000): 115–133.

In this article Collins describes a study he did to learn more about how biracial individuals develop a sense of ethnic identity. He interviewed 15 adults (ages 20-40) with one
parent who is Japanese and the other non-Asian. In the results/discussion section,
Collins lays out patterns he found in psychological stages these subjects went through,
and he also discusses factors that he thinks affected the experiences of these subjects.
Specifically, he talks about the environments they grew up in, and, then, when they were
older, the environment they sought for themselves—either by literally moving somewhere else, or perceiving the "old" environment differently. Collins ends this article by
talking about "clinical implications" of his study, which leads me to think that his primary
concern is with the mental health of biracial people, and that his research is intended to
help counselors understand what biracial people (students?) are going through.

　　In looking into the experiences/identity issues of Japanese Americans, I have been
defining Japanese Americans as people whose racial/ethnic heritage is Japanese, and
how these people have coped, as an ethnic group, in predominantly Anglo-European
communities. I was going to say that I'm not studying biracial individuals, but it occurs
to me that third-generation Japanese Americans such as Noda could easily have a non-
Asian parent. So this study could be very helpful to me not only in considering the issue
of identity in a psychological way, but also in the specific light it throws on the ways two
cultures conflict internally.

Noda, Kesaya E. "Growing Up Asian in America." *Making Waves: An Anthology of Writing
    by and about Asian American Women.* Ed. Asian Women United of California.
    Boston: Beacon Press, 1989. 243–51.

Noda's short piece is one of fifty-one in which women from a broad spectrum of Asian
countries and backgrounds write about their experiences in the United States in the
1970s and 1980s. The editors have divided these firsthand accounts by topics, Noda's
appearing in the section on identity. Talking to us through details from her life, Noda, a
third-generation Japanese American, reflects on her attempts to reconcile those parts of
her heritage that connect her to Japan and mark her as Other with those experiences and
attitudes that make her family American. Most difficult, she tells us, has been making
connections with her mother, who seemed to be the antithesis of the "model of
strength" (248) Noda was looking for as she came of age in an America permeated by
feminism. Noda speaks explicitly of the struggles I feel in Nakanishi's article, and
complements Kessler's chronicle by giving us the perceptions of both third-generation
Japanese Americans and the women in this community.

H. Recording Specific Pieces of Information

Before I go into detail about this form of notetaking, let me offer some cautions:

- You should take notes on specific parts of a source only after you've read the source actively and critically and written a summary of it.

- While you are in the process of educating yourself generally about your subject, you should probably keep these types of notes to a minimum. As you develop a clearer sense of the dialogue that is going on among the experts, and your inquiry becomes more focused, you'll find yourself taking more of these notes because you'll have a clearer sense of the sources you deem important and because you'll have a clearer sense of the specific evidence you need.

- Experienced researchers know that they will be returning to certain sources more than once as the research process goes on; thus you shouldn't feel as if you need to "get it all" the first time you work with a source. On the other hand, library books often need to be returned before you have a chance to study them further; if you foresee problems in putting your hands on an item after you've returned it to the library, consider photocopying those parts you know you'll want to have available.

The types of notes I'll be discussing here fall into two categories:

- "building block" evidence, facts or data such as dates, names and identities of people, definitions of terms, pieces of common knowledge, and so on;

- specifics related to the points of view of the author of a source (the specific hypothesis tested, his/her precise conclusions, comments on particular matters, and the like).

1. Facts or data

When you are recording basic facts and figures, you can usually just abstract the pertinent facts you want and jot them down for yourself in shorthand fashion (see Notes 1 and 2). But you should make a couple of distinctions here. The first

NOTE 1

Subjects of study = 75 high school students

1/2 = SAT verbal scores over 600

1/2 =   "   "   "   under 400

Instrument used = Howard Smith Reading Comprehension Test

                      Sorensen
                      "Comprehension & Thinking"
                      pp. 40–41

NOTE 2

Some stats on unemployment rates—U.S.

	All civilian workers	Men over 20	Women over 20	Whites	Blacks	Persons of Hispanic origins
1973	4.9	3.3	4.9	4.3	9.4	7.5
1992	7.5	7.1	6.3	6.6	14.2	11.6
Dec. 2001	5.8	5.2	5.2	5.1	10.2	7.9

Business Statistics
Strawer, ed.
p. 130, Table 8.3

is between facts and figures that come directly from the work the author has done and facts and figures he or she has taken from somewhere else. Your reading of the text—the context of the fact—will normally tell you which is which. Obviously numbers given in the methods section of a study or experiment, for example, or the numbers in the results section of such a work, are the author's own. When I talk about facts and figures that the author has taken from somewhere else, I mean facts and figures like those italicized in the statements below:

When the battle of Sanchez was over, *1,500 men lay dead* on the field.

Because *anything above 5 parts xenocane per million will kill plant and animal life,* xenocane should not be dumped in landfills; it can too easily seep into water sources.

Here you want to pay close attention to context. If the author you are reading gives no source for this fact, *and* if it is clear that this is not the author's own "fact," then you can consider this information a commonly accepted fact in the field and make a note like Notes 3 and 4. But if the author gives a source for this information (in a note or citation), you should deal with it the same way you deal with material the author has taken from other sources (see subsection H.3).

NOTE 3

1500 died in the Battle of Sanchez

Vandervoort
Glorious Victory
p. 176

NOTE 4

Xenocane--lethal above 5 parts per million

Samuelson
"Xenocane"
in Greene & Walters
Protecting Our Water
p. 87

NOTE 5

Samuelson considers anything above 5 parts per million
of xenocane lethal

> Samuelson
> "Xenocane" in
> Greene & Walters
> Protecting Our Water
> p. 87

In some cases, what looks like a simple fact is really the author's interpretation of data. Let us say, for example, that the context makes clear that when the author says that anything above 5 parts xenocane per million can kill plants and animals, this figure is the *author's* estimate of the danger level of this chemical; in such cases, your note should read accordingly (see Note 5).

2. Specifics about the author's views

Taking notes on an author's general interpretation of factual material and those parts of texts in which an author is clearly stating his or her general views on a topic can present us with a real challenge. Students often try to paraphrase such passages, but it is difficult to do legitimate paraphrases of two or three concurrent sentences. What too often occurs is that the notetaker changes a word here, a phrase there. Since, however, the note still essentially follows the author's thought pattern, the note is an *illegitimate paraphrase*. To avoid any possibility of having such illegitimate paraphrases in your notes, you are going to have to do *legitimate paraphrases,* or quote directly the author's words.

Legitimately paraphrasing an author's point of view requires the same techniques you used in reading actively and writing your summaries; and it works best for extended parts of texts (those covering several pages). Read, for comprehension, the segment you want to paraphrase; **put the original aside;** think about what the author is doing and saying here; write a gist of this in your own words; reread the original and compare it with what you've written, making any changes necessary to assure yourself that your note correctly reflects the author's meaning. Such notes (see Note 6 for an example) will resemble the summaries you've written except that they will be more focused and the information in them more concrete and specific.

NOTE 6

DiMarco shows how traditional readings of Williams' poem "Victory" are
generally religious interpretations and emphasize the Christian symbolism.

> DiMarco
> "Poetry of Williams"
> pp. 776–82

Otherwise, you will want to quote the author directly. Taking down critical ideas in the author's own words has several advantages. Not only do you not have to worry about illegitimate paraphrases, but when you read over your notes later, you know precisely what the author said. As you are writing your paper, you have the choice of using the full quotation, part of it, or simply alluding to this idea, depending on how this information fits into the argument you are making.

While quoting the author directly has its advantages, you don't want to turn into a passive sponge, copying out sentence after sentence of the text. What I do is to ask myself which of the author's words I consider to be important enough to quote and *why* I think I should record these exact words in my notes. Sometimes I will take down a full sentence because it captures, in a nutshell, an author's views; if the purpose and the importance of this sentence is self-evident, that's all I'll have in this note. Usually, however, I find myself isolating key words or parts of sentences that nutshell the author's views; I will quote these directly, putting them in context by explaining to myself, in my words, how this quoted material fits into the author's general argument. Notes 7, 8, and 9 give you some concrete examples of notes that result from using this technique. Before you look at them, though, let me caution you that you must be very careful whenever you copy the words of authors in your notes. In the general advice I offer for taking notes, I give you more details for certain "rules" you must follow for quoting others.

NOTE 7

> As Jamison sees it, there are two main schools of historians: The " 'I was there' school," with the historian attempting to "record a past event as if the historian were an eye witness" (p. 240) and the "analytical school," where "all historical data become grist for the statistician's mill" (p. 241).
>
> Jamison
"History Today"

NOTE 8

> Valdez sees the anthropologist as "walking the fine line between objectivism and subjectivism" (p. 876). Her solution: "observational subjectivism . . . the ability to watch both what is happening outside oneself and to observe one's own reaction at the same time" (p. 890).
>
> Valdez
"Dilemma"
in White and Campbell
Anthro. Today

Some General Advice about Taking Notes

- To give yourself maximum flexibility in reviewing and sorting your evidence, each note you record should be a discrete, self-contained whole.

This means that each note should contain only one piece of information and that it has sufficient bibliographic information about the source so that, if you choose to use this item of evidence in your final paper, you will be able to document it. If you are not keeping a working bibliography, you will be forced to record *all* bibliographic information about the source with *each* note. If you are keeping a separate record of your sources, it is usually sufficient to include the following information with each note:

- the last name of the author(s);

- a short title of the work;

- the page number(s) from which this evidence is taken.

I have developed the habit of putting this bibliographic information in the same format and in the same place on each note so that I am less likely to forget to jot down any of this vital information.

- In Notes 4, 5, and 8 I give an author and a title and then, after "in," another set of authors and a title. These are references to collections of articles. Valdez's article, with the shortened title of "Dilemma," was published in a book edited by White and Campbell titled *Anthropology Today*. Whenever you are taking notes from a part of a book, you must be very careful that you take down all the bibliographic information you will have to have in order to document this source in your final paper. I talk in more detail about this matter in Section 8.D.3. If you are using one of the documentation styles I cover in the appendixes, look for the subsection "Part of a Book" in the "Forms for Sources" section. Generally speaking, you will need the following information:

  - complete name(s) of the author(s) of the part;

  - complete title of the part;

  - pages on which this part is printed;

  - complete bibliographic information about the book, including author or editor(s).

- If you are quoting the author's words, be very careful that you quote accurately and completely.

  - Be sure to put the quoted material in quotation marks (if you don't, you won't know that these words are quoted).

  - Copy the phrase, sentence, or sentences *exactly* as they are in the text— capital letters, punctuation, spelling, and all.

  - If you want to leave out a word or words, indicate their omission with ellipsis points (. . .). Be sure that the material you omit does not leave a statement that misrepresents the author's message.

  - If you need to add any information or words, put this added material in brackets [ ]. Note that brackets have square corners. They are not parentheses ( ). The author whose work you are reading may have used parentheses. Thus, if you put your own words in brackets, you always know they are your words, not those of the author. (See Section 6.B.4 for a more detailed discussion of conventions for omitting and adding words in quotations).

Check Notes 9, 10, and 11 and compare the quoted material in the note with the original passage to see how these guidelines work in practice.

NOTE 9

After summarizing the controversy over the glass pyramid I. M. Pei designed for the new entrance to the Louvre (pp. 193–94).
Sutcliffe concludes that "[t]he core opposition to Pei and his works . . . came mainly for artistic conservatives. . . . [who] were poor judges of modern architecture."

Sutcliffe
Paris
p. 194

THE ORIGINAL PASSAGE

The core opposition to Pei and his works therefore came mainly from artistic conservatives such as the senior preservationist author, Yvan Christ. These people were poor judges of modern architecture.

Anthony Sutcliffe, *Paris: An Architectural History* (New Haven: Yale University Press, 1993), 194.

NOTE 10

"A military scholar who had written and translated several works on strategy . . . , [General Henry W.] Halleck was a cautious general who waged war by the book."

James McPherson
Ordeal by Fire
p. 158

THE ORIGINAL PASSAGE

A military scholar who had written and translated several works on strategy (which earned him the sobriquet "Old Brains"), Halleck was a cautious general who waged war by the book.

James M. McPherson, *Ordeal by Fire: The Civil War and Reconstruction* (New York: Alfred A. Knopf, 1982), 158.

NOTE 11

Commenting on the traditional drug treatment of depression, Leavitt writes: "For the approximately 30% of depressed patients refractory to TCAs [tricyclic antidepressants], MAOIs [monoamine oxidase inhibitors] provide a useful alternative. The MAOIs irreversibly inactivate MAO, an enzyme of major importance in the metabolism of epinephrine, norepinephrine, dopamine, and 5-HT [serotonin]."

> Fred Leavitt
> Drugs and Behavior
> p. 248

THE ORIGINAL PASSAGE

For the approximately 30% of depressed patients refractory to TCAs, MAOIs provide a useful alternative. The MAOIs irreversibly inactivate MAO, an enzyme of major importance in the metabolism of epinephrine, norepinephrine, dopamine, and 5-HT.

> Fred Leavitt, *Drugs and Behavior*, 2nd ed. (New York: John Wiley and Sons, 1982), 248.

3. Dealing with material an author has taken from other sources

When I discussed, in Section 1, what research is about, I said that researchers build on the work of others. So in the reading that you do, you will find that the authors of your sources are themselves referring to the work of others. These references may be summaries, or they may be direct quotations.

EXAMPLE 1

More recently, a series of longitudinal studies (Fergusson & Horwood, 1995; Fergusson, Horwood, & Lynskey, 1993; Fergusson, Lynwood, & Horwood, 1997) conducted with a sample of over 700 children in New Zealand has demonstrated clear linkages between ADHD behaviors in elementary and middle school (based on maternal and teacher ratings) and later levels of academic achievement (middle school through age 18).

> George J. DuPaul and Gary Stoner, *ADHA in the Schools: Assessment and Intervention Strategies*, 2nd ed. (New York: The Guilford Press, 2003), 86.

EXAMPLE 2

Habitat choice has been demonstrated in many insects, lizards, rodents, and birds (Jones 1980; Rosenzweig 1981, 1991; Jaenike 1982; Rausher 1984; Cody 1985; Morris 1994; Brown 1998; Hanski and Singer 2001).

> F. John Odling-Smee, Kevin N. Laland, and Marcus W. Feldman. *Niche Construction: The Neglected Process in Evolution* (Princeton, NJ: Princeton UP, 2003), 123.

EXAMPLE 3

Andrew D. White asserted in 1890 that "with very few exceptions, the city governments of the United States are the worst in Christendom—the most expensive, the most inefficient, and the most corrupt."

Richard Hofstadter, *The Age of Reform From Bryan to F.D.R.* (New York: Random House, Vintage Books, 1955), 176.

When you run across such references (summaries or direct quotations) that are relevant to your subject, you will probably be tempted to take this information from the source that you are reading and be done with it.

I must warn you that experienced researchers don't stop here. Instead of copying the information into their notes, they plan to find the author's sources and to look at these works firsthand. You should do the same.

Thus, when you see a reference to a list of studies (as in the first and second examples), you should copy the bibliographic information for each source from the author's reference list or bibliography. This information goes into the Sources section of your Researcher's Notebook, with a note from you about what to look for in these sources.

If and when you come across a direct quotation (as in Example 3) that you think you might be using in your final paper, it is particularly important for you to locate and read the original work from which the quotation has been taken. Although there is a method for quoting from secondary sources, you should be aware that this practice is frowned upon in academic circles. Hofstadter, for example, has selected this passage from White to make a point that he, Hofstadter, is developing. Until and unless you read White for yourself, you do not know how this statement fits into White's overall argument. You don't want to be quoting White, or even alluding to his idea in this quotation, until you've developed your own interpretation of his point of view and seen this quotation in its original context.

So, while I will show you how to make notes of such quoted material, let me urge you to take down all the information the author of the secondary source gives you about the original (check his or her notes, bibliography, and/or reference list), put it in the Sources section of your Researcher's Notebook (as well as including it with your note), and make every possible effort to locate this work.

If, in your final paper, you quote something from a secondary source, these quotations should come from sources that are truly inaccessible—rare books that don't circulate, or unpublished papers in a library or private collection, or personal communications (letters, phone conversations, and the like) that the person you are quoting had with the author of the secondary source. Trusting that you are going to track down the original work, here's the way you should record the material now in your notes:

• Be sure to put *your* source's words in double quotation marks and the material your author quotes in single quotation marks.

- Include all bibliographic information about the original source as well as the necessary information about your source.

Your note for Example 3 would look like this:

"Andrew D. White asserted in 1890 that 'with very few exceptions, the city governments of the United States are the worst in Christendom—the most expensive, the most inefficient, and the most corrupt.' "

> White, *Forum*, Vol. X (Dec. 1890), p. 25,
> quoted by Richard Hofstadter,
> *Age of Reform*,
> p. 176

As the authors you read give credit where credit is due, so must you when you write your paper. Under no circumstances may you imply in your final paper that you have read and studied works which, in reality, you have only seen referred to in works of others. Your notes must clearly indicate the source of all ideas and the authors of specific words.

I. Summary

Because reading critically and thinking about the evidence you gather is the heart of the research process, I'd like to make a few final summary remarks about this stage of the research process.

You need to have a good system for keeping track of your evidence. After all, this evidence is essential: you will be using it to test your original assumption about your subject, you will be using it to answer the questions you've posed for yourself, and thus you will be using it to develop a picture of your subject that makes most sense to you. For these reasons, you want to be sure that the evidence you have is accurate, that you can quickly put your hands on specific items of evidence, that you can sort and manipulate individual items of evidence in a variety of ways. And you want to be sure that you have complete bibliographic information about each of the sources you've looked at. But if all your energies are focused on the techniques of taking notes, you have missed the whole point of this stage of the research process. Your collection of notes should be nothing more than reminders of what you've learned; what counts are the intellectual activities your brain has been engaged in as you read your sources actively and digest their contents.

> At this stage in the research process, the most important work you are doing is in your Researcher's Notebook.

In the Reading section of your Notebook, you are critically examining the work of others. You are asking questions of the texts you are looking at; you are digesting the work of others, comprehending it, comparing it with what you've learned about your subject. In the Working Thesis section of your Notebook, you are writing to yourself about the picture that is forming in your mind as you put the pieces of the puzzle together, take these same pieces apart and put them together in different ways, decide which pieces in the puzzle are missing, and ask the questions that will allow you to find those pieces.

> If you use your Researcher's Notebook wisely, you will realize
> that you have started writing your research paper
> *as* you read and study your evidence.

The writing you do in your Researcher's Notebook is a very important part of the writing process. You are figuring out what you want to say. The final paper you are going to produce, I remind you, is *not* going to be a "memory dump" paper. You are *not* going to *list* what others have said (John Doe says this about X, and Mary Brown says that about X, and Sally Smith says something else again). Rather, your paper is going to focus on the conclusions *you* have reached about X from your critical reading of John Doe, Mary Brown, Sally Smith, and everyone else who can help you draw this conclusion. If you gather all of your evidence first and then attempt to make some sense of it, you will be over-whelmed. I've seen it happen too often to students I've worked with. Besides, as I've now said over and over again, how do you know what evidence you need if you have not, throughout the entire research process, been asking questions, if you have not been the one to give your research direction?

This sense of direction, I repeat, is critical to you as a researcher. As you have already discovered for yourself, the process of gathering evidence is not as straightforward and neat as all of us would like it to be. Experienced researchers know that their first visit to the library will not be the only visit they will make in the course of a research project. They will return as they come across the titles of promising sources in the bibliographies and reference lists of the books and articles they are reading. As their research changes direction, or as they realize that they are finally zeroing in on the real question they want to ask, they return to databases, reference materials, and library catalogs. I have found myself in the library, tracking down the answers to one or two final questions, when I have been in the second or even third draft of my papers. If your experience is like that of other researchers, you will also find yourself rereading important sources several times at different stages of your research, gleaning more information from that source as your knowledge of the subject grows and deepens.

Finally, I should alert you that the research process rarely ends naturally. You will feel that you have more to learn, more sources to read, more to think about, more directions to explore. Experts have spent years, even decades, inves-tigating a subject. As time passes and you get more deeply into your research, you will want to make a conscious effort to isolate and narrow down the area of investigation you want to focus on. Be prepared for the fact that, approxi-mately three weeks before the final paper is due, you will have to say, "The major portion of my research is finished. I must now decide what I am going to say in my paper." Obviously, by this point the major portion of your research must be finished; you must have found and studied all the sources you ought to have read. If you are doing a study or experiment, you must set a deadline for the time when all your raw data will be in your hands, a deadline that leaves you plenty of time to analyze those data, draw your conclusions, and write your report.

Use your time during this collecting/reading/studying stage of your project wisely. Plan to spend an hour here, a couple of hours there, *every day*, reading, searching, thinking, writing in your Researcher's Notebook. Give your brain as much time as possible to mull over what you are putting into it.

Then, about three weeks before the final paper must be handed in to your instructor, when it is time to start work on this paper, turn to the next section of this book.

5

Writing Your Paper

If you are on schedule, you should have about three weeks before your final paper is due. I cannot say that it is time for you to begin writing because you have already been doing a great deal of writing over the past weeks in your Researcher's Notebook. But in your Researcher's Notebook you have been writing to yourself, for yourself. As you have tested your working hypothesis/thesis, you have been making sense of your subject. If the Researcher's Notebook has worked for you the way it should, by this stage your own view of your subject ought to be fairly clear to you. This doesn't necessarily mean that the learning process is finished. The final test of how clear your ideas are to you comes in this last stage of the research project, presenting your view of your subject to other people. In showing others how you make sense of the subject, in showing others one way to put the parts of the puzzle together, you will be determining the exact shape of each piece of the puzzle and carefully and precisely fitting the pieces together. As you work on presenting your ideas to others, you will be honing and refining your own thinking.

In some very important ways, writing a research paper is no different from writing other kinds of prose. In this paper you will be talking to other human beings, and your main concern is going to be that they understand what you are saying. You have had enough experience with writing to know that one of the significant differences in addressing others on paper and talking with them face to face is that your readers can't interrupt you when they become lost or confused. Thus, one of the major challenges now before you is finding a mode of presentation that your readers will find clear, coherent, and convincing.

The shape a paper takes is determined by a writer's answers to four sets of basic, interrelated questions:

- What do I want to say about my subject? What is the message I want to convey to my readers?

- Who are my readers? What do they know about my subject? What do they assume that I will say? What do they know about the specific idea I am trying to express?

- What persona or voice do I want to adopt in this paper? What kind of person do I want my readers to hear speaking to them from this paper?

- What is my purpose in writing this paper? What impact do I want to have on my readers? What do I want my readers to think or feel when they have finished reading my paper?

Often the answers a writer develops for these questions lead him or her to use a particular genre. Genre, which means "type" or "kind" in French, is a term usually used to categorize literary works, but it can also apply to nonfiction writing. Book reviews, biographies, ethnographies, poetry analyses, grant proposals, even various forms of business documents could be called genres. A research paper is not a genre, but certain types of papers based on research are: reviews of the literature and reports on primary research in the social and natural sciences are definite categories of academic writing, conventional modes of conveying ideas and information. I am raising the issue of genres here for two related reasons. The first is to alert you that I am breaking down my discussion of the writing process into separate sections: reports on studies and experiments, reviews of the literature, and critical papers. The second reason accounts for these divisions. A genre is not a mold or an equation into which the writer mindlessly inserts ideas or information. A more reasonable way to conceptualize a genre is to see it as a conventional form of language use, like the greeting "How are you?" It is a form of verbal shorthand adopted by a particular group of people to facilitate the exchange of common types of messages. Just as all of us recognize "How are you?" as a gesture to acknowledge another person and make contact with him or her, so a genre automatically signals to readers the general intentions or purposes a writer has for a particular piece of writing. When a reader recognizes that a text is a primary research report in the natural or social sciences, he knows not only that the writer wants to describe a study or experiment she did but that she will follow a pattern that makes it easy for the reader to locate certain kinds of information, to evaluate the writer's work, and/or to set up a similar study.

I've divided some of my discussion of the writing process according to genres because advice I may give you if you are writing a critical paper will differ from the advice I'd give you if you are writing a report on a study or experiment. But one point about writing is general enough that it applies to all three kinds of papers: Composing a paper is the process of making decisions. And the only way for you to make the numerous "micro" decisions you will need to make—about which word to use, about how to structure a sentence, about how to organize a paragraph, about which evidence belongs where—is for you to have a clear sense of the overall purpose you have for the paper as a whole. In subsections B, C, and D you will find a great deal of discussion about purpose. At times I will be informing you about purposes that are built into a genre—what readers will expect you to be doing. At other times I will be offering strategies that will enable you, by adopting these generally accepted purposes, to decide the most effective way to present your ideas and points.

There are a few more general words of advice I can offer about the writing process that you are now beginning, so before you turn to the subsection relevant to the paper you are writing, read "The Writing Process: An Overview."

A. The Writing Process: An Overview

1. Writing for readers

It's hard to tell why so many students seem to think that research papers have to be dull and dry. Perhaps it has something to do with the pointlessness of those "reports" on dinosaurs you copied out of encyclopedias in the seventh grade. Or maybe it is because, for you, "formal" means "dull and dry." For me, dullness and dryness have nothing to do with subject matter or style per se, and everything to do with my sense of the writer's involvement with his or her material, and the writer's interest in me, the reader. The whole process you've been following up to this point has been intended to involve you with your subject matter. Now you must attend to the challenge of getting your readers equally involved.

When experienced researchers write a paper, they are usually addressing an audience of other experts who are interested in the general subject the writer is writing about. The purpose of these writers is to inform this audience about the work they've done and the conclusions they've reached. By presenting their work as thorough and their conclusions as logical, sound conclusions, they therefore wish to persuade their readers to see their subject as they see it. These writers usually, then, present themselves as serious, thoughtful, reasonable people, confident that the work and thinking they have done is worthy of consideration.

You are not an experienced researcher speaking to other experts. But you will write a much more successful paper if you can imagine yourself in a situation like the one just outlined. You will write a much more successful paper if you can avoid the traps of "writing for the teacher." If you think of your reader only as your instructor, two bad things may happen to you as a writer:

- You may fall into the trap of feeling that your purpose in writing the paper is to prove to the instructor that you have done your research properly. You will be tempted to drag in every source you have examined, whether it applies to your main point or not, just to show your instructor that you read this material. In other words, thinking that your purpose is to prove to your instructor that you did your research properly may cause you to write a "memory-dump" paper.

- You may fall into the trap of feeling that you have no right to say anything about this subject because your reader (the instructor) knows far more about your subject than you do. This perception will hurt the paper you produce because you will be tempted to leave out some essential information since, you will say to yourself, "My instructor already knows what X is." This perception will hurt the paper you produce because you will fail to explain ideas that need to be explained, simply because you assume your instructor already knows what you are talking about.

The best way to avoid the traps inherent in writing only for your instructor is not to think of your instructor as your audience (reader).

Plan to address your paper to other students.

The students you address may be either other students who are enrolled in your class or students who are majoring in the field or department in which your course is offered. Assume that these students are interested in your general subject; surely they have demonstrated their interest by taking the course or majoring in this field. Because you have been going to class regularly and reading the required material, you know what your fellow students in the class already know. But remember that they have not done the research you have done and that they certainly do not know what your conclusions are. Therefore, you legitimately have to assume that you will have to show these readers what the parts of your idea look like, and you will have to explain clearly how the parts fit together. Addressing an audience of your peers will put you in the position of experienced researchers, whose purpose is to inform their peers about the work they've done and the conclusions they've reached. Because you want to persuade other students to accept your view of your subject as a valid and legitimate view, you will present yourself as a serious, thoughtful, reasonable researcher. You will have a sense of confidence because you know that you have done a thorough job of researching and you have given your subject much thought, and you will not be intimidated because you know that you know more about your subject than your readers do.

2. Working from whole to part

Your readers are going to expect your paper, in the words of my students, "to flow"; they will expect your paper to be clear and coherent from beginning to end. In my experience as a writer, clarity and coherence do not just happen; they are the result of conscious effort. Too many students I talk to think that the mark of a good writer is "getting it right" in the first draft; they seem to feel that the need to do a series of drafts—the need to revise—is a clear sign that they are unskilled writers. If that's true, then you'll have to classify me as an unskilled writer because what I want to say rarely comes out "right" in my first attempt to put it on paper. My major concern, like that of all experienced writers, is to be sure that my readers understand exactly what I mean. I am willing to experiment with different organizational patterns, to try out various ways of expressing an idea, to look for just the right word or phrase—to go through as much revising and rewriting as necessary to reach this goal. Considering all the time and effort you have expended on this research project up to this point, I hope that your goal, too, is to do as much revising and rewriting as is necessary to develop a paper that precisely and clearly reproduces the ideas you have in your mind.

Ironically, the goal of getting it right in the first draft runs counter to everything we know about effective problem solving. Trying to make all kinds of decisions at once ties your brain into knots, potentially leading to a major case of writer's block. The reasonable way to write is to focus your attention on one thing at a time, writing first to discover your answers to "macro" questions, and in subsequent drafts working your way down to the "micro" ones.

- Your first concern should be the *general shape* of your presentation, which means translating your purpose into a skeleton of the paper as a whole. At this stage you want to work on deciding what your main points will be, where they should be placed, and, generally, what type of support you will need for each.

- After you are satisfied that you have a meaningful, coherent overall shape, then you can focus on sharpening and outlining individual sections. Your attention in these first two steps is on your ideas—getting them into words that come closer and closer to expressing what you have in your mind.

- When you have a good sense of what a particular section is supposed to do, you can give your attention to each paragraph, considering its organization, working with specific sentences, concentrating on word choice, being sure you provide transitions that link this paragraph to what you said earlier, and preparing the reader for what is coming next.

- Finally, when the paper has reached the point at which all these earlier problems have been satisfactorily resolved, you can worry about editing and proofreading. Don't waste time early in the process correcting spelling, punctuation, subject–verb agreement, and the like. There can be real dangers in polishing your prose too soon. The more you polish, the less willing you will be to throw out a paragraph or do a major revision, even though you know what you have isn't right.

I want to introduce two basic strategies that will give you a way to focus on the shape of the entire paper. One strategy is making a map of the territory; the other is writing an abstract of your paper. They are slightly different means of achieving the same end: enabling you to make the macro decisions upon which your micro decisions will be based.

a. Maps of the territory

You are no doubt familiar with outlines—in theory, if not in practice. Traditional outlines are one kind of map. I prefer the broader term *map of the territory* because it so precisely expresses the functions of this strategy. Like a road map, a map of your paper gives you a detailed picture of your entire paper at one glance. With a map you represent to yourself

- the *direction* of your ideas (what idea comes first, second, third, etc.);

- the *level* of generalization of each idea (what is a main point and what is a subordinate point, what is illustration, evidence, explanation);

- the *relationships* of ideas (Y causes Z, or Y is part of Z, or if Y, then Z).

Outlines are essentially a verbal map. The common division markers

I.

A.

1.

a.

indicate the relationships of ideas, both temporal and logical. Concepts marked by the same number or letter are of equal importance (I = II = III); the letter or number that follows in the pattern indicates a subordinate idea (A is a part of I, 1 is a part of A, and so on). You can express items in an outline as topics (II. Gender differences) or by making full grammatical statements (II. From an early age, girls and boys learn to use language for different purposes).

Writers who are more visual than verbal may prefer maps that represent temporal and logical relationships in forms that look like diagrams. To see what visual maps might look like, turn to subsection D.3; there you will also find two samples of sentence outlines. What is important for you to recognize are the main purposes and advantages of making a map:

- At a glance, a map enables you to plot out your paper as an organic whole. A map is an easy way to work out what will be your major points, what are subordinate concepts, and, most important, how they are connected to each other. With a map, you are deciding what needs to be said, what should go where, and why. It doesn't really matter if your map doesn't make much sense to another person, but it must make perfect sense to you.

- It is much easier to try out different organizational patterns by shifting around the small units of a map than by trying to push around chunks of written prose.

- Perhaps the greatest advantage of a map comes when you are writing. You probably know how easy it is to lose track of what you are doing when you are writing a particular section or paragraph of a paper, how easy it is to go off on tangents. If you have a map to guide you, you can always check on

where you've been,
where you are going,
and where you should be now.

b. Writing an abstract: Your first rough draft

Over the years that I've spent consulting with student writers about their papers, I've come to put more and more stress on the very early stage of the writing process, and particularly on the abstract as an excellent strategy for it.

An abstract is a map of the paper in prose form.

When you look at the examples of abstracts that I provide in subsection D.2, you'll see that the abstract is an obvious transition from the Working Hypothesis/ Thesis section of the Notebook to the final, polished draft intended for an audience. In the abstract there are obvious signs that you are still, in one sense, writing for yourself. The prose is still rough. In a number of sentences you are addressing comments to yourself. But you are starting now to think of another audience, the readers to whom the final paper will be addressed. And your focus now is going to be on structuring and organizing. In the abstract, as in the map of the territory, you are working on and with the **bare bones of the paper, the skeleton of your thinking.** That's why I've chosen to call it an abstract, even though I risk confusing you a bit. "Abstract" is the term used for brief summaries that authors provide of their studies, summaries that are printed at the beginning of articles when they are published in journals, or used in bibliographic databases. While the general nature of these formal summaries and your first rough draft is similar, these two types of abstracts are very different in other respects. The abstract for publication is written for readers, after the text of the article is finished. **The function of the abstract I'm describing here, this first rough draft, is to test your organizational pattern in order to see if it is coherent and cohesive.** The function of this abstract is **to test your line of reasoning to see if it is logical and clear.**

I said a moment ago that the abstract is a map in prose form. But it goes a step beyond the map. As a writer I've found that my ideas can look perfectly reasonable and coherent in an outline, but when I start to write the text, huge crevasses open up between point A and point B, or I reach a paragraph in which my prose becomes hopelessly tangled up as I try to explain three major but interrelated ideas. I've come to realize that I can save myself a lot of time and frustration if I can spot and resolve these problems or challenges long before I have pages of lovely prose that, in the face of the need for a major revision, transform themselves into an impenetrable mass that weighs me down.

So, here's what you are going to do in composing your abstract:

- write quickly;
- write roughly;
- talk to yourself
- about the overall structure of your points;
- about issues, problems, concerns you see.

I particularly recommend writing the entire abstract at one sitting, and not looking at your notes or any other material. The philosophy here is that, if a paper has coherence, its coherence comes from the mind of the writer. In the abstract, you are trying to capture the outline of this coherence. Since you are still writing for yourself, your prose can and should be rough. The more time you spend on a sentence, the less likely you are to throw it away. Since the paper is in a testing phase, you need to be able to throw things out, or tinker with them at a macro level. You don't need your notes at this stage because you are doing a sketch, and, moreover, you want your mind to transmute the knowledge you've gained from the evidence into that coherent whole we are talking about. Moreover, because this abstract is a sketch, the whole text will be short. My abstracts are usually about a quarter of the length of the final paper.

The content of your abstract is, as I've noted, the shape of your thinking. So in this abstract you'll be laying out for yourself three things:

- where you are going to discuss specific main ideas;

- very generally, the kinds of supporting evidence and explanations you'll be supplying for each central point;

- most importantly, the rationale for this organizational pattern; in other words, you will be explicitly telling yourself *why* you are discussing a particular idea in a certain place and *how* it is related to other points.

In writing the abstract, your critical thinking faculties should be on high alert, and your conscious focus should be on **making sense.** Making sense, at this point in the process, has two important meanings.

You need **to make sense at an intellectual level**: Does my thinking here make sense? Is what I am saying logical? Do these pieces *really* fit together the way I am saying they do? Does A really lead to B?

Making sense at an intellectual level now has to translate into **making sense at a communicative level.** If your ideas do make sense, then you ought to be able to explain them to other human beings in such a way that these ideas make sense to them, too. So you need to be concerned with how you present your ideas: What does my reader need to know in order to understand this point? Which should I talk about first, A or B? This idea is complicated; how can I pull it apart so that readers can understand as they read?

As a first step in getting started on a paper, writing maps and abstracts makes a lot more sense than spending three days struggling to craft a beautifully polished introduction for a paper that doesn't as yet exist. The purpose for writing such an introduction is the same as that for doing a map and an abstract, but the abstract and map are a much more efficient means to the same end. Ease yourself into the writing stage of the process by doing a quick map, then spend forty-five minutes writing an abstract; or write an abstract first, and then do a map. Do whatever feels best for you. At all times remember that maps and abstracts are strategies; *you* are using *them* to achieve a goal, which is now your final paper. They are here to keep you on track by constantly reminding you of the big picture, and they are here to enable you to resolve problems at the macro level in the easiest and most meaningful ways. The longer the paper is going to be and/or the more complex its structure, the greater are the advantages of having a map to use at all stages of drafting and revising. Plan to work back and forth between your draft and the map. They can and should change as the picture becomes clearer and clearer to you. Just make sure that changes in one are reflected in the other.

3. Reviewing your evidence

The point in the writing process when you should review your notes will depend on the type of paper you are writing and other factors. In general, however, you will be better off if

you put your notes aside as you develop the shape of your own thinking.

Still focusing on what is going on in your mind and the way you see the puzzle, you will be transforming the intellectual work you've done in the Working Hypothesis/Thesis section of your Researcher's Notebook into a map and an abstract of your paper. Looking at your notes before you've crystallized your own view of your subject can seduce you into becoming a passive sponge. As hard as you've worked up to this point to prevent your sources from using you, you don't want to fall into the trap of feeling as if you have to include *all* the evidence you've collected in your paper or choosing an outline that is nothing more than a mindless catalog of what the experts have said.

Of course, the evidence you've gathered is important to your paper. In Section 6 you will find a detailed discussion about how to decide which evidence to use and how to incorporate it into your draft. But in the initial stages of the drafting process, you want your mental energies solidly focused on refining your own line of thinking and expressing it clearly and cogently. So you need a system (!) that enables you to keep track of the sources of the evidence you incorporate in your paper without this mechanical matter distracting you from the central task of formulating and expressing your own ideas. In other words, looking ahead, you have to remember that, once your paper has found its shape and you have a good, solid draft, you are going to have to

- double-check the evidence you've used in the paper against your notes to be sure that the content is accurate;

- document all this evidence, which will require knowing the source from which each item of evidence comes and, where required, the appropriate page numbers;

- and you want to be able to handle this task of documentation with a minimum of wasted time and energy.

Probably the simplest way to meet these criteria is to include information about sources of evidence in parentheses right in the body of your paper. One variation of such a system closely resembles the final citation form of the MLA and author-date documentation styles. Immediately after a sentence containing material you've taken from a source, you'd write

- the last name(s) of the author(s);

- an abbreviated title;

- the page number(s).

You'd include all this information for each source you make use of.

EXAMPLE

> Several experts in the field of diplomatic history have pointed out that the United States tends to take a confrontational rather than a conciliatory stance in its dealings with other countries (Williams, *Dip. Hist.*, 497; Samuels, *Looking*, 297–300; Carter, *US*, 406). Confrontation certainly characterizes the way the United States handled the Cuban missile crisis. US actions included the creation of a blockade around Cuba to prevent the delivery of more missiles from the USSR and a threat that the firing of these missiles would be met with full military retaliation (Corwin, *Cuban*, 905–30). . . . .

Once you've decided on a system, you are ready to turn to subsection B, C, or D, depending on which type of research project you have been engaged in.

- If you have designed and carried out an experiment or study, turn to subsection B, "A Report on a Study or Experiment."

- If you have concentrated on discovering exactly what's been done recently in a specific area of a field so that you can write a review or a review of the literature paper, turn to subsection C, "A Review or a Review of the Literature Paper."

- If the paper you are writing will focus on your answer to the research question you have posed for yourself, turn to subsection D, "A Critical Paper."

When you have accomplished the part of the writing process covered in subsection B, C, or D, then turn to subsection E, "Drafting and Revising."

B. A Report on a Study or Experiment

The type of paper described here applies only to primary research projects in the natural and social sciences. This is the way you report on studies or experiments in which you have gathered raw data directly from sources through a carefully designed series of tests or procedures, and in which you have analyzed your raw data by using objective, accepted procedures in the field.

1. General format

In these reports, the researcher is laying out his or her study or experiment for the reader in the order in which the study was conceived and carried out. The diagram on page 138 provides a picture of the overall shape of the report. The report breaks down into three major parts (a, b, c, on the left of the diagram).

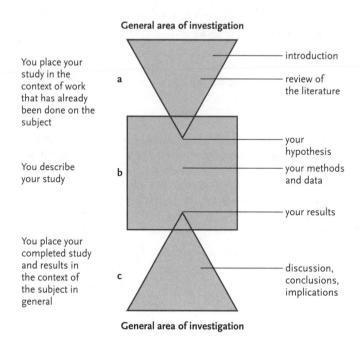

General area of investigation

You place your study in the context of work that has already been done on the subject — a — introduction / review of the literature

You describe your study — b — your hypothesis / your methods and data / your results

You place your completed study and results in the context of the subject in general — c — discussion, conclusions, implications

General area of investigation

a. The first section: Introduction, review of the literature, statement of the hypothesis

In the diagram, the first section of the report is an inverted pyramid because, in this part of the report, you begin by introducing your reader to the general area of investigation (the general subject) and then gradually lead your reader to the specific hypothesis you tested. The purpose of this opening segment of the report is to put your study or experiment into the context of other work that has already been done in the field.

If you have worked as other experienced researchers have worked, before you designed your specific study or experiment you investigated the theories that are current in the field and you looked carefully at the studies and experiments that have been carried out by others. Thus, your specific study evolved out of your reactions to these previous studies and experiments, reactions such as "Smith and Jones's hypothesis needs to be tested further with more subjects" or "Dr. X's theory needs to be tested by doing a study that would . . ." or "I wonder if procedure Y would give me more information about the way that DNA. . . ." In other words, you did your study to fill a hole or gap in the knowledge base that has already been accumulated about your subject.

In the first part of your report, then, you are accomplishing two things:

- You are *informing* your reader about the theories that your study is based on and about published research projects that you have drawn on to develop your hypothesis and methodology.

- You are *explaining* to your reader where your study fits in the general picture of the current theories and the work that has been done.

An abstract of this section of your paper would go something like this:

> I need to tell my reader that my general area of investigation is learning styles. Then I need to say that there are 3 basic views of learning styles: view Y, view X, and view Z. I'll briefly describe X and Y and say that I'm not following these views. I'll then explain Z's theory in more detail because, as I'll tell the reader, this is the theory I'm using. Briefly I'll show the reader what kinds of testing procedures have been used to test Z's theory, stressing Smith and Wesson's work. I'll point out that these studies haven't considered age as a variable. I will say that I think age is an important variable, and I will prove it by pointing to studies that have focused on the relationship of age and both learning and cognitive development (like Johnson, Wilson, and Smedley's study; I have more). Then I will say that age should also be considered when talking about learning styles, which will lead me right into my hypothesis that. . . .

In the reading you have been doing, you have probably already noticed that primary research reports are divided by headings in the text. Sometimes this first section is headed Introduction. Sometimes, particularly if this part of the report is long, the writer will use several headings (Introduction, Review of the Literature, Statement of Hypothesis) or will subdivide the introduction, using subheadings or headings that specifically describe the content of that section (Z's Theory of Learning Styles, Age, and Learning).

b. The second section: A description of your study, including data and methodology

The second general segment of the report is a description of the study you did. It includes a description of the material or subjects you used as your source for raw data, the procedures you used to acquire your data, the data themselves. The common headings for this section are Methods, Methods and Procedures, Materials and Methods, or Experimental Section. Use the heading or headings that best describe the work you did. Check the published reports you read as you were doing your research.

In the sciences and social sciences, one purpose of writing up a study is to allow other researchers to replicate or redo a study or experiment exactly as it was first done. This principle, then, can provide you with a good rule of thumb in writing the methods section of your report. Ask yourself what another researcher would need to know about your materials (and/or subjects) and your research procedure in order to reproduce your study or experiment exactly as you did it.

After you have jotted down this information, try to organize it so that this part of your report is easy to follow. You could, for example, first talk about your materials—the chemicals, instruments, and apparatus you used—then describe your research design.

You will notice that experienced researchers sometimes divide this section with several headings or subheadings if it is complicated or long.

c. The third section: Results, discussion, conclusions

The final section of the body of the report is devoted to a presentation of the results you came up with when you analyzed your data and a discussion of the results and the study as a whole. It begins with a straightforward report of your results or findings and an explanation of the procedures you used to obtain those results. Once this is accomplished, the researcher is free to step back from the study or experiment he or she did and comment on the study as a whole, or on parts of it. This section allows you to critique your work and the results of your work (thus Discussion) and to draw conclusions or to discuss the implications of your study for the field as a whole.

In preparing to write this section, then, what do you want to say about your results? What do you want to say about the whole study? If you feel that your procedures were flawed in any way, discuss that here. If you wish you had used other instruments or tests to generate more data, say so here. If you feel that you should have analyzed your data in other ways, say so here. You will want to compare your results with your original hypothesis. Do your results support the hypothesis? Were they inconclusive? Have your results suggested certain implications for the direction further research should take?

In other words, after you have described your results, you will be doing what you did in the beginning of your paper—you will be putting your specific study and the information you obtained from it back into the context of the general search for knowledge in this area of investigation. Thus, on the diagram, this segment appears as a regular pyramid. You are moving from your specific study back to the general area under investigation. In the Discussion and the Conclusion sections of this segment of your report, you will be telling your reader what you learned, in more general terms, by doing this study. If you look at the published studies you read as you were doing your library research, you will notice that some researchers label this part "Results and Discussion" and that others divide their reports into separate Results and Discussion sections.

d. Appendixes and the reference list

Your report will end with your reference list, and any notes or appendixes you decide to include. I talk more about explanatory notes in Section 8.E.4. There I point out that an appendix is really just a long note. In these kinds of reports, appendixes typically include more details about the data that were collected, copies of surveys or instruments or procedures that were used in gathering data, and the like. The reference list is the list of all the sources you make reference to in the body of your paper. If you are using one of the documentation styles I cover in the appendixes of this book, look there for a sample reference list. Otherwise, for more information on these matters, consult your instructor and, if necessary, the manual for the documentation style you are using.

e. The abstract

After your report is finished, you should write an abstract of the entire report, which you will type on a separate sheet of paper and insert between your title page and the first page of the body of your report. Clearly the abstract I am talking about here is not the preliminary draft that I've recommended as a strategy in the writing process, but a formal summary of your finished paper. Authors of published papers often preface their articles with these succinct overviews of the main points in their papers to allow readers to determine quickly whether an article contains material of interest to them. To get started, you can try writing one sentence each on the basic area of the study, your hypothesis, your methods, and your results. Work with it until you have one, tight paragraph.

One of the sample student papers at the end of this book, "A Paradigm of Social Sorting Rituals: Differences between Leaders and Outcasts," is prefaced by an abstract; you might want to take a look at it.

✳ 2. General guidelines for writing the report

As you can see from the general description of the order in which you present your information, you are approximating the order in which you conceived and carried out your study. In this report, you are telling your reader what you did and explaining why you did it. Your information is complete enough that your reader, if he or she wished to, could do the same study and compare his or her results with yours. The text is divided by headings so that the reader can quickly distinguish the parts, and the headings allow a reader who is most interested in your methodology, or results, to go straight to that specific part of the study.

Here are some pointers that will help you produce a coherent, readable report:

- The three divisions I've just described give you the basic outline of your paper, but it would be wise to "fill in the blanks" by creating a map of each section. In my experience, many students have trouble with the review of the literature section of these reports. Starting with an abstract of this section, and of your discussion section, would be particularly helpful. Plan on writing several drafts, working from whole to part in each section. Once you have your first rough draft of one or more of the divisions, read over subsections E, F, and G and continue to write with the issues and suggestions you find there in mind.

- Because your report is divided into separate segments, you can begin to write the introduction and methodology sections even while you are analyzing your data and considering your conclusions/discussion.

- Because this paper is a formal, scientific report, you will want to use a style appropriate to such a report. Do *not* write in an informal, chatty way. This does not necessarily mean, however, that you cannot use the first person. Perhaps you've noticed in the reading that you've been doing that scientists and researchers do use the first person where and when they deem it appropriate. I say more about this in subsection F. Obviously, if you aren't sure what is appropriate for your paper, consult your instructor.

- Use technical language where and when you need it, but keep your audience in mind. Will your readers know what these terms refer to? There are graceful ways to include definitions in your paper, and often the definition becomes an integral part of the point you are making.

  > If Freud (19XX) is right, and the id is xxxxxx, then it would be reasonable to expect that . . .

  > . . . this mechanism, which Lee (2011) calls "the linchpin."

- Throughout your report, your goal is to be as clear and precise as possible. Even if your instructor helped you design your study and analyze your data, you may not assume that your readers know what you did in this study. Think of your readers as people who had no idea that you were working on any research project until they picked up this report.

- You must be precise and specific, but you do not want to overwhelm your reader with details to the point that your reader can't see the forest for the trees. Try these techniques:

  - In each division of the text, begin with a summary statement of the material in that section, then go into more detail. Use this same summarize-then-explain pattern in each subdivision, and even each paragraph. For example, your results section might begin, "Results indicate that males prefer tasks that require physical activity and interaction with other people, while females prefer to work alone in sedentary jobs. On the Hansen Job Inventory Scale, 92% of the male subjects ranked 'Be physically active' as their first priority; the other 8% ranked this criterion either second or third (see Table 3)."

  - Whenever possible, use graphs and charts to report results or to summarize data. In your text, do not simply present your data in prose. The prose parts of your text should be statements you make to draw your reader's attention to numbers you consider important or significant and to tell your reader why you consider these numbers important.

  - Do not attempt to put all your raw data in the body of your paper. If you feel obliged to give data that cannot be represented in summary charts and graphs, put these data in appendixes at the end of your report. If and when you want to refer to these data, you can refer your reader to the proper appendix.

  - If you were gathering data from people by using tests or instruments that your reader could not easily obtain (such as a questionnaire that you made up), you should include a copy of this test or instrument. However, place this material in an appendix at the end of the paper and refer your reader to the appropriate appendix when you talk about this material in your text.

- Whenever you refer to the work of other researchers and experts, you must document your sources. See Section 8.

- As suggested in subsection B.1, your text should be divided by headings. If you are not sure how to divide your text, either look at the studies you have read as you were doing your research, or ask your instructor. Mainly, in cases like this, you should use your common sense. Your objective is to isolate the important parts of your report so that readers can go directly to those specific portions of your study that particularly interest them.

✳C. A Review or a Review of the Literature Paper

In addition to describing one section of a report on a study or experiment, the term "review of the literature" also applies to an entire research paper, one that is based on material you have gathered from books and articles. In the natural sciences, this type of paper is often called simply a review. Don't confuse this type of review with an evaluation of a specific book, play, or film. The review that I am describing here is a review of the research that has been done in a specific field.

A review of the literature, or review, is a summary of the "state of the art" of a particular area of investigation. A researcher selects a particular subject (clinical treatments for depression, definitions and causes of autism, methods of teaching foreign languages in middle school); the objective is to point out to readers the patterns and trends that have been developing in research done on this subject. Unless the writer has a particular reason for doing an historical study, she is usually interested in the most recent trends and patterns of research (what has occurred in the past ten, or even five, years).

Reviews of the literature are a common form of paper in academic disciplines. As the knowledge explosion increases and experts become more specialized, these experts find it difficult to keep abreast of developments in areas outside their own fields of interest. Reviews help them stay informed about scholarly work in their discipline that lies outside their areas of specialization. An instructor may ask students to write reviews on topics outside his or her area of specialization as one means of keeping informed about developments in the field in general.

If you were going to publish a review of the literature, then your obligation would be to find and to read everything available on your topic. Often, in assigning a review of the literature paper, instructors ask students to base their review on a specified number of works (ten, perhaps, or fifteen). Even if your search has been limited in this manner, your obligation is still to give your readers a clear sense of trends and patterns in the research. Thus, if you find that a great deal has been published on the general subject with which you began, I would expect you to narrow the topic. The two most common ways are to narrow the area of investigation (methods of teaching foreign languages in middle school is narrowed down to methods of teaching Japanese in middle school) or to restrict your research to a given period of time (what clinical therapies for depression have been used in the past five years?).

When you write a review or review of the literature paper, the most valuable evidence you have are the summaries of books and articles that you have written (see Section 4.G.).

The trickiest part of writing a review of the literature is deciding how to organize your paper. The one thing you *do not* want to do is simply to *list* the studies you have read. Let me remind you that your purpose in writing a review is to tell your reader about the main *trends* and *patterns* you see in the work that has been done on this subject. Thus, as you have researched, you should have been looking constantly for trends and patterns (and considering these in the Working Thesis section of your Researcher's Notebook). In determining the overall structure of your paper, you should use the basic trends and patterns you see as the focal point of the paper.

Here are some strategies you can use in determining what the basic trends and patterns are:

- What theory or theories seem to be the most popular? (Which theories are referred to most often? Which theories are the basis for most of the studies or experiments you looked at?) Has there been a shift in the popularity of theories?

- What basic assumptions do most of the researchers seem to be making about the subject?

- Can you categorize the research reports you've read according to the test procedures used in the studies and experiments?

- Can you categorize the research reports you've read according to the kinds of subjects or material tested or observed?

- Can you see any patterns in the results reported?

- Are there any patterns in the conclusions drawn by the researchers?

- What experts' names pop up most frequently? Are certain experts associated with certain types of research, certain theories, certain areas of investigation?

If it helps you, make actual charts by putting these questions in categories at the top of the page and the works you've read along the left-hand side; then fill in the blanks. Or create a chart by putting the following categories at the top: theories used, hypothesis, methods, results, major points made in the discussions section. Then list each article along the left-hand side, and fill in the blanks. Here are some other strategies to use in writing your paper.

- When you have determined what you consider to be the two or three most important trends or patterns in the subject you've researched, you need to summarize these trends or patterns in one sentence (your thesis statement) and use that sentence as the key to the organizational pattern of your whole paper. Some of the strategies I give in subsection D for critical papers could be helpful to you. But if you read subsection D, remember that in a review of the literature your purpose is *not* to focus on your personal ideas about the topic. Your thesis statement must be a statement of the conclusions you have reached about *the major trends and developments you see in the research that has been done on your subject.* I urge you to do a map and abstract of the whole paper; use as your major points those aspects of the studies that reveal the trends or developments you've nutshelled in your thesis statement.

- Another note of caution: In a review of the literature, your obligation is only to indicate the *type* of work that is being done or has been done and the most *influential* theories. Of course you will illustrate and support your argument by referring to specific works, but this can be done with summary statements and *some* descriptions of actual studies. Do *not* turn your paper into a list in paragraph form, giving a summary of one work in one paragraph, then a summary of the next work in another paragraph, and so on. It is not necessary for you to give a complete description of every study or book you looked at. Use detail where it is important to make your point. A review is not a memory-dump paper.

- At the end of your review, you should devote a few paragraphs to your conclusions about the work that still needs to be done in the field. You won't be able to do this unless you have thought about the general picture you have seen emerging in the research to date.

- Obviously, your reader will expect you to refer to specific books and articles as you support and illustrate the points you are making (it would be very difficult indeed to write a review of the literature without a large number of these references, since your job was to survey the field). All works you refer to must be documented in your paper, so see Section 8 and the appropriate appendix.

- Plan to write several drafts, working from the overall shape of your paper to specific parts. Once you have a rough draft of your paper, read subsections E, F, and G, and keep in mind the suggestions and strategies there as you continue to pull your paper into its final form.

D. A Critical Paper

The most common type of research paper assigned to students in college courses falls into the broad category of critical papers. The focal point of a critical paper is an assertion or claim the writer makes about a particular subject:

Sergeant Pepper marked the high point of the musical artistry of the Beatles.

The power of the military in Outer Slabovia has been the greatest obstacle to the development of a democratic government in that country.

Clothes and hairstyles in the 1920s reflect the social and psychological liberation that women in the United States were pushing for during that decade.

Clearly you don't need eight or ten pages to write out a statement like these. What constitutes the body of a critical paper—and holds the key to its purpose— is nicely explained by Stephen Toulmin:

> Whatever the nature of the particular assertion may be . . . we can challenge the asser-
> tion, and demand to have our attention drawn to the grounds (backing, data, facts,
> evidence, considerations, features) on which the merits of the assertion are to depend.
> We can, that is, demand an argument; and a claim need be conceded only if the argu-
> ment which can be produced in its support proves to be up to standard.[1]

In the paper you are now starting, your readers will expect you to make one central claim or assertion about your subject. Because they value critical think- ing, their willingness to accept your claim will be based on your providing grounds for this assertion; in other words, your readers expect you to provide an argument.

Writing your paper, then, involves two central tasks: first, determining the specific claim you'll be making in this paper, then working out an argument. Actually, you've already spent a great deal of time doing the necessary ground- work. Your whole investigation has been directed by a tentative assertion, which we've been calling your working thesis. Determining your claim simply involves moving from a "working" thesis to a final thesis statement. The terms "thesis" or "thesis statement" are probably more familiar to you than "claim" or "asser- tion"; as I continue my discussion, think of the four terms as synonymous. In your Researcher's Notebook you've been continually testing—and perhaps changing—your working thesis by organizing the evidence you've found into patterns that make sense to you. Now you'll be taking the lines of reasoning you've been working out in your Researcher's Notebook and transforming them into the argument you'll present to your readers. The specific shape your argu- ment takes will be the overall shape—the organization—of your whole paper. And since the argument you work out is, in turn, determined by the assertion you decide to focus on, let's go now to strategies for developing your thesis statement.

1. Developing your thesis statement

In this process of developing your thesis, it could be helpful to think about the claim or assertion you will make as the statement of a conclusion you've arrived at about your subject after all these weeks of studying and thinking about it. It's now time to determine exactly what conclusion you feel strongly enough about that you want to base your paper on it. So take out your Researcher's Notebook, and in the Working Thesis section answer these questions:

- Was my original assumption/working thesis valid?

- Based on the evidence I have found, what conclusions have I drawn about my subject?

---

[1] *The Uses of Argument* (Cambridge: Cambridge University Press, 1958), 11–12.

• What statements do I feel comfortable making about my subject? (You want inferences and judgments here, not factual statements.)

Freewrite on these questions.

Don't worry if you decide that your original assumption or working thesis was not correct; don't worry if you find that the conclusions you are drawing cover only part of the general area you began investigating. You should know by now that the more you research, the more you realize how broad and complex a subject is.

As you are developing your thesis, let me address two common fears that seem to drive students to write poor critical papers. Do *not* try to find a conclusion that will cover everything you read just so you can refer to all your research in your paper. If you have done a thorough job of investigating your research assumption or working thesis, you will find yourself referring to a variety of sources as you develop the argument of your paper, even though your thesis seems narrow. But the main thing to remember is that the *quality* of the assertion you make and the argument you present is the real test of a critical paper. The more evidence you studied, the more time you spent thinking about your subject, the higher will be the quality of the thesis you develop.

Your objective, at this stage, is to express your thesis in one sentence.

When I insist that the thesis be expressed in one sentence, my students often groan and complain and beg for a couple of sentences or a paragraph—but I stand firm, and here's why. You could draw many conclusions about your subject, as you've already discovered in the freewrites you've been doing. If you want to end up with a successful paper—one that presents one, sharp, clear-cut argument—you must begin with one, sharp, definite point. The strategy of expressing your point in one sentence forces you (1) to decide exactly *which* claim you want to make, and (2) to bring that claim into sharp focus. The task won't be very difficult at all if you remember a couple of things. First of all, a thesis statement by definition is a summary statement. It is not self-explanatory; in fact, you are going to write eight or ten or fifteen pages to explain what it means. Second, the structure of sentences in English allows you to qualify assertions made in the main clause with all sorts of dependent clauses, phrases, adjectives, and adverbs. Your thesis statement probably won't be a flat assertion such as "The moon is blue." I assume you'll qualify it by saying something like this: "Under certain atmospheric conditions the moon can appear to be blue"; or, "The moon can appear to be blue because of X, Y, and Z." To see how much you can say in one sentence, take a look at the sample thesis statements I offer below.

It may take a while to come up with the sentence that feels exactly right. Don't put it off. Here are a few strategies to follow:

• What claim do you feel confident in making about your subject?

• You may come up with several statements. In these cases you will have to choose one. Which statement comes closest to expressing what you want to say about your subject?

- Don't just stare at a blank page, forming and dismissing statements in your head. Write down something, anything. If the first statement you write is "wrong," don't erase it or scratch it out. Move down on the sheet of paper and write another statement.

- If you write a statement that is not quite right, underline the parts of the statement that are wrong and rewrite those parts until they say what you want them to say.

- As you write and rewrite these statements, keep saying to yourself, "*Exactly* what do I want to say about X in this paper?"

- Be sure the statement you end up with covers only what you want to say in your paper and that it does cover what you want to say, precisely and completely.

Your thesis should look like this:

> When men and women in our society talk to each other, they can fail to communicate because research indicates that men and women have different concepts of what "communication" means.

> Among the many risks associated with genetically modified organisms (GMOs) is the "genetic pollution" that could occur if GMOs reproduced themselves in the wild. An obvious solution would seem to be the terminator gene, a strategy being pursued in genetic use restriction technology (GURT). I will show, however, that the terminator gene is not a viable response to the threat of genetic pollution.

Once you have a statement that you are sure states clearly and precisely the assertion you want to make, you are ready to begin sketching out your paper.

Don't let the spector of "how can I write ten pages on this?" get to you now. You now *know* that you have a great deal of knowledge of your subject. Never forget that it takes a great deal of space to make your ideas clear to other people. And the abstract you will write in the next step will immediately calm your fears because you will begin to fill in pages with your prose.

2. Writing an abstract of your paper: Your first rough draft

I believe that writing an abstract is a very important strategy to use in doing a critical paper. Having a clear sense of your line of reasoning is crucial for two reasons. First, the success or failure of your paper depends on your argument; if your readers find your thinking logical, they will be willing to accept your claim or assertion. Moreover, the line of reasoning you choose automatically becomes the organizational pattern or outline of your paper. So the more you concentrate on the skeleton of your argument—which is what you are doing in the abstract—the higher your chances of writing an A paper.

This is probably a good place to say a few more words about arguments. Let me begin by talking about what an argument is not. An argument is not a story. It is neither the story of what you've been reading over the past few weeks (John Doe says this and Mary Brown says that . . .), nor is it the history of your subject (first this happened, and then that happened). In certain sections of your paper you may use a few short stories to explain or illustrate a point, but the overall organization of the paper has to mirror some pattern of **logical, analytical thinking.**

The claim you are making, expressed in the thesis statement you developed in the last step, is your whole paper in a nutshell. You know what the statement means to you, but nobody else but you knows all those "meanings." Therefore you must write a paper that will be a full explanation of how and why you arrived at this conclusion. That is, you will now be reconstructing, in all its detail, the way you've put this puzzle together.

Do not use your notes at this stage of the process; do not even look at them.

Write your thesis statement on a card or a slip of paper so that you can have it in front of you at all times. Then, as you've been doing in the Working Thesis section of your Researcher's Notebook, write your abstract by using only the ideas and information you have in your head. A few more words of wisdom:

- Very often an organizational pattern is built into your thesis statement; see if yours has one, and if so, start with it.

- After you sketch out a possible introduction (which probably should include your thesis statement), go to your first central point. Avoid giving us "background" material; it is a trap that can lead you into telling us the story of your subject. The odds are that relevant background material is really an explanation of or evidence for one of your main points, and should be presented as such.

- Remember: If you find, as you sketch out your thinking, that your thesis statement is not quite right, stop and revise the thesis statement.

- And don't try to write polished prose. You are still writing for yourself, attempting to discover what you mean by the claim you've summarized in your thesis statement.

In writing your abstract, you have two objectives:

- to express the *major* ideas or parts of your argument;

- to express clearly the ways these ideas are related to each other.

Here are examples of abstracts for the two thesis statements I gave in the last section:

ABSTRACT FOR THE PAPER ON GENDER AND COMMUNICATION

A good way to start this paper would be to find an actual short dialogue between a male & female that my readers would recognize as familiar and that would illustrate my central point about problems in communicating. Then there are two things I need to do in this opening section—(1) establish that enough research has been done to show that men and women do communicate differently—(2) give my thesis statement. ALSO, somewhere in this paper I need to DEFINE communication. Tricky, since my whole paper is about definitions of communication, but I need some measure of effective communication. Should I put this here, or wait until section 3, where I go into talk between males and females? Anyway, I'll say that just because a person hears the words another person is uttering, it doesn't mean that the listener interprets the speaker's messages the way the speaker intends them to be interpreted. Effective communication = hearer tries to interpret the message the way the speaker intends, then tries to respond along the same lines. I'll use this basic idea as a touchstone for effective and ineffective communication.

I'll start right in, then, with the different ways that boys and girls learn to use language when they are young because my point is that these different styles are established early in life and are practically unconscious. I'll break this section into 2 parts, one about research in boys' language use in all-male groups and one about girls' talk in all-female groups. For boys, my main point is they use language in larger groups to establish their place in the hierarchy, to dominate and control the group. In these groups boys attempt to "hold the floor" with stories meant to impress their peers. Goal: to complete the story in spite of challenges and heckling from others. Boys' style: competitive and aggressive. Be sure to illustrate, provide evidence. Then on to girls, where my main point is that, in contrast to boys, girls use talk to form and maintain personal relationships. Girls' talk is in smaller groups (2 or 3), topics are their feelings and everyday lives. Girls' style: cooperative, inclusive. Give illustrations, evidence.

If I devote quite a bit of space to the section above, this next section, on adult communication styles, can focus mainly on evidence. My main point: By the time we are adults, males and females have established definite and different concepts of communication. I'll again break down into males in all-male groups, then females in all-female groups. Main point about males: communication = establish status and authority. Main point about females: communication = establish and maintain personal relationships. Use this section to give lots of evidence that these are the definitions that males and females operate on.

This third major section is probably the most important—may be the longest. Using what I've said in the first 2 sections, I can now say that it isn't surprising that a man and a woman may run into trouble when they want to communicate with each other. I want to break this section down into (1) relationships at work; (2) relationships "at home" (romantic, marriage). I want to make the point that male-female relationships in the workplace are more and more relevant as women move into positions of authority in businesses and corporations. Here I want to tie the research I've done on women's managerial styles in with this research on male/female communication styles; my point—you "manage" people through communication, verbal and nonverbal! So, if your messages are misinterpreted, that will lead to poor working relationships. Then I'll go into intimate relationships. Here I think I'll break it down into "male's view," then "female's view," focusing on females' frustrations. Male view—if talk establishes status and control, no need to talk much at home unless he feels need to re-establish dominance or control. Not interested in mate's desire to talk about feelings, mundane experiences—sees it as idle chitchat. Female view—talk about feelings, mundane experiences creates and maintains relationship. VERY frustrated if mate not interested in what she says, if he shows no interest in talking about his feelings, how his day went. TROUBLE is brewing.

Right now, I come to a paradoxical conclusion. Conflict resolution tends to stress the need for "more communication," "talking it out"—but this isn't going to work very well in male-female relationships—intimate or working relationships—if males and females see different purposes in talk! Is "talking it out" a "female" form of conflict resolution? Does "talking it out" just mean different things for all-male, all-female groups? HMMMM. Something else to think about: Do I want to reword my thesis statement slightly so that the "frame" is conflict resolution between males and females? The paper then would be about the limitations of the approach of "talking it out" when it comes to problems in male-female relationships because of gender differences in definitions of communication.

ABSTRACT FOR THE PAPER ON THE TERMINATOR GENE

From the very beginning of this paper I need to make it VERY, VERY clear that I want to talk about the <u>SCIENCE</u> of GMOs and the terminator. My research has shown me, though, how controversial GMOs are, and how political the controversy gets. A natural place to start my intro. would be to talk about the controversy since it is what people (my readers, who are the general public) are most familiar with. I'll use accounts I have from the public press to make two points at once: (1) GMOs are a controversial issue, and (2) the kind of controversy they cause (health risks, farmers' control of their crops, big companies making big bucks, patenting genes, etc.). I can also use some stuff I got from Web sites of those groups totally opposed to GMOs. I'll end the list of controversies with genetic pollution. That will let me move into the scientific approach, so I can give my thesis. I want to be sure I put lots of emphasis here on "gene" and "genetic," since that's my real focus.

I do need to let readers know what GMOs are and how the genetic engineering works, but I think the paper might flow better if I start this section by talking about the benefits of GMOs. These benefits will also let me narrow GMOs down to plants, and specifically crop plants. I can quickly lay out the three main benefits: more nutritious food, higher yields, pest- and disease-resistance. I'll say a little something about how such crops would particularly benefit the Third World. The benefits are a perfect bridge because I can use Bt corn and "golden" rice to get into the science of genetic modification. Here I'll be fairly superficial since I will be getting into more detail later (or will I? Something to think about). I'll just say that advances in molecular bio & biochem and our increasing understanding of how DNA works within a cell have enabled scientists to add a gene from one species into the genome of another and to adjust its regulation within the new genome. I'll have to decide what other details I want to introduce here. This could be an excellent place to go into the basics of how genes work—transcription factors, the promoter sequence, DNA/RNA, etc. Yes, I like that. Really keeps the science in the forefront. Wherever I do get into these details, I want to use lots of pictures and diagrams to help me. My objective is to see if I can explain the basics of these mechanisms so that people without much science can understand them.

OK, this is looking good. I was worried that the "background" stuff would take over, but if I follow this pattern, I'll be in the "science" pretty much from the start (or at least page 3!). The next step is to talk about the potential for genetic pollution—the spread of altered genes into the wild gene pool. I will have to make it clear that this is only one of many concerns people have about GMOs, but I'll point out that it is potentially a really major problem, since the end result could be changing whole species, at least in certain parts of the world. I need to (briefly) explain the basics of plant reproduction and seeds, since that's where the terminator comes it. Then I'm ready to explain that the terminator addresses the threat of genetic pollution by producing plants that are sterile—that cannot reproduce themselves.

Before I get into the terminator, I want to spend a paragraph (maybe two) on GURT itself. Somewhere in here I will have to acknowledge that this technology is probably driven mainly by the profit motive (companies protecting their patents, forcing farmers to buy seeds every year) but I do have a couple of quotes where the GURT scientists *say* that one reason for the terminator is to protect against genetic pollution. I'll explain t-GURT (one specific trait—traitor technology) and how that works, and then go into v-GURT, restriction for a whole variety, which is the one that the terminator falls into. I'll certainly credit all the sources I've used, but I want to explain my understanding of these mechanisms in my own words. If I have already talked about the basic mechanisms of genes and even genetic splicing, then here I can focus on details of the terminator.

I'll start by saying that this GURT has to allow the plant to produce one generation of fertile seeds—otherwise, the company would have no GM seeds to sell to farmers—but then the terminator is activated to ensure that all second generation seeds are sterile. Then I'll explain how all this works.

The terminator gene creates sterile seeds by encoding a protein such as ribosomal inactivating protein (RIP) whose expression results in cell death. The RIP gene is downstream of a transiently active promoter sequence, which is selected to be active only in the late stages of embryogenesis. This allows the selective killing of cells which are not involved in normal plant development but are required only for the production of viable embryos. Thus the plant can produce viable endosperms, which in the case of rice and corn, for example, is the desired crop product. However, when embryogenesis begins, the RIP gene is expressed and kills the embryo cells, resulting in sterility.

Now I can get into the way scientists inactivate the terminator gene in the first generation of reproduction so seeds are produced that can be sold to farmers. Inactivation is achieved by placing a spacer between the promoter sequence and the RIP gene. The spacer has a lox site at each end, allowing its removal by the Cre recombinase enzyme. The Cre recombinase enzyme, which has also been added as part of this GURT, is not produced in the first generation of this GM crop because its gene is silenced/repressed by a repressor protein that has also been added. The gene for this repressor protein has been given a unique promoter. The promoter ensures that this gene is always on (so there is always repressor protein available) UNLESS a specific chemical is present. After the plant produces the first generation of seeds, these seeds are sprayed with a chemical which represses the recombinase repressor. The recombinase is then expressed and removes the spacer sequence. So when this seed is planted it grows just like a normal plant, except that when it begins embryogenesis, the RIP gene is expressed and kills the embryo cells. The seeds that this second generation plant produces are sterile.

Then, my conclusion: The terminator gene is not a viable strategy for preventing gene pollution in the wild because it is not reliable; a naturally occurring mutation could nullify the terminator sequence. Genetics itself will be my bridge from the way that the terminator is supposed to work to my objections to it as a possible solution to the risk of genetic pollution. I'll explain that mutation is a natural part of genetics—in the wild, over long periods of time, and in various places, genes can (and do) randomly and spontaneously change. A mutation in the targeted crop could nullify the terminator gene, thus allowing this altered crop to reproduce alongside wild types or creating hybrids with wild-types. The GM species could, for example, out-compete the wild type for resources, causing extinction of the wild type. If GMOs do reproduce in the wild, the results could be those feared by individuals opposed to GMOs in general: that is, risks to human health, and changes in the entire species of a particular plant.

When you are satisfied that you have all the main points of your argument in their proper places, and when you have explained to yourself how the parts fit together (the argument "flows" smoothly from one point to the next), you have your first rough draft. Before you do any more drafting, I encourage you to make a map of the territory.

3. Creating a map of the territory

You are now going to take what you've learned from your abstract and put it into the form of a map so that, from now on, you have a convenient way of keeping the overall shape of your argument before you as you continue the writing process. On the following pages are samples of two more visually oriented maps (Samples 1 and 2), as well as a couple of sample sentence outlines (Sample 3). Try each to see what works best for you, although it is very likely that you will develop your own particular form.

When I help students write outlines for arguments, I insist that they write sentence outlines, outlines in which each item is a full grammatical statement. My reason is simple. Topic outlines, the kind of outline that uses only key words, such as,

     I.   Gender differences

    II.   Girl talk

   III.   Boy talk

are often a hindrance rather than a help because **the writer fails to tell herself what she wants to say about the key word(s)**. With this type of topic outline you could easily be inclined to natter on about everything you have learned about gender differences, boy talk, and girl talk, thus creating a sprawling mess rather than a tight, focused argument. Topic outlines work for writers if and when the writers remember what they intend to say about each of those key words. Writers who are still getting used to generating cogent, tight arguments usually function better with sentence outlines since a sentence, by definition, forces them to say something about those key words.

     From an early age, girls and boys learn to use language for different purposes.

     Boys use language in larger groups to establish their place in the hierarchy.

     Girls use language to form and maintain personal relationships.

The sentence outline, as a good map should, reproduces your central argument and thus keeps the argument on track. Another aid in keeping your argument on track is to repeat key words in the statements you write. Those repeated words increase the coherence of the argument, and your prose. They provide a solid base for the development of your ideas, which, in the example below, are differences in the use of language:

     I. From an early age, *girls* and *boys* learn to *use language* for different purposes.

        A. *Boys use language* in larger groups to establish their place in the hierarchy.

        B. *Girls use language* to form and maintain personal relationships.

When you have a map and an abstract you are satisfied with, read subsections E, F, and G, and continue to write with the issues and suggestions there in mind.

A MAP OF THE TERRITORY: SAMPLE 1

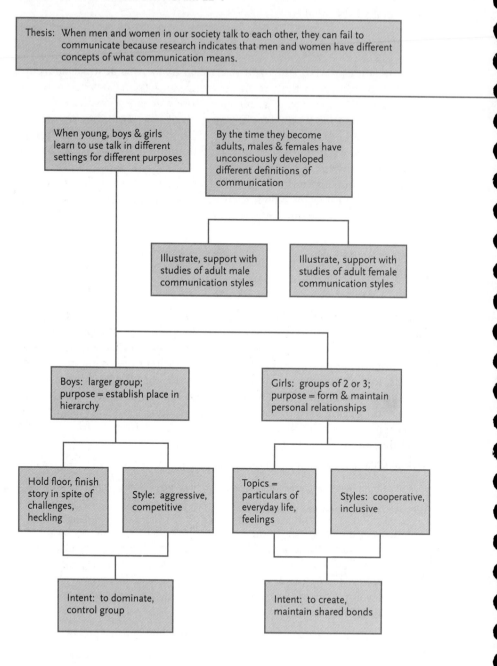

Thesis: When men and women in our society talk to each other, they can fail to communicate because research indicates that men and women have different concepts of what communication means.

When young, boys & girls learn to use talk in different settings for different purposes

By the time they become adults, males & females have unconsciously developed different definitions of communication

Illustrate, support with studies of adult male communication styles

Illustrate, support with studies of adult female communication styles

Boys: larger group; purpose = establish place in hierarchy

Girls: groups of 2 or 3; purpose = form & maintain personal relationships

Hold floor, finish story in spite of challenges, heckling

Style: aggressive, competitive

Topics = particulars of everyday life, feelings

Styles: cooperative, inclusive

Intent: to dominate, control group

Intent: to create, maintain shared bonds

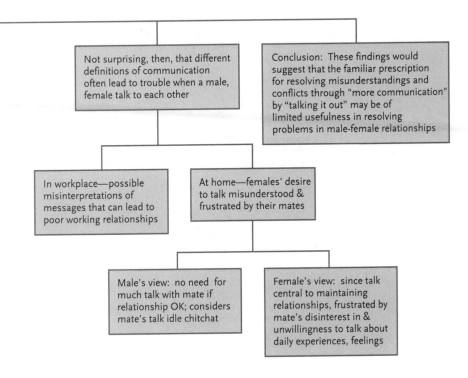

A MAP OF THE TERRITORY: SAMPLE 2

Thesis: Among the many risks associated with genetically modified organisms (GMOs) is the "genetic pollution" that could occur if GMOs reproduced themselves in the wild. An obvious solution would seem to be the terminator gene, a strategy being pursued in genetic use restriction technology (GURT). I will show, however, that the terminator gene is not a viable response to the threat of genetic pollution.

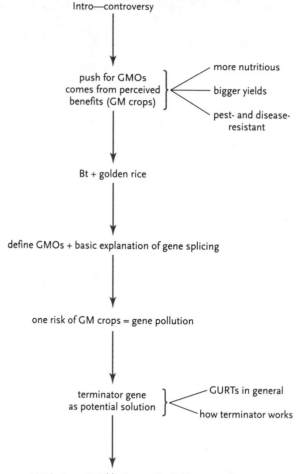

Intro—controversy

push for GMOs
comes from perceived
benefits (GM crops)
— more nutritious
— bigger yields
— pest- and disease-
resistant

Bt + golden rice

define GMOs + basic explanation of gene splicing

one risk of GM crops = gene pollution

terminator gene
as potential solution
— GURTs in general
— how terminator works

terminator not viable since not reliable

A MAP OF THE TERRITORY: SAMPLE 3

Thesis: When men and women in our society talk to each other, they can fail to communicate because research indicates that men and women have different concepts of what "communication" means.

I. When they are young, boys and girls learn to use language in different settings for different purposes.
   A. Boys use talk in groups of three or more other boys for the purpose of establishing their place in the group's hierarchy.
      1. In these settings, boys attempt to "hold the floor" with stories meant to impress their peers; their goal is to complete the story in spite of challenges and heckling from other members of the group.
      2. Boys' communication style in these settings is competitive, and verbally and nonverbally aggressive.
      3. Thus, boys learn to use language to dominate and control groups.
   B. In contrast, girls use talk in smaller groups of two or three other girls for the purpose of forming and maintaining personal relationships.
      1. In these settings, "girl talk" revolves around details of everyday life and what the girls are feeling as well as thinking.
      2. Their communication style is cooperative and inclusive.
      3. Thus, girls learn to use language to create and maintain shared bonds with one another.

II. As a consequence of this early socialization, adult males and females have unconsciously developed different definitions of what "communication" means.
   A. Studies of men's communication style in all-male groups reveal that the objective of talk is to establish status and authority in the group, which men do in talk about activities and things (cars, football, fishing trips, sexual conquests, etc.).
   B. Studies of women's communication style in all-female groups reveal that the objective of talk is to establish personal relationships which they do by sharing personal experiences and feelings.

III. It is not surprising, then, that these different definitions of communication can lead men and women into trouble when they attempt to communicate with each other in both working relationships and intimate relationships.
   A. In the workplace, differences in male and female communication styles can lead to misinterpretation of messages and thus to poor working relationships.
   B. In intimate relationships, females' desire for "more communication" with their mates can be misunderstood and frustrated by their mates.
      1. Since males view language essentially as a means to establish their status and authority, they will tend to talk less when they judge their relationship with their mate to be satisfactory; they will dismiss the talk of their mates about daily experiences and feelings as idle chitchat.
      2. Since females view language as an essential means of establishing and maintaining personal relationships, they will be frustrated by their mate's disinterest in and unwillingness to engage in talk about daily experiences and feelings.

IV. These findings would suggest that the familiar prescription for resolving misunderstandings and conflicts through "more communication," by "talking it out" may be of limited usefulness in resolving problems in male-female relationships.

Thesis: Among the many risks associated with genetically modified organisms (GMOs) is the "genetic pollution" that could occur if GMOs reproduced themselves in the wild. An obvious solution would seem to be the terminator gene, a strategy being pursued in genetic use restriction technology (GURT). I will show, however, that the terminator gene is not a viable response to the threat of genetic pollution.

A. The continuing push for GM crop plants comes from perceived benefits to consumers and farmers, especially those in the Third World.
  1. Genetically modified organisms (GMOs) are organisms whose genetic make-up has been changed by scientists to produce specified effects.
  2. Some of these specified effects are benefits that include:
    a. more nutritious food;
    c. higher yields;
    d. pest- and disease-resistance.
  3. Scientists create GMOs by adding a gene from one species into the genome of another and adjusting its regulation within the new genome.
B. One of the potential risks of GM crops is "genetic pollution"—the spread of altered genes into the "wild" gene pool.
C. The terminator gene could be a solution to the threat of genetic pollution.
  1. Terminator genes are one strategy being pursued in GURT, genetic use restriction technology.
  2. Inserted into the genome of a crop plant that has already been altered to produce one of the beneficial effects noted above, the terminator gene is designed to disable the plant's ability to reproduce.
D. The terminator gene is not a viable response to the threat of genetic pollution because it is not reliable; a naturally occurring mutation could nullify the terminator sequence.

E. Drafting and Revising

No matter which type of research paper you are writing—a report on a study or experiment, a review of the literature, or a critical paper—you should **plan on working through several drafts.** Writing your paper will be far easier if you focus on one mental activity at a time rather than trying to accomplish several tasks at once. In the overview of the writing process, I advised you to work on your paper from whole to part, and what I say now is premised on the assumption that you have already created a map and/or an abstract and that you have a first draft. But just as the research process is not a neat, clean progression from one step to the next, so the writing process tends to be recursive. Some sections of your paper may work according to your plan. But it is also possible that as you develop specific sections and paragraphs, you will discover that your original scenario isn't going to work—or, more interestingly, that you are writing new insights, making connections you hadn't anticipated. As you write, your ideas can change. This happens to writers all the time. The trick is to avoid being over-whelmed by these new possibilities, to avoid feeling as if you are losing control. You can avoid this trap by going back to the whole, going back to the macro level, and making some conscious choices. If a new idea feels "right," revise a main point to accommodate it; change things on your map; try out new connections by sketching a quick abstract. If you remember that the most important thing is to have a coherent picture of the whole paper based on some central purpose, you will always have a sense of direction, even if the particular direction changes. In fact, my major piece of advice as you move into this drafting and revising stage is this: **Be prepared to keep moving back and forth from whole to part and part to whole.**

- After you have a map and/or an abstract that pleases you, you are ready to decide what evidence you are going to use. Review your notes and the summaries of sources that you have written. Read each section of your abstract or outline to remind yourself of the major points you want to make in each section. Select the specific evidence you want to use in each section by using these criteria:

  - What information or evidence helps you *explain* this point?

  - What information or evidence helps you *substantiate* this point?

  - What information or evidence helps you *illustrate* this point?

  Your goal is to end up with separate stacks or groupings of notes that correspond to each section of your paper; these stacks or groupings should include *only* that information or evidence directly relevant to each section. It is very possible that when you have finished sorting you will have notes "left over" that you will not use in the paper. That's fine. Your goal is to write a cogent argument, not to squeeze in everything, whether it fits or not. At the same time, you should be aware that you can substantiate a point with evidence from more than one source, and the more sources you can use to substantiate a point, the stronger your point becomes.

  If you've looked at the table of contents of this book, you will have noticed that I've devoted a separate section to the topic of how to, and how not to, incorporate evidence into your paper. The topic deserves extended discussion because there are ways of incorporating your evidence into your text that can make you seem like a passive sponge. Since you have taken such pains to avoid this trap in the research process up to this point, you don't want to fall into it now. You want to handle your evidence in your paper the way the experts do. When your draft has reached the stage at which you are ready to start using your notes and after you've decided how you are going to keep track of your sources as you write, you've reached a good point to stop and read Section 6.

- Some people prefer to write their papers by hand; others find it easier to compose on the computer. Whichever method you use, once you start the second draft of your paper you have the same objectives. You want a draft that is, at all times, easy to read from beginning to end. And you want to have a flexible, open attitude toward the draft, being ready, willing, and able to make changes that will strengthen your paper—even if these changes involve radical moves such as reordering segments of the text, eliminating or adding paragraphs, or doing major revisions within paragraphs.

Keeping your draft clean enough to read is easy if you are composing on a computer, but if you are writing with pen and paper I'd advise you to write on only one side of each sheet of paper and only on every other line. By writing on every other line and leaving wide margins, you give yourself room to neatly reword sentences or add material without having to recopy the prose you intend to keep. Similarly, if you decide to change the order of paragraphs, you can simply cut apart the sheet of paper and paste or staple the paragraphs as you want them.

Maintaining control of your draft at the same time that you keep a flexible attitude toward it might be easier if you do your drafting in physically separable sections that accord with major divisions of your map. Thus, if you are writing by hand, you could begin each division on a separate sheet of paper. If you are composing on the computer, you could create a separate file for each division. Or, if you prefer to have the entire draft in one file, you could insert page breaks before each division. No matter which method you use, at the beginning of each division, copy over the statement from your map that tells you the purpose of this section of the paper and reminds you what central point you intend to make in it. Composing in this manner helps you to focus your attention on developing the specific point at hand. Because you are working in smaller segments of text, it is easier to revise and reorder parts without losing a sense of their coherence. And, finally, it is easier to change the order of major divisions if such reorganization becomes necessary.

Maintaining control of your draft will also be facilitated by your taking the simple step of numbering the pages of your draft (if you are composing in sections, add a section designation before the page number). A critically important writing strategy (I'll elaborate on it in a minute) is frequently reading your draft from beginning to end. If your pages are numbered, it will take no time to put the draft together in its proper order.

- Moving from section to section, write a more elaborated, although still rough draft of the whole paper. If you realize that you don't have a clear picture of some section, take time to map it out, or do a brief abstract of it. At this stage you should be writing in complete sentences, and you should be looking for the words and sentence structures that best express your ideas—but your focus should still be on capturing those ideas and the flow of your thinking. Don't distract yourself by worrying about spelling or punctuation; if a sentence is clumsy, mark it in some way, so that you can revise it later, and keep moving ahead.

Remember that you are explaining to other people what your ideas are and how they are related. If you expect your readers to understand the point you are making, then you must explain clearly what you are talking about, and you must *show* your readers *exactly* how each idea is related to the others. **Never assume that your readers know what you mean.** Even if these readers are acquainted with your subject matter, they cannot know how you see this subject until you *tell* them how you see it. Such explanations apply to all parts of the paper.

Never introduce facts or information unless you have shown your readers what to do with these facts or this information. Each section, each paragraph of your paper should include a statement (the sooner, the better) that clearly states the point you are making there. As you complete one point and move on to the next, show your readers how the two points are related. Don't assume they know; spell it out. If you feel at any point that you are going off on a tangent or that you are getting lost, refer back to your map. Say to yourself, "What is the point I want to make here?" Or go back and reread the two or three pages that precede the paragraph. Remind yourself where you are going.

• When the various sections have taken on a very solid shape, you will want to be sure that the relationships between the sections are absolutely clear. Spend time developing transitions for the beginning of each section that accomplish these goals: (1) summarize the central point you will be making in this section; (2) tie the central point of this section back to the thesis statement or central idea of your paper; (3) connect the upcoming section with the one that precedes it. Sometimes these objectives can be achieved with one sentence; sometimes you'll need to write a full paragraph.

• Plan to reread the entire draft frequently, matching it against your outline or abstract. As you reread, you are checking to be sure that each section is fitting properly into the overall shape of the paper. When you see a problem, write a note to yourself in the margin, telling yourself what the problem is. You should finish your reading before you stop to revise. Keep working in this fashion, from whole to part to whole, until you feel you have a draft that is ready for a final polish.

• Here's another strategy to help you maintain a picture of the whole. You can use it at any stage of the drafting process. We'll call it the "bird's-eye view." You'll need a paper copy of your entire draft, printed on only one side of each sheet of paper. You'll need a place to lay out this draft so you can see it all at a glance. Large tables in the library work well, as do big bulletin boards, or even walls (if it is legitimate to stick pins into them). Once the draft is all laid out, you need to have a certain physical distance from it, so stand back from the wall, or, if the text is on a table, read it from a standing position. What this exercise enables you to do is to look at sentences and paragraphs in their larger context. It is truly amazing what this bird's-eye view allows writers to see that they were not able to see before. A problem the writer was trying to solve by revising—and revising—two or three sentences turns out to be a problem that will be solved by rearranging ideas on the map! In addition to enabling you to see your text as a whole, this strategy also makes revising as easy as moving pieces of paper to new places. The ease with which you can move pieces of paper to new places also provides an easy way to test different patterns of organization. You can play out the hypothetical "What would happen if. . . ."

- This strategy is one that you can use at any stage of the drafting process. It is particularly helpful if and when you "feel" something is going wrong, but you aren't sure exactly what the problem is. Again, you'll need a paper copy printed on only one side of each sheet of paper, and two pens with different colored ink (the brighter, the better). Go through the draft—or the problem sections of the draft—paragraph by paragraph. In the left margin, write out **the main idea** the paragraph is supposed to be expressing (if it is already expressed in the paragraph as a topic sentence, underline the sentence). In the right margin, write the **purpose or function** of this same paragraph; **what it is supposed to be doing?** For example, in the right margin of this paragraph I would write "Providing another concrete strategy in the hope that it will inspire real revision!" This strategy is a good way to diagnose problems. This exercise may show you, for example, that you are not expressing the main point of the paragraph as clearly and explicitly as you need to. You may find discrepancy in the saying and doing: a paragraph is not saying what it is supposed to say. At other times, when you read down the right margins, you may become aware, from what the paragraphs are doing, that you have abandoned your map and gone off on a tangent. Again, taking this macro view helps you to see more clearly what types of changes you need to make.

- Since you are going to be addressing your paper to your fellow students, you may want to involve one or two of them actively and directly in your writing process. Think about asking one or two members of your class, or someone you know who is a major in the field, to read and respond to your paper as you are writing it. While you can ask for help in spotting mechanical problems (spelling, punctuation, grammatical errors), help of this sort should be requested late in the process, when you consider your paper almost finished. Earlier in the process, while your paper is still in draft form, ask a classmate to *read*—not to edit or to proofread—it to see whether your ideas are coming across clearly and to see how convincing your presentation is. If you ask for help of this sort, tell your reader to concentrate on what you are saying; tell him or her that you are most interested in whether or not your draft is making sense. Some of the points you could ask this reader to respond to are listed below. You will probably want to add to the list, especially requesting information on sections of your draft that don't seem to be working or that you are worried about. Your readers could give their responses to you orally, but if you asked your readers to write their responses, you would have them in front of you when you sit down to revise. And a word of caution: Since your purpose here is to "test" your draft to see whether it is saying what you want it to say, don't prejudice your readers by explaining ahead of time what your main point is or what you are trying to accomplish in this paper. Let the draft speak for itself.

Responses to ask of your reader:

- Tell me the main point of my paper.

- After you have read my paper, sketch out the general direction of and the main points of my argument.

- Did you understand all of my technical terms and language? Were there any that I could have made clearer?

- If there are any places in my paper where you were confused, even for a short period of time, point them out to me and explain to me what confused you.

- Are there any places where you are not convinced by what I say? Where? Why weren't you convinced?

- Do you have any advice or suggestions that you think would make my paper stronger?

Don't feel as if you are obliged to follow every suggestion but do pay close attention to the responses you receive from these readers because they will give you a good notion of the way other readers will process or comprehend your words. Compare your readers' reactions with your intentions for your paper, and make any changes that will clarify your points and make your ideas easier to follow.

F. May I Use the First Person in My Paper? and Other Issues Related to Style

One question that students often ask me when they are writing their research papers is, "May I use *I* in this paper?" I cannot always answer the question for them. Because conventions of style differ from discipline to discipline and from type of paper to type of paper, your instructor is the person who can tell you whether the first person is appropriate in the specific paper you are preparing for him or her. So your safest course is to address specific questions about style to your instructor. However, there are general guidelines that experienced writers use for determining the style and tone of papers (not only research papers but all types of expository writing). In the rest of this subsection I'll briefly discuss some of these guidelines; they could help you determine the most appropriate style for your paper.

   At the beginning of this section I talked about the audience for whom you are writing your paper and the image of yourself that you want to project to this audience. If you think of yourself as a speaker and think about the audience you are addressing, you put your paper in a communication context. If, when you write, you consider yourself communicating with a group of readers, an issue that then arises is, "What is my relationship with the members of my audience?" Determining the relationship between themselves as speakers/writers and their audience/readers helps experienced writers decide the style and tone of the prose they are composing. Let us say, for example, that you are a senior psychology major who has done a research project on teenage drug abuse. You would discuss your work differently if you were writing a letter to a close friend, if you were talking to a class of junior high students, and if you were presenting your work at a conference of social workers, psychologists, and school officials. The differences in the way you present your work are determined by the differences in your relationship with each of these groups.

In writing a letter to a close friend, you would probably be casual. You might use slang and colloquial expressions. You probably wouldn't worry about your sentence structure and punctuation. Instead of presenting your ideas in a tight, logical fashion, you'd probably dash off ideas as they came into your mind. It would be natural to make connections between what you've learned in your study and instances of drug abuse that you've noticed among the people you know. You'd probably refer to events that you and your friend have shared. In other words, a casual or informal style is most appropriate for this communication context because you are "talking" to someone you know very well, someone with whom you share a certain intimacy.

However, in making a presentation on this same study on teenage drug abuse at a conference, your style and tone would change because you have a different relationship with this audience. In a group of psychologists, social workers, and school officials, there would be many people you do not know. Even if some of the members of the audience are friends of yours, this is a "professional" communication situation and you are playing the role of "budding professional." You want the members of the audience to see you as a knowledgeable, reasonable, thoughtful researcher. Because the situation is more formal, you would use a more formal style.

The communication context of the research paper you are now writing is much closer to the presentation of the study on teenage drug abuse at a conference than to writing about the subject to a close friend. Thus your paper will be in a more formal style.

In writing your paper in a more formal style, here are some of the features of your prose that you will want to pay attention to.

- You will want to avoid slang, colloquialisms, and such informal speech mannerisms as "well," "you know," "as I was saying," etc.

  This diction is usually inappropriate in a more formal communication situation because it implies a casual, more intimate relationship with your audience than actually exists. Even if you address your paper to your classmates, you are speaking to them in the more formal context of the classroom. You want them to take you and your work seriously. In formal situations, slang will work against your efforts to communicate, not only because some of your readers may not know what the slang words mean but also because slang tends to be very vague and thus imprecise. Some instructors may consider contractions (*don't, wasn't*) too informal; it would be wise to ask your instructor about this and other stylistic matters before you polish your final draft.

- You will use the technical terminology associated with your subject because it is the most precise language to use; at the same time, in using this language of the discipline, you will always consider the amount of knowledge your audience has about this subject.

  If you are positive that your readers know what a term means (and thus know the concept that it represents), you will use the term without explaining it. If you know your readers do not know the term (and thus the concept it represents), you must be prepared to educate your readers about this concept as you make your own point. And remember: explanations need not be exhaustive. You can tell your readers only what they need to know in order to understand the point you are making.

- In deciding whether to use the first person in your paper, Mary-Claire van Leunen offers a nice rule of thumb: "When you're a part of your story, bring yourself in directly, not in a submerged or twisted way. . . . When you have nothing to do with your story, leave yourself out."[2]

  This simple guideline can also help you decide whether your own personal experiences belong in your paper. From the beginning, were you and your experiences meant to be a part of the subject you were researching? If they were, then references to yourself are an appropriate part of your paper and should be presented in the first person. If you and your personal experiences were not intended to be a part of the subject you were researching, then they probably do not belong in your paper.

  Many of you may have been taught not to use the first person in any expository prose. This ban on the first person is all tied up with the development of the modern scientific method and an approach to knowledge that could be summed up this way: The role of the scientist or researcher is to observe and record phenomena that have no connection with the scientist or researcher herself. Thus, in reporting what she has observed, the researcher or scientist will obviously not appear in the paper. If you are writing a critical paper, however, you are certainly a part of that paper since the inferences and judgments you have made—your ideas—are the major informing element of the paper. This fact does not automatically mean that each of your inferences or judgments should be prefaced with "I think," "I feel," or "It is my opinion." Your readers will assume that inferential and judgmental statements are your inferences and judgments unless you indicate otherwise. It is for this reason that I urge you in Section 6.B.2 to name in your sentences the authors of the ideas that you have taken from your sources.

  If you feel comfortable that you know which ideas are yours and which belong to your sources, and if you realize that your readers will assume that an inference or judgment is yours unless you tell them otherwise, you should find that you really won't have to use the first person very often. You will probably notice that frequently, when you are not reiterating the opinions of

---

[2]*Handbook for Scholars* (New York: Alfred A. Knopf, 1978), 39–40.

other authors, you are saying that the facts speak for themselves; the most accurate way of expressing this idea is, "However, it is clear from the evidence that . . ." or "There is no substantial evidence for these positions." On those few occasions when you feel that you need to tell the reader directly that a certain idea is yours, you should feel free to do so in the first person. If your instructor has told you not to use the first person, you will have to refer to yourself in the third person: "This author has concluded. . . ."; "It is the opinion of this author that. . . ."

- Be very careful about the use of the first person plural (*we, us, our*).

    Such pronouns are appropriate only when they are used to represent a specific group of which you are actually a member and only when you have made it clear to your reader which group you are referring to. If a music teacher is addressing other music teachers about common teaching experiences, he or she could appropriately write, "We music teachers often find that our students . . . ." But don't use the editorial *we* as a roundabout way of saying *I*. And, if the group you are referring to is the human race, it is clearer to say *people* or *human beings* than *we*, at least in initial references to this group.

- Whether or not you use the second person (*you, your*) will again depend on your relationship with your readers and the purpose you have in writing your paper.

    A *you* in a paper automatically means *me* to the reader; if the remark seems to me, the reader, to apply to me, all is well; but I resent it when you make a remark in your paper about *you* (*me*) that I don't think applies to me. Perhaps you've noticed that the second person is usually found in prose intended to instruct readers how to do something or to exhort them to think, feel, or behave in a particular way. If the purpose of your paper is to instruct (as is the purpose of this book) or if it is to exhort your readers to change their ways, then the second person is appropriate. If your paper is not a "how-to" paper or a piece of exhortation, the second person probably isn't appropriate. In my experience students usually use *you*'s in papers because English doesn't have a really satisfactory indefinite third-person singular pronoun. Informally, we use *you* to represent *everybody* or *anybody*, as in "You would think that . . . ." In more formal writing, it is better to use *a person* or *one*— "When embarrassed, *a person (one)* is likely to become hostile or defensive."

- Finally, formal style is usually characterized by paragraphs and sentences that are self-explanatory.

    Because your readers cannot know how you have put your ideas and evidence together, all of these relationships must be made absolutely explicit. This is the reason that writers, in formal communication contexts, usually use a topic sentence that gives their readers an overview of the point that is being introduced; this is the reason that sentences in formal writing tend to be longer and to fall into the category of complex sentences (sentences with one or more dependent clauses).

In talking to a friend, you might appropriately say, "I left the party early. I was sick" and to leave it to the listener to infer a cause–effect relationship. In formal writing, you don't want to take the chance that the reader might not see the cause–effect relationship, so you make it explicit: "I left the party because I was not feeling well."

The need for precision is the other reason that sentences tend to be longer in formal writing. You want to qualify your point so that the statement is exact: "In this case, Outer Slobovia concluded that if it did not send troops to the Isle of Herron, it risked losing the support of its allies, Inner Slobovia and Alcimene."

As a writer addressing a group of people whom you do not know very well, your major objective is your readers' complete understanding of your exact point. Thus, above all, you want your prose to be clear and precise. You can judge the clarity of your prose by asking, "Will my readers comprehend my point after one reading of this sentence or paragraph?" You can judge the precision of your prose by asking, "Will my readers see exactly what I mean here?" Because it is not always easy to answer these questions on your own, you can see the advantage of asking one or two other students to read and respond to your drafts.

Before I leave this issue of formal style, I must warn you that formality of style is not measured by the "look" or the "sound" of the words on the page. To put it another way, you are not making your paper more formal if you simply search around for the longest, classiest words you can find and then string them together in phrases that have a certain "ring" to them—"the proposition of annihilation tactics"; "integrated monitored hardware."

I realize that you may be tempted to throw big words around in long, convoluted sentences because such sentences seem to look and sound like the sentences of the authors you've been reading. It is natural for you to assume that you need to impress your readers and that the best way to impress them is to sound impressive. I see papers every day that are collections of such impressive-sounding sentences; unfortunately, very often they don't communicate any ideas. A few years ago when I was discussing a collection of such sentences with Tony Abena, the student who had written them, he had a flash of insight: "I'm writing to impress, not to express," he said. I am borrowing Tony Abena's phrase because it says so well what many students do when they are trying to write in a formal style.

My usual response to the student who is working harder to impress me than to communicate with me is this. Words carry meanings for me. If a particular group of words doesn't make sense to me, I'm not impressed; I'm confused, frustrated and irritated. What impresses me is the idea that is expressed, the idea that is carried by the words. So if you want to impress your readers, choose those words and phrases that best represent the idea you have in your mind. Those people who are worth impressing are too smart to be snowed by an avalanche of meaningless verbiage.

G. Summary

Some students tend to lose momentum when it comes time to write the paper that ends the research process. When they feel they have figured out their answer to their research question, it seems bothersome, boring, or redundant to have to put it all down on paper. The pressure of the deadline doesn't help, especially since other papers, tests, or assignments are usually due about the same time. If you find yourself being tempted to slack off at this stage, here are some things you should tell yourself.

First, writing the paper is still a very critical part of the thinking process. You may "feel" you know what you think, but you won't really *know* until you say it to yourself or another person. Writing the paper gives you the opportunity to go through this process. It is the final and crucial "sharpening" phase of the whole thinking/research process. I know this from my own experiences with writing and from the hours I have spent with students. Students tell me they know what they think, but as they try to express their ideas, they often just give me disconnected bits and pieces. Our talking together about a paper has the effect of bringing these pieces into a unified whole and often brings to light connections they didn't realize they saw. What students and I are doing together in these conversations is going through the same mental processes that a writer goes through in composing a paper. So think of the whole formal writing process, from determining the paper's overall shape and purpose through the various drafts, as an important intellectual challenge—the challenge of refining your ideas into a form that is clear and meaningful and the challenge of giving other people good reasons for accepting your view of your subject.

Second, it is also very important for you to attend to details that may be more mechanical than creative. When you have read over the entire draft from beginning to end and are satisfied that your ideas are spelled out so clearly that your readers will have no trouble following you, you have a final rough draft. Only two steps remain:

- The first involves formally documenting all the material you've taken from your sources. I cover this topic in detail in Section 8, and, in Appendixes A through D, I provide the basics of four documentation styles used in academic texts.

- The second involves transforming your final rough draft into the polished text of your paper. This step will require your setting aside sufficient time to thoroughly copyedit and proofread the final rough draft, attending to matters from format to smoothing out rough sentences to correcting errors in spelling, punctuation, grammar. If you've done your composing with pen and paper, this step will include the typing of the paper. In the polishing phase of the writing process your attention will be focused on surface features of your text, being sure your paper is free of all errors.

I cover the topic of polishing your draft in Section 7. When you reach the point that you are satisfied that you have said what you need to say—or when your deadline forces this decision upon you, turn to that section.

If you need encouragement to save enough time and energy for this polishing step, call upon your pride of ownership, or the value you place on putting your best foot forward, or the perfectionist in you—the one who says, "If it's worth doing, it's worth doing well." Attention to detail is important in writing. Misspelled words, errors in grammar, and sloppiness in documentation form can dominate readers' perceptions—and judgment—of your work. At best, these technical problems will irritate readers and distract their attention from what is being said in the paper. At worst, readers can interpret a writer's lack of attention to such details as a sign that the writer doesn't put much value on his or her work. Thus, readers may conclude that they shouldn't take the work very seriously either. You have put a great deal of time and energy into developing your views of your subject. I would assume that now you want your readers to focus on what you have to say, that you want to hear what your readers think about your ideas. Is it worth taking the risk that your readers' first comments will be about technical mistakes?

SECTION

6

How to and How Not to Incorporate Your Evidence into Your Paper

A. If You Don't Use and Acknowledge Your Sources Properly, You May End Up Plagiarizing

I don't like beginning this section with an unpleasant subject, but plagiarism is a serious offense and, considering all the efforts you have made to develop and express your own views of your subject, you certainly do not want your instructor to accuse you of having plagiarized parts of the paper you hand in. In my experience in working with students who are writing research papers, I have found that much plagiarism is unintentional. Papers, or parts of papers, are plagiarized not because the student intended to plagiarize but because the student either did not know how to use sources properly or because the student did not know how to acknowledge sources properly. To express it negatively, the purpose of this section is to save you from falling into unintentional plagiarism; to express it more positively, the purpose of this section is to show you how experienced writers follow the basic rule of using the ideas and works of others: giving credit where credit is due.

1. What plagiarism is

Quite simply, plagiarism is theft. Common thieves take cars, stereos, silverware, and other material goods that legally belong to others. Plagiarists steal the words, the ideas, and /or the work that rightfully belong to others. Plagiarists then present these words, ideas, and/or work as if this material were their own words, ideas, or work.

Just as there are laws against taking the material goods that belong to another, so there are laws against plagiarism. If you were to copy an article or a section of a book and publish this work under your own name, clearly implying that this work was yours, you could be taken to a court of law. But you do not have to publish plagiarized material to be in serious trouble. College instructors put plagiarism in the same category as cheating on exams, and offenders may be punished with stiff penalties.

I hope it is obvious that you would be guilty of plagiarism if you intentionally passed off the work, the ideas, or the words of another person as your own. You'd be guilty of plagiarism if you put your name on a paper that you found in the file of your fraternity, or one you purchased from a paper mill, or one you downloaded from a Web site. You would also be guilty of plagiarism if you failed to put quotation marks around words that you copied from one of your print sources, or that you copied-and-pasted from a Web site, even if you cite the source! You'd be in trouble if all or part of your paper was illegitimate paraphrase (see subsection B.3).

Occasionally, students are guilty of premeditated or intentional plagiarism. They consciously attempt to pass off the work of others as their own, or they buy a term paper written by someone else. But as I've said, many cases of plagiarism are cases of unintentional plagiarism. I am sure that you don't want to be one of those students who plagiarize without realizing that they are plagiarizing.

2. Common sources of unintentional plagiarism

If plagiarism is the act of presenting the words, ideas, or work of others as if they were your own, then the proper use of the work of others requires that you

always give credit where credit is due.

Or, to put it another way, in our papers we frankly tell our readers that we are making use of the material of another, and we give our readers all the information they need to find and read the original source. In academic circles the two basic ways we give credit where credit is due are these:

- We frankly acknowledge to our readers that a certain idea or work has been taken from other sources by saying so in the text of the paper and/or by documenting the sources of these ideas in our papers. In Section 8 and the appendixes that follow, I introduce you to four styles of documentation commonly used in academia. Although there are differences among them, each is an accepted method of giving credit where credit is due.

- We frankly acknowledge to our readers that the words we are using are the words of another person by putting these words in quotation marks *and* documenting that source by using one of the accepted styles of documentation. I talk more about the proper ways of quoting material in subsection B.4.

Often students neglect to follow these simple procedures for giving credit where credit is due. Here are some of the reasons I've discovered for unintentional plagiarism:

- **One major source of unintentional plagiarism is carelessness in the research process.**

  In Section 4, you'll remember, I stressed the importance of having systems for keeping track of your evidence and being very careful when you take notes. One reason for such measures is to avoid the risk of unintentional plagiarism.

  You can, if you are sloppy, fail to make a record of the source of a piece of evidence (forgetting to record the author or the title of the work or the page number on which this information was given). Or you could fail to keep a complete record of the necessary bibliographic information for the source. If, when you write your paper, you want to use this information, you are going to have trouble giving the credit you are expected to give.

  In Section 4, I also stressed how important it is to put quotation marks around the exact words of an author when you are taking notes. If your note doesn't indicate that the words are the words of the author, you will assume that these words are yours and thus fail to give credit where credit is due. If you are not careful to paraphrase properly, you may have notes that are illegitimate paraphrases (see subsection B.3)

  Thus, carelessness in the research process can lead to inadvertent plagiarism.

- **Another source of unintentional plagiarism is sloppiness while writing your paper.**

  You may fall into plagiarism if you fail to keep track of the sources of your evidence in your drafts as you write and revise your paper. You can avoid this source of unintentional plagiarism easily by developing a system of noting your sources as you write (see Section 5.A.3).

- **A more general source of unintentional plagiarism is ignorance of the "giving-credit-where-credit-is-due" rule.**

  Many students fall into plagiarism because they do not know that they are obliged to give credit where credit is due or because they do not know the proper ways to give such credit.

- **Perhaps the most common source of unintentional plagiarism is the "passive-sponge" approach to research.**

  If a student mindlessly gathers great quantities of information without digesting, thinking about, and assessing this information as she researches, it is very easy for her to plagiarize because she can easily assume that everything she reads is, somehow, *the truth*. She will not see a need to document sources or to give credit to specific experts because she will assume that all the evidence she gathered falls into the category of received truth or common knowledge.

Or a passive sponge may panic when he sits down to write his paper. Suddenly he may realize that all he has is material that belongs to others. Because he has not been developing his own ideas, he is trapped into following the ideas in his sources. He may conclude—probably accurately—that everything in his paper will have to be acknowledged as belonging to others. He may find himself using long passages from his sources, either quoting directly or falling into illegitimate paraphrase. Overwhelmed and oppressed by the idea of having to document everything in the paper because the paper actually belongs to his sources, he may rebel and document haphazardly.

Throughout this book I have attempted to save you from falling into the traps that lie in wait for passive sponges. Saving you from unintentional plagiarism is only one reason why I have stressed taking control of your research project from the very beginning of the process. But obviously one of the advantages of taking control of the research process from the beginning is that, when you reach the point of writing your papers, you have a clear sense of your own ideas and the debts you owe to others. Thus, if you have taken your notes carefully and systematically, if you have maintained a working bibliography, and especially if you have used your Researcher's Notebook as I have advised you to do, you have the necessary basic foundation for avoiding plagiarism.

However, you may still have questions about the best way of incorporating your evidence into your text and the best way of giving credit where credit is due. These are the issues I will discuss in the rest of this section. So when you have a good, solid first rough draft of your paper, when you have developed a system for keeping track of your sources as you write and revise, and when you have reviewed your evidence and decided what you want to use, you should stop and read all of the subsections of this section.

B. Using and Acknowledging Your Sources . . . Properly

Obvious signs of plagiarism are not the only problems instructors find in the way that students use, or abuse, sources. Whenever I read a student paper that includes a large number of direct quotations, particularly a large number of *long* direct quotations, I worry that I am reading the paper of a student who has allowed herself to be used by her sources. Instead of writing a paper in which she expresses her own point of view, supported by evidence from various sources, she is letting others write her paper for her. Whenever I read a paper in which the same source is cited in paragraph after paragraph, or page after page, I worry that I am reading another paper in which a student has allowed himself to be used by his sources. Instead of developing and formulating his own point of view, this student is content to repeat the argument of one of his sources.

Throughout the research process your goal has been to use your sources, rather than having your sources use you.

Now, at this last stage of the research process, you do not want to fall victim to your sources. So I will repeat, one last time, that in your paper you are articulating and presenting *your* perception of the subject you have been investigating. The phrase "your perception of the subject" should not be read as "a completely new, original, unique perception of the subject." Your conclusions will probably not be startlingly new; but coming to radically new perceptions of a subject isn't the ordinary experience of experts, either. Teachers do not expect your papers to be original in this sense. Rather, what they will expect to see in your papers are obvious and clear signs that *you* have made *your own decisions* about the way the intellectual puzzle you have been working on should be put together. A passive-sponge paper sounds like a person who would say to you, "Mom has told me not to major in chemistry because. . . . " A researcher-as-detective paper sounds like the person who says "I have decided to major in geology because, as my dad says, geology is. . . . Also, as Aunt Jane points out, a geology major would. . . . Besides, several people who have majored in geology have found that. . . . "

Confidence is the key, the confidence that you have drawn your own conclusion and that there is a solid basis for it. Just as it is natural for my hypothetical student to explain her decision to major in geology by calling on arguments and facts offered by her father and her Aunt Jane and other majors, so in your paper you should find that you automatically refer to the sources from which you have drawn to form your conclusion. You should find it natural to say, "After considering the theories of X, Y, and Z, I find that Z's argument is most convincing because . . . " or "I agree with Doe's assessment of the problem." Because you have worked out your own picture of the puzzle, you won't be tempted to present Doe's or Z's argument in great detail because you know that their arguments are their perceptions of the puzzle and, while you agree with their general perceptions, you have your own reasons for doing so. You will use Doe's work, or Z's, and that of your other sources as it suits your needs.

I urged you to do your first full draft without your notes so that you would have the confidence that I've been talking about. Now that you have this confidence, let's talk about using those sources you've decided are relevant.

1. Use what you need, where you need it— and document what you've used

In most cases, as you write your paper, you should find that the evidence you are using is either

discrete pieces of information from your sources

or

summaries of the conclusions, work, or opinions of one or more of the experts you've read.

Using sources does not imply quoting the sources directly and, in fact, you should be very judicious in using direct quotations. **Look upon direct quotations** only as supporting evidence, never as a substitute for your own expression of the point you want to make. You should use the exact words of others *only* when the expert's words are the best or most direct illustration of the expert's point of view. In subsection B.4, I talk at length about how to quote your sources effectively and properly. But here, let me illustrate what I mean when I say that in most cases you will be using discrete pieces of information or summarizing the work or conclusions of others.

a. Using discrete pieces of information

EXAMPLE 1 (DOCUMENTED IN THE CMS NOTES & BIBLIOGRAPHY STYLE)

THE BODY OF YOUR PAPER

> Unfortunately, these experiences of Kashay, Leroy, and Juan are far from unique, as unemployment rates over the past thirty years clearly show.[12] Back in 1973, for example, the unemployment rate for whites was 4.3%, but for persons of Hispanic origins it was 7.5%, and, for African Americans, it was over double the figure for whites, standing at 9.4%. Almost thirty years later, in December 2001, the rate for whites was 5.1%, that for Hispanics was 7.9%, and that for African Americans, again, was double the figure for whites, at 10.2%. In 1992, when the U.S. was experiencing a recession, unemployment for whites rose to 6.6%. But the rate for Hispanics was almost twice as high, up to 11.6%, and that for African Americans was a steep 14.2%. In spite of the ups and downs of the economy, the trend has been for unemployment rates for Hispanics to be a third again as high as they are for whites, and those for African Americans to be double the rates that whites experience.

YOUR NOTE

Some stats on unemployment rates—U.S.

	All civilian workers	Men over 20	Women over 20	Whites	Blacks	Persons of Hispanic origins
1973	4.9	3.3	4.9	4.3	9.4	7.5
1992	7.5	7.1	6.3	6.6	14.2	11.6
Dec. 2001	5.8	5.2	5.2	5.1	10.2	7.9

Business Statistics
Strawer, ed.
p. 130, Table 8.3

YOUR FOOTNOTE

12. The unemployment figures in this paragraph taken from *Business Statistics of the United States*, ed. Cornelia Strawer, 8th ed. (Lanham, MD: Bernan Press, 2002), 130, table 8.3.

Example 2 (documented in the MLA style)

The Body of Your Paper

In considering the dilemmas faced by Iranian women who consider themselves both feminists and Muslims, one must keep in mind two central points about the Islamic religion. The first is that the essence of Islam is submission (Goldziher 3–4). The other is that the Islamic religion pervades all aspects of the state. Whereas in Western countries one can distinguish between the laws of a particular religion and the secular laws of the state (i.e., civil and criminal codes), in an Islamic state all the laws of the country are dictated by the religious laws (Goldziher 54).

Your notes

"Islam means submission, the believer's submission to Allah. The word expresses, first and foremost, a feeling of dependency on an unbounded omnipotence to which man must submit and resign his will. . . . Submission is the dominant principle inherent in all manifestations of Islam: in its ideas, forms, ethics, and worship."

> Goldziher
> Islamic Theology & Law
> pp. 3-4

"But the conduct of life in conformity to the law includes more than ritual. For in Islam, religious law encompasses all legal branches: civil, criminal, and constitutional."

> Goldziher
> Islamic Theology & Law
> p. 54

Your List of Works Cited

Goldziher, Ignaz. Introduction to Islamic Theology and Law. Trans. Andras and Ruth Hamori. Modern Classics in Near Eastern Studies. Princeton, NJ: Princeton UP, 1981.

b. Summarizing the work of others

Example 1 (documented in the APA style)

The Body of Your Paper

Recent studies indicate that direct intervention by a teacher can reduce disruptive behavior in the classroom (Hall & Jenkins, 2005; Klein, Jerome, & Fielding, 2002; Smith, Watkins, & Hemingway, 2006).

YOUR NOTES AND DOCUMENTATION

You arrived at this generalization after reviewing the summaries you wrote of the articles by Hall and Jenkins, by Klein, Jerome, and Fielding, and by Smith, Watkins, and Hemingway. You specify the studies to which you are referring by giving the author and date of each article. In the reference list at the end of your paper you will have a separate entry for each in which you give full bibliographic information for that source.

EXAMPLE 2 (DOCUMENTED IN THE CMS NOTES & BIBLIOGRAPHY STYLE)

THE BODY OF YOUR PAPER

H. N. Hirsch's study of the life of Supreme Court Justice Felix Frankfurter illustrates one way in which psychobiography can be used by historians and political scientists.[21]

YOUR NOTES AND DOCUMENTATION

Either at the bottom of the page or in a list of notes at the end of your paper, you provide the following reference:

21. H. N. Hirsch, *The Enigma of Felix Frankfurter* (New York: Basic Books, 1981). See pp. 3-10 for Hirsch's views of psychobiography.

Since your reference is to the entire book, the note in your paper need not give any specific page numbers. However, the notes you took while reading Hirsch's book remind you that Hirsch discusses the how's and why's of his use of psychological theories in the first chapter of this biography. Since this general approach to biography is the theme you are pursuing in your paper, you suggest that your readers look at this first chapter (pp. 3–10).

EXAMPLE 3 (DOCUMENTED IN THE MLA STYLE)

THE BODY OF YOUR PAPER

According to most film critics, there is nothing special about Richard Carlsbad's Rest on Sunday. Henry Griffin doesn't even mention it in The Top Movies of the 70's, even though he singles out two other Carlsbad movies as worthy of high praise. In her exhaustive study of Carlsbad's work, Sally Smith dismisses Rest as one of his more mediocre efforts (215–17). However, while Rest on Sunday may not be a great example of cinema, I'd suggest it has value as social commentary. Renata Silverstein has made a convincing argument in "What Movies Tell Us" that popular entertainment is like a mirror, reflecting a society's mores and values. Following Silverstein, I will show that Rest gives us some important insights into the culture of America in the 1970s.

YOUR NOTES AND DOCUMENTATION

The basic method of citing a source in the MLA style is to use the name of the author in the body of your paper. In the list headed "Works Cited" at the end of your paper, you will give full bibliographic information for the books and articles written by Griffin, Smith, and Silverstein as well as for Carlsbad's film *Rest*. Since you are alluding only to the general points of view of these particular authors, there are no specific pages to which you need to refer your readers. The one exception are the pages on which Smith analyzes *Rest*; you include these to enable readers to quickly find the place in Smith's book where she discusses this film on which your paper focuses. Because your list of works cited includes only one work by Griffin and Silverstein, you aren't required to mention the titles of these sources, but you chose to do so because these titles reiterate and reinforce the point you are making in this paragraph.

2. Experts openly acknowledge their sources in the body of their papers; so should you

Defense Minister Jose Pampuro said that [President Nestor] Kirchner planned to remove more than 20 army generals, 13 admirals and 12 air force generals—half of the armed forces' top command. Pampuro said the changes were the most comprehensive over-haul since the military returned power to civilian control in 1983.

The move came only three days after Kirchner was sworn in as Argentina's presi-dent and political and military analysts here said the effort was intended to assert his authority, ensure stability and put into key positions younger officers loyal to him who have demonstrated little interest in civilian politics.

"Kirchner knows that the military is no threat to his leadership," said Oscar Rezende, a political analyst here.

> Jon Jeter, "Commanders Purged in Argentina," *Washington Post*, May 29, 2003, A22. Copyright © 2002 *The Washington Post*, reprinted with permission.

In his autobiography, *Seventy Years in Archaeology*, published in 1932, Sir William Matthew Flinders Petrie, one of the towering figures in the recovery of the Near Eastern heritage, observed ominously that "the perils of discoveries are by no means over when they reach a museum."

> Jed Perl, "Raping Beauty," *New Republic*, June 2, 2003, 26. Copyright © 2003 by *New Republic*. Reprinted with permission.

Journalists must indicate the sources of their information in the body of their stories because this is their only opportunity to document their sources. But if you look at the scholarly books and articles you've been reading, you will see that the experts also take every opportunity to name the source of their information in the body of their texts, as well as giving complete bibliographic information in notes or reference lists. They recognize a principle that journalists have long been aware of—naming the source of certain information not only acknowledges the source of the information but also lends more credibility to the information.

Thus, as you work on the drafts of your paper, whenever possible you should name the source of the information you are using in the sentence you write. Particularly, you should give the names of the experts whose opinions you are summarizing or quoting.

Here are a few examples from published works that show how the experts acknowledge the sources of their evidence in the body of their texts.

In his brilliant, if unfortunately posthumous, essay, "The Heroic Paradox,"[63] Cedric Whitman meditates on the hardest center of Greek heroism, Akhilleus, who in his view alternates between a search for a "divine" autonomy and the desire to be reconnected to humanity: "A man may assert his divine absolutism and thus in some sense 'become a god,' but then also after some fashion he ceases to be a human being, and he has no communication with anyone."[64]

> Dean A. Miller, *The Epic Hero* (Baltimore: The Johns Hopkins Press, 2000), 378.

According to the NRC, one of the dominant activation products and a major source of radioactivity aside from the fuel is cobalt 60.

> Matthew L. Wald, "Dismantling Nuclear Reactors," *Scientific American,* March 2003, 65.

Examples of opposing theories can be found in Köhler and Moscovitch's (1997) outstanding review on unconscious visual processing.

> Alberto Zani and Alice Mado Proverbio, *The Cognitive Electrophysiology of Mind and Brain* (New York: Academic Press, 2003), 7.

Anecdotal evidence is also provided by Morton (1996), Graham (1995) and MacDonald, Brooker, and Hewitt (1995), which suggests that taking into account the views of students has proven helpful in changing teaching practices and restructuring formal evaluative reports.

> Deborah Lee and David Gavine, "Goal-Setting and Self-Assessment in Year 7 Students," *Educational Research* 45 (Spring 2003): 51.

The spectacular light and color of *A Twilight in the Catskills* caught the eye of many of the critics. "The brilliance of this picture almost fills the room, and we doubt if any one enters without his eyes being attracted involuntarily to the spot," remarked the writer for the *New York Daily Tribune.*[6] Another correspondent described the painting's sky as "delicately woofed with opalescent and topazescent clouds, culminating in tufts of ruby or fading into an enriched saffron purple in a celestial twilight of pyrotechnic that glows a moment and then is lost forever."[7] The critic for the *Times* was impressed by the "deep plum color foncée of the mountain ridge" and "richest orange and crimson of the late Summer-glory."[8]

> Adam Greenhalgh, "'Darkness Visible': *A Twilight in the Catskills* by Sanford Robinson Gifford," *American Art Journal* 32, no. 1 & 2 (2001): 47-48. Copyright © 2001 American Art Journal. Reprinted with permission.

It is interesting that, despite the advent and great success of relativity theory and quantum mechanics, the classic problems of light and action at a distance remain, as Wilczek has illustrated in his essay on *The Persistence of Ether.*[60]

> Colin Pask, "Mathematics and the Science of Analogies," *American Journal of Physics* 71 (2003): 533.

As an alternative, we draw from scholars who have developed similar ironic frames in approaching the theory and practice of law (Facher, 1999; Lewis, 1994; Patten, 2000; Rorty, 1989, pp. 73-78; Strickland & Strickland, 1994).

> Marouf Hasian, Jr., and Geoffrey D. Klinger, "Sarah Roberts and the Early History of the 'Separate but Equal' Doctrine: A Study in Rhetoric, Law, and Social Change," *Communication Studies* 53 (Fall 2002): 270.

Thus Durkheim's argument according to which every society needs shared beliefs that "belong to the group and unify it" is still valid.[27]

> Gilbert Rist, *The History of Development: From Western Origins to Global Faith*, trans. Patrick Camiller, rev. ed. (London: Zed Books, 2002), 227.

After conferring with his like-minded attorney general, James Brown, on January 13, 1794, Governor Shelby dispatched a forceful letter to the secretary of state. "I have great doubts," he wrote, "whether there is any legal authority to restrain or punish" Clark and his expedition.

> Jon Kukla, *A Wilderness So Immense: The Louisiana Purchase and the Destiny of America* (New York: Alfred A. Knopf, 2003), 175.

The mode of relationship that Miller calls instrumental association is embodied in the economy.

> Daniel Attas, "Markets and Desert," in *Forms of Justice: Critical Perspectives on David Miller's Political Philosophy*, ed. Daniel A. Bell and Avner de-Shalit (Lanham, MD: Rowman & Littlefield Publishers, 2003), 87.

A significant and informative study of this type is that performed by Timothy Bradley, Michael Rose, and their coworkers on desiccation resistance in the fruit fly *Drosophila melanogaster* (e.g., Gibbs et al. 1997; Chippindale et al. 1998; Bradley et al. 1999; Folk et al. 2001).

> Albert F. Bennett, "Experimental Evolution and the Krogh Principle: Generating Biological Novelty for Functional and Genetic Analyses," *Physiological and Biochemical Zoology* 76 (2003): 5. Copyright © 2003 University of Toronto Press.

Certainly, some critics, such as Susan Carlson, do suggest that optimism characterizes not only feminist comedies, but female-authored comedies generally. Other critics, like Gloria Kaufman, argue that feminist comedy contains an explicit, and sometimes implicit, didactic and revolutionary purpose: "The persistent attitude that underlies feminist humor is the attitude of social revolution—that is, we are ridiculing a social system that can be, that must be changed" (13).

> Celeste Derksen, "A Feminist Absurd: Margaret Hollingsworth's *The House That Jack Built*," *Modern Drama* 45 (Summer 2002): 223.

To live for the moment is the prevailing passion—to live for yourself, not for your predecessors or posterity. We are fast losing the sense of historical continuity, the sense of belonging to a succession of generations originating in the past and stretching into the future. It is the waning of the sense of historical time—in particular, the erosion of any strong concern for posterity—that distinguishes the spiritual crisis of the seventies from earlier outbreaks of millenarian religion, to which it bears a superficial resemblance. Many commentators have seized on this resemblance as a means of understanding the contemporary "cultural revolution," ignoring the features that distinguish it from the religions of the past. A few years ago, Leslie Fiedler proclaimed a "New Age of Faith." More recently, Tom Wolfe has interpreted the new narcissism as a "third great awakening," an outbreak of orgiastic, ecstatic religiosity. Jim Hougan, in a book that seems to present itself simultaneously as a critique and a celebration of contemporary decadence,

compares the current mood to the millennialism of the waning Middle Ages. "The anxieties of the Middle Ages are not much different from those of the present," he writes.
Then, as now, social upheaval gave rise to "millenarian sects."

> Christopher Lasch, *The Culture of Narcissism: American Life in an Age of Dimin-*
> *ishing Expectations* (New York: W. W Norton and Co., 1978), 5.

Look at each of these examples. Notice how, in each, the author includes at
least the last name of the expert whose work he or she refers to and makes it
clear in the body of the text that the ideas outlined or the words quoted belong
to the person named. These published writers show you how you can acknowledge your sources directly in the body of your paper.

I have included the longer example from Christopher Lasch to show you
how one expert, Lasch, uses other experts to make his point. Lasch's point is
stated in the third sentence: "It is the waning of the sense of historical time—in
particular, the erosion of any strong concern for posterity—that distinguishes
the spiritual crisis of the seventies from earlier outbreaks of millenarian religion,
to which it bears a superficial resemblance." He points out that others (Fiedler,
Wolfe, and Hougan) have seen a resemblance between the cultural revolution of
the seventies and millenarian movements of the past but continues with his own
argument that the resemblance is superficial by arguing that Fiedler, Wolfe, and
Hougan fail to see important differences between the previous millenarian
movements and the cultural movement of the seventies. In the paragraph following the one I have quoted, Lasch shows what he considers the flaws in their
thinking. But first he must establish that these three men do see the current spiritual crisis as a religious awakening. The purpose of this paragraph is to make
Lasch's idea clear to his readers; he uses Fiedler, Wolfe, and Hougan to make his
own argument.

3. Summarizing the work and ideas of another expert: How experienced writers do it

Because, in your paper, you are using the work of others, rather than having the
work and ideas of others use you, in most cases you will need only a sentence or
two to summarize the work and ideas of others. You will have selected what you
need from these sources and you will put this material into a paragraph, similar
to the one I quoted from Lasch in the last subsection, in which you are developing your own idea. Occasionally, however, you may decide that you need to give
more information about the ideas or argument of a particular author.

If you find yourself giving a detailed, extended summary of an author's idea
or argument, be very careful. In these situations you run the risk of letting your
source take over your paper, which can all too easily lead you into a form of
plagiarism that I call illegitimate paraphrase. Let us say, for example, that you
are reading a paper on the American Civil War and you come across this passage:

> Eighty-seven years earlier the Founding Fathers had brought forth a new nation on this
> continent, born in liberty and dedicated to the idea that all men are created equal. But

this nation was now engaged in a great civil conflict, testing whether the United States or any country set up on the principles upon which the United States was founded could continue to endure. People on the Union side met on a famous battlefield of the civil war. They were there to dedicate part of this battlefield as a final resting-place for those who gave their lives that the nation might live. They were there to dedicate themselves to a large task that still remained before them. From those who died they would take increased devotion to the cause for which these men died. They resolved that these dead should not have died in vain; that this nation, under God, should have a new birth of freedom; and that government of the people, by the people, for the people should not perish from the earth.

Your first reaction will probably be, "Why, that's Lincoln's Gettysburg Address!" You recognize Lincoln's famous speech because this passage is the Gettysburg Address with only a few words and phrases changed here and there. If I ran across this passage in a paper, I would consider this passage plagiarized. I would consider it plagiarized first of all because there is no mention of Lincoln or his speech. But even if the author of this passage had prefaced the passage by saying, "As Lincoln said at Gettysburg," I'd still consider the passage an illegitimate paraphrase because what are expressed in this passage are essentially Lincoln's ideas and words, not the writer's. The ideas are introduced in the same order in which Lincoln introduced his ideas, and the relationship among the ideas expressed here is exactly the relationship Lincoln expressed. The writer has done nothing but change a few words and phrases; the difference between Lincoln's address and this paraphrase is that the passage is slightly less precise than the actual Gettysburg Address, and much less eloquent.

In your efforts to understand the ideas of others you may find it helpful to take a passage from a work and do a paraphrase like the preceding one. Your purpose would be to change unusual language into words that are more meaningful to you in order to increase your comprehension of the author's ideas. But such direct paraphrases do not belong in the papers you write. You would go through the exercise of doing a paraphrase so that you could ultimately express your understanding of the author's idea, so that you could reach your own conclusions about what the author means. Having digested the basic ideas of another person, in your paper you will want to express, in your own words, your understanding of what this author is saying. In your paper you will use summaries, not paraphrases; and in these summaries you will clearly indicate to your readers that you are talking about the ideas of another person, and you will put in quotation marks those phrases and sentences that are taken directly from the source.

A legitimate summary of Lincoln's address would look like this:

In his short but eloquent dedication of the cemetery at Gettysburg in 1863, Lincoln focuses his audience's attention on the Union's cause, the preservation of the United States as it was constituted eighty-seven years earlier. Time and again he returns to ideas formalized in the Declaration of Independence and the Constitution, reminding the audience that the United States was "dedicated to the proposition that all men are created equal" and that it is a "government of the people, by the people, for the people."

If, as you are writing your paper, you find yourself slipping into close paraphrase of one of your sources, it is time to step back from your paper and ask yourself why you are following your source in such detail. Is this author's argument or idea central to *your* argument? How? What is your point? What is the relationship between the author's point and your point? You should not continue with a detailed summary of an expert's argument until you know exactly why you are using this material and until you know what point you want to make about it.

If, after considering the issues I have just raised, you decide that a more extensive description of another person's idea is critical to your argument, follow these guidelines in doing your summary:

- Determine what *your* point is. Write your point in a sentence (that sentence would probably make a good topic sentence for your paragraph). If you have decided that the author's analysis of the problem is the most convincing analysis, then I would expect you to write a statement like "Richard Jones's analysis of the problem of welfare fraud is the most convincing analysis because Jones stresses the role that desperation plays in the lives of people who are likely to commit such fraud."

- Acknowledge the source of the idea in your paragraph by naming the person to whom the idea belongs.

- Do not get caught in the trap of simply reiterating the author's argument. Pull out those points that are critical to the point you want to make. Use only those ideas that you want and need.

- Throughout your summary, explicitly indicate which ideas belong to your source ("according to Smith," "he notes," "Smith goes on to say"), so that your readers recognize what is yours and what belongs to your source.

- Put quotation marks around words and phrases that are taken directly from the source.

To illustrate ways to follow these guidelines, I am including some examples of ways that published writers gave more extended summaries of the work of others. Study these examples carefully. Note how each writer follows the guidelines I have just laid out.

EXAMPLE 1

Virgil Whitaker, in his biographical–analytical study, *Shakespeare's Use of Learning*, asserts this current religious view of Shakespeare's comic and tragic art with admirable boldness. Shakespeare as a man of the Renaissance, he assures us, had accepted the basic religious training of his youth and had never experienced "a genuine skepticism." It follows from such a premise that Shakespeare "did believe profoundly that God had made man in His own image and that, as all men had fallen once in Adam, so each man might fall again if he disobeyed the fundamental laws of God."[4] Whitaker, when he turns to aesthetics, is therefore led to argue, for example, that "Macbeth's sin is so awful simply because, like Shakespeare, he knows and believes in the foundations of human morality and in their ultimate basis in the mind and will of God."[5] This is no doubt to praise Shakespeare and Macbeth as sternly religious men, rather than as superlative playwright and brilliantly conceived character. Moreover, the implications seem to be that the sternness of the religion begot the strength of the play. And some such assumption of a highly self-conscious, febrile religious orthodoxy, both in Shakespeare and in his audience, seems to underlie the critical comments on Shakespeare by the whole contemporary school of Christian aesthetics.

> David Lloyd Stevenson, *The Achievement of Shakespeare's "Measure for Measure"*
> (Ithaca: Cornell University Press, 1966), 94–95.

The first and last sentences of Stevenson's paragraph indicate very clearly why he is summarizing Whitaker's work. Stevenson wants us to see the Christian approach to Shakespeare in detail. Stevenson's point is that the critics who take this approach assume that Shakespeare, Shakespeare's characters, and Shakespeare's audience were highly conscious of Christian teachings and that these Christian ideas were the essence of the meanings of the plays. So that we see clearly what he is talking about, and in order to support his argument, Stevenson summarizes the argument of one of these Christian critics, Virgil Whitaker, and quotes passages from Whitaker that illustrate this religious view.

Example 2

> Shaw and McKay never claimed that they were the first to investigate the geographical distributions of juvenile delinquency. In their introduction to the 1942 volume, they cite not only the spatial work of European criminologists (especially in France and England; see Morris [1957] or Phillips [1972) but also the American research of Breckenridge and Abbott (1912), Blackmar and Burgess (1917), and McKenzie (1923) that preceded their first major report in 1929. However, Shaw and McKay were not satisfied with the descriptive emphasis found in these studies and sought to interpret the spatial distributions within a general macroscopic theory of community processes. It was this important empirical/theoretical synthesis that gave the Shaw and McKay research its significance. Broadly stated, they proposed that the spatial distribution of delinquency in a city was a product of "larger economic and social processes characterizing the history and growth of the city and of the local communities which comprise it" (1942, p.14).[2]

> Robert J. Bursik, Jr. and Jim Webb, "Community Change and Patterns of Delinquency," *American Journal of Sociology* 88 (July 1982): 25. Copyright © 1982 by University of Chicago Press. Reprinted with permission.

In this paragraph, Bursik and Webb's major point is that although Shaw and McKay were not "the first to investigate the geographical distributions of juvenile delinquency," Shaw and McKay's research is very important because they "sought to interpret the spatial distributions within a general macroscopic theory of community processes." The body of the paragraph provides specific illustration and support for this major idea. Notice how Bursik and Webb constantly refer to their source (Shaw and McKay never claimed . . . they were . . . their introduction . . . they cite . . . their first major report . . . Shaw and McKay were not satisfied . . . the Shaw and McKay research . . . they proposed . . .).

EXAMPLE 3

The idea of writing the earlier essay on the "Utility of Religion," its title and its specific theme, had first originated with his wife. Her proposal was clear in intention if incoherent in expression:

> Would not religion, the Utility of Religion, be one of the subjects you would have most to say on—there is to account for the existence nearly universal of some religion (superstition) by the instincts of fear, hope and mystery etc., and throwing over all doctrines and theories, called religion, and devices for power, to show how religion and poetry fill the same want . . .—how all this must be superseded by morality deriving its power from sympathies and benevolence and its reward from the approbation of those we respect.[4]

The essay, as Mill then wrote it, reflected most of these views. Religion, he wrote, was indefensible both on the grounds of truth and of utility, the appeal to the latter being a form of "moral bribery or subornation of the understanding."[5] There was, he concluded, nothing in Christianity that was not better supplied by the Religion of Humanity. At the same time, using her very words, he subtly altered their effect: religion, he suggested, had a more honorable origin than fear; the idea of religion as a device for power was only the "vulgarest part" of his subject; and religion, while comparable to poetry, was also distinct from it, for it addressed itself to reality in a way that poetry did not.

> Gertrude Himmelfarb, "The Other John Stuart Mill," in *Victorian Minds: A Study of Intellectuals in Crisis and of Ideologies in Transition* (New York: Harper & Row, Harper Torchbooks, 1970), 151–52.

Himmelfarb's focus in this paragraph is an early essay written by John Stuart Mill titled "Utility of Religion." Using a proposal for the essay by Mill's wife as a convenient summary of the major ideas in the essay, Himmelfarb shows us major changes Mill made in the essay he wrote. In the paragraph that follows this one in "The Other John Stuart Mill," Himmelfarb goes on to compare "Utility of Religion" with an essay on religion that Mill wrote later in his life. Himmelfarb's overall concern is the way Mill's thinking changed and evolved.

EXAMPLE 4

In June 1905, *Annalen der Physik* published an article by Einstein entitled "On a Heuristic Viewpoint Concerning the Production and Transformation of Light." Physicists usually refer to this as "Einstein's paper on the photoelectric effect," but that description does not do it justice. Einstein himself characterized it at the time as "very revolutionary," and he was right. This is the paper in which he proposed that light can, and in some situations must, be treated as a collection of independent particles of energy—light quanta—that behave like the particles of a gas. Einstein was well aware that a great weight of evidence had been amassed in the course of the previous century showing light to be a wave phenomenon. He knew, in particular, that Heinrich Hertz's experiments, carried out less than twenty years earlier, had confirmed Maxwell's theoretical conclusion that light waves were electromagnetic in character. Despite all this evidence Einstein argued that the wave theory of light had its limits, and that many phenomena involving the emission and absorption of light "seemed to be more intelligible" if his idea of quanta were adapted. The photoelectric effect was one of several such phenomena which he analyzed to show the power of his new hypothesis.

> Martin J. Klein, "Einstein and the Development of Quantum Physics," in *Einstein: A Centenary Volume*, ed. A. P. French (Cambridge, MA: Harvard University Press, 1979), 134.

Klein is clearly not reproducing Einstein's argument in detail. Rather, in the last five sentences he abstracts the main points in the argument, beginning with Einstein's hypothesis (light is a collection of particles of energy) and then giving, in their logical order, the major points that Einstein makes in his article. Notice that Klein constantly reminds us that this is Einstein's argument by using either "Einstein" or "he" in each of these five summary sentences. Notice also that Klein tells us first of all, in sentences three and four, why this article is important and thus worth summarizing.

4. Using direct quotations properly

If you review the examples I have given in the last two subsections of this section, you will see that published authors occasionally quote directly from their sources. You will notice, however, that they don't use direct quotations as a way of letting other people write their essays for them. Rather they quote the words of another person when the idea they are developing involves the perspective or point of view of another person, a point of view that is best established or illustrated by this person's exact words. You will also note that in most cases this point of view can be established or illustrated by quoting just a few words, or perhaps a sentence, and these few words are always integrated into a statement or sentence by the writer, a sentence that usually includes a direct acknowledgment of the source of the words quoted.

> "The anxieties of the Middle Ages are not much different from those of the present," he writes.
>
> Christopher Lasch, *The Culture of Narcissism*, 5.

> Religion, he wrote, was indefensible both on the grounds of truth and of utility, the appeal to the latter being a form of "moral bribery or subornation of the understanding."
>
> Gertrude Himmelfarb, "The Other John Stuart Mill," in *Victorian Minds*, 152.

> Broadly stated, they proposed that the spatial distribution of delinquency in a city was a product of "larger economic and social processes characterizing the history and growth of the city and of the local communities which comprise it."
>
> Bursik and Webb, "Community Change and Patterns of Delinquency," 25.

> Einstein himself characterized it at the time as "very revolutionary," and he was right.
>
> Martin L Klein, "Einstein and the Development of Quantum Physics," in *Einstein: A Centenary Volume*, ed. A. P. French, 134.

From these examples, we can develop our first four guidelines for using quoted material.

Guideline 1

Do not use the words of the author of one of your sources to express a point or an idea that you should be expressing in your own words for your own purposes. Quote directly from a source **only when**

1. the point you want to make involves calling the reader's attention to the point of view of the author you are discussing,

   and

2. the author's point of view is *best* established or illustrated by using this person's exact words.

Guideline 2

Quote only those words, phrases, or sentences necessary to make *your* point about the author's point of view. Leave out any and all parts of a quotation that introduce ideas or points of view that have nothing to do with what you are talking about. If you leave this extraneous material in, it will confuse your readers! Instead, insert words or phrases from your source into your own sentence:

> Johnson's poem is full of images of light. The face of the beloved "glows like the moon" (line 12), the poet "arose like the sun" on his wedding day" (line 15), the church "is softened . . . [by] yellow candle flickers" (lines 17-18).

In those cases where you want to quote a longer segment from the original, it is acceptable to modify parts (leave out words, add words for clarification or grammatical correctness) as long as you do not misrepresent the ideas in the original. For standard methods of making slight alterations in quotations, see Guideline 6.

Guideline 3

Quoted material should never stand alone in your paper. Always incorporate the words of others in your own sentences.

- *Avoid* using quotations this way:

> The value of many diet drugs is highly questionable. "Starch blockers are a fraud."[14] "Many hunger suppressants are dangerous because they raise the blood pressure."[15]

- Use this approach:

> The value of many diet drugs is highly questionable. Based on a series of studies he has conducted, Dr. Benjamin Stokely flatly states that "starch blockers are a fraud."[14] Tests of other diet drugs reveal potentially dangerous side effects. A report by the Science Research Institute concludes that "many hunger suppressants are dangerous because they raise blood pressure."[15]

Guideline 4

Punctuation before and after direct quotations is determined by the grammar of your sentence.

> Dr. Carl Smith (2010) has stated that "there is no evidence that large doses of vitamin C have any beneficial effect" (179).

> Dr. Carl Smith (2010) doubts the value of taking large amounts of vitamin C; "there is no evidence," he states, "that large doses of vitamin C have any beneficial effect" (179).

> Dr. Carl Smith (2010) doubts the value of taking large amounts of vitamin C: "There is no evidence that large doses of vitamin C have any beneficial effect" (179).

Guideline 5

There are **two standard ways of letting your reader know that you are quoting the words of another.** When quotations are short (a few words, a sentence), put **quotation marks** in front of the first word you quote, and don't forget to put them around the last word you quote. Longer quotations are **set off** in **block quotation** format. Setting off these quotations involves creating a new paragraph for the quoted material, and indenting this paragraph sufficiently from the left-hand margin that it is obvious that this material is separate from the text of the body of your paper.

EXAMPLE

> Much of the material that Smith used in his novel about Napoleon is based on historical fact. In a letter to his friend Sam Spade in 1924, Smith explained that
>
>> I am starting work on a novel on Napoleon that I've spent the last six years researching. Don't misunderstand. I do not intend to write an historical romance, those so-called novels that pretend to be historical by piling up all sorts of accurate detail about furniture and clothes and architecture. Such bits and pieces of history do not add up to any real sort of authenticity. My novel is going to be a novel that re-creates Napoleon himself. When I am finished, I will have made Napoleon a living, breathing person that the reader will feel he has met and lived with for years and years. I can do it. I've read everything that has been written about the man, and everything he wrote.[8]
>
> Smith did not have to worry about someone who actually knew the Emperor calling his portrait into question, since all those people have long ago turned into dust; but ignoring the issue of the authenticity of the portrait for a moment, there is no doubt that Smith has created a three-dimensional character.

Style manuals vary in both in their criteria for "longer" quotations, and in their recommendations for formatting them. Check the style manual you are using if you are following its manuscript style. Otherwise, these are my suggestions (you should also read over what I have to say about single- and double-spacing in Section 7.C).

- In **defining longer,** I'd suggest following the *MLA Handbook.* Use the block format if a quotation runs more than four lines in your normal paragraph style. Use the block format if you are quoting more than three consecutive lines of poetry.

- As far as **the format itself** is concerned:

  - Leave a line of space before and after the block quotation;

  - Indent the block quotation *at least* five spaces from the left margin; you can go up to ten spaces, which is what the MLA style calls for.

  - If it is acceptable to your instructor, single-space the paragraph.

ALERT!

- **DO NOT** put quotation marks around the words in a block quotation! Setting this material off in a block format is the signal that the material is quoted. If you put quotation marks around these words, you are saying that these words are quoted in the source that you are quoting!

- As I urge you to do in Section 7.C, format block quotations electronically (not with tabs and the return or enter key!)

- As in all matters of style, be consistent. Use the same format for all quotations you set off.

Guideline 6

Occasionally it will be necessary to alter quotations slightly to meet the needs of your prose. Such modifications are acceptable only if you do not misrepresent the meaning of the original words and only if you use the accepted means of indicating that quoted material is being modified.

- Indicate *omission* of a word or words by inserting ellipsis points (. . .) where a word or words are omitted.

ORIGINAL

In the corporate structure as in government, the rhetoric of achievement, of single-minded devotion to the task at hand—the rhetoric of performance, efficiency, and productivity—no longer provides an accurate description of the struggle for personal survival.

> Christopher Lasch, *The Culture of Narcissism: American Life in an Age of Diminishing Expectations* (New York: W. W. Norton, 1978), 61.

MODIFIED

In the corporate structure as in government, the rhetoric of . . . single-minded devotion to the task at hand . . . no longer provides an accurate description of the struggle for personal survival.

- Indicate *additions* or changes of certain words by putting your changes in brackets [ ].

ORIGINAL

After the November 1963 coup in Saigon that took Diem's life, Kennedy regretted encouraging an action that, he now believed, would deepen rather than reduce U.S. participation in Vietnamese affairs.

> Robert Dallek, "JFK's Second Term," *Atlantic Monthly*, June 2003, 65.

MODIFIED

According to Dallek, "After the November 1963 coup in Saigon that took [Ngo Dinh] Diem's life, [President] Kennedy regretted encouraging an action that, he now believed, would deepen rather than reduce U.S. participation in Vietnamese affairs."

ORIGINAL

Knipling believed the most significant implication of his theoretical results was that the two complementary techniques allowed a pest controller to overcome the law of diminishing returns.

> John H. Perkins, *Insects, Experts, and the Insecticide Crisis: The Quest for New Pest Management Strategies* (New York: Plenum Press, 1982), 118.

MODIFIED

Perkins writes: "Knipling believed the most significant implication of his theoretical results was that the two complementary techniques [of using insecticides and releasing sterile male insects] allowed a pest controller to overcome the law of diminishing returns."

PLEASE NOTE:

- Do not use parentheses for making changes in a quotation. Authors can and do use parentheses. To make sure that there is always a distinction between what an author has said, and changes that you are making, put your additions in **brackets,** which have squared-off corners and are clearly different from parentheses.

- Modifications or additions to quotations **should be limited to changes made for clarity, completeness, or grammatical correctness**—changes of pronouns to nouns, changes of verb tense, additions of the first name of a person, and the like. If you find yourself making a patchwork quilt of a quotation with all the changes you are making, step back from the situation. Write the statement you want to make, and then put quotation marks around those words that you have taken directly from your source.

- Normally, when you are quoting only a phrase or a part of a sentence from a source, it is obvious that you are quoting only part of the author's original sentence. It is, therefore, **not necessary to put ellipsis points** at the beginning and end of these quotations. But remember that your primary objective is **never to misrepresent the ideas and the meaning of the author** whose material you are using. It would be wise to use such ellipsis points in those few cases where it may not be obvious from the context that you are using only part of what is a larger whole. See the first example in Guideline 7.

Guideline 7

There are a few things you should know about **quoting from novels, short stories, poetry, and plays.** In general when quoting from a work of literature, you should use the same guidelines I have just outlined. Thus, you should quote from the actual text of a piece of literature only when the specific words of the text are essential to the point you are making. Otherwise, as in using other kinds of sources, you will find that the most effective way for you to make your point is to summarize, in your own words, the material in the text to which you refer.

If you decide that you must quote the exact words of the text in order to support your point, be sure to introduce the quotation by giving your readers enough information to put the quotation into its proper context. If you are quoting the words of a character in a novel or a play, for example, be sure to tell us which character is speaking. Similarly, the words you quote often will be more meaningful if you tell your readers, briefly, the circumstances that led that character to speak those words.

EXAMPLE 1

As he draws toward the end of his story of the "great" Jay Gatsby, Nick Carraway passes judgment on Daisy and Tom Buchanan—"they were careless people," Nick decides; "they smashed up things and creatures and then retreated back into their money or their vast carelessness, or whatever it was that kept them together, and let other people clean up the mess they had made . . ."[11]

> 11. F. Scott Fitzgerald, *The Great Gatsby* (New York: Charles Scribner's Sons, 1953), 120.

EXAMPLE 2

In *To the Lighthouse,* Mrs. Ramsey is constantly giving of herself to her husband, her children, her neighbors. This self-giving is what brings other personalities into harmony and communion. At the dinner with which section I ends, Mrs. Ramsey surveys the group seated around the table: "They all sat separate. And the whole of the effort of merging and flowing and creating rested on her."[7]

> 7. Virginia Woolf, *To the Lighthouse* (New York: Harcourt, Brace, 1927), 126.

EXAMPLE 3

Richard's helpless self-pity is eloquently expressed as he prepares to give up his role as king, and his identity:

> What must the King do now? Must he submit?
> The King shall do it. Must he be depos'd?
> The King shall be contented. Must he lose
> The name of king? a' God's name let it go. (3.3.142–145)

As example 3 illustrates, several lines of poetry may be quoted by setting them off from the text in a block quotation. Shorter passages of poetry, however, should be put in quotation marks and integrated into the prose of your text. If the passage you quote runs from one verse line to another, you should indicate the end of the verse line with a slash mark (/) and the beginning of the next verse line by capitalizing the first letter of the first word.

Example 4

The tragedy in the story of Michael is that his only son, heir to his land and to his life, is forced to apprentice himself to a kinsman, "a prosperous man, / Thriving in trade" (Wordsworth, "Michael," lines 249–50).

Guideline 8

Numerous times throughout this book I remind you that, when you come across references to (or quotations from) material that really interests you in one of the sources you are reading, you need to make every effort to locate the original source and read it for yourself. If you have followed this advice, if and when you quote such material, you will yourself be quoting from the original.

There will be times, however, when it will be impossible for you to put your hands on the original source. If you decide you want to quote this material, you will be **quoting from a secondary source**, and there are forms you must follow to make sure your reader knows that this is what you are doing.

- In the body of your paper, you must give at least the name of the person whose words you are quoting. It would be best to give us as much information as you can about the author of these words and the circumstances (or text) in which they were first used. This admonition is particularly important if you are documenting your sources in a parenthetical citation style.

- Put the material in quotation marks. If you quote words of the author of the secondary source as well as words from the original, put double quotation marks around the material from the secondary source, and single quotation marks around the material quoted *in* the secondary source. If you use *only* words quoted in the secondary source, you may use only double quotation marks.

- Documentation styles have explicit forms for indicating that you are using material from a secondary source.

In his biography, Nelson makes much of Lady Martha's intelligence. One of her early beaux, he tells us, described her as "sharp and brilliant as the most perfectly cut diamond in the world" (qtd. in Nelson 156).   **MLA**

> In 1926 Fredericks (as cited in Smith, 2004) insisted   **APA**
> that "intelligence is invariably fixed by age three"
> (p. 47).

Be aware that the **page numbers you give** in such citations are the pages on which you found the quotation in the secondary source that you were reading.

For more information on this matter, read over Section 8.D.7. If you are using one of the documentation styles I cover in the appendixes, check there for specifics and/or consult the relevant style manual.

SECTION

7

Polishing Your Final Draft

At this point, the intellectually challenging work of your paper is done, but you aren't finished. When you began revising the text of your paper, you started shifting your focus from developing your own conclusions about your subject to communicating those conclusions to other people. The three steps you have left—all part of polishing your final draft—are undertaken with your readers' needs and expectations in the forefront of your mind. You want to make sure that your readers' attention is completely immersed in what you have to say. So you need to eliminate all those flaws in formatting, style, grammar, and mechanics that, if not corrected, have the potential of distracting or irritating your readers. I said this at the end of Section 5, and I'll repeat it again. Think about how far you've come since you started this research project months ago. Do you want to risk having all your hard work ignored or downgraded because your instructor is exasperated by typos, spelling errors, stylistic inconsistencies, grammatical errors, and/or other flaws that keep interfering with his or her efforts to focus on what you have to say?

Unfortunately, I see too many final drafts that are marred by small but bothersome lapses in these areas. In my experience, there are two basic reasons why students fail to attend properly to this last stage of the process:

- They do not give themselves the necessary time—and "distance"—to copy-edit and proofread the way they should.

- They don't have appropriate strategies for finding and fixing problems in these areas.

Let's see if we can change this situation.

A. Copyediting and Proofreading: Some Strategies

The final polishing stage of your paper begins when you declare your draft finished. This is both an arbitrary and a conscious decision that you must make, but making it is critical because with it you will shift from "writing" and "revising" to "copyediting." The distinction I make between writing and the tasks of copyediting and proofing is the distinction between making changes that affect the content of the paper, and making changes that assure you that your manuscript conforms to the conventions of style and mechanics developed by members of the academic discipline in which and for which you are writing. In other words, you will be making changes that assure you that your paper is "correct."

In the remainder of this subsection I'm going to make concrete suggestions for carrying out the task of copyediting and proofreading.

Preliminary Steps

- First of all, time. The issue here is not so much quantity as it is quality. You are more likely to be successful in copyediting and proofing if you have "distanced" yourself from the paper. Experienced writers know that they can't really trust the proofreading they do of a text immediately after they have written it, simply because they know that they are looking at what's in their heads, not what's on the screen or on the page. As I've suggested in the series of deadlines I've given you, you should *start* this task at least two days before you turn in the polished text to your instructor. However, you aren't going to need large blocks of time to complete it. In fact, you'll probably be more successful if you copyedit/proof in shorter blocks of time—say, half-hour or hour-long segments—throughout the two-day period.

- Second of all, concentration. Your copyediting and proofing will be successful only if you give it your full and undivided attention. Take whatever steps are necessary to be sure that, in the periods you set aside for this task, you **know** you will not be disturbed (or distracted).

- The third requirement is a style sheet and a proofing sheet (which you could probably combine into one). A style sheet is simply one's personal style guide for a particular manuscript. On it, you record decisions you have made about specific stylistic and/or formatting issues (to capitalize "Web," for example, or to represent all italics with underlining). You will then use this guide to be sure you've been consistent in following this style throughout your text. A proofing sheet, in contrast, covers basic grammatical and mechanical matters. The model I have given you here covers the most common problems I see in students' papers.

Model of a Proofing Sheet

Feature	Check off when completed
Spelling/Word Choice	
Spelling (be sure to run *final* copy through the spellchecker; check proper names against sources; if the spellchecker gives suggestions for misspelled words, be sure to choose the word you intended to use; BE SURE to check the paper for typos—i.e., correctly spelled words that are not the word you intended to use)	
then/than (then is the time word)	
affect/effect (verb = affect)	
Punctuation (check *all* punctuation)	
Make sure direct quotations are either enclosed in quotation marks or are set off in block form	
Compound sentences must be joined either with a coordinating conjunction or a semicolon	
When checking commas, be sure nonrestrictive clauses, phrases, and words are properly set off	
Possessives (be sure all possessive nouns are indicated with apostrophes)	
Quotation marks come AFTER periods and commas	
Double-check all it's/its (it's = it is)	
Grammar	
Subject/verb agreement	
Fragments	
Pronoun agreement	
Base tense	
Parallel structure	

The wise thing for you to do would be to create a proofing sheet for yourself in a file in your word-processing program. You can then tailor it to fit your needs (each of us has a set of errors we seem to make with alarming regularity, and rules that we cannot seem to follow properly). Moreover, you can print a copy to use every time you need to polish a paper, whether it is a research paper or not. In my Researcher's Notebook right now I have started a style sheet, and, when it comes time to proof this typescript, I will be definitely using it and a proofing sheet.

- In addition to your own style sheet, you need a dictionary, and a handbook that covers basic rules in English grammar and mechanics; if you own a copy of the manual for the documentation style you are using, having that close by also makes a lot of sense.

- The last prerequisite is a colorful pen (bright red or green or purple) with which to make your corrections. The bright color increases the likelihood that you will not miss any corrections you need to make.

The Process Itself

- My first piece of advice is that you do your copyediting/proofing on a paper copy of your text. If you run it through the spellchecker before you print it, you will reduce the spelling errors and typos you'll need to attend to. If you have been doing your drafts with pen and paper, I'd advise copyediting and proofing on the paper copy before you type, although you will have to proofread the typed copy and make any changes necessary.

  Doing your copyediting and proofing on a paper copy has, from my point of view, two major advantages. The first advantage is one that I experience constantly, which is that I am much better able to spot errors on paper than on the screen. I've had a number of students tell me that they have the same experience. Secondly, and perhaps more importantly, copyediting on paper helps you to avoid segueing from copyediting back into revising. When you are on the computer, it is just too easy to begin by changing a word, which may lead to rewriting a sentence, which, since you have changed the meaning and focus of this sentence, may require revising the whole paragraph. This move back into revising/writing can become an endless regression. It is probably one of the main reasons that students never really get around to editing and proofreading. Such wholesale rewriting is less tempting on paper simply because it is a lot more work!

- Do whatever you need to do **to see what is literally on the page**. This means stopping yourself from "reading" the text. It is true that, to determine the correct punctuation for some constructions, you will have to read the sentence. But generally, if and when you start reading, the odds are you will be "seeing" what you want to see. Professional proofreaders have told me that they begin at the bottom of a page and work their way up to the top line-by-line, or they start at the right side of each line and work to the left. Something that works for me is putting the point of my pen on each word as I move along, and subvocalizing the word, so I can tell if what I am saying is what is written, and if what is written is the word I intended.

- You are going to resist this piece of advice, but it is based on both experience and logic. Using your style sheet or proofing sheet as your guide, check the entire manuscript for one "rule" or "issue" at a time. If you work on a haphazard basis, it's just too easy to correct one error, only to overlook one or two others. Besides, you will quickly discover that, if you are focusing on one issue, it takes very little time to check the entire text!

- Those of you who learned the proofreaders' marks as part of a journalism class are at a real advantage in doing your corrections. If you do not know the proofreaders' marks, be **bold** in indicating those points where a correction needs to be made (use your colorful pen and circle the area, or underline it). Write the correction, cleanly and legibly, in the right-hand margin. Just to be very, very sure that I do not overlook any corrections that need to be made, I put a small x in the left margin for every correction that I need to make in a manuscript line.

- If you decide to rewrite a phrase or a sentence, I suggest writing the revision on a slip of paper which you can then staple to the left margin of the manuscript. It looks like a little flag. The revision is physically where the correction needs to be made, but the slip of paper can be folded back so you can read any text that's under it.

- Finally, take advantage of features of your word-processing program designed to help you edit papers. One that I particularly value is Replace, a part of my program's Edit menu. As its name implies, this feature allows me to make stylistic or spelling changes (west to West, Hagel to Hegel, International Business Machines to IBM) with just a few keystrokes and in very little time. Best of all, from my perspective, the computer, unlike my fallible eye, will find every instance of this word or phrase.

- When it is time to make these various changes in your electronic draft, again, take whatever steps are necessary to be sure that you will not be disturbed (or distracted). And carry out this operation in a systematic fashion so that you know that all the necessary changes have been made.

B. Copyediting and Proofreading: Issues to Consider

The following list is indicative of the types of stylistic and mechanical features you must attend to. Add any rules or conventions that you know you need to check for.

When it comes to written conventions and style, consistency is central!

In the area of written conventions you will find that there are instances in which more than one form is acceptable. For example, it is correct to put a comma after the penultimate in a series, but it is also correct to omit such a comma; in some manuals or dictionaries a particular word is capitalized; in others, it is not. You will need to decide which form you will follow, and then make sure you use that form consistently throughout the paper.

- Be sure each sentence leads the readers clearly from one idea to the next.

- Check your word choice. Be sure the words you've used are words that precisely reflect the ideas you are trying to convey. Eliminate slang and expressions that are too casual for formal papers.

- If you are using numbers in your paper, you should be aware that the commonly accepted style is to spell out numbers if they can be expressed in one or two words and to use numerals if more than two words are necessary.

two hundred books   1,512 subjects

a million dollars   412 ships

You should never begin a sentence with a numeral. If you are writing a scientific paper in which there are many numbers, check the APA *Publication Manual, The Chicago Manual of Style,* or the manual for the CSE style and systems for their recommendations about the proper style for numbers.

- If you want to use abbreviations in your paper, be sure you have told your reader what the abbreviation represents. The first time you refer to the company, chemical compound, or organization, give the full name first and put the abbreviation after it in parentheses:

Dimethylsulfoxide (DMSO) is a chemical compound . . .

A leader in this field is International Business Machines (IBM), a corporation that . . .

- To be sure your quotations are in a proper form, check Section 6.B.4.

A Note on Punctuation and Quotation Marks   Commas and periods are always put *inside* quotation marks:

Marble and other cold objects are central images in his poem "Death."

Describing the loss as "overwhelming," General Smith promptly resigned his post.

Semicolons and colons are placed outside the quotation marks. Question marks and exclamation points are placed inside the quotation marks if they are part of the quotation; if they punctuate your sentence, they are placed outside the quotation marks:

The speech ends with a question: "What is real?"

Did anyone hear him say "I give up"?

- Be sure titles in your paper are in their proper form. The rule of thumb is very simple. If a work was published originally as an independent, separate unit, the title should be underlined or formatted in italic type. This is the proper form for the titles of books, journals and magazines, CDs, films, operas. If a work was originally published within a larger, independent unit, its title has quotation marks around it. The titles of poems originally published in magazines or collections should be put in quotation marks, as should the titles of chapters of books, the titles of essays and articles, and the titles of songs or selections on a CD or tape.

A Note on Capitalization in Titles   *The Chicago Manual of Style* gives the following guidelines for capitalizing words in the titles of works.

CAPITALIZED	NOT CAPITALIZED
the first word in a title	articles (*a, an, the*), unless first word in a title or subtitle
the last word in a title	
all nouns	coordinate conjunctions (*and, but, or, for, nor*), unless first word in title or subtitle
all pronouns	
all adjectives	prepositions (*from, during, to, at, of,* etc.), unless first or last word in title or subtitle
all verbs	
all adverbs	the *to* in an infinitive (*to be, to go, to work,* etc.)
all subordinate conjunctions (*because, since, unless, before, after,* etc.)	

- Be sure the grammar of each sentence is correct.

  - Do pronouns have antecedents? Do the pronouns agree with their antecedents? (. . . the company. It . . .; Scientists . . . They . . .).

  - Do subjects and verbs agree in number?

  - Is the base tense of your paper consistent? If you are treating an event or events as if they occurred in the past, always refer to these events in the past tense; if you are treating an event or events as if they are occurring now, always use the present tense. What you want to *avoid* is referring to such events in the past tense in one sentence or paragraph, and then switching to the present tense in another sentence or paragraph:

    Hamlet *was* very upset by his father's death, so upset that he *contemplated* suicide . . .
    In this play, Claudius and Gertrude *are* unwitting villains. They *act* as if they *are concerned* about Hamlet's welfare, at least at first . . .

- Proofread; correct all errors in spelling and punctuation.

- Finally, take the time required to double-check the accuracy of your citations for content and form. You'll find detailed steps for this procedure in Section 8.E.1.

C. The Format of the Paper

When you consult one of the formal style manuals I discuss in Section 8, you will find that these manuals cover much more than the proper form for documenting sources. Normally they give guidelines for three categories of stylistic issues. One, of course, is documentation style. Another comprises those matters I've just outlined in the subsection on copyediting. The third has to do with the appearance of the final paper, what I call the manuscript style. Manuscript style is concerned with such things as the order of the units of the text (title page, abstract, notes, and so on), content and form of the title page, page headers and numbering, and all sorts of formatting issues from the width of margins to line spacing to the format for headings.

> In all matters of style,
> find out—and follow—the preferences of your instructor.

Formatting Electronically

Whenever you are working in a word-processing program, do all formatting electronically (not manually). In the old days, when we used typewriters, we had to format with tabs, the space bar, and the return key because this was the way the machine worked. Computers do not work the way typewriters do, and if you format on the computer with the tab key, the space bar, and the return key, you are probably creating a lot of problems for yourself.

Formatting electronically means using the format menu and the ruler in your word-processing program to create "the look" you want your text to have when it is printed—that is, to set the margins for the text, to create page numbers and headers, and especially to format individual paragraphs, including headings, block quotations, footnotes or endnotes, entries in the final list of sources. You can capitalize on these formatting features of your program even further if your program allows you to create "styles" for specific types of paragraphs. Once you have formatted a particular type of paragraph to look the way you want it to—including line-spacing, margins for first and subsequent lines, lines of space before and after the paragraph, and the like— you can define this as the "style" for that feature of your text, be it block quotations, certain headings, or entries on your final list. Thereafter, all you need do is to attach this style to other paragraphs in your paper that you want formatted identically. An additional advantage of these electronic styles is that, if you decide at some point to make a change in a style, you need change only one paragraph; your program will automatically change all other paragraphs to which you've attached this style. Clearly it is worth finding out if the word-processing program you are using has this capability—and learning how to use it.

To Double-Space or to Single-Space, That Is the Question

Guidelines given for manuscript style in the manuals of professional organizations and publishing houses can be problematic for students because these manuals are addressed essentially to authors preparing manuscripts for publication. Their guidelines for the appearance of the paper are governed by the need to make the text easy to copyedit, proofread, and otherwise prepare for the final step of setting it in type. In contrast, you will be presenting your instructor with a paper in its final form, comparable to the printed version of the published author's work. Moreover, the technology that most students have available to them these days—sophisticated word-processing programs, even desktop publishing programs—makes it possible for you to produce a text that very closely resembles works that have been formally published. One area in which differences between manuscript style and final printed form is most obvious is spacing, particularly line spacing. Most style manuals advise authors to double-space everything in the manuscript because double-spacing makes it easier for editors to proofread and for compositors to read the text accurately. Double-spacing the body of your paper makes sense because it enhances readability. If, however, readability is a central criterion for the appearance of a paper—as it is in decisions made about the format of printed materials—then I believe that single-spacing certain elements of your paper will enhance its readability. Specifically, single-spacing block quotations, notes, entries in bibliographies and reference lists makes student papers easier to read because this is the form in which we are used to seeing these elements in published works. The issue for you, then, is to decide whether you should format your paper according to the guidelines in the style manual you are using, or if your objective is to produce a paper that, in its appearance, approximates the look of printed texts.

Other Formatting Matters

Since your top priority is to allow your readers to focus their full attention on what you have to say, choose a font (typeface) for your paper that is clean and readable. Most people favor the classics—Times, Palatino, Garamond in the serif category; Arial, Helvetica, or Geneva in the sans-serif category. Please, stay away from cursive fonts and the experimental ones that obviously look much better in headlines on Web sites than in blocks of prose you are trying to read. Twelve-point is the size designed for the body of texts and this is the size you should use for all elements of the paper. Print or type your paper on standard white, twenty-pound bond paper, making sure that your printer (or typewriter) is making sharp, even copies. If you try to get "fancy" with any aspects of text (using a variety of fonts or type sizes, using special paper, printing your paper in purple), you risk distracting your reader's attention from your paper's content, and such efforts to be creative graphically can clash sharply with the image of the thoughtful, logical researcher you want to project.

Title and Title Page   In my view, your research paper should have a separate title page. The title of the paper itself should give the reader a clear picture of the content of the paper, even though you may consider such a title boring. Clever titles are fun to create, but they may be very frustrating to the reader, as you yourself may have learned when you were using bibliographic databases and the library catalog.

FRUSTRATING

Fun and Games

BETTER

Using Game Theory to Analyze the Ethiopian–Somalian Conflict

There is no widely accepted form for a title page. If your instructor specifies no preferred format, I recommend this format. Center your title about one-third of the way down the page. Capitalize only the first letters of central words (see note on capitalization in titles on p. 200). In some aesthetically pleasing fashion, give the following information:

your full name

the number and title of the course

the full name of the instructor

the due date of the paper

Margins   While specific widths for margins vary in the recommendations of different style manuals, any margin less than 1 inch would be unacceptable. I suggest 1¼ (or 1½) inches on the left and 1 inch on the other three sides. Although I have encouraged you to use these same margins for note pages, bibliographies and reference lists, you should be aware that some style manuals require deeper top margins for these pages and, sometimes, for the first page and title page of the paper.

Page Numbers   Do not forget to number all the pages of your text, and consider using a "running head" or "headers." These consist of some kind of text that precedes the page number, most commonly the author's last name or the first two or three words of the paper's title. I prefer such headers to be formatted in the upper right-hand corner of each page. Setting up such headers with a word-processing program is quite simple:

Williams   4

Using Game Theory   4

The numbering of nontextual material (endnote pages, bibliography, appendixes, etc.) varies; I would recommend simply numbering all pages in your paper consecutively. Thus, if the last page of your text is page 14, the first page of your endnotes would be page 15, and so on.

Headings and Table of Contents   If you are doing a report on an experiment or study, you will use headings in the body of your paper (see Section 5.B). Otherwise, determining the appropriateness of headings for your paper will depend on the length and nature of the paper. Headings break the readers' attention, signaling a major transition. Therefore, headings would be obtrusive in the middle of a tightly organized argument. On the other hand, if your paper is very long and the argument rather complex, headings can be helpful to the reader. Again, if you are not sure if it would be appropriate to use headings, consult your instructor.

If you decide that headings are appropriate for your paper, your outline should suggest what headings you should use and where they should be inserted. All headings should follow the parallel-structure rule: Express all headings in the same grammatical form (all phrases, or all sentences). Moreover, each level of heading should be formatted differently, so that the format itself signals the nature of the division that follows it. Levels of headings are comparable to typical divisions in a formal outline:

    I. Major divisions of the paper (level 1 head)

       A. Subdivision of major divisions (level 2 head)

          1. Subdivision of subdivision (level 3 head)

Most style manuals recommend formats for each level.

You should be aware that a heading should *never* be the last line of type on a page. If the first two or three lines of a paragraph following a heading will not fit on a page, type the heading and the paragraph on the following page. With a word-processing program, it is easy to avoid this problem of "orphans" by using the command in the paragraph-formatting menu that tells your printer to keep the heading paragraph with the paragraph that follows. In fact, if you are using a word-processing program that allows you to create styles for certain paragraphs, you can save a lot of time and assure consistency in the appearance of your headings by creating styles for each level of headings and attaching the appropriate style to the paragraph in which you have typed the content of the heading. When you create a style, you can choose the "keep with next" command as well as establish the number of lines of space you want before and after each heading. If your paper is divided into a number of divisions and subdivisions, a table of contents might be useful to the readers.

Tables, Charts, and Graphs   If you are giving your readers statistical information, charts and graphs can be useful visual aids. To be most effective, such charts and graphs should be placed in the body of the paper at those points where you refer to the information on these charts and graphs. If you plan to use charts and graphs and are composing your paper on a computer, be sure to check into the capabilities you have for electronically creating and placing these items in your paper. For guidelines about the appropriate format of tables, charts, and graphs, consult the style manual for the documentation form you are using.

Appendixes   An appendix is what we might call a very long explanatory note. If you wish to include detailed information relevant to some part of your paper, information that does not belong in the text of the paper, you may place it in an appendix, which will be put at the end of your paper. If you are writing a report on a study or experiment, your instructor may want you to include raw data you compiled, or other elements of your investigative procedure (such as a questionnaire used to gather evidence); such material belongs in an appendix or appendixes. In books and articles in the humanities, you will sometimes find documents, like letters or legal documents, reproduced in appendixes; and sometimes authors use appendixes to elaborate on a point mentioned in the body of the paper. If you decide that you have material that should be put in an appendix, consult the style manual for the documentation form you are using.

Congratulations!

You've come a long way since the day weeks ago when you made your first, tentative efforts to formulate your research question. No doubt, like most researchers, you've taken a route that has had a number of unexpected twists and turns, and you've experienced periods of frustration and discouragement. But my hope is that you are proud of the paper you are about to hand in, and that you are also feeling a very real sense of intellectual accomplishment. Let yourself experience the confidence that comes from knowing that your ideas are the product of serious thought and assessment of the evidence; and realize that whatever questions or uncertainties linger in your mind are positive indications of how your understanding of this complex subject has deepened and grown in the past weeks.

Above all, my hope is that you no longer consider the task of doing research papers overwhelming or intimidating. If I have reached the objectives I had for this book, you now possess a good sense of the various steps you need to take to complete a research project, and are confident that you can write an effective paper because you now have various strategies that enable you to accomplish each step successfully. Since the research and writing processes are no longer mysterious, you are now in a position to welcome such assignments in the future: to approach them as opportunities to grapple with the intellectual puzzles that intrigue and motivate members of various disciplines, and thus to enhance your educational experience by working and thinking the way experts do.

SECTION

8

Documenting Your Sources: The Basics

A. Choosing a Documentation Style

One of the important decisions you are going to have to make at some point in the process of doing this research paper is choosing the style you will use to document your sources.

Documenting sources in a paper involves letting readers know, in the body of your paper, that certain information and ideas have been taken from others (your sources), and then giving readers complete information about each of these sources, information that will enable readers to locate and read a source themselves if they choose to do so. To meet this basic objective, you will need to select a standard method of documentation, which I'll be calling a **documentation style.** In Section 4, I encouraged you to make this decision fairly early in the process so that you could save yourself time and effort by recording bibliographic information about your sources in the form you will be using in the final draft of the paper.

SO—how do you decide which documentation style to use? The short answer—and the best answer—is

ask your instructor.

The most logical, the most direct, and the most foolproof method of selecting a documentation style is to find out which style your instructor prefers or, very often, requires that you use. When you ask for this information, be sure your instructor gives you a name that makes sense to you. In a few pages I will be giving you the names of four documentation styles commonly used in academia. If your instructor gives you a different name, do not hesitate to ask for the title of a style manual or a style guide that provides detailed information both about the system and about particular forms for specific types of sources. In other words, you want to be sure, from the outset, that you fully understand what your instructor wants. Probably the best way to ask the question is this: "Which style or style manual do you want me to follow?"

The answer your instructor provides, however, may not really resolve the issue. If you are like many students with whom I work, you face the prospect of documenting your sources with a mixture of dread and confusion. Perhaps in the past you have struggled to do your documentation "right," only to have your instructor spill red corrections all over your efforts. Perhaps on the course syllabus your instructor requests that you use the APA style (or Chicago or the CSE), but you haven't the foggiest notion what APA or Chicago or CSE means, and you certainly haven't a clue about the styles they represent.

Why, you may well ask, can't there be just one, simple method of documentation? Why can't I use the system I know, or, better yet, make one up? And why, oh why, are instructors so nit-picky about how I give information about sources?

Not only are these questions very natural responses to what, on the surface, seems to be a bewildering array of styles, but they also raise very legitimate issues. However, until and unless there is a major revolution in the world of publishing and/or in professional organizations, variations in systems and styles of documentation will remain a fact of life. Be prepared to find that the style your psychology instructor expects you to use will not be the same as the style your literature instructor wants, and the style recommended by your biology teacher will differ from both of these. If the research you have been doing for this particular paper has taken you across disciplinary boundaries, you have already noticed differences in the way authors of books and scholarly journals have documented their sources. There are very good reasons why you are going to have to choose an established style of documentation, and there are also very good reasons why you are going to have to follow that style exactly. Using an established style appropriate to an academic field—appropriate, that is, to your subject and audience—and following that style exactly are important parts of learning how to be a responsible detective-researcher. You do not want to undercut the quality of the intellectual work you've done thus far by not acknowledging the debt you owe to others in a form understood by people in the field.

I can't promise to make this step of the process fun. Let's be honest: documenting sources is not a creative nor a very exciting task. But I think I can make documentation much less confusing. Moreover, I can provide you with information that ought to make the process less time-consuming, or, at least, less frustrating. Here's how.

- In the **four appendixes** that follow this section, I give you specific information about four documentation styles (my coverage of the CMS and the CSE styles involves presentation of two different systems in each style). I have tried to set up these appendixes so that you can quickly see how a style works, and so that you can use them as quick reference guides for finding the required form for a specific type of source.

- In **the remainder of this section** I have three objectives:

  - To educate you about the simple and **fundamental principles upon which all documentation systems are based.** If we step back from the minutiae that tends to make documentation so confusing and exasperating, a simpler and meaningful picture emerges. First of all, I will show you that there is an easy-to-understand logic that drives any system and style of documentation. Moreover, beneath superficial differences in mechanical conventions and typography, most styles share similarities that are, again, very logical and easy to understand.

  - To provide general information about **conventions that have been established for providing information about texts.** Subsection D follows up on my comments in Section 3.C.2. I envision it as a reference to be used when you need it, whether for reading citations you find as you do your research, or for understanding the documentation style you've been asked to use in a paper.

  - To give you concrete advice about **steps to take in documenting your sources.**

> When you are ready to start thinking about documenting your sources, I urge you to look over all of this Section 8 so you know what kind of information is available to you if and when you need it.

You may protest that you have no need—and even less desire—to become some sort of expert in documentation. So let me spell out what I see as the advantages of your understanding the basic principles of documentation and the underlying similarities in documentation styles.

- As you are doing your research, having this knowledge makes it much easier for you to read citations you find in bibliographic databases and in the bibliographies and reference lists of sources you read.

- When it comes to documenting sources in your paper, having this knowledge makes it much easier for you "to see" and thus to follow the forms for basic categories of sources in any one style.

- Having this knowledge makes it much easier to phrase questions you have about documenting a particular source, and thus for finding the right answer (by looking it up in a manual, or asking your instructor or someone in the writing center).

- Having this knowledge enables you to use your problem-solving skills to deduce the appropriate form for unusual sources that don't easily fit the standard categories.

- Having this knowledge makes it much easier to proofread the documentation in your final paper to be sure it is complete and accurate in both content and form.

- In the future, having this knowledge will make it much easier for you to "learn" a new documentation style.

If I am successful in achieving my goals for Section 8, what once looked like gibberish to you ought to start making sense, and feelings of dread and confusion ought to be replaced by a sense of competence and confidence. If I am successful, I will have convinced you that, while documenting sources may not be fun, or terribly challenging intellectually, it is a task that must be done, and done correctly!

Styles General and Academic

Now, back to the issue of choosing an appropriate documentation style. Your instructor's concern that you document your sources appropriately is, in part, an expression of her concern that you understand the first premise of documentation—giving credit where credit is due. But her concept of what constitutes an appropriate style for your paper will most definitely be influenced by the discipline or academic field of which she is a member. That is, the style she recommends or requires will undoubtedly be a style used by authors in her field when they write articles and books. And, as we will see very shortly, the really major distinctions in documentation systems and styles are directly attributable to distinctions between what are called the "hard" and the "soft" sciences; the differences are differences that have developed from different disciplinary practices and needs.

To this point I have been talking about documentation style, but you need to be aware that all of the styles I'll be talking about or referring to in this section and the appendixes cover a much broader spectrum of issues. In other words, documentation is only part of the picture.

Style, in this broader sense, refers to all aspects of a manuscript or the final, polished draft of a paper. Style in this broader sense covers all those conventions and standards that a publisher requires of manuscripts submitted to it for publication.

Thus, **a style manual** typically contains three types of information: (1) the forms an author is to use in documenting sources in a manuscript; (2) rules for written conventions or mechanics, including such matters as punctuation, capitalization, representations of numbers, and so on—the sorts of issues I cover in Section 7.B; (3) requirements for manuscript format—the sorts of issues I cover in Section 7.C.

In the academic world, there are four well-known style manuals, one produced by a university publishing house, and the other three the products of professional academic organizations.

Common Name	stands for	The Formal Manual
APA	The American Psychological Association	*Publication Manual of the American Psychological Association*, 5th ed. Washington, DC: APA, 2001.
MLA	The Modern Language Association	*MLA Handbook for Writers of Research Papers*, by Joseph Gibaldi. 6th ed. New York: MLA, 2003.
CMS	*The Chicago Manual of Style*	*The Chicago Manual of Style*. 15th ed. Chicago: University of Chicago Press, 2003.
CSE (or CBE)	The Council of Science Educators (formerly the Council of Biology Educators)	*Scientific Style and Format: The CBE Manual for Authors, Editors, and Publishers*. 6th ed. Cambridge: Cambridge University Press, 1994.

Of all these manuals, the oldest (first edition published in 1906!), the most widely-known, and the heftiest is *The Chicago Manual of Style*. It has become accepted as *the* authoritative manual for people who write scholarly books in academic disciplines and beyond. For this reason, be prepared for your instructors—and even other style guides—to refer you to this manual for some answers to questions you may have, particularly questions about conventions of written English. In its efforts to be a comprehensive manual, CMS presents two documentation systems, one for humanists and one for scientists. I outline both in this book (in Appendixes B and D respectively), along with the documentation style of the MLA (Appendix A), that of the APA (Appendix C), and both the name-year and citation-sequence systems as they are given in the CSE manual.

Odds are very high that the style your instructor has asked you to use is one of these four documentation styles. You should be aware, however, that in addition to these basic styles/style manuals, professional organizations in other disciplines, or the publishers of academic journals, can have developed variants of these basic styles and require authors submitting manuscripts to use them. Here are a few:

American Chemical Society. *The ACS Style Guide: A Manual for Authors and Editors*. Ed. Janet Dodd. 2nd ed. Washington, DC: ACS, 1997.

American Institute of Physics. *AIP Style Manual*. 4th ed. College Park, MD: AIP, 1998.

American Medical Association. *AMA Manual of Style: A Guide for Authors and Editors*. Ed. Cheryl Iverson et al. 9th ed. Baltimore: Williams and Wilkins, 1998.

American Political Science Association. *Style Manual for Political Science*. Rev. and updated. Washington, DC: APSA, 2001.

In some cases, an instructor will ask you to follow the style used in a particular academic journal. In such cases, check any issue of the journal for information it provides for authors (usually near the table of contents for the issue). The journal may well send you to the publisher's Web site, which is always a good place to look for information about style. Publishers of print manuals will also use their Web sites to provide updates of their style, and to answer frequently asked questions. After you have located the official site of the publisher, the keyword for your search is "style." Typically you can find this information by following links to publications; then look for "information for authors."

Now that you know what the style acronyms stand for, let's continue to dissipate the mystery that stands in the way of your understanding documentation by considering the two fundamental premises upon which all of these specific documentation styles have been built.

B. Understanding Documentation Systems and Styles

1. The two basic premises of documentation

PREMISE 1

A writer must give an obvious sign, in the body of the paper, at each point where he or she is using material taken from someone else, and this writer must also give readers full information about each source so that readers, if they choose, can locate each source themselves.

Regardless of the specific form it takes, each documentation style is designed to allow you to give credit where credit is due. In addition to paying your debt to your sources by acknowledging them, you are also being a generous researcher. In giving your readers full information about each of your sources, you are sharing these sources of information with your readers. By allowing them to locate and read this material themselves, you are enlarging their knowledge of your subject. If you think about it, you yourself have profited from the generosity of other researchers when you have taken the titles of books and articles from their notes, bibliographies, and reference lists.

PREMISE 2

The information about the writer's sources should be given in a form that is least obtrusive and that takes the least amount of space without sacrificing completeness or intelligibility.

As the costs of publishing books and journals have risen, space itself has become an increasingly valuable commodity. Publishers would rather devote as much space as possible to an author's ideas, limiting the amount of space necessary for documentation to a minimum. The result of this need to save space in documentation has been the development of systems of shorthand. Thus many citations seem to be mysterious series of words and numbers:

> Proc. Nat. Acad. Sc. 7:186.

But this shorthand system allows this author to say "you will find this article in volume 7 of *The Proceedings of the National Academy of Sciences* on page 186" in much less space than it took me to write all that. Instead of writing:

> The ideas I'm using are those of Jane Hawkins which I found in an article entitled "Lives of the Saints." It appeared in the scholarly journal *News from the Vatican,* in the second issue published in 1999, and you can find it in the 56th volume of this journal on pages 256 through 273.

a documentation style allows you simply to write

> Hawkins, Jane. "Lives of the Saints." *News from the Vatican* 56 (1999): 256-73.

Since a citation such as this is a form of shorthand, every element in it becomes crucial. That is, there is meaning in the placement of information, in the way that certain pieces of information are presented (italics/underlining and quotation marks, for example), in mechanical features such as punctuation and capitalization. Individuals acquainted with styles in the humanities, for example, know that this is an article published in a periodical because a title in quotation marks is followed by a title in italics that is followed by a number. Similarly, the word "volume" does not have to be used since these same people know that the number given before the date is the volume number.

These two premises of documentation, particularly the second, should help you to appreciate both why you want to use an established style, and also why my mantra is going to be that **you must follow the form exactly.** Shorthand systems don't work unless there are rules that govern the "code" and unless both readers and writers know the code. You could, of course, develop your own system of shorthand, but that would involve working out a complete system and then providing your readers with the key. Why reinvent the wheel? Groups of people who regularly communicate with one another—scholars in a particular academic field, for example—have developed styles that allow them to provide exactly the kind of information they deem important in what seems to them to be the cleanest way. For people such as your instructors, who have worked in an academic field for a number of years, the documentation style of their fields is as transparent and meaningful as the English language.

For outsiders, however, it can be as obscure as a cryptographer's code. Let's continue our effort at breaking it!

2. Basic systems and styles of documentation

a. Systems of documentation

As I indicated a minute ago, a system of documentation is the basic mechanism that an author uses to satisfy the first premise of documentation. Figure 1 illustrates basic mechanisms of four of the common academic styles to which I have introduced you in subsection A. This picture makes a couple of points immediately clear.

Figure 1

Signal		Full Information about the Source
In the Body of the Paper	**Note**	**List at the End of the Paper**
	Called a footnote if placed at the bottom of the page; called an endnote if placed at the end of the paper	(Variously called a bibliography, reference list, list of works cited, depending upon the documentation style)
Number (note number or reference list number)	… in this way.[1] → 1. John M. Doe, *Seascape* → (New York: NoPress, 2007), 23.	Doe, John M. *Seascape.* New York: NoPress, 2007.
	… in this way(1). ──────────→	1. Doe JM. Seascape. New York: NoPress; 2007. 452 p.
In-text citation (or)	… in this way (Doe 23). ──────→	Doe, John M. <u>Seascape</u>. New York: NoPress, 2007.
Parenthetical citation	… in this way (Doe, 2007). ─────→	Doe, J. M. (2007). *Seascape.* New York: NoPress.

First of all, systems can be divided into those that use **numbers** as a **signal** that the writer has used a source, and those that provide this information in an **in-text** or **parenthetical citation**. Secondly, we notice that while the number in the first example leads to a note, where information about the source is given, the other three "skip" this step. These latter systems have each developed a method of moving readers directly from the signal in the body of the paper to a list of sources at the end of the paper.

Let's consider these systems in a bit more detail to understand both how they work and some technical language that goes with them.

(1) Numbers

Notes and Bibliography   Until the early 1980's, notes and bibliography was the standard method for documenting sources in the humanities (literature, philosophy, history), in areas of the fine arts, and in areas of the social sciences where a humanist approach was taken. In this system, the writer signals readers that she is making use of a source by placing a number at the end of one of her sentences, raised one-half space above the line (like this[1]). Traditionally, the notes that corresponded to these numbers were printed at the foot of the page where the number appeared (hence, **footnote**). Because setting notes at the foot of the page could be costly, some journals and book publishers began collecting these notes and printing them all together at the end of an article, a chapter, or the entire book (hence **endnotes**). Wherever the note is situated, it provides readers with information about the source, including the page or pages from which the writer has taken material. Full bibliographic information about these sources is also included in a list that is printed at the end of the text, called a **bibliography**. Here the sources are listed in alphabetical order according to the last name of the first author of the source. All works cited in the body of the paper appear on this list, but it can also include works that the author consulted in doing her research, but which she does not directly refer to in the body of her paper.

Only a few scholarly journals continue to use footnotes. Most books in the humanities provide notes, although they may not always be signaled with a number in the text. I provide more detailed information about this system in Appendix B, where I introduce you to the notes & bibliography system of CSM.

Numbered Reference Lists, including the Citation-Sequence System   To my knowledge, this variation of the number system is used exclusively in the sciences. Within this general category, however, there are several variations. The number in the body of the paper may be a superscript, or it may be placed in brackets or parentheses on the same line as the text. The number may correspond to a reference printed at the foot of the page (like a note), or it may take the reader to a list at the end of the paper. Each citation on this list will have a number in front of it, and the list will be in ascending numerical order, but again there is variation. The author may first make a list of all the sources he refers to in the body of the paper, then alphabetize the list according to the last name of the first author of the sources, and then number the list. Or the numbers may be assigned according to the order in which sources are cited in the text. In Appendix D, I give one of these variations, the citation-sequence system in the CSE style.

(2) In-text or parenthetical citations

In these systems, the signal in the text is the same thing as the basic citation. That is, the writer both signals the reader that he is making use of a source, and gives the reader sufficient information about that source so that the reader can go straight to a list of all sources at the end of the paper. Hence **in-text citation**. These in-text citations can also be called **parenthetical citations** if the standard method of providing information about the source is to give it in parentheses. In the list at the end of the paper the writer provides complete bibliographic information about each source. Unlike a bibliography, however, this final list includes *only* works that the writer has explicitly referred to in the body of the paper. In the MLA style, the list is called a **list of works cited;** otherwise, it is usually called a **reference list**. In the appendixes that follow this section, I present four styles that use parenthetical citations.

Obviously, in order for this system to work, the in-text or parenthetical citation must correspond to one and only one entry on the final list.

Parenthetical Citations: Author-Date Styles   The parenthetical citation system was first developed in and for the sciences, where it is still widely used. As you can see in the last example in Figure 1, the salient information the writer provides about the source in the body of the paper are the last names of the authors of a source, and the year in which the source was published (hence **author-date**). Typically, in this general system page numbers are provided only when the writer quotes directly from a text. These three features of this system— authors' names, year of publication, and lack of page numbers—all point to the nature and interests of scientific disciplines. Writers are making reference to the *work* of their peers (meaning the overall study or experiment and its results), not to any one part of the published text. Dates are important because they indicate the currency of a work in fields where the assumption is that meaningful knowledge is always evolving and scholars want to stay on the cutting edge. To readers, authors' last names and dates are important information in themselves, and are also keys to entries in the final list (**the reference list**). As you will note in the last example in Figure 1, the reference list gives the author's name first, followed by the year of publication. To find full bibliographic information about a citation in the text, readers must first match last names and then match dates with an entry in the final list. In Appendix D, I give two versions of the author-date system that can be found in scientific literature, the name-year system of the CSE style and the author-date system of the CMS style. I should note that CMS recommends this author-date system for the social sciences as well as the natural and physical sciences. And speaking of the social sciences . . . the author-date system was adopted (and adapted) by the American Psychological Association, which has become popular as the APA style. The APA style is used not only in almost all publications in the field of psychology, but can also be found in texts in related social sciences such as education, communications, linguistics. I go into detail about the APA style in Appendix C.

Parenthetical Citations: The Author-Page System of the MLA   Until the early 1980's, the MLA (the Modern Language Association) style was a system of notes and bibliography, one very similar to that of the notes & bibliography system in CMS. When the MLA decided to move to a parenthetical citation system, it is not surprising that they chose author's name and page number as the salient information to be provided as the citation in the body of the paper. Humanists are not necessarily concerned about the currency of a work, particularly that of a primary source, so dates are not necessarily of paramount interest. On the other hand, page numbers are important since scholars are usually focused on specific ideas or language within long texts. As is the case with other styles in this general category of systems, the list at the end of the paper (headed **Works Cited**) contains full bibliographic information about sources, but the only sources listed here are those that have been cited explicitly in the text. The last name of an author is the key to the appropriate entry on the final list.

    The MLA style is used by scholars in literature (English, American, French, Spanish, and so on), and can be found in journals and texts in other areas of the humanities. I cover the MLA style in Appendix A.

> ## ALERT!
>
> More lingo, this time, mine. From here on out I will be calling the list at the end of the paper the **final list.** I have been forced into this expediency by the variety of terms used for it in specific styles. The sciences and social sciences are fairly consistent in calling it a **reference list,** but the MLA has insisted on calling it the list of **works cited** (which essentially means the same thing). That is, in all of these cases the term is intended to let the reader know that the list contains only works that the writer has cited in the body of the paper. As I have indicated, the term **bibliography** says something different. This type of list can include all works that the author read, whether she actually refers to them in the body of her paper or not. In other situations, a bibliography may be intended to provide an exhaustive list of works published on a topic.

b. Styles of documentation

As I noted earlier, a **system** of documentation refers to the general mechanism by which a writer signals his or her use of sources. The term **style** refers to a system as it has been specifically defined by a publishing house, a professional organization, the publisher of scholarly journals. So, obviously, a **style of documentation** falls into one of the category of systems we've just discussed. In addition, though, a style includes all sorts of specific "rules," rules about

- what information the writer is to provide in a parenthetical citation or a note;

- how the writer is to provide this information;

- how bibliographic information about sources is to be given in the final list.

It is documentation styles that are so picky because it is here that the shorthand nature of documentation comes to the fore, as you can see in Figure 2, where full bibliographic information about a journal article is given in the four commonly-used academic styles.

Figure 2

Smith, Darlene. "The Name of the Game." <u>Journal of American Disciplines</u> 34 (2008): 234-87.	MLA
Smith, Darlene. "The Name of the Game." *Journal of American Disciplines* 34 (2008): 234-87.	CMS Notes & Bibliography
Smith, D. (2008), The name of the game. *Journal of American Disciplines* *34,* 234-87.	APA
Smith D. 2008. The name of the game. J Am Dis 34:234-87.	CSE Name-Year
Smith, D. 2008. The name of the game. *Journal of American Disciplines* 34:234-87.	CMS Author-Date

As I have noted—and will continue to remind you—the shorthand aspect of documentation is the reason that you must be meticulous with mechanical conventions such as capitalization, punctuation, quotation marks, boldface, italic type or underlining, and the like.

But we will get to these picky details in the appendixes. In the meantime, I want to stay with the big picture. Take another look at Figure 2, but this time look at the examples from a macro perspective. You should notice right away that, in spite of differences in mechanical details, they resemble each other quite closely, both in the information that is provided about the source, and in the order in which this information is provided (with the exception of the date in the author-date systems). You should also have noticed the similarities between these citations and the citation of sources that you have found in bibliographic databases, the library catalog, and other such resources.

Staying at this macro level reinforces one of the central points I made in Section 3:

Across disciplines and fields, scholars and experts "see" texts in very similar ways.

Thus my effort in all of this Section 8 is to educate you about the fundamentals of this basic, shared way of looking at texts (and even, as we shall see, texts in media other than print on paper, and materials not comprised of words in graphic form). I'll repeat. Having the general knowledge I'm presenting here should take you a very long way toward having a sense of control and thus of confidence when it comes time to document sources in any paper you write—this semester, in your college years, in your career or profession.

This general knowledge is my particular focus in subsection D, which you should skim just to get a sense of the information you can find there. But first, as a transition from choosing an appropriate style to more information about elements of documentation covered in style manuals, I want to give you some general pointers about using those manuals.

C. What You Need to Know about Style Guides and Manuals

I know, from my own personal experience and from the experiences of students, that "formal" style manuals—the ones written for scholars publishing in journals and books—can be tremendously intimidating and overwhelming to novices. This is particularly true of *The Chicago Manual of Style* and the *Publication Manual of the American Psychological Association,* but I find it also the case for the *MLA Handbook,* even though the latter has been written for students like you. The problem is that

- these manuals cover **so much material.** As I've indicated, style manuals go into issues of formatting manuscripts and writing mechanics/conventions (punctuation, spelling, abbreviations, capitalization, and so on) in addition to covering documentation style.

- these manuals attempt to address **so many different issues.** Formal manuals, particularly, attempt to be exhaustive in their coverage of every issue, since the manual is a reference work intended to answer all possible questions that publishing writers might have.

- these manuals presuppose quite a bit of "background knowledge" on the part of the user about the material they cover.

I've already started to address this last issue and I will continue to do so in this subsection and in the next. But at this point let me make a few initial recommendations:

- If the style you have been asked to use is one you've never used before, your best bet is to find a short and succinct guide to the style written for novices. The appendixes in this book have been prepared for precisely such a purpose and audience. A number of handbooks used in composition courses also provide this type of introduction to the most commonly used documentation styles.

- Using the general information I'm providing here in Section 8, determine how the basic system works, and get a feel for the particulars of the style.

- Using examples provided in the guide for novices, do a "practice run." Take a few of your sources (a book and an article from a scholarly journal), and create an entry for your final list using the style as you understand it. If you are insecure about the correctness of these entries, take them to your instructor, or someone in the writing center who knows this style.

Earlier, I noted that one of the problems with formal style manuals is that they presuppose quite a bit of background knowledge. Ironically, some of the knowledge they presuppose that users have is knowledge of the way that a style manual or guide presents information about documentation! These manuals can also presuppose that you already know what types of information you are expected to provide about sources.

I don't presuppose you have this knowledge, so let me continue my effort at educating you here. The information that follows applies not only to formal manuals, but even to guides for novices, such as this one!

How Documentation Forms Are Presented in Style Guides and Manuals

- Methods of citing sources in the body of the paper (e.g., notes or parenthetical citations) will usually be discussed in one section, and in another you will find information about preparing entries on final lists.

- The section on entries on the final list will be subdivided according to **types of sources.** I will go into more detail about these types in a moment.

- A section on a type of source will probably include extended commentary, commentary that is subdivided according to the elements in the citation. So, for example, in the subsection that tells you how to provide full bibliographic information about a book, you will find commentary on the author, then on titles, then on parts of books, then on particulars about that book (editors, or translators, or series), and so on.

- In giving the proper form for a specific type of source, manuals always illustrate with examples. If you rely on an example, be sure that you understand the example.

  - That is, be sure you understand what kind of information you are being asked to provide where (which title is the title of the article and which is the title of the journal; which number is the volume number and which number is a page number). If and when you aren't sure how the example works, check the commentary in the manual, or use subsection D of Section 8 here.

  - Also be aware that an example is usually intended to illustrate one point. For example, how to cite a book with an author and an editor. If your source is a multivolume work with a translator as well as an author and an editor, you may have to consult several examples in order to obtain all the information you need to cite this source appropriately.

- Because these manuals are designed as reference works, sections and subsections are assigned numbers (Section 4, subsection 10 will be represented as 4.10). These shorthand numbers are used in the text for cross-references— "see 17.8"—and in the index, although the index may also include a page number.

- The smart user of a style manual will open the manual at one of two places: either the **table of contents** for the documentation section, or the **index**. The **table of contents** will lay out the divisions and subdivisions of sources that I am covering here. You will use this resource when you need to find the appropriate form for specific types of sources. You can use the **index** (at the back of the manual) for the same purpose, but the index is particularly helpful when you have a "specialized" question (How do I give the English translation of the title of a book in another language? When am I allowed to use et al. in my citations?)

Categories of Sources in Style Manuals

As you look over what I say here, I hope Section 3.C.2, "Bibliographic 'Filing' Systems," is resonating in your mind. The form that has been developed for documenting a source is determined by the category into which the source falls, and thus that part of a style manual in which such forms are given is set up according to **types of sources.**

- The first two categories of sources covered in manuals are almost always **books** and **periodicals.** Forms for **parts of books** will be found in the section on books. Sections on periodicals cover **scholarly journals, magazines,** and **newspapers,** but, not surprisingly, the section will begin with scholarly journals and most of the space in this general category will be devoted to a consideration of them. Manuals for styles designed for the sciences, in fact, usually begin with forms for scholarly journals, since these are the sources that predominate in the reference lists of publishing scientists. Manuals for disciplines in the humanities, on the other hand, typically begin with a consideration of books.

- In manuals for styles in the sciences look for a specific section on **reports— scientific, technical, research.** Specifics required for documenting these texts not only inform readers about the sponsors of the work being reported on, but also provide important information critical in locating them.

- **Government** or **public documents** also constitute a category of sources. This category contains material produced by governmental bodies in the United States—federal, state, and local. This is the category you want to look for if you need to document a bill passed by Congress or the report of a committee in the House of Representatives. *The Chicago Manual of Style* covers this topic most exhaustively, providing forms not only for materials from governmental entities in the United States but also abroad, and telling us also how to cite material from international bodies such as the United Nations. Forms for documenting **legal documents** are usually nearby.

The material covered to this point in manuals is, typically, verbal texts in print form. The rest of the sources for which forms are given fall into one of three main categories. You will have to check the table of contents of your specific manual to determine where a specific type of source is discussed. Here I'll try to give you the terminology that is typically used for these types.

- **Electronic sources/media/publications** are the terms generally used for materials created for or transmitted by means of computers. These are the terms to look for when you want to know how to cite material from Web or Internet sites, texts you accessed in databases, material from online forums or discussion groups, or e-mail messages. In those cases where an electronic text had or has a parallel life as a print text, you will usually have to turn back to the appropriate print category to complete documentation of this source.

- Forms for **nonprint material** will usually be grouped together. **This general section** might be divided into **audio** and **visual, mechanical** and **live.** Look here for forms for music on CDs, forms for first-run movies, videotapes, and DVDs. Forms for documenting live performances—music concerts, plays, other types of entertainment—will also be in this same vicinity, along with those for public lectures. If you need to document the reproduction of a painting, a cartoon, or the advertisement from a magazine, look in this general area for a form for doing so.

- Finally, you will find a section on **unpublished print material.** Traditionally the sources that fall into this category are papers presented at professional conferences, poster sessions at such conferences, doctoral dissertations. Look also for terms like **informally published** and **publications of limited**

circulation. These terms indicate that style manuals are recognizing that scholars are using materials that fall into a gray area between books and truly "unpublished" material. Certain pamphlets, brochures, and leaflets would fall into this gray area.

- As you will see from my appendixes, there are particular documentation forms for **standard reference works**, particularly **dictionaries** and **encyclopedias.** However, style manuals typically don't give much space to this class of sources because scholars don't typically use them. If your list includes such a work, check the index of your style manual under "dictionary" or "encyclopedia." Entries from **specialized dictionaries** and **encyclopedias** can often be documented using the form for part of a book; see subsection D.3.

Earlier, I noted that these general sections on types of sources can include commentaries on elements in the citation (author, titles, dates of publication). In the subsection that follows, I am using a similar format. At the end of subsection B.2, I encouraged you to skim subsection D so that you have a good sense of what it contains. You can use subsection D in two ways. Reading individual parts will build your background knowledge of those issues that style manuals often take for granted. But it is also here for you to use as a quick reference on those occasions when you have specific questions about authors, or titles, or periodicals. I've crosslisted it in Section 3 so that you can also use it if and when you are confused by a citation you find in a database or in the final list of one of your sources.

Before we leave this section on manuals, though, I have to repeat a point that you need to adopt as a mantra:

When you get to a specific form for a particular type of source in a style guide or manual, it is **CRITICAL** that you follow the form that is given **EXACTLY.** This means both placing information in the specified order, and paying close attention to mechanical and typographical matters: capitalization, quotation marks or italics, abbreviations, punctuation. If you need a good reason to be hyper-detail-oriented, review my discussion of the principles of documentation.

D. What You Need to Know About . . .

1. What you need to know about authors

The first piece of information that is always given in a citation is the **author** of the text.

The author is the person or group who wrote the text being cited. The **author** is the person or group **responsible for the words, ideas, or information** that you are using in your paper.

In most cases the identity of the author is straightforward, but here are some issues related to authors that you should be aware of.

Authors of Parts of Books

Perhaps the area in which students are most likely to get confused about authors is in cases where a text (a poem, a play, an essay, an article) is published within another text (an anthology, a collection of works, an edited collection). For this reason, I have devoted a whole section to such cases; see subsection D.3.

Authors and Editors

This issue is related to the previous one, as you can see from a term such as "edited collection." You need to be sure you understand the difference between authors and editors since these terms pop up frequently in discussions of documentation styles, and also because it can affect your search for certain books. **Authors** write essays and articles, poems and plays. **Editors** are the people who create books that are comprised of texts that have been written by authors. Editors are the people, for example, who decide which poems should be printed in an anthology of twentieth-century verse, or which essays should appear in a collection of essays on modern Mexico, or which letters should be included in a collection of letters written by Dwight D. Eisenhower. Although most of the work that editors do is "behind the scenes," they may also do some writing of their own, usually in introductions or afterwords; see subsection D.3, Documenting Parts of Books. Any person considered an editor is clearly noted in citations:

Edited by John Doe	John Doe, editor
Ed. John Doe	John Doe, ed.

In library catalogs and databases, citations of an edited book (an anthology, a collection) will give the editor's name in the "author" position. Or, to turn that around, if you do an author search for this book, you will need to use the name of the editor.

Some texts are part of what is called a general series and there is a series editor, or editor-in-chief. In most cases, you can simply disregard this information.

Multiple Authors

When you have a text that was written by more than one person, here are a few things you need to be aware of:

- Be *very careful* to copy the authors' names down in the **SAME** order in which they are given on the title page (or in a citation from a database). This is the order in which you *must* always give these names (in your own citations, when you use the authors' names in sentences in your paper).

- In the sciences, it is not unusual for texts, especially articles in periodicals, to have many authors. Multiple authors, however, can make parenthetical citations in papers very long and cumbersome:

  . . . this study (Halberstam, Wong, Keebler, Ito, Murray, Greenberg, & Perez, 2006).

  So, to shorten such long citations, most documentation styles in the social and natural sciences have use et al. Et al. is the abbreviation for the Latin phrase that means "and others." Thus, "Halberstam et al." means "this text was written by Halberstam and others," and this is the way that et al. is generally used. That is, in the citation the last name of the first author is given, followed by et al.

  . . . this study (Halberstam et al., 2006).

  In citations, et al. is typed in the same font as the rest of the paper, and the "al." is followed by a period, since it is the abbreviation of the word "alii." Different documentation styles have different conventions for the use of et al., so if you have one or more works by multiple authors, check your style manual to be sure that you use et al. correctly.

Group Authors, Organization as Author, Corporate Authors

There will be cases in which you come across texts whose "author" is not a person or persons, but rather a group. The group may be an organization (The American National Red Cross). It may be a political party or a lobbying group (the NRA). It may be a government agency or body (the U.S. Forest Service). It may be a company or corporation (Johnson & Johnson). It could also be the page on the Web site sponsored by such a group or corporation. In these instances, you will use the name of this group in the author position for the text (for further discussion of unsigned Web pages, see subsection D.6). Style manuals tell you how to cite sources of this type; in the index, look for one of these terms: corporate author, group author, organization as author. Here are some basic hints:

- If the name of the group **begins with an article** (*the, a, an*), disregard the article when you alphabetize your final list. In some cases, the style you are using may recommend omitting the article completely.

- The names of some organizations are pretty long, and most organizations have developed (well-known) acronyms—WHO for the World Health Organization. Some documentation styles allow you to use these acronyms, but each has specific guidelines that you must follow in doing so. Check the manual.

- You will probably run into cases where a group or organization is the publisher of a text and this same group or organization could also be considered its author. It would never be incorrect to spell out the name of the organization in both the author and the publisher positions, but check your style manual for other possibilities.

- When and if the group author is a **government body,** you really do need to check the style manual you are using for citations of **government documents** or **public documents.** There are special styles for citing sources that fall into this category.

Representation of Names

One of the major distinctions between styles in the humanities and those in the sciences lies in the way that authors' names are represented in citations. In the humanities, (1) only the name of the first author is inverted in a citation, and (2) the author's full first name is given (if it is available), along with a middle initial (if available):

> Bradford, Herman L., and Alfred E. Newman

In the sciences, however, (1) only the first (and middle) initials are typically used, and (2) often the names of all authors are inverted:

> Bradford, H. L., & Newman, A. E.

This is one of those details you need to watch for when you are doing your documentation.

TIP

In the Sources section of your Researcher's Notebook I'd suggest that you write out the full first name of every author and that person's middle initial (if given). This information makes searching for texts much easier, and you have the information you need for any of the documentation styles.

Authors of Introductions, Entries in Reference Works

It is conventional for authors of introductions to put their names at **the end** of the introduction. In the case of anthologies in which introductions to sections of text have not been signed, it would be reasonable to assume that these portions of the text have been written by the editor (or editors) of the text as a whole. Check the style manual you are using. Generally, you have the option of using the editors' names as the authors of the introduction, or you can simply start with the title.

> Witherspoon, Alexander M., and Frank J. Warnke, eds. "John Donne: Introduction." *Seventeenth-Century Prose and Poetry* . . .

> OR

> "John Donne: Introduction." *Seventeenth-Century Prose and Poetry.* Ed. Alexander M. Witherspoon and Frank J. Warnke.

If and when you put the names of the editors in the author position, it is not necessary to repeat their names where the names of the editors are normally given.

It is also conventional for the names of authors of entries in reference works (encyclopedias, dictionaries) to be placed at the end of the entry, so be sure to check here for this information. Just to make life interesting, some entries are "signed" only with initials. If and when you run across this situation, you will have to check the master list of authors for the name that corresponds to the initials.

Texts with No Author

If no author is listed next to the title of a text, don't assume that the text has no author until you have considered the various alternatives I've just discussed above. If you have assured yourself that you do not know who should be legitimately considered the author of a text,

- the CSE styles will ask you to list Anonymous as the author (see Appendix D.C.);

- other styles will have you begin the entry with the title or the headline of the text; see subsection D.2;

- in instances where you find pages on a Web site that have a title but list no author, see my discussion of this matter in subsection D.6.

2. What you need to know about titles

Always give the title **EXACTLY** as you find it on the title page of the work!

Titles and Subtitles

Generally speaking, when you give the title of a work, you should **always give the FULL title;** this means giving us any subtitles. The main title is the part that is given first; subtitles are the parts that come next (usually after a colon). In punctuating the title, follow the punctuation used in the original. If none is given, it is customary to separate the main title and the subtitle with a colon. When in doubt, I check the title in a library catalog record or the record in a database to see how the cataloger punctuated it!

The Dream of Eternal Life: Biomedicine, Aging, and Immortality

The History of Development: From Western Origins to Global Faith

"Phantom Menace: Is Washington Terrorizing Us More Than Al Qaeda?"

"Modernist Memory; or, The Being of Americans"

Titles within Titles

There are many cases in which a complete text is published inside the "covers" of another text. It is imperative that readers of citations know which title is which. The issue is handled in all documentation forms first of all by placement or order of information, and, frequently, by representing the two kinds of titles in different typographical forms.

Author of Words	Title of the Text by the Author	Title of the Text in Which This Shorter Text Has Been Made Public
Frost, Robert	"Birches"	*The Norton Anthology of American Literature*
Webb, Arachne	"Spiders"	*Journal of Science*
Smith, Charles	"Man Bites Dog"	*Smalltown Gazette*
Harper, Ben	"Beloved One"	*Burn to Shine*

As the examples here illustrate, the author and title of the text published "inside" the more inclusive text always come first because the material being cited is the responsibility of the author, and the title that follows the author's name must be the title of the text in which the author presented this material. The title of the more inclusive work (and its editor, if relevant) is given next. The title of the more inclusive work and its author or editor is critical information, because it is the more inclusive text that is cataloged in the library, as well as in the catalogs of bookstores (or music stores).

Representation of Titles

- In most documentation styles, the differences in these two kinds of titles is emphasized by the use of different typographical representation. Thus, in most documentation styles, the title of the more inclusive text is italicized; one exception is titles in the CSE style. In styles in the humanities, the title of the work included within the larger text is enclosed in quotation marks.

- You need to be aware that there are major differences in the way that titles are represented in styles in the humanities and those in the social and natural sciences: quotation marks, for example, are not used in the scientific styles, and few words in titles are capitalized.

This is an area in which you need to be very self-conscious about following a documentation style exactly. Your vigilance will be particularly critical if you are familiar with the humanities style but are now using a scientific style, or vice versa.

- In cases where there are words in quotation marks in the original title, and you are putting this whole title in quotation marks, put the material that was originally quoted in single quotation marks: "The Typical 'Soccer Mom.'"

- In cases where you are italicizing a title, and the original title has a word or words already in italics, simply present these words in regular roman type.

Original: Tragedy in *King Lear*

Your Citation: *Tragedy in* King Lear

Italics and Underlining

When it comes to titles, underlining and italics really "say" the same thing, but usage varies. Some style manuals may advise you to underline; others may recommend that you represent these titles in italic. See Section 7.C for further discussion of the issue. Your instructor's preferences must also be considered. **As in all matters of style, what is most important is consistency.** Once you have decided on a way to represent a title, use that same style for ALL titles in your paper (whether they appear in the body of your paper, in a note, or in your final list).

A Few More Words about Titles in Scientific Styles

If and when you are using a scientific style, you should be alert to the following:

- The titles of journals may be abbreviated. You'll notice that this is the case in the CSE style, and it is the form I've found in most journals and books in the hard sciences that I have looked at.

- In some cases, the titles of articles published in journals are simply omitted.

When a Citation Begins with a Title

When a text has no author, most documentation styles have you begin the citation with the title of the text. All guidelines for titles apply in these cases. The one thing you need to remember is that you will disregard initial articles (*the, a, an*) in alphabetizing your final list: "The Name of the Game" will be alphabetized under "Name."

3. What you need to know about documenting parts of books

I am hoping that you are reading this section early in the research stage of your project. That way, I can help you both to find texts that are parts of books, as well as to enter parts of books properly in the working bibliography you are setting up.

From my own experience I know that students typically run into trouble citing essays or articles or stories that are published in edited collections of works. However, if you understand the fundamentals of documentation systems, you should have no trouble figuring out how to document a part of a book without even having to look at a model.

The basic questions you need to ask yourself (and answer) should, by this point, sound very familiar:

- Who wrote the words or ideas that I using in my paper?

- What is the title of this segment of the book?

- What further information would the reader need in order to locate the book?

If you are looking at a book whose entire content was written by the same person or persons, and the divisions of the book are normal chapter divisions, then you usually don't need to cite the part. On the other hand, if the book is comprised of parts that are independent texts that could have been (and probably were) published in different places at different times, then you will want to provide further information about these parts. Providing information about the part is essential if the book is made up of parts written by different authors.

> ## NOTE
>
> Examples in this subsection are given in the MLA style. While the basic order of information in citations remains the same in most styles, other details will differ. See the manual of the style you are using. The type of book I'm talking about here goes by a number of different names; it may be called a collection of works, an anthology, an edited collection, or an edited work. In the style manual you are using, look for information about citing part of a book, or for citing a text in an anthology, an edited work, or an edited collection.

Part and Book by the Same Author

Let us say that you are looking at an anthology of poems by Emily Dickinson or a collection of essays by Tom Wolfe. The divisions in these books are not simple chapters, but are complete texts that may have been or could have been published in places other than this book. Giving us the title of the poem or the essay, then, becomes important because it is the specific text that you are using. Notice how the citation moves from specific to general publication information.

> Dickinson, Emily. "A Diamond on the Hand" (No. 1131). 1867. *The Poems of Emily Dickinson*. Ed. R. W. Franklin. Variorum ed. Vol. 2. Cambridge, MA: Belknap-Harvard UP, 1998. 985.

> Wolfe, Tom. "Sorry, but Your Soul Just Died." *Hooking Up*. New York: Farrar, 2000. 89-109.

Part and Book by Different Authors

Edited collections are books comprised of essays (articles) by a group of different authors. Here is the citation of one essay in such a collection.

> Quandt, William. "New U. S. Policies for a New Middle East?" *The Middle East and the United States: A Historical and Political Reassessment*. Ed. David W. Lesch. 3rd ed. Boulder, CO: Westview Press, 2003. 459-66.

If you tried to find this book in a library catalog by entering Quandt's name, your search would fail, even if the library owned the book, because Quandt is not its author. Rather, in the catalog record the author field is filled with the name of the editor of this collection, David Lesch. So, in cases where a collection of articles have been brought together by a person or persons who is considered the editor, you will need all the information I have given above in order to locate the text for yourself. And if you use an article from such a collection in your paper, you will need to provide your readers with the same information.

Introductions, Prefaces, Afterwords

Finally, let us consider parts that are entitled Preface, Introduction, Afterword. Introductions (or afterwords) are common in contemporary editions of classic works, like Dante's *Inferno*. These parts of a book are often written by the editor or the translator, although occasionally an "outside" scholar is asked to provide such a commentary. Below is a citation of the introduction of a recent edition of the *Inferno*. Notice how it follows the typical pattern that I have described, moving from specific part to whole and providing sufficient information about the book itself so that you and other readers could find this particular edition in searches of library or bookseller catalogs.

> Hollander, Robert. Introduction. *Inferno*. By Dante Alighieri. Trans. Robert and Jean Hollander. New York: Doubleday, 2000. xvii-xxxiii.

Entries in Reference Works

In the appendixes in this book, I cover the citation of material from dictionaries and encyclopedias in the section on parts of books. Forms for citing this type of material do differ from style to style, and you should check the appropriate style manual for proper forms. But here are a few general issues you should be aware of.

- If the entry in a reference work is signed, you should use the name of that person as the author. See my discussion of this issue in subsection D.1. under "Authors of Introductions, Entries in Reference Works."

- Most style manuals make a distinction between what they call standard reference works and specialized ones. A standardized reference work is a well-know text that has been in print for a number of years and is periodically updated. For these reasons, less publication information is typically required in citing them. *The Encyclopedia Britannica* and *Webster's Third New International Dictionary of the English Language, Unabridged* fall into this category. Full bibliographic information, however, is usually required for less well-known, specialized dictionaries and encyclopedias.

- Treat the term or phrase of the entry in the reference work as the title of this source. Represent this title exactly as it is in the original: Eisenhower, Dwight David. Since reference works are set up like dictionaries, with entries in alphabetical order according to the first word in the entry phrase, your readers will not be able to find the entry you used unless you give it to them exactly as it is in the original.

- Since entries in reference works are presented in alphabetical order, you really don't have to give page numbers; this is definitely the case with standard reference works.

- While it makes good sense to find and use definitions of specialized vocabulary in specialized dictionaries, you will need a very good reason for quoting a definition from a common English dictionary. As I note in Section 3.B.3, the *Oxford English Dictionary* (OED) does not fall into this category. It is a specialized, authoritative reference work that you should not hesitate to quote in appropriate circumstances.

Tips and Advice for Citing a Part of a Book

- In most cases, any and all information that you are required to give about a book will need to be given about anthologies and edited collections; see the next subsection, D.4. If the text you are citing comes from a book that is part of a multivolume set, you will have to provide volume numbers. See the Dickinson example above, and my discussion of multivolume words in the next subsection, D.4.

- If you are using an in-text or parenthetical documentation style, each part of a book that you use will have to be entered on your final list as a separate entry. This requirement comes simply from the way these systems work. However, the copy and paste features of your word-processing program relieves you of the need to retype bibliographic information about the book. Type it once, then copy and paste it into other relevant entries. Be careful, though, about any information that differs from part to part, such as page numbers in the CMS style.

- If the text you are using was published much earlier than the copyright date of the book where you found it, you should give us the original publication date. (See the Dickinson example above). Check the style manual you are using for details.

4. What you need to know about documenting books

In documentation styles, a book is an entity that has been printed and bound for durability and wide distribution. What typically defines a book is the fact that it has been formally copyrighted. **Pamphlets** and **brochures** may exist on the periphery of the category of book, or fall into the category of unpublished material. One determinate would be whether or not the text provides what I call facts of publication. **Technical or research reports,** again if they have facts of publication, are essentially cited the way books are. Specifics of the report simply fall into the category of particulars of publication. Manuals of styles in the social and natural sciences usually have explicit discussions of technical or research reports, so check the table of contents or the index. If you are not sure how to categorize a particular text you have, check with your instructor.

In order to satisfy the first premise of documentation, you'll need to give your readers complete publication information about each book you have used.

This publication information is typically broken down into two segments of the citation; they are given in the following order:

- **Particulars of publication**
- **Facts of publication**

You will find most of this information on the title page of the book. Often you'll have to turn the page to find the year of publication.

Particulars of Publication

As you have probably already noticed, some books have multiple existences. A novel in Spanish can have been translated into English; a famous Spanish novel may have been translated into English by different people in different years! Or the author of a particular book decides to revise what he said earlier, and so publishes a second (or third) edition of it. Some works are so long that they need to be published in a series of separate books (volumes). Any and all of this information about the specific book you used is important to the reader and thus you are expected to include it in your citation. Such information is given after the title of the book and before the facts of publication, often in the following order:

Name of an editor and/or a translator

Edition used, if not the first

If a multivolume set, information about volumes

Title of series, with volume or number

The way in which you represent this information will vary according to the documentation style you use. If the book you are citing has more than one of these particulars, and you want to be absolutely sure you have the citation right, you may need to check a couple of examples in the style manual, since examples tend to focus on one particular at a time.

Publication Information for Books in Multivolume Sets

Books in multivolume sets fall into three different categories: sets with volumes with the same title by the same author/editor; sets with volumes by the same author/editor with different titles; sets with volumes by different authors/editors and different titles.

If you are using material from a book that is part of a multivolume set, you will (obviously) check your style manual for the appropriate form for your citation. Here are the underlying issues.

If all volumes in the set have the same author and the same title, then your citations will obviously have to include the number of the volume you are using; since each volume in the set begins with page 1, page numbers alone will not take your readers to the material you are citing. The issue is amplified if, in your paper, you use material from more than one volume in the set.

Less problematic are multivolume works that fall into the next two categories, since titles and/or authors are different. In these cases, your citation may or may not indicate that the book you are using is part of a larger set. Here are a couple of examples given in the MLA style.

MULTIVOLUME SET WITH SAME EDITOR AND TITLE

"Robin Hood Rescuing Three Squires" (Child No. 140). The Traditional Tunes of the Child Ballads with Their Texts, according to the Extant Records of Great Britain and America. Ed. Bertrand H. Bronson. Vol. 3. Princeton, NJ: Princeton UP, 1966. 53-57. 4 vols. 1959-72.

OR

"Robin Hood Rescuing Three Squires" (Child No. 140). The Traditional Tunes of the Child Ballads with Their Texts, according to the Extant Records of Great Britain and America. Ed. Bertrand H. Bronson. Vol. 3. Princeton, NJ: Princeton UP, 1966. 53-57.

MULTIVOLUME SET WITH DIFFERENT TITLES

Wellek, René. French, Italian, and Spanish Criticism, 1900-1950. New Haven: Yale UP, 1992. Vol. 8 of A History of Modern Criticism: 1900-1950. 8 vols. 1955-92.

OR

Wellek, René. French, Italian, and Spanish Criticism, 1900-1950. New Haven: Yale UP, 1992.

NOTE

Frequently, multivolume sets are published over a series of years (2003-10). When you list the entire set, give the dates in this way. If the title page of the book itself does not contain such information, you can find it in the record of the work in a library catalog. If and when you cite only one volume, be sure the year you give is the year in which that volume was published.

Facts of Publication

The facts of publication include the city of publication, the publisher, and the copyright date. Placement of the date varies among systems. Here is general information about these "facts."

- What comes in front of the publisher is the *city* in which the publisher has offices (*not* the state); "New York" means "New York City." If multiple cities are listed, you do not list them all. Check your style manual. Usually you will use the first city listed. The name of the state may be *added* if the city is not well-known, or if there are multiple cities with the same name:

Portland, ME: Stenhouse Publisher

- The date of publication is the copyright date. In some cases, you'll find it on the title page of the book. If not, on the reverse side of the title page look for the most recent year next to the copyright symbol ©.

- And speaking of dates, there are times that you will be citing a work that is being reprinted; its original copyright date or year of publication may be much earlier than the copyright date of the edition you are using. I'd encourage you to give the original date. You can, of course, include it in the body of your paper. But most documentation styles also have forms for providing this information in the entry in your final list. Check your style manual.

- As far as the publisher is concerned, you should be aware that some styles like to truncate the names of publishers. Also, if the text you are using is a paperback edition, this information could be important. Obviously it is important if the "plates" used for the hardback and those used for the paperback are different, because page numbers in the two editions will be different. Watch for these matters, and check your style manual's discussion of publishers.

- If any of these three pieces of information—city of publication, publisher, copyright date—is not given in the book, you must so indicate (otherwise, we think you simply forgot to include it). Check your manual, but the traditional way to indicate missing information is to write n. p. (no place), n. p. (no publisher), or n. d. (no date) in your citation where this information would normally go.

5. What you need to know about periodicals

By the time you finish this section on periodicals, you should feel confident that you can read citations that you find for articles in both the bibliographic databases you search and in the bibliographies and/or reference lists of sources you consult. You should also feel confident that, when you are documenting your own sources, you understand the terms that the style manual is using when it is showing you how to document periodicals.

I will remind you that periodicals are materials that are published on a regular basis; they include magazines, newspapers, and scholarly journals. One of the areas in which the shorthand aspect of documentation styles can be most evident is in citations of articles that have been published in scholarly journals.

Journal of American History 109 (2023): 958-983.

Am J Phy 2023 June; 91(6):533.

Am J Phy 91(6):557.

Journal of Cognitive Psychotherapy, 17, 94-97.

You have to "crack these codes" in order to find the articles you want to read, and you'll have to understand them in order to cite periodical literature in your paper. But cracking these codes is not difficult if you understand a few basic things about periodicals.

In most citations, the title of the periodical will be given in full. In those cases when it is abbreviated and you want to be sure you have the correct full title, check with your instructor or a reference librarian. But using the title or name of a periodical to locate an article published in it will get you only so far. To find a specific article, you need more publication information.

Three types of publication information are key:

- the inclusive pages on which the article is printed;

- the volume (and issue) number of the issue;

- the date (or year) of the issue.

About Volume and Issue Numbers

Volume (and issue) numbers are, in my experience, the elements of periodicals that are least understood by students. The concept, however, is really pretty simple. All you have to do is to think of a periodical as a very long book that is being published in segments, the segments being **issues** and **volumes.** To grasp the way volumes work in periodicals, think in terms of the volumes of an encyclopedia. (And throughout this explanation you are going to have to think in terms of print-on-paper versions of these materials, because all the conventions I'm talking about here were devised for, and dictated by, the fact that these materials were printed on paper and, like other physical material in the library, had to be stored in an organized fashion.)

Print encyclopedias are published in volumes because all of the material the editors wanted to include in them would not fit into one book that could be lifted by a normal human being. Thus, an encyclopedia is broken down into separate books or bound volumes. The separate volumes of encyclopedias are usually divided into alphabetical units (A-C, D-G, etc.). The **volumes** of a periodical are, on the other hand, determined by annual increments, and the volume number is calculated from the first year a periodical is published. So, for example, let's say the (fictional) periodical *Fantasia* was first published in September of 1980, and that, in its first year of publication, it brought out four **issues** (four separate versions of *Fantasia,* each with a different date on the cover and different material inside). Those four issues together make up volume 1, and the issues would have been numbered in the order in which they were published. In September of 1981, *Fantasia* started its second year of publication, and the issue it produced that September was volume 2, issue 1. Meanwhile, in December of 1981 the librarians took the first four issues of *Fantasia* off the shelf, and had them bound together. On the spine of the binding, we find the volume number (roman numeral I or arabic numeral 1) and, perhaps, the calendar years

(1980–81). If you take a trip around your library, you will see that all the paper copies your library has of journals and magazines are collected and stored in such bound volumes.

You should understand, now, that to locate an article in a bound periodical, you will always need the volume number. However, if you are searching for an article in a scholarly journal, you may not need the issue number because scholarly journals are typically **paginated consecutively through a volume year.** In the case of our fictional *Fantasia,* volume 1, issue 1 contained pages 1–65, issue 2 was paginated from pages 66 to page 92, and so on through the end of issue 4. The next volume year started again with page 1. Thus, the volume number and the inclusive pages numbers are usually sufficient to find the article being sought.

Examples of Citations of Scholarly Journals

Author. "Article Title." Journal of Literary Surprises 34.4 (2023): 356-75.

Author. "Article Title." *Journal of American History* 109 (2023): 958-983.

Author. (2023). Article title. *Journal of Cognitive Psychotherapy, 37,* 94-97.

Author. 2023. Article title. *American Journal of Physics* 91:557.

Author. 2023. Article title. Am J Phy 91(6):557.

Author. Article title. Am J Phy 2023 June; 91(6):557.

Author. Title. Brief Treatment and Crisis Intervention 23, no. 2 (2023): 245-76.

Author. Title. Journal of Child Psychology & Psychiatry & Allied Disciplines. Vol 64(6) Sep 2023, 765.

Scholarly Journals

With this information in mind, let's return to the examples of citations of scholarly journals. Earlier I said that three types of publication information are key:

- the inclusive pages on which the article is printed;

- the volume (and issue) number of the issue;

- the date (or year) of the issue.

Can you find each of these pieces of information in the sample citations?

Here are some hints:

- In almost all citations **the last numbers given are the page(s) on which you will find the article.** Typically, the page numbers are **inclusive,** which means the numbers of the pages on which the article begins and ends. However, in some citations in bibliographic databases you may be given only the number of the first page of the article.

- **Volume numbers** are usually given immediately after the title of the journal, although you will notice a bit of variation in some citation formats. The letter "v" and "vol." are the common abbreviations for volume; any number that comes after these abbreviations is the volume number.

- When **issue numbers** are given, they always immediately follow the volume number. Most commonly, they are placed in parentheses or the abbreviation "no." is written in front of them. In the MLA style, the issue number is separated from the volume number with a period: 34.4.

- Most documentation styles also include **the year** in which an article was published, although that information is usually provided mainly to let the reader know how current the material is; the month or season of publication may be included, but is usually not required. The year of publication is the piece of information whose placement can vary most widely. You ought to be able to recognize it in the citations, though, simply by reason of your familiarity with recent calendar years.

Popular Magazines and Newspapers

If you check the table of contents of popular magazines or the masthead of newspapers, you'll see that they, like scholarly journals, have volume numbers and issue numbers. Among the four styles I cover in this book, however, only the CSE asks you to give volume and issue numbers in the citations of **popular magazines.** In the other styles, simply the date of the issue and the page numbers of the article are given, and they are usually sufficient to locate the article.

In the case of **newspapers,** however, there are a few things you need to be sensitive to both for citing and retrieving articles.

- Some newspapers are published throughout the day in **different editions;** other well-known newspapers, such as the *New York Times,* create different editions for different locales. Since the content of pages in different editions may vary, when you are using a print newspaper as a source, pay close attention to the edition and plan to include this information in your citation. Check the manual of your documentation style, but the logical place for this information is after the date and before page numbers.

- Again, pay close attention to **page numbers.** Many newspapers divide an edition into segments (front section, sports section, business section), each of which begins with page 1. Thus the section designation is a vital part of the page number: B3. It is not unusual for a newspaper article to begin on one page and continue on another. One way of indicating this information is to place a plus sign after the number of the first page of the article: B3+. But check your style manual for the proper way to handle nonconsecutive pages.

- When the material you are using falls outside the category of a news article, it can be helpful to let the reader know **what type of article this is.** You'll notice that bibliographic databases usually provide this information. So, if you are using material from a letter to the editor, an editorial, a review of a play or movie, check your style manual for the proper way to cite.

- When you are giving the name of newspapers that do not include the city (or state) of origin, you will want to add this information to your citation. Usually you do that with parentheses or brackets:

Oregonian [Portland]

Times Herald [Smalltown, ND]

ALERT!

Whenever you download an article from a computer (full-text database or other source), you must provide readers with full information about where you located it, even though the article originally appeared in print (or seems to have originally appeared in print). See section D.6., Documenting Material Downloaded from Computers.

Other Information regarding Periodicals

- Although volume numbers in periodicals themselves may be written as roman numerals, citations almost always express these numbers as arabic numerals (33 instead of XXXIII).

- Some documentation styles express dates in the American fashion (June 24, 2007) but some prefer the European style (24 June 2007). Similarly, some styles ask that you abbreviate months of the year.

- Regarding page numbers. Inclusive page numbers are used when an article starts on one page and continues on the pages that follow. In these cases, you give the first page of the article and the last page of the article, with a hyphen (n-dash) in between. If an article starts on one page and jumps to a later page, check your manual for the way to represent nonconsecutive pages.

- As the examples I have given illustrate, when you are documenting your own sources you will have to pay very close attention to typographical representation in citations of periodicals, especially of scholarly journals. If you are moving from a humanist style to a scientific one, or vice-versa, you will have to be particularly vigilant because typographical aspects of these citations are so different.

6. What you need to know about documenting material downloaded from computers

The category of sources I am going to be discussing here covers any material transmitted through a computer; thus, it includes everything from textual material on CD-ROMs to material from any and all online sources, public and restricted, edited and unedited (databases, Web and Internet sites, newsgroups, discussion groups, online forums, e-mail messages and the like). When you go into style manuals and guides, you will find that the common term for these materials is **electronic** (electronic publications, electronic sources, electronic media), but, in my experience, this is not necessarily a term students know or use. The heading I have used in the appendixes, derived from the words students typically use in asking me for such information, is "Web Sites and Other Electronic Sources." But here I am using the clumsier phrase "downloaded from computers" because it encompasses not only Internet sites but also a category of electronic sources that students make constant use of—full-text databases—without recognizing that they must document these texts as electronic sources.

Before we move into this matter, let me say a few more words about this category in general. First of all, these electronic sources have become a prominent and ordinary part of the lives of researchers only in the past fifteen or so years, and they will undoubtedly continue to evolve and change at an equally rapid pace. The speed with which the technology progresses presents two basic challenges as far as documentation is concerned: (1) developing meaningful ways to document such material; (2) recognizing that one fundamental premise of documentation—enabling readers to find and see material for themselves—may not be possible in an environment in which material regularly comes and goes, and an environment in which material can be easily and regularly revised and changed. At the point that I am writing this subsection, all the standard documentation styles that I cover in this book, with the exception of the CSE, have been updated, in large part to explicitly address the issue of electronic sources and to provide "official" forms for documenting these sources, or at least the most common categories of these sources. We should all be alert, however, to the probability that these documentation forms will change, either because of changes in the technology itself, or because of the needs of scholars, or both. In creating examples for the appendixes of this book, I have sometimes had questions about citing electronic sources that the manual did not answer, and at other times my sense of what should be said about an electronic source in a citation did not accord with what the manual asked me to record. So in this area of documentation all of us are involved with a "work in progress." Our obligations as responsible researchers, however, are very clear. We have to cite all electronic sources from which we have taken words, ideas, and/or factual material, and we are most likely to meet this obligation fully and correctly by making use of (1) our knowledge and understanding of the fundamentals of all documentation, and (2) our understanding of the basic principles governing the style of documentation that we are using, as well as seeking the form that best matches each source in question.

Secondly, let me remind you that, to document electronic sources correctly, there is information you need to be sure that you record **WHEN** you are accessing or downloading this material.

> For detailed discussion of the information you need to record when you access or download electronic sources, see Section 3.E.

Now, let's turn to an area that my experience tells me is problematic for students.

Electronic Versions of Print Material

Here I am speaking of texts that were originally published in print form, or texts that are currently available in both a print and an electronic form. The issue is very simple, and I ought not to have to provide the rationale.

POINT ONE

Even if versions of this material are available in paper form, if **you** found it in an electronic source, you must give us full information about the electronic source where you found it.

POINT TWO

If this text was originally published on paper, in your citation you should give us as much information as the electronic version provides about the print version.

You provide information about the print version both to acknowledge that what you read was based on—or is a reproduction of—a text that was originally available to the public in print (a nineteenth-century magazine, for example, or an essay no longer in print), or, in the case of periodicals that are publishing in both formats, to give readers information about the alternate print version. You provide us with full information about the electronic source where you found this article *quite simply because this is where you found it*. Providing full information about this electronic source, of course, gives readers the information they need to access the same text from the same place if they wish to. But providing this information is equally important for another reason. You should be aware that, unless the material you have accessed is a literal reproduction of the original print text (e.g., a PDF document), the electronic version and the print version may not be the same. It is not unusual for there to be differences in newspaper articles in the two formats, especially articles produced by news services.

Material Available Only in Digital Form

In a conference I had last semester, a student showed me the bibliography of a paper that included research. The list was nothing more than a series of URLs. In one sense, this student's instincts were right on the mark. The URL is *the* piece of information that will take us directly to the source. But my own immediate reaction was, what is this? Where do these addresses take me? What exactly have you been making use of? Her list would be analogous to a bibliography that gives us nothing more than the call numbers of books! Yes, we need precise information that will tell us how to locate sources, but we also want and need to know what these sources are, who is responsible for their dissemination, when they were written, and so on. So it is not surprising that documentation of electronic sources follows the same basic principles—and even the same basic order—of documentation of print sources.

Specific forms used in various documentation styles differ, but generally you will see that they follow this general pattern, moving from left to right in the citation:

Author of material	Title of material	As much information as you have about this particular material	Information about where and when you located it

This general pattern applies, regardless of where you found the material, whether on a full-text database, on a government or agency Web site, on the site of an academic library that is making a collection of old documents available in digital format, or in an online dictionary or encyclopedia. Information about the particular material, for example, will include full information about the print version if it was originally published in print. It will include the date when this material was written or created. It can include information about the nature of this material (e.g., that this text is a review of a book or a movie). To tell us where and when you located the material, you will give us such information as the URL of online sites, the name of a database or a Web site, the sponsors of a Web site, the date on which you accessed the material, and the like.

Issues Raised by Electronic Sources

- One problematic area of documentation of electronic sources that does not seem to have been resolved is the issue of **page numbers.** In texts that are over a page or two long, how do we tell readers where they would find a quotation or a fact or an idea? If you download print material that is an exact reproduction of a print text, or if the material is a PDF document, you should be able to use the page numbers in the document since the format of these documents is stable. But other page numbers do not have such authority, especially when they are determined strictly by settings on your browser and/or printer. Over the years, I've seen it recommended that paragraph numbers be used as an indicator of the location of material within a text, and I've come across online journals that do number the paragraphs in their articles. But I don't know many people with the patience to number the paragraphs themselves, especially if the document runs ten or twenty pages long, nor readers who would be willing to go through the same operation.

- Another area that could be problematic is determining the **authorship of unsigned pages on a Web site.** In some examples I've provided in the appendixes, I have assigned authorship to the organization on whose site I found them (the American National Red Cross and the World Health Organization). I did so because I felt very confident that material on these pages was either written by members of the staff of the organization, or that the material was written at the request of the organization. In either case, my assessment was that what was said on these pages was something that the organization as an organization would say publicly, that it would take full responsibility for its contents. But you will come across material on Web sites that has been posted there by the sponsors of the site. In other words, this would be material written by someone with no affiliation with the site. We could assume that the sponsor posted it because the point of view of the material was consonant with the sponsor's point of view, but if we knew for a fact that this material was not written by or for the sponsors, we would not list the sponsor as the author. So, my advice: if you have any question about who should be given responsibility for a text, go with anonymous. In other words, skip the author position and start your citation with the title of the piece or the name of the page. It would have been equally proper for me to have cited the two examples I'm talking about that way.

- In Section 6, I stressed the value and importance of **integrating your sources into your paper,** bringing authors into dialogue with you: "Sally Kelly has argued in her book *Christmas Bells* that . . . . Recently, however, Mark Wong took issue with this whole reading. . . ." This strategy can be particularly useful to you and to your readers when you introduce material from certain electronic sources because it allows you to say things about the source that may not be required by your documentation style or made clear in a citation in your final list.

This has become a topic of heated debate among music students, as can be seen in recent postings on the American Musicology Society e-mail discussion list for students. The views of Kara Hendricks are typical of those who favor. . . .

I found a number of Web sites for the fans of this group. Most were highly informal; the main pages of the sites were nothing more than a series of links to other pages in the site and/or to related sites. On one of them <http://xxxxxxxxxxxx>, I found a review of a concert posted by "Jenny." In it, Jenny rhapsodized about . . .

In the last example the address of this Web site is included because, given the dearth of information available on the site, there is little information to put in a formal citation. This would be a case in which complete bibliographic information (the full citation) is simply given in the body of the paper. From my perspective, a citation such as this is a perfectly legitimate documentation of the source in question. If you have such sources that you want to include in your paper, it would probably be best for you to consult your instructor as well as the manual of the style you are using to determine the best way for you to cite the material.

7. What you need to know about documenting other types of sources

The main message I have for you here is:

If you used it, you must document the source!

In some cases it has taken a while, but the people who create and update documentation styles now fully recognize that scholars and experts make use of many types of materials that fall outside the traditional categories of printed books and articles. They have responded by developing forms for citing non-traditional sources and/or material from various media. If and when you have such sources, I trust that subsection C gives you sufficient information so you know where to look for the proper form in your style manual, or that you understand the style you are using well enough to deduce how the source ought to be cited.

But let me reiterate two basic principles that follow from Premise 1 of documentation.

- If it is available to the public, give readers the information they need to locate it themselves.

- If it is not available to the public, then tell us where you located it.

A Few Reminders and Pointers

- **Using material from a secondary source.** I'm speaking here of material that you find in a source you are reading (the **secondary source**) that comes from another source (the **primary** or **original source**). This material may be a direct quotation, or it may simply be a paraphrase or even a reference to the original. I'll remind you that your obligation is to make every effort to locate the original so that you can read it yourself. If putting your hands on the original is impossible (because it is, for example, an unpublished letter in the archives of a library two thousand miles away), then you will make it very clear in your paper that you have found this information in a secondary source. Documentation styles that use in-text parenthetical citations typically word such citations this way:

A study by Johnson and Johnson (as cited in Murphy 2005) . . .

In a lecture in Boston in 1910 for the Woman's Christian Temperance Union, Samantha Hadley raged on about the evils of alcohol, calling it "the water of hell" (qtd. in Monroe 46).

In the body of your paper, make an effort to give readers as much information about the original as you can, and remember that, under no circumstances, do you want to give your readers the impression that you have been in possession of the original. **Check your style manual for the proper way to do such citations.**

- There are forms for various types of **unpublished print material** and **print material with limited circulation.** Such material includes papers given at conferences, material from poster sessions at such conferences, masters theses and doctoral dissertations, leaflets and brochures, and the like. If the index of your style manual does not include "leaflet" or "brochure," then follow the basic guidelines for unpublished print material, especially any category for such material that is informally published, or that has limited circulation.

- **Information and material you obtained in a class in which you were enrolled**—whether handouts or notes you took—should be documented. If print materials your instructor made available are copies of parts of books or articles from periodicals, follow the standard form for such published materials. If the instructor failed to include full bibliographic information on the material, you'll need to ask him or her for it! If the material in question was written by or developed by your instructor, follow the guidelines for unpublished material. If you are using information from your notes of lectures or class discussions, look in your style manual for forms for documenting public lectures or addresses. When you are making reference to the course, give us the full name of your instructor, the full title of the course, the name and location of your school, the specific date of the lecture, or, in the case of printed material, the term and year you took the course.

- **Information you received directly from another person** (interviews, e-mail or snail-mail correspondence, one-on-one conferences with a professor) is usually categorized under the label "personal communication." Check your style manual. Such material is always cited in a parenthetical citation or note, but usually it is not included on your final list since this source would not be available to your readers. However, you should ask your instructor about his or her preferences. This would be particularly important if you did a number of interviews or much of your evidence falls into this category.

E. When It's Time to Document Sources in a Paper

From now on out in this process of documenting your sources there are a few vital and basic concepts that you must keep in mind at all times.

- Be sure you have a good understanding of the basic principles on which the documentation style you are using are based. With this understanding, it is going to be much easier for you to "see" the forms for individual types of sources, and you are much less likely to make mistakes, especially the kind of mistakes that will greatly irritate your instructor.

- Throughout this process, you are going to have to draw upon that part of yourself that is methodical and detail-oriented. You will need to be sure, first of all, that you properly categorize each of your sources so that you choose the proper form for each source. I have revised and expanded this section of *Writing Research Papers* precisely to help you out in this regard. But if you are still not sure how to document particular material, you should not hesitate to ask your instructor, or someone in your writing center, for assistance.

- Once you've found the proper model for a source, you must **follow that model exactly,** down to punctuation, capitalization, abbreviations, typography (boldface, underline, etc.).

- Remember, remember, remember that in-text or parenthetical citation systems will work if, and only if, the citation in the text provides the information necessary to take the reader immediately

  - to an entry on the final list

    AND

  - the citation matches one, and only one, entry on the list.

- When and if you have questions about documentation, do not hesitate to consult your instructor or someone in the writing center who knows the style you are using. When you are making such inquiries, you'll need to have complete information about the source with you, and, to make sure you are communicating effectively, plan to use the terminology I've been giving you.

1. The steps to take

The advice and suggestions in this section assume two things:

- that you have now almost completed this entire research project; that you have a draft which, although it still needs to be documented and polished, is finished as far as content is concerned;

- that you have, following my recommendations in Section 4, a working bibliography of sources you have consulted during this project. If you have been lax in creating such a working bibliography, then the steps that follow will involve creating your final list as you go along.

Completing the documentation process involves three operations:

- making sure that all material you have used from your sources is cited in the body of your paper, as well as adding documentation that will support or further support points you are making;

- checking your paper, your citations, and final list to be sure the *content* is accurate;

- making sure your citations and final list follow your documentation style *exactly*.

Preparing Yourself for This Stage of the Process

- These steps can be time-consuming, and they certainly demand concentration. Find a quiet place where you are not going to be interrupted. You can carry out this step in several shorter blocks of time if:

  - you follow the steps I give you in the order in which I give them, completing one before you begin the next. This expedient will make the process easier, and you are less likely to miss things or make mistakes.

  - you have a system for keeping track of what you have finished and what still needs to be done. Brightly colored pens work nicely for checking off tasks completed, and for making copyediting changes in written material.

- To go through these steps, you will need the following materials: your notes, the Sources section of your Notebook, this book (or the style manual you are using), your working bibliography, and a draft of your paper. Since you are going to be moving back and forth between the draft and the working bibliography, I'm going to strongly suggest that you carry out all these procedures using paper copies of your draft and bibliography.

Some Advice regarding the Documentation Itself

- If you are using either the MLA style or the CMS notes & bibliography style, you will want to be careful that the citations in the text (note numbers or parentheticals) don't distract your readers. Whenever possible, place them at the end of sentences. In those rare instances when a citation must come inside a sentence, try to place the number or citation at a natural resting point (such as the end of a clause).

- In all documentation styles there is a form for citing more than one source at a time. Use it!

- If some of the information required in the citation is already in your text (for example, you have used the author's name and given the title of the book in the sentence you wrote), you do **not** have to repeat this information in the note or the parenthetical citation. In parentheses or the note, simply provide the next required piece(s) of information.

- In cases where you are making extended use of one source, you do not have to keep citing that source as long as **you have made it perfectly clear that you are still making use of this source** (see Section 6.B.3). However, you will have to add citations if and when you quote directly from this work or you make reference to a specific part of the text, requiring page or section references.

The Steps

Step 1:   Print copies of your draft and your working bibliography. You will be creating your final list as you go through this process. Have paper available, or open a file for this purpose; create entries on this list in the order in which sources come up in these steps. You will formally order the list when it is complete.

Step 2:   Before you turn to your paper, it would be wise to do a quick scan of all your notes and the summaries you have written of the various sources you have used. If you refresh your memory about what you've read, you are more likely to add more supporting evidence.

Step 3:   Starting with the first page of your paper, you are going to locate every point that requires documentation. In other words, you are making sure you have a citation for every direct quotation you've used, for all the material you have taken from sources, for all the views of the experts you've made use of. Where relevant,

- you can, and should, add citations for other sources that make the same point. The more sources you can provide for a particular point, the stronger that point is going to be.

- elaborate on a point by creating an explanatory note (see subsection E.4).

For each point that requires citation, follow steps 3a through 3f. Complete all these steps before you move to the next point requiring a citation.

Step 3a: In this step you are checking the **accuracy of the content of the material you have used**. This requires:

- checking each quotation against your notes (or the original) to be sure it follows the original exactly. Be sure you have indicated that this material is quoted, either by blocking it off or by using quotation marks. If you have made any changes, be sure you've followed the conventions for doing so (see Sec 6.B.4).

- checking factual information against your notes (or the original) to be sure it is accurate.

- checking the ideas and views of others against your notes. You want to be particularly vigilant that you are not inadvertently plagiarizing. If your wording is too close to the original, you are going to have to quote directly, or do some major rewording.

- in all cases that require page numbers, making sure your page numbers are there, and that they are correct.

Step 3b: Using the style manual, create a citation in the correct format. Make sure that the citation begins with (or makes clear) the name of the person or group responsible for the material you have used.

Step 3c: On your working bibliography, make sure you have an entry for this source **that begins with this author's name** (in other words, that the citation takes readers to the correct entry). If no such entry exists, create one now.

Step 3d: Double-check the accuracy of the **content of the entry** on the working bibliography. Use material from the Sources section of your Notebook, or the actual source, if you have a copy.

Step 3e: If you are citing more than one source at this point in your paper, go through steps 3a through 3d for each of those sources.

Step 3f: Using your system, indicate that you have completed this citation. Put X's next to the entries on the working bibliography that correspond to these citations.

Step 4: The final step is to turn your working bibliography into a polished final list, one in which entries are in their correct order and in the correct form. I'd suggest you keep your working bibliography file for reference. Duplicate it, rename it as your final list, and proceed from here.

- If you are using a style whose final list includes only sources explicitly cited in the body of the paper (which includes all but the CMS notes & bibliography system), your first step is to eliminate sources you have not cited in the paper.

- Go through each entry on the list, attending now strictly to the form:

  - Make sure that you have given the required information in the proper *order*.

  - Pay very close attention to the mechanics and typography (italics, quotation marks, capitalization, punctuation, etc.).

- If you aren't sure if you have set up an entry correctly, make a note of your question(s) and consult your instructor or someone in the writing center.

- Once you are sure each entry is correct, use the next two subsections to order entries on your list and to learn how to format the entries properly. If you are using one of the styles I cover in the appendixes, check the section titled "The Final . . . , including a Sample" for complete information about formatting this segment of your paper.

You have one more step, but this one should take little time and can be reserved for the proofing stage. Again, with paper copies of your draft and your final list, go through your paper. Make sure that each citation in the paper takes the reader directly to an entry on the final list, and that the citation refers the reader to one and only one entry on the list.

Right now, you deserve a break. Sit back and congratulate yourself. The work you have just completed was tedious, but you have proved yourself to be a responsible and conscientious researcher who has fulfilled the obligations outlined in two major premises of documentation:

- **You have given credit where credit is due!**

- **You've done so in an appropriate standard form that gives readers all the information they need in the most unobtrusive and space-saving manner.**

  Hurrah for you!

2. Putting together your final list

I am assuming that either you have turned to this section from the previous section, where I talked in detail about steps to take in finalizing documentation in your paper, or else you have turned here from Section 4.F., having decided that you want your working bibliography to work as a bibliography!

Formatting Your Final List

There are two types of formatting issues you'll need to consider in preparing your final list.

The **overall appearance** of your final list (font, margins, and so forth) depends, in part, on requirements your style manual, or your instructor, or both have for your manuscript. I discuss **manuscript style** in some depth in Section 7.C. If you are using one of the styles I cover in the appendixes, check the last subsection in that appendix. There I will tell you more about the specific format requirements for that style.

The other formatting issue is the **format of each entry on the list.** Entries on the final list are in a paragraph style called a hanging indent (or hanging indentation). In this style, the first line of the paragraph is flush with the left margin.

The second and subsequent lines are indented, typically one-half inch (on a computer) or five spaces (on a typewriter). A hanging indent looks like this:

left margin ⟶ Adamson, Rachel, and Harry Schmidt. *A History of the Americas from 1492, with a Focus on the Native People of the Andes.* NewYork: NeverNever Press, 2050.

If you are doing your paper with a word-processing program I *urge* you to format these paragraphs electronically. By that I mean:

Do NOT format with the return or enter key and tabs.

DO format using the formatting menu and/or the ruler.

If you format the hanging indents electronically, they will "wrap" the way your ordinary paragraphs do. Thus you can add or delete material from an entry, you can change the font, or the font size, or both, and the entry will always look—and print—exactly as it is supposed to! Moreover, if you format these entries so that the entry paragraph includes a line of space after it, your program will also be able to sort your list for you.

Word-processing programs have been designed to make life easy on typists, and you should take advantage of this fact. Find out how to format **all** the entries on your list in one, quick operation, and also find out how to have your program alphabetically sort your list. Be aware, however, that you may have to tweak the list after the program sorts it. Your program may not understand, for example, that, when entries begin with an article—*a, the,* or *an*—the article is to be disregarded in alphabetizing!

Ordering Entries on Your Final List

First of all, several basic principles:

- Entries on your list always begin with the **last name** of the first **author.** If you have any questions about who (or what) should be considered the author of a source, see 8.D.1.

- The principle used by most documentation systems for ordering lists is ascending alphabetical order (that is, A's come first, then B's, then C's, and so on).

- When you do your first sorting of your sources, use only the letters in an author's last name; ignore his or her first name or initial. If your list includes works by Stephen Green and Aaron Greenberg, the work by Green will come first.

- Typically, if a source has no author, it is listed by its title. The exception is the CSE name-year style, which uses Anonymous as the author of such works.

- When you alphabetize anything that begins with an article (*the, a,* or *an*), always disregard the article and alphabetize according the first main word.

Look over this list carefully to see these principles at work:

Abrams, Zechariah.

Abramson, Adam.

"The Beauty of the Great Outdoors."

The Council of Educators.

Cullens, Alice.

Zimmerman, Charles, and Adam Abramson.

ORDERING YOUR LIST: THE MLA AND CMS NOTES & BIBLIOGRAPHY STYLES

Use the following principles to sort your list:

- Sort your entire list first by using the last name of the first author of each source.

- If more than one first author has the same last name, sort alphabetically according to the authors' first names. If first names are the same, sort then by middle initial.

- If your list contains more than one work by the same author, sort alphabetically using the first main word in the titles of the sources.

- If your list contains several works by the same author or set of authors,

  - list first the works this person wrote by him- or herself;

  - then list any works the person edited;

  - then list any works this person co-authored or co-edited. Sort alphabetically according to the last name of the second author/editor, and so on.

SAMPLE ORDERING OF SOURCES: THE MLA AND CMS NOTES & BIBLIOGRAPHY STYLES

Johnson, Carl X.

Johnson, Frances H.

Johnson, Frederick J.

Johnson, Frederick S.

Jones, John. "The Abolitionists. . . ."

Jones, John. Conventions at Dawn.

Jones, John, ed. Papers of the Continental Congress.

Jones, John, and Herman Gotz. America during the Revolution. . . .

Jones, John, Stephen Greenberg, and Alfred Lutz, eds. The Papers of Jefferson. . . .

Jones, John, Stephen Greenberg, and Louisa Smith. "American Lives."

Jones, John, and James Jackson. Seven Years. . . .

ORDERING YOUR LIST: AUTHOR-DATE AND NAME-YEAR STYLES

Use the following principles to sort your list:

- Sort first using the last name of the first author of each work.

- If more than one first author has the same last name, sort alphabetically according to the authors' first initials. If first initials are the same, sort then by middle initial.

- If you have a series of works by the same person (let's say B. C. Smith):

  - List all works written by B. C. Smith alone first.

  - Then list works that B. C. Smith has co-authored with others, alphabetizing these co-authored works according to the last names of the second author.

- If you have a series of works by the same author(s), list the works chronologically according to the year of publication, starting with the oldest work and ending with the most recent. If an author (or authors) published more than one work in the same year, sort alphabetically according to the first main word in the titles, and then differentiate the works by putting a lowercase 'a' after the date of the first work, a lowercase 'b' after the date of the second work, and so on. This 'a' or 'b' will always be included when this work is cited in the body of the paper.

ALERT!

The list below illustrates principles of ordering *only*. The way that names and dates are presented depends on the requirements of a specific style. Consult the appropriate manual.

SAMPLE ORDERING OF SOURCES: AUTHOR-DATE AND NAME-YEAR STYLES

Smith, B. C.

Smith, B. C., R. J. Green, and S. Spade

Smith, B. C., and A. W. Weinberg. 2001.

Smith, B. C., and A. W. Weinberg. 2004.

Smith, B. C., and A. W. Weinberg. 2005a. Effects of carbon monoxide. . . .

Smith, B. C., and A. W. Weinberg. 2005b. *Pollutants in the Great Lakes.*

Smith, C. F.

Smith, H. A.

Smith, H. B.

3. Some general comments on in-text or parenthetical citations

First of all, terminology. When and if you go to the formal manual of the style you are using, be aware that names used for these citations can differ. However, the terminology usually includes the word "citation," so this is the word to look for in the table of contents or the index.

I have already made this point on several occasions, but this is an area in which I see students constantly making mistakes, so I consider it worth repeating. In-text or parenthetical citation systems will not work until and unless the following **three criteria** are met:

- When the name of the author is key to the citation, the name must be that of the person or group directly responsible for the material being cited.

- The information in the in-text citation must take the reader directly to an entry on the final list; that is, the name of the author, or the name of the author and the date, in the body of your paper must be the same name (or name and date) with which an entry in the final list begins.

- The information you give in the in-text citation must take the reader to one and only one entry on the list.

In my experience, the areas in which students tend to make most of their mistakes are with essays, articles, poems and other texts that are parts of books, and with material they download from computers. If your paper contains any sources that fit these descriptions, be sure to read over subsections D.3 and/or D.6 in this section, and then pay very close attention to the forms used for such sources in the documentation style you are using.

If you are using one of the **scientific systems** (and I include APA in this grouping), you need to realize that **most citations are made to the work as a whole.** In a shorthand fashion, the writer is saying: These researchers have done studies in this area, or these researchers have come up with certain findings. For this reason, you'll use page numbers only when you quote directly from such texts. On those occasions when you are making reference to a section of a book, it may be acceptable to give section designations or page numbers. Check the manual of the style you are using.

In the **MLA system,** since the author's last name is the only key to the final list, you will have to provide additional information when and if your list includes entries for more than one author with the same last name, or, more typically, you use more than one work by the same author. See my discussion of parenthetical citations in Appendix A.

If you have been reading texts that have parenthetical citations, you have probably noticed that such citations always have the potential to become **obtrusive,** making it difficult to follow the author's point. The general solution is to **place parentheticals—particularly if they are long—at the end of the sentence.** If such placement would be misleading, the solution would be to word your sentence so the parenthetical can come at a natural "resting place."

> Even though Carter has suggested that Flynn is a villain (34), most critics believe . . . .

In this category of long, and thus potentially obtrusive, citations are those with **multiple authors.** The typical solution to this problem is et al. If you have sources in your text with three or more authors, see my discussion of multiple authors in subsection D.1. Check your style manual both for the appropriate form for citing multiple authors and also for proper placement of parenthetical citations.

Group authors, especially if they are **governmental bodies,** can present similar problems. In some cases, acronyms can be substituted (WHO for the World Health Organization). If you have authors in your list that present such problems, check your style manual for solutions it offers.

In those cases where your citation is to the **title of a work** (or includes the title of a work), keep the citation short by using the first main word in the title, or a short opening phrase. It should be obvious that you may not change the actual words or the order in which the words appear. Thus, if the entry in your list begins with the title "The Church of England at the Crossroads," your citation would be either "Church" or, perhaps, "Church of England," but never "English Church." Check your manual for the appropriate typographical representation of such titles (e.g., in quotation marks, underlined or italicized).

Here are other aspects of the in-text or parenthetical system that you should be aware of. Most of these issues, if you think about it, are commonsensical.

- If and when your final list contains a **multivolume work** with the same author and title, you will have to include the volume number in citations, or readers will not know which volume you are citing (Carlson 2: 456). If you are taking material from only one volume in the set, your best bet is to create your entry for that volume only; see subsections D.3 and 4.

- There is **no need to repeat information** in parentheses that you have already given in a sentence you have written.

- The same general principle applies when you are giving the **summary of a work** that takes three or four sentences in your paper. If you have followed my advice about making it clear whose ideas you are recounting, you do not have to keep giving us the same citation over and over again. The exceptions would be if you quote directly from the source, or if (in the MLA style) you move from one part of a source to another. Boldface used for emphasis only.

> The narrator tells that his mother hated Lassie from the day he brought the stray home with him (**Murphy 243**).

> In "My Dog Lassie," the first short story Harold **Murphy** ever wrote, the narrator tells us that his mother hated Lassie from the day he brought the stray home with him (**243**). By the end of the tale, however, she is won over (**255**).

- It is perfectly acceptable to cite more than one source in one parenthetical; in fact, if you've done any reading in the scholarly literature of the social or natural sciences, you realize that citing multiple sources is a regular occurrence. Check your style manual for the proper way to do such multiple citations.

- If and when you are citing a source that you yourself have not read, you must make it absolutely clear in your text and in your citation that you are citing from a **secondary source**; see subsection D.7.

4. Some general comments about explanatory notes

These days, fewer and fewer publications are using notes as the method for citing sources. For this reason, I'll restrict my comments on notes used for this purpose to Appendix B, where I lay out the specifics of the CMS notes & bibliography style.

But even if you are using an in-text or parenthetical system to document your sources, you may want to include **explanatory notes** in your paper. Once in a while you may feel the need to elaborate on a particular point, or to refer readers to more detailed discussions of a particular topic.

EXAMPLES

2. Throughout the play the word *cold* is used in reference to chastity, inactivity, and death, So, for example, in speaking of the postponement of the sentencing of the Duchess's young son, Spurio says. . . .

4. For more detailed information about the Smith raid, see Johnson, *Indian Wars,* 75-83; John Halvorsen, *The Wild West* (San Francisco: Nonexistent University Press, 2040), 120-35.

It is perfectly acceptable to include explanatory notes, but you must use your common sense to determine if such a note is appropriate. Material that your reader must have in order to understand a point you are making should never be hidden in a note; this information has to be part of the body of your paper. And readers can become very irritated if you use the note system to introduce material that you think is interesting but which is really tangential to, or outside the bounds of, the paper you are writing. **So use explanatory notes where they are really needed. Do not use explanatory notes to show off everything you know about a topic.**

If you decide that an explanatory note is in order, check the manual of the style you are using for its recommendations about placement of such notes. You will signal a note in the text of your paper with a number raised one-half space at the end of the relevant sentence. If you are going to print notes at the bottom of the page on which they appear (**footnotes**), I'd recommend using the footnote feature of your word-processing program. It makes formatting footnotes a snap.

However, if the manual wants you to print notes at the end of your paper (**endnotes**), especially if these notes are supposed to be on a separate sheet of paper, the footnoting feature may cause more problems than it is worth. It is easy enough to add note numbers in the body of your paper by formatting them as superscripts. You can then type your notes wherever you want to place them.

A long explanatory note becomes an **appendix.** Appendixes are typical parts of reports on studies and experiments in the social and natural sciences; this is particularly true in college courses, since instructors usually like to see not only copies of questionnaires or surveys that the student researcher distributed, but also full sets of data collected, transcripts of interviews, and the like. If you want to create an appendix or appendixes for a paper, check the manual for the style you are using. It will tell you how to set up appendixes, what to put in particular appendixes, how to head them, how to make references to them in the body of your paper, and related matters.

APPENDIX

A

The MLA Style

A. How the MLA Style Works

The MLA style is a parenthetical citation system that lists all sources cited on a separate sheet at the end of the paper.

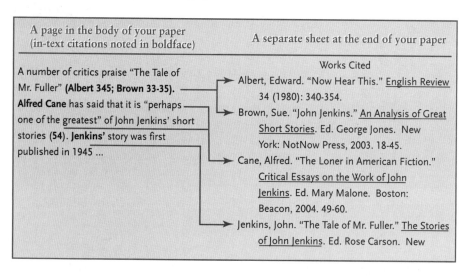

A page in the body of your paper (in-text citations noted in boldface)	A separate sheet at the end of your paper
A number of critics praise "The Tale of Mr. Fuller" **(Albert 345; Brown 33-35)**. **Alfred Cane** has said that it is "perhaps one of the greatest" of John Jenkins' short stories **(54)**. **Jenkins'** story was first published in 1945 ...	Works Cited Albert, Edward. "Now Hear This." <u>English Review</u> 34 (1980): 340-354. Brown, Sue. "John Jenkins." <u>An Analysis of Great Short Stories</u>. Ed. George Jones. New York: NotNow Press, 2003. 18-45. Cane, Alfred. "The Loner in American Fiction." <u>Critical Essays on the Work of John Jenkins</u>. Ed. Mary Malone. Boston: Beacon, 2004. 49-60. Jenkins, John. "The Tale of Mr. Fuller." <u>The Stories of John Jenkins</u>. Ed. Rose Carson. New

    To cite a source in the body of your paper, you provide the last name of the **author(s)** of the source and the **page number(s)** on which the relevant information or words will be found. The last name of author(s) takes the reader to the appropriate entry on the list of works cited. The illustration here shows you the various ways in which this principle is applied.

At the end of your paper, on a separate sheet or sheets, you will provide readers with a list, headed **Works Cited.** This list contains full bibliographic information about each source you have referred to (cited) in the body of the paper. The sources are listed in alphabetical order according to the last name of the first author of the source.

> When you are ready to document your sources using the MLA style, turn to Section 8.E., where I give you important advice and information regarding this process.
>
> * * *
>
> If you are not familiar with the fundamental principles of documentation and the terminology that goes with it, I'd recommend that you look over the whole of Section 8.

The purpose of this appendix is to provide basic information about how to document a paper using the MLA style. Here I am following the style as it is laid out by Joseph Gibaldi in the *MLA Handbook for Writers of Research Papers,* 6th edition (New York: Modern Language Association, 2003). If you do not find information you need in this appendix, check the *MLA Handbook.*

This appendix is laid out in the following way:

- Subsection B provides information about parenthetical citations.

- Subsection C provides forms for basic types of sources as they will appear on your list of works cited.

- Subsection D discusses the format for the final list of works cited, and provides a sample.

Some Particulars of the MLA Style

- Double-space all elements of your paper, including block quotations and entries on your list of works cited.

- In cases where italic type is called for (titles of books and the like) you may either underline the relevant words or put them in italics. Ask your instructor for his or her preference. Whichever option you select, you must use it consistently throughout the entire paper for each and every instance where italic type is required.

- Block quotations are indented one inch (ten spaces) from the left margin. End the quotation with a period, space, then add the parenthetical citation. No punctuation after the end parenthesis.

- Within quoted material, place any ellipsis points (. . .) you add in brackets ONLY if the author of the passage you are quoting uses ellipses in the passage.

- In entries on the list of works cited, MLA prefers abbreviations—for editors, for translators, for publishing companies, and so on. I use some of the abbreviations in examples in this appendix; for a complete list, check the *MLA Handbook*. Abbreviations are conveniently collected in Chapter 7.

- If the text you are citing was originally published much earlier than the copyright date of the edition you are using, you will want to acknowledge this fact. Typically, you will do so by giving the original date of publication immediately after the title of the work.

B. Parenthetical Citations

1. The basic form

You cite a source in the body of your paper by giving the author's last name and the page number(s) in parentheses, normally at the end of your sentence. Please note that the period is *always* placed after the parentheses.

> The poet Wilson was a recluse with odd ideas (Stark 24–30).

If you have used the author's name as part of your sentence, as I encouraged you to do in Section 6, you need to add only the page number(s).

> Sheila Stark points out that the poet Wilson was a recluse with odd ideas (24–30).

Similarly, if the context makes it clear whose ideas or words you are using, it isn't necessary to repeat the author's name.

> These musical instruments came into vogue about the time of King Henry VI (Harvey 134). The viola da gamba, for example, was being played in court in 1453 (140).

If you are referring to an entire work, the author's name is enough; no page number, obviously, is necessary.

> Shakespeare's Richard II is full of images of the sun.

2. Placement of citations

As you can see, these parenthetical citations have the potential of becoming obtrusive and thus interfering with your readers' ability to pay attention to what you are saying. For this reason, keep these guidelines in mind when you place your citations in your text:

- Within the rules of the MLA form, keep your parenthetical citations as short as possible. One simple solution to this problem is to use the names of authors in your sentence proper, as I advised in Section 6. If you use the author's name directly in your sentence, you need to add only the page number(s) in parentheses.

- The citation must be placed so that it is clear which ideas have been taken from a source; at the same time, you do not want to impede the flow of your sentence. Whenever possible, place your parenthetical citation at the end of the sentence. If you are finishing a quotation, place the parentheses after the quotation mark and before the period. If it is not possible to put the citation at the end of the sentence, try to place it next to a natural "rest" point in the sentence.

As she wrote in her journal in May, "inspiration ravishes me" (56).

This policy, although strongly opposed by Carlson (Hindman 14–16), eventually was adopted by the court.

- If you are using the block style of quoting, place your citations after the concluding punctuation of the quotation.

Describing the battle as he witnessed it from his bedroom window. Kendall wrote to a friend:

> It was fierce and bloody. Bullets flew. Blood was everywhere. The noise was deafening. Bodies lay on the sidewalk. (34)

3. Variations of the basic form

More than One Source by the Same Author

If your list of works cited contains more than one work by the same author, be sure that it is absolutely clear to your reader which of the works you are citing by giving a short title of the work along with the author's name:

In his novel <u>Kingdom Come</u>, Withers often uses the phrase "cold death" (68, 97, 110).

This form of poetry was most popular at court (Hall, Introduction 48)

Use commas to separate nonconsecutive page numbers.

Source with More Than One Author

If a source has two or three authors, the last names of all must be given each time you cite the source in your paper. List the names in the order in which they appear in the entry in your list of works cited; even if two authors have the same last name, both names must be repeated. If you have a source with more than three authors, see the *MLA Handbook* for advice about citing.

Felltham was a fanatic about the royalist cause (Witherspoon and Warnke 317).

Robertson and Robertson argue that . . .

Source with a Corporate Author, or Organization as Author

Since the entry on your list of works cited will begin with the name of the corporation, the organization, or the government body, this is the name that you will have to use for your citation. Particularly if the name of the organization is long, a parenthetical citation could be cumbersome. So, whenever possible, try to use this name directly in your discussion of the material:

> The World Health Organization has finally recognized the crisis that HIV/AIDS is creating in certain sub-Saharan countries in Africa.

Source with No Author

Works with no authors will be entered in your final list by the title. To cite in your paper, you can incorporate the complete title in your narrative. Or, in parentheses, you can use the first two or three main words of the title in the order in which they appear in the original. In either case, represent the title appropriately (quotation marks or underlined or in italic type). If you are citing a source that is only one page long and this page number is given in the entry on your list, you need not repeat the number.

> Such were the times that men earned less than a dime a day ("Breadlines").

Citing a Work of Literature (Poem, Play, and the Like)

If you are quoting from or referring to a poem, play, short story, or novel, it is helpful to your readers if you include in your citation division markers used in the work itself (e.g., chapter numbers, book numbers, line numbers, etc.). In your parenthetical citation, give the page number first; then use a semicolon to separate it from the division reference. Abbreviate chapter, book, and section, but spell out the word "line" since a lowercase l can be confused with the number 1. If you are citing a classic poem or play, you can omit page numbers completely and just give the conventional division markers used in the work itself. If an act or book number precedes a line number, you don't have to spell out "line"; convention tells us this is a line number.

> It is not until the middle of the novel that we meet the heroine (200; ch. 6).

> When Keats writes "what soft incense hangs upon the boughs" (line 52), we can almost smell this dark garden.

> Satan's return to hell was greeted by "a dismal universal hiss" (bk. X. 508).

> The psychological aspects of Richard II become most obvious in the moving soliloquy of the deposed and imprisoned king (5.5.1-45).

Citing Material from a Multivolume Set

If your list of works cited includes an entry for a multivolume work with the same author and title, each time you cite this work you will have to include the number of the volume (in arabic numerals) in front of page number(s). For more information regarding multivolume sets, see Section 8.D.4. and subsection C.1.

> According to Jones, this was the high point of the dynasty (3: 122).

Citing Material Found in a Secondary Source

In Section 4.H.3, I stressed the importance of seeking out the original source any time you find mention of a work in one of the sources you are reading. If you have not been able to put your hands on the original, provide as much information about the original work as you can in the body of your paper (see Section 8.D.7), and then cite the source in which you found it. Use the phrase "qtd. in" when the original was quoted in the secondary source, or "cited in" if the material was paraphrased or mentioned. Only the secondary source (in this case, Wallace) may be included in your list of works cited.

> In 1850 a man who signed himself only "Tom Angry" wrote a fierce letter on the subject to the editor of the Times (qtd. in Wallace 67).

Citing Several Sources at a Time

If you found the same information in more than one source, include all sources in the same parenthetical citation, separating different sources with semicolons.

> (Smith 645; Clark and Hillsdale, "Keats" 47).

If such citations prove cumbersome, put them in a note (see below).

Notes and Explanatory Notes

In addition to using notes for citing a number of sources at once, you can use notes on those occasions when you want to say something further about a point or topic, but such information or discussion does not belong in the body of your paper. If you are using a note for documentation, simply use the same form you would in the body of your body, but without the parentheses. For more detailed discussion of explanatory notes, see Section 8.E.4.

C. Forms for Sources on the List of Works Cited

1. Books

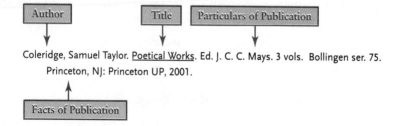

Coleridge, Samuel Taylor. Poetical Works. Ed. J. C. C. Mays. 3 vols. Bollingen ser. 75.
Princeton, NJ: Princeton UP, 2001.

Author

- The entry begins with the last name of the first author, followed by a comma. Give first name and middle initial. If the source has two to four authors, give *all* names in the order in which the names are listed on the title page of the original. Invert the name of the first author only. Write "and" before the name of the last author. If a source has more than four authors, see the *Handbook* for advice about citing. End with period.

- If an editor is being entered in the author position, follow the style for authors. After the final name listed, put a comma and add "ed." for one editor or "eds." for more than one.

  Jacobs, John, ed. The History of . . .

  Anderson, Sally, Nina Wilkerson, and Mona Perkins, eds. Women in the Arts . . .

Title

- Give the complete title of the book (including any subtitles) exactly as it appears on the title page of the book. Typically, the main title is separated from the subtitle with a colon.

- Underline (or italicize) the complete title. Capitalize main words; see Section 7.B. Use quotation marks around words in quotation marks in the original. Any words italicized in the original should *not* be underlined.

- End with a period.

Particulars of Publication

- After the title and before the facts of publication, record relevant information about this book noted on the title page that is not provided elsewhere in the entry. Record this information in the following order; each of these units is separated from others with a period:

- editor and/or translator. Put Ed. in front of the name(s) of editor(s). Put Trans. in front of the name(s) of translator(s). Put a period after each unit.

- edition, if not the first. Represent as follows: 2nd ed., 3rd ed., 4th ed., and so on.

- if multivolume set, number of volumes or volume number and title (see examples below and in subsection C.2. For a fuller discussion, see Section 8.D.4.

- if a series, the name of the series.

- Always use arabic numerals (4), not roman numerals (IV), except for page numbers in roman numerals.

Facts of Publication

This unit is composed of three pieces of information, punctuated as follows: the place (city) of publication, colon, the publisher, comma, the copyright date, period.

- If more than one city is listed, use only the first. Please note that the place is the *city* in which a publisher has offices, *not the state or country.* The state or country may be *added* if the city, by itself, is not well known or could be confused with another city. Use the Postal Service abbreviations for states in the U.S.; see the *MLA Handbook* for appropriate abbreviations of countries.

- Shorten the name of the publisher as much as possible. The names of university presses are shortened as follows: Harvard UP, or U of Georgia P. Use your common sense in shortening titles, or, to be absolutely correct, see the list of abbreviations in the *MLA Handbook.*

- If the book you are using is a paperback, give the paperback imprint, a hyphen, and the publishing house: Vintage-Random.

- The copyright date is the most recent date next to the copyright symbol © on the reverse side of the title page.

CORPORATE AUTHOR, ORGANIZATION AS AUTHOR

For more information on this type of author, see Section 8.D.1.

National Education Association. Teaching with Technology. Washington, DC: NEA, 1999.

PAMPHLET

National Education Association. Teaching with Technology. Washington, DC: NEA, 1999.

A Brief Wrap on Ethics. Washington, DC: GPO, 2000.

BOOK IN A MULTIVOLUME SET

In citing a book that is part of a multivolume set, the issue is to be sure that your reader always knows which volume you are citing! Typically, if you are using a multivolume work, you are citing a discrete part or parts of one or more books. For a full discussion of citing books in a multivolume set, see Section 8.D.4. For more examples, see Part of a Book, C.2.

ENTRY FOR THE COMPLETE SET

> Bronson, Bertrand H., ed. The Traditional Tunes of the Child Ballads with Their Texts, according to the Extant Records of Great Britain and America. 4 vols. Princeton, NJ: Princeton UP, 1959-72.

ENTRY FOR ONE VOLUME, SAME TITLE

> Bronson, Bertrand H., ed. The Traditional Tunes of the Child Ballads with Their Texts, according to the Extant Records of Great Britain and America. Vol. 3. Princeton, NJ: Princeton UP, 1966.

or

> Bronson, Bertrand H., ed. The Traditional Tunes of the Child Ballads with Their Texts, according to the Extant Records of Great Britain and America. Vol. 3. Princeton, NJ: Princeton UP, 1966. 4 vols. 1959-72.

ENTRY FOR ONE VOLUME, DIFFERENT TITLE

> Caro, Robert A. Master of the Senate. New York: Knopf, 2002.

or

> Caro, Robert A. Master of the Senate. New York: Knopf, 2002. Vol. 3 of The Years of Lyndon Johnson. 3 vols. to date. 1982-.

2. Part of a book, including reference works

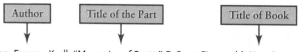

Ring, Frances Kroll. "Memories of Scott." F. Scott Fitzgerald: New Perspectives. Ed. Jackson R. Bryer, Alan Margolies, and Ruth Prigozy. Athens: U of Georgia P, 2000. 18-21.

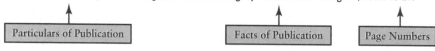

Author

- This is the name of the person(s) responsible for the words or ideas you are using in your paper.

- Entry begins with last name of first author, followed by a comma. Give first name and middle initial. If the part has two to four authors, give *all* names in the order in which the names are listed on the title page of the original. Invert name of first author only. Write "and" before name of last author. If the part has more than four authors, see the *Handbook* for advice about citing. End with period.

- If there is no author, begin the entry with the title of the part.

Title of the Part

- Give the full title of the part, including any subtitles, ending with a period. Capitalize all main words; see Section 7.B.

- Enclose the title in quotation marks with the following exceptions:

  - Titles of plays are underlined (italicized), as are the titles of other works that were originally published as a book.

  - Introduction, Afterword, Foreword, and Preface are simply capitalized (see example below).

- If the title is in quotation marks:

  - the period is placed *inside* the end quotation mark.

  - put single quotation marks around any word/words in quotation marks in the original.

- Underline any word(s) that are italicized in the original.

Title of Book

Follow all the guidelines for the title of books (subsection C.1). End with a period.

Particulars of Publication

- In the case of anthologies or edited collections, the name of the editor(s) of the collection comes next. The unit begins with a capitalized "Ed.," which stands for "edited by." Names are given in their normal order.

- If the book was written by a person whose name has not yet been given, provide that information immediately after the title of the book. Begin the unit with "By," capitalized.

- If any other information about this book needs to be given, provide it here. See Particulars of Publication for a book (subsection C.1).

Facts of Publication

Follow the guidelines for Facts of Publication of a book (subsection C.1).

Page Numbers

At the end of the entry, set off by commas, give the inclusive page numbers of the part (the pages on which the part begins and ends). Note that page numbers in roman numerals in the original must be given in roman numerals; otherwise they'd be confused with other pages in the book.

PART AND BOOK BY SAME AUTHOR

> Wolfe, Tom. "Sorry, but Your Soul Just Died." Hooking Up. New York: Farrar, 2000. 89-109.

PART AND BOOK BY DIFFERENT AUTHORS

> Prida, Dolores. Botánica. Puro Teatro: A Latina Anthology. Ed. Alberto Sandoval-Sánchez and Nancy Saporta Sternbach. Tucson: U of Arizona P, 2000. 7-45.

> Lowell, Robert. "For the Union Dead." 1960, 1964. The Norton Anthology of American Literature. Ed. Nina Baym. Vol. 2. New York: Norton, 1998. 2538-39.

INTRODUCTION, AFTERWORD, PREFACE

> Hollander, Robert. Introduction. Inferno. By Dante Alighieri. Trans. Robert and Jean Hollander. New York: Doubleday, 2000. xvii-xxxiii.

PART REPRINTED FROM EARLIER PUBLICATION

> Smith, Hedrick. "9-Block Area Lies Devastated; Buildings Still Burn after Riot." New York Times, 13 May 1963. Rpt. in American Journalism 1941-1963. New York: Library of America, 2003. 809-812. Vol. 1 of Reporting Civil Rights. 2 vols. 2003.

ENCYCLOPEDIAS, DICTIONARIES, AND OTHER REFERENCE WORKS

When you are citing a standard reference work—the kind that is updated every few years—there is no need to provide particulars or facts of publication beyond the edition and/or the most recent copyright date. To cite other reference works, follow the form for part of a book. Check the end of the entry in the reference work to see if it is signed; if so, begin with this person's name. If not, begin with the title of the entry. Since the entries in most reference works follow the model of a dictionary, (a) give the title of the entry exactly as it appears in the original and (b) there is no need to include page numbers. For further discussion of these matters, see Section 8.D.3.

STANDARD REFERENCE WORK

> Nettl, Bruno. "Folk Music, American." Encyclopedia Americana. International ed. 1999.

> "Pullman Strike." Encyclopedia Britannica Online. 2003. Encyclopedia Britannica. 8 Aug. 2003 <http://www.search.eb.com/>.

> "Silly." Def. Adj. 1.a. Oxford English Dictionary Online. 2nd ed. 1989. Oxford English Dictionary. 15 Aug. 2003 <http://dictionary.oed.com/>.

SPECIALIZED DICTIONARY OR ENCYCLOPEDIA

> Robinson, Roxana. "O'Keeffe, Georgia." The Dictionary of Women Artists. Ed. Delia Gaze. Vol. 2. London: Fitzroy Dearborn, 1997. 1039–41.

> "Leave It to Beaver." Encyclopedia of Television. Ed. Horace Newcomb. Vol. 2. Chicago: Fitzroy Dearborn, 1997. 939–41.

3. Articles from journals and magazines

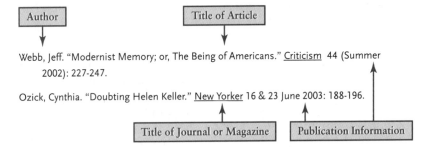

Author

- Entry begins with the last name of the author, followed by a comma. Give first name and middle initial. Use initials if first name not given. End with period.

- If the article has two to four authors, names of *all* must be given in the order in which they appear on the title page of the original. Invert name of first author only. Names of all others are given in the normal order. Write "and" before the name of last author. If an article has more than four authors, see the *Handbook* for advice about citing. End with period.

- If there is no author, begin the entry with the title.

Title of Article

- Give the full title of the article, including any subtitles, ending with a period.

- Enclose the title in quotation marks; the period is placed *inside* the end quotation mark.

- Capitalize all main words; see Section 7.B. Underline any word that is italicized in the original. If any words in the original are in quotation marks, place in single quotation marks.

Title of Journal or Magazine

Spell out the full title, capitalize main words, and underline (italicize). Notice that there is no punctuation after the title.

Publication Information

- In citing journals, give volume number immediately after title. If the journal begins each issue with page 1, also include the issue number. Volume 27, issue number 1 is represented this way: 27.1. In parentheses, give year of publication; you may add the season or month of publication. End with inclusive page numbers of the article (the pages on which the article begins and ends). A colon and a space separate the date from the page numbers; otherwise, there is no punctuation.

- For magazines, give the date of the issue (month and year; or date, month, and year); do so in the European style. Abbreviate all months except May, June, and July. End with the inclusive page numbers of the article (the pages on which the article begins and ends). Year and page numbers separated by a colon; otherwise, there is no punctuation.

ALERT!

If you downloaded an article from a database or an online site, you must include this information after your citation of the print version; see subsection C.5, Web Sites and Other Electronic Sources. For more discussion of the issue in general, see Section 8.D.6., Documenting Material Downloaded from Computers.

4. Articles from newspapers

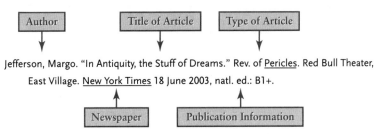

Jefferson, Margo. "In Antiquity, the Stuff of Dreams." Rev. of <u>Pericles</u>. Red Bull Theater,

East Village. <u>New York Times</u> 18 June 2003, natl. ed.: B1+.

Author

- The entry begins with the last name of the author, followed by a comma. Give first name and middle initial. Use initials if first name not given. End with period.

- If the article has several authors, the names of *all* must be given in the order in which they appear on the title page of the original. Invert name of first author only. Names of all others are given in the normal order. Write "and" before the name of last author. End with period.

- If there is no author, begin the entry with the title of the article or the headline.

Title of Article

- Give the title of the article or the main headline as it appears in the original.

- Enclose in quotation marks; capitalize all main words; see Section 7.B. Any words in the original in quotation marks should be put in single quotation marks.

- Put the end period *inside* the quotation marks.

Type of Article

- In the case of special types of articles—reviews, editorials, letters to the editor, and the like—it is very helpful to include this information. Insert the appropriate word(s)—Editorial, Letter, Rev. of—between the headline and the name of the newspaper; end with period.

Newspaper

- Articles (*the, an, a*) are not included as part of the name; underline (italicize).

- If you are citing a local paper whose name does not give the city of origin, add that information in square brackets after the newspaper name: Oregonian [Portland].

Publication Information

- The date immediately follows the name of the newspaper. No punctuation. Give in European fashion; abbreviate months except for May, June, and July.

- If the newspaper comes out in various editions, tell us which edition you used; abbreviate; place after the date, separated with a comma.

- Take care with page numbers in newspapers. Since various sections tend to begin with page 1, you'll need to give us the section along with the page number.

- If an article begins on one page and is continued on a non-adjacent page, give the number of the first page and a plus sign.

ALERT!

If you downloaded an article from a database or an online site, you must include this information after your citation of the print version; see subsection C.5, Web Sites and Other Electronic Sources. For more discussion of the issue in general, see Section 8.D.6., Documenting Material Downloaded from Computers.

---

5. Web sites and other electronic sources

In this section, I'm using the term "electronic source" to cover any material transmitted through a computer; thus, electronic sources include textual material from CD-ROMs, and material from any and all online sources, public and restricted, edited and unedited (databases, Web and Internet sites, online journals and magazines, newsgroups, discussion groups, online forums, e-mail messages, and the like).

For more detailed discussion of issues related to documentation of electronic sources, read over Section 8.D.6. Information I'm giving here should be sufficient for you to create appropriate entries for such sources in the MLA style. If it is not, consult the 6th edition of the *MLA Handbook,* which is the one I am following. Be aware, however, that forms for electronic sources may be updated at any time.

Material from a Web or Internet Site

Swartz, Carl. "Concept Formation and Problem Solving: Understanding and Managing
    Two Key Components of Higher Order Cognition." All Kinds of Minds. 1999-2003.
    28 July 2003 <http://www.allkindsofminds.org /articleDisplay.aspx?categoryID=
    10&articleID=18>.

Where and When You Located the Material

Print Text from a Database

Smith, David H. "After 100 Years, Museum Finds Room for Change." Christian Science
    Monitor 28 Feb. 2003: 17. Newspaper Source. EBSCO. Watzek Lib., Lewis & Clark
    College, Portland, OR. 28 July 2003 <http://web16.epnet.com>.

Where and When You Located the Text

Author and Title

- Begin with the name of the author, or the person or organization responsible for the material you are using; see Section 8.D.6. for further discussion of this issue. Follow standard MLA style for authors. End with a period. If no author is given or discernable, start entry with title.

- Provide the title of the text or material. Underline (italicize) titles of books, plays, and other independently published works; titles of articles in periodicals, articles posted on a page, and titles of Web pages should be placed in quotation marks. End with a period (*inside* quotation marks).

Particulars about the Text

- If the text was originally published in print form, or is available in a print version, provide any information you are given about the print version. Use standard MLA form for a print version of this material.

- If the material you are citing seems to have been generated for, or is available only on, this Internet site, provide the date of the material and any other information about it that the reader would find helpful (for example, if this is a review of a film or a book).

Where and When You Located the Text

You will now give information about where and when you located this material.
MLA provides the following list, asking for this information in the order given.
Obviously, give only that information relevant to the type of source you are
citing, and only if the information is available. Each of these segments is
followed by a period.

- Give the title of the Web or Internet site. If the site does not have a name,
  provide a description of it—e.g., Home page. Underline (italicize).

- Some academic sites that are formal collections of materials have editors; if
  you are citing such a site, provide the name(s) of editor(s) in this form:
  Ed. John Doe and Sally Smith.

- If your material is an online publication (an e-book, for example, or an article in an online journal), give particulars of its electronic publication
  (volume, issue, date), following standard MLA form for print versions of the
  same type of material.

- Give the date of electronic publication. This would be the copyright date of
  the material, the copyright date of the page on which the material is posted,
  or the date on which the page was most recently updated.

- If the material was downloaded from a subscription database (such as those
  full-text databases you find in the library), MLA wants you to provide three
  pieces of information:

  - the name of the database, underlined (italicized);

  - the name of the service or company that provides this database;

  - the subscriber to this database (which, if you accessed the database in a
    library, will be the name of the library and its geographic location).

- If the material you are citing comes from a forum or discussion group, give
  the name of that forum or group here.

- If the material you have downloaded has paragraph numbers or page
  numbers, provide them here. Be careful; use only those page numbers that
  would remain consistent no matter the settings of a printer or a browser; see
  Section 8.D.6.

- If the information you have already given in your citation does not name the
  sponsor of the Web or Internet site, provide that information here.

- Give us the date *you* downloaded this material.

- Give us the URL of the page on which you found this material. If the address
  is especially long and complex, provide the address for the search page. In
  the case of subscription databases, you need provide only the address for the
  search page, or, alternatively, the keyword you used to reach the site or the
  links to the text.
  Keyword: McGraw
  Path: Articles; Differences in Learning (General).

More Examples of Print Texts from a Database

> Melmer, David. "Bill Could Add Legal Clout to Protection of Lands Sacred to American Indians." Indian Country Today. 23 July 2003. LexisNexis Academic Universe. LexisNexis. Watzek Lib., Lewis & Clark College, Portland, OR. 28 July 2003 <http:// web.lexis-nexis.com>.

> Schminke, Marshall, Maureen L. Ambrose, and Jeffrey A. Miles. "The Impact of Gender and Setting on Perceptions of Others' Ethics." Sex Roles 48 (Apr. 2003): 361-76. Expanded ASAP. Gale Group. Watzek Lib., Lewis & Clark College, Portland, OR. 28 July 2003 <http://web6.infotrac.galegroup.com>.

More Examples of Material from a Web or Internet Site

> Henry, Dewitt, and Geoffrey Clark. "An Interview with Richard Yates." Ploughshares. 2003 (originally published Winter 1972). 4 Aug. 2003 <http://www.pshares .org/issues/article.cfm?prmArticleID=128>.

> The American National Red Cross. "A Brief History of the American Red Cross." 2001. The American National Red Cross. 30 June 2003. <http://www.redcross.org/ museum/briefarc.html>.

Text from an Online Publication

> Goldberg, Brian. "Byron, Blake, and Heaven." Romanticism on the Net. Issue 27 (Aug. 2002): 40 pars. 28 July 2003 <http://www.erudit.org/revue/ron/2002/v/ n27/006561ar.html>.

> Joyce, Cynthia. "The Salon Interview: Russell Banks." 5 Jan. 1998. Salon.com 15 Aug. 2003 <http://archive.salon.com/books/int/1998/01/cov_si_05int.html>.

Notes

- For examples of online reference works, see Part of a Book, C.2.
- For e-mail messages, see Interviews in Other Types of Sources, C.6.

6. Other types of sources

Here are a few, quick samples of forms for other types of sources. If I do not cover a type of source you are using, check the *MLA Handbook*.

In some of the categories of sources below, a number of individuals have contributed to the work you are citing. In such cases your entry should begin with the person or aspect of the piece to which you are referring in the body of your paper. Thus, if the focus of your paper is Alfred Hitchcock as a director, your citation of *Rear Window* should begin with Hitchcock. If, however, you are using this movie as an example of suspense films, then begin the citation with the title.

SOUND RECORDINGS

Repilado, Francisco. "Chan Chan." Perf. Buena Vista Social Club. Buena Vista Social Club. World Circuit/Nonesuch. 1997.

Gritton, Susan. "Die Ersehnte." Op. 9, No. 1. By Fanny Mendelssohn. With Eugene Asti, Piano. Fanny Mendelssohn Songs. Hyperion, 2000.

RADIO AND TELEVISION PROGRAMS

This Far by Faith: African-American Spiritual Journeys. Part I. PBS. KOPB-TV, Portland, OR. 24 June 2003.

Poggioli, Sylvia. "Restoring Michelangelo's David." Morning Edition. Natl. Public Radio. KOPB-FM, Portland, OR. 11 Aug. 2003. Transcript.

FILMS, VIDEOS, DVDS

Hitchcock, Alfred, dir. Rear Window. Perf. Grace Kelly and Jimmy Stewart. Paramount, 1954. Collector's Edition. DVD. Universal, 2001.

Rashomon. Dir. Akira Kurosawa. Perf. Toshira Mifune, Masayuki Mori. 1950. Video-cassette. Embassy, 1986.

LIVE PERFORMANCES

Kretzu, Jon, Dir. Copenhagen. By Michael Frayn. Artists Repertory Theatre, Portland, OR. 6 June 2003.

Blue Man Group. Keller Auditorium, Portland, OR. 2 June 2003.

PUBLIC ADDRESSES, CLASS LECTURES

Thurow, Lester. MIT Professor of Management and Economics. "Ensuring a Solid Foundation for Education: The Stakes for America and Our Future." Dolores Winningstad Theatre, Portland, OR. 29 June 2003.

Smith, Sally. Lecture. English 100: Introduction to the Novel. State University, Anywhere, NY. 5 Nov. 2010.

CARTOONS

Smaller, B. Cartoon. New Yorker 27 Jan. 2003: 58.

ADVERTISEMENTS

Parliament cigarettes. Advertisement. Time 18 Aug. 2003: 38-39.

INTERVIEWS

(The following are examples of interviews you have conducted with the person whose name begins the citation. For published interviews, see the *MLA Handbook* and an example in subsection C.5).

Walton, Jeff. Personal interview. 12 Dec. 2011.

Kaplan, Elvin. E-mail interviews. 13-15 Sept. 2008.

D. The Final List of Works Cited, including a Sample

- Two central reminders:
  - The author's name (or authors' names) in your text or parenthetical citations must take the reader to one, and only one, entry on your list.
  - Only those sources cited in the paper may be included on the list.
- For important information about ordering entries on your list, turn back to Section 8.E.2. Follow the guidelines under "MLA and CMS Notes & Bibliography Styles."
- For information on electronically formatting individual entries on the list, see also Section 8.E.2.

Format for the List of Works Cited

- Print (type) on separate sheet or sheets of paper using the same font, font size, and margins as those used in the body of the paper.
- The list will follow immediately after the body of the paper, and that followed by explanatory notes and appendixes. Number all pages consecutively with the body of the paper.
- Head the list "Works Cited." Center this heading one inch from the top of the page. Leave a line of space, and begin your first entry.
- Leave a line of space between entries on the list.
- Format individual entries as hanging indents—first line flush with the left margins; subsequent lines indented one-half inch (five spaces). Double-space.
- If your list includes more than one work by the same *first* author, you may substitute a 3-em dash (three hyphens, no space between them) followed by a period for the author's name in subsequent entries. In using this device, keep in mind that the dash stands for the name of the author (or authors) in the first entry, and only for the name (not roles, such as editor). If you have questions, consult the manual.

Works Cited

A Brief Wrap on Ethics. Washington, DC: GPO, 2000.

Caro, Robert A. Master of the Senate. New York: Knopf, 2002.

Coleridge, Samuel Taylor. Poetical Works. Ed. J. C. C. Mays. 3 vols. Bollingen ser. 75.
    Princeton, NJ: Princeton UP, 2001.

Hollander, Robert. Introduction. Inferno. By Dante Alighieri. Trans. Robert and Jean
    Hollander. New York: Doubleday, 2000. xvii-xxxiii.

Kretzu, Jon, Dir. Copenhagen. By Michael Frayn. Artists Repertory Theatre, Portland, OR.
    6 June 2003.

"Leave It to Beaver." Encyclopedia of Television. Ed. Horace Newcomb. Vol. 2. Chicago:
    Fitzroy Dearborn, 1997. 939-41.

Lowell, Robert. "For the Union Dead." 1960, 1964. The Norton Anthology of American
    Literature. Ed. Nina Baym. Vol. 2. New York: Norton, 1998. 2538-39.

Melmer, David. "Bill Could Add Legal Clout to Protection of Lands Sacred to American
    Indians." Indian Country Today. 23 July 2003. LexisNexis Academic Universe.
    LexisNexis. Watzek Lib., Lewis & Clark College, Portland, OR. 28 July 2003
    <http://web.lexis-nexis.com>.

National Education Association. Teaching with Technology. Washington, DC: NEA, 1999.

Ozick, Cynthia. "Doubting Helen Keller." New Yorker 16 & 23 June 2003: 188-196.

Poggioli, Sylvia. "Restoring Michelangelo's David." Morning Edition. Natl. Public Radio.
    KOPB-FM, Portland, OR. 11 Aug. 2003. Transcript.

"Pullman Strike." Encyclopedia Britannica Online. 2003. Encyclopedia Britannica. 8 Aug.
    2003 <http://www.search.eb.com/>.

Schminke, Marshall, Maureen L. Ambrose, and Jeffrey A. Miles. "The Impact of Gender and
    Setting on Perceptions of Others' Ethics." Sex Roles 48 (Apr. 2003): 361-76. Expanded
    ASAP. Gale Group. Watzek Lib., Lewis & Clark College, Portland, OR. 28 July 2003
    <http://web6.infotrac.galegroup.com>.

"Silly." Def. Adj. 1.a. Oxford English Dictionary Online. 2nd ed. 1989. Oxford English
    Dictionary. 15 Aug. 2003 <http://dictionary.oed.com/>.

Smith, Sally. Lecture. English 100: Introduction to the Novel. State University, Anywhere,
    NY. 5 Nov. 2010.

Webb, Jeff. "Modernist Memory; or, The Being of Americans." Criticism 44 (Summer 2002):
    227-247.

Wilde, Oscar. Picture of Dorian Gray. 1891. New York: Penguin, 2003.

---. Salome. 1893. Illus. Aubrey Beardsley. New York: Three Sirens P, n. d.

APPENDIX

B

The CMS Notes & Bibliography Style

A. How the CMS Notes & Bibliography Style Works

The notes & bibliography style uses numbers to signal citations in the body of the paper. The citations themselves are given in notes. In addition, all sources the writer has used or consulted are included on a separate list attached to the end of the paper.

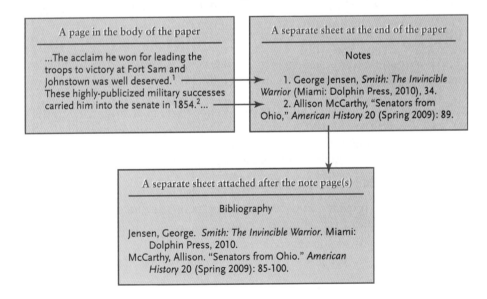

A page in the body of the paper	A separate sheet at the end of the paper
...The acclaim he won for leading the troops to victory at Fort Sam and Johnstown was well deserved.[1] These highly-publicized military successes carried him into the senate in 1854.[2]...	Notes 1. George Jensen, *Smith: The Invincible Warrior* (Miami: Dolphin Press, 2010), 34. 2. Allison McCarthy, "Senators from Ohio," *American History* 20 (Spring 2009): 89.

A separate sheet attached after the note page(s)

Bibliography

Jensen, George. *Smith: The Invincible Warrior*. Miami: Dolphin Press, 2010.
McCarthy, Allison. "Senators from Ohio." *American History* 20 (Spring 2009): 85-100.

To cite a source in the body of your paper, you insert a number that is raised half-a-space above the line (a superscript number). That number corresponds to the number of a **note** where bibliographic information about the source is given. Notes can be printed at the bottom of the page on which the note number appears (**footnotes**) or they can be gathered together on separate sheets of paper attached after the last page of the body of the paper (**endnotes**). Most word-processing programs have a feature that automatically handles the creating and printing of such notes. If you are using a typewriter, you most definitely want to do endnotes!

In addition to these notes, a list is attached to the end of the paper called a **bibliography.** Here we find sources listed in alphabetical order according to the last name of the first author of the source. In the bibliography, you must list all the sources you cite in your notes, but you may also include any and all sources that you read, even though you do not refer to them directly in your paper.

CMS stands for *The Chicago Manual of Style,* perhaps the most influential style manual in academic circles. This notes & bibliography variant of the CMS style would be appropriate only for papers in the humanities, or papers in the social sciences that approach a subject from a humanistic perspective. Although this style continues to be used in books (with certain variations) and a few schol-arly journals, it is considered rather old-fashioned, so check with your instruc-tor to be sure this is the style he or she wants you to follow.

When you are ready to document your sources using the CMS notes & bibli-ography style, turn to Section 8.E., where I give you important advice and information regarding this process.

* * *

If you are not familiar with the fundamental principles of documentation and the terminology that goes with it, I'd recommend that you look over the whole of Section 8.

The purpose of this appendix is to provide basic information about how to document a paper using the CMS notes & bibliography style. Here I am follow-ing the style as it is laid out in *The Chicago Manual of Style,* 15th ed. (Chicago: University of Chicago Press, 2003). If you do not find information you need in this appendix, check the CMS. Specific forms for sources are given in Chap-ter 17. For appropriate forms for first notes, look for examples marked N; for appropriate forms for entries in the bibliography, look for examples marked B.

This appendix is laid out in the following way:

- Subsection B provides information about notes, including the form for making subsequent references to a source.
- Subsection C provides forms for basic types of sources. In each of these cate-gories, I give you the proper form for both the bibliography entry and the first note (your first citation of a specific source).

- Subsection D discusses the format for the bibliography and includes a sample bibliography.

Some Particulars of the CMS Notes & Bibliography Style

- In cases where italic type is called for (titles of books and the like) you may either underline the relevant words or put them in italics. Ask your instructor for his or her preference. Whichever option you select, you must use it consistently throughout the entire paper for each and every instance where italic type is required.

- If the text you are citing was originally published much earlier than the copyright date of the edition you are using, you will want to acknowledge this fact. Check CMS under "reprint editions."

- All numbers in your notes and your bibliography entries should be expressed in arabic (13) rather than roman (XIII) numerals. The one exception would be page numbers of prefaces or introductions, which, if expressed in roman numerals in the original, will have to be expressed in roman numerals in your citation.

B. Notes

1. Basic information about notes

- **All notes are numbered consecutively** through the paper, beginning with number 1 for your first note and ending with the number that reflects the total number of notes in your paper. If you are using a word-processing program that includes a footnote feature, let the program number your notes. When and if you add notes, delete notes, or shuffle them around, the program automatically renumbers and keeps the content straight.

- In the body of your paper, **the note number is raised above the line** (no punctuation) and should be placed at the end of a sentence. As in the case of the Johnson example below, it is easy in notes to provide a clear reference to Johnson's work and then, in the same note, to cite those other historians. If it is *absolutely* necessary to put a note number within a sentence, do so after a point of punctuation.

  According to Richard Allen, the poem is based on a traditional Navaho myth.[4]

  Although James Johnson has argued that this battle was "the most decisive of the war," other historians disagree with Johnson's assessment.[10]

- **If you have used an author's name in your narrative,** or given the author's name and the title of the work, it is not necessary to repeat this information in your note. Just begin the note with the next required unit of bibliographic information. Be aware, however, that in your sentence you must give *all* the information that would be required in the note—i.e., the author's *complete* name, the *full* title of the work. It is never incorrect to repeat such information in the note.

- There are **different forms** for the first reference you make to a source and subsequent references to the same source. See the next two subsections.

- Never, never, never insert **two different note numbers at the same point** in your paper. If you need to cite more than one source, do so in the *same* note. If you are concerned that your readers may not understand exactly what you are citing, just explain ("The statistics about marriage were taken from Helen Thurber . . ."). The various citations will be separated with semicolons. Use the form for a first note if this is your first citation of a source; use the shortened form if you have already cited this work in a previous note.

> 14. Charles B. Long, *The Civil War* (New York: Never Press, 2010), 116-17; Curtis, "Lee and Grant," 108; James G. Gillingham, *A History of the War between the States* (San Francisco: Nosuch Press, 2003), 2:35-70.

- When you are making **extensive use of one of your sources,** or when you have drawn factual information from several sources in a paragraph, explain this to your reader in a note:

> 10. Information in the following paragraphs on the Battle of the Bulge has been taken from John W. Sweet, *World War II.* . . .

> 4. My recounting of the basic events of the Pullman strike relies on information found in Harding, *Unions,* 34-78; Purcell, "Union Movements"; and Lee, *The Railroad Empires,* chap. 6.

Such notes spare you from having to put note numbers after every sentence! I recommend placing a note such as this early in the paragraph, so your instructor gets your message right away. If and when you quote directly from a source, each quotation will have to have a separate note. If you are using one work extensively in a paper, you have some other options; see subsection B.3.

- If there are certain points you would like to elaborate on but they are not directly a part of your argument, consider creating an **explanatory note;** see Section 8.E.4 for more details.

- Information given directly to you personally (face-to-face, over the phone, or in an e-mail message) would be considered a **"personal communication."** In CMS, you do not list personal communications in your bibliography; rather, you will give necessary information about them in the body of your paper or in a note. As is generally the case, information you provide in your own narrative does not have to be repeated in a note. Thus, if you give us full information about your informant and the occasion in your text, no note will be required. **NOTE:** It is always helpful to give your reader any and all information about your informant that would increase the authority of that person to speak on the given issue.

I had an extended telephone conversation with the CEO of Clean-Up Environments, Judy Hawk, on November 11, 2005. In that conversation Ms. Hawk . . .

OR

     11. Judy Hawk, CEO, Clean-Up Environments, telephone conversation with the author, November 11, 2005.

- **Citation of material found in a secondary source.** In Section 4.H.3 and again in Section 8.D.7, I talk about the importance of seeking out the original source any time you find mention of a work in one of the sources you are reading. If you have not been able to put your hands on the original, provide as much information about the original work as you have, and then give full bibliographic information about the source in which you found it. Below I give the full citation for the note. It would be best, however, to give as much information as possible about the original in your text.

     15. Henry D. Lloyd, *Wealth against Commonwealth* (1894; ed. 1899), quoted in Richard Hofstadter, *The Age of Reform from Bryan to F. D. R.* (New York: Random House, Vintage Books, 1955), 141.

Obviously, the Hofstadter text must be included in your bibliography. If you followed the CMS style exactly, you would also list the original source (Lloyd) on your bibliography with information about where you found the pertinent information. I would recommend **not** listing the original source in your bibliography. But consult with your instructor. If he or she wants you to include the original in the bibliography, you must check CMS for the proper way to do so (Section 17.274).

- As I indicated in the introduction to Appendix B, you may choose to print (or type) your notes at the bottom of the page on which the note numbers appear (**footnotes**), or you can print or type all notes on separate sheets of paper that will be inserted between the last page of your paper and your bibliography (**endnotes**). If you choose endnotes, here are some suggestions for formatting. Number pages consecutively with the body of the paper. Use the same margins, font, and type size you've used in the body of your paper. Center the heading, Notes, at the top of the page, leaving one line of space between the heading and the first note. The first line of the note may be indented (three to five spaces) or it can be flush with the left margin. The note number may be a superscript, or it may rest on the text line. You may leave a line of space between notes or not. You may double-space notes or not. The two major determinants of the format you follow should be (1) the preferences of your instructor; (2) the defaults and capabilities of the footnote feature of your word-processing program. In my experience with this feature in the word-processing program that I and most of my students use, it is possible to change the formatting of notes, but you really need to know what you are doing. I would advise you do a test document in your word-processing program and work out all the bugs *before* you actually start creating notes in your paper file.

2. First and subsequent notes

The first time you cite a source in your notes, you must give full bibliographic information about the source; this is your first note. If you refer to that source again later in your paper, this is a subsequent note. In the next subsection, I talk in more detail about subsequent notes. Here's a picture of what your notes will look like.

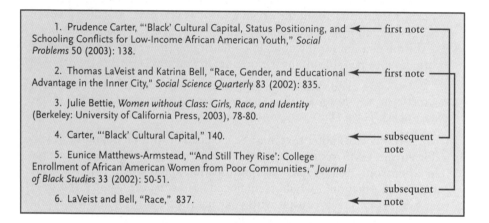

The form for subsequent notes is given in the following subsection. Forms for first notes are given along with forms for bibliography entries in subsection C.

3. Forms for subsequent notes

The Shortened Form

After you have given your readers full bibliographic information about a source in a first note, and you have occasion to cite that source again, CMS recommends that you use the shortened form for this and other subsequent notes. In the shortened form, you will give the author's last name, the title of the text from which you have taken the information, and the relevant page numbers. The function of this shortened form is to enable the reader to turn from the note immediately to the bibliography, so keep in mind that the information you provide in this shortened form must correspond exactly with the author and title as given in the entry in the bibliography. See below for further commentary on this point.

> 15. Caro, *Master of the Senate*, 45.

> 16. Kroll, "Memories of Scott," 19.

> 17. Webb, "Modernist Memory," 194.

> 18. Hollander, introduction, xxii.

Some Advice on Using the Shortened Form

- Use only the author's last name unless you have more than one entry for works by authors with the same last name; in these cases, add the author's first name and initial to all notes.

- In the shortened form, the title of the work is the title that is given immediately after the author's name in the bibliography. If this title is five words or fewer, use the complete title; otherwise, shorten by using the first four or five words, in the exact order and form in which they appear in the original.

- In those cases in which your bibliography entry is to multiple volumes of the same work by the same author, your note must always include the appropriate volume, expressed in an arabic numeral and placed in front of the page number, separated with a colon.

> 15. Hegel, *Aesthetics*, 2:118.

- When you are using a part of a book as a source, you have two options in listing this work on your bibliography: you can list the part as its own entry (which is the form I follow in subsection C.3), or you can list only the book itself. If you list only the book on the bibliography, you will have to give full information about the part each time you cite it. However, once you have given full bibliographic information about the book itself, this information may be given in shortened form. In this shortened form, the editor's name is given in the author position because this is the way the collection is entered in the bibliography.

> 17. "Robin Hood Rescuing Three Squires" (Child No. 140), in Bronson, ed., *Traditional Tunes*, 56.

> 5. Dolores Prida, *Botánica*, in Sandoval-Sánchez and Sternbach, eds., *Puro Teatro*, 8-9.

Ibid.

The term Ibid. (an abbreviation for *ibidem*, which in Latin means "in the same place") is a throwback to a whole series of Latin terms that used to be used in footnotes. I will spare you the gory details about the problems that were caused by these references back to previous notes. Here I'll simply *urge* you to jettison ibid. and, in the few cases where you would use it, use the shortened form instead. If you follow my advice about appropriate methods for making extensive references to one work in Section 6.B.2 and 3, and in this appendix, you won't even need it! But if you insist on using ibid., please do so correctly. Ibid. can be used *only* when the note in which it appears refers to the source in the note that immediately precedes it, *and* there is only one source cited in that preceding note. Ibid. used alone means "in the same source on the same page." If you want to cite the same source but different pages, you will have to add the relevant page number(s).

> 14. Jeff Webb, "Modernist Memory; or, The Being of Americans," *Criticism* 44 (Summer 2002): 230.

> 15. Ibid.   [meaning Webb, page 230]

> 16. Ibid., 235.   [meaning Webb, page 235]

Extensive References to One Source

If you have written a paper in which you use one work extensively—if, for example, you have written a paper on Karl Marx in which you refer frequently to his book *Capital*—you will have many notes that cite this work. An alternative is to put these citations in the body of your paper. Here's the procedure for citing a work in the text.

- The first time you refer to this work, you must give a normal first note. After you document the source, it would be wise to inform your reader that further citations in your paper will be given in the body of the paper.

  > 1. Sigmund Freud, *Interpretation of Dreams*, 1900, in *The Standard Edition of the Complete Psychological Works of Sigmund Freud*, trans. from the German under the general editorship of James Strachey (London: Hogarth Press and the Institute of Psychoanalysis, 1953), 4:136-38. All references to Freud's works in this paper are references to this edition of the *Complete Works*; citations will hereafter be given in the text.
  > 2. Karl Marx, *Capital: A Critique of Political Economy*, trans. from the 3rd German ed. by Samuel Moore and Edward Aveling, ed. Frederick Engels, rev. according to the 4th German ed. by Ernest Untermann (New York: Random House, Modern Library, 1906), 106. All references to *Capital* are references to this edition; citations will hereafter be given in the text.

- Each time you refer to this work in the body of your paper, you will put your citation in parentheses at the end of the relevant sentence. The reader must be given the same information that would be given in the normal shortened form. If part of this information (like the name of the author and the title of a specific selection) is given in your sentence or is obvious from the context, this information need not be repeated. If the work is part of a multivolume set, don't forget that you must include the volume number.

According to Marx, capital is "essentially the command over unpaid labour" (*Capital*, 585).

Freud covers this subject in the first sections of *Interpretation of Dreams* (*Complete Works*, 4:134-62).

C. Forms for Sources in First Notes and Bibliography

1. Differences between first notes and the bibliography entry

In the pages that follow, I will be giving the form for first notes and that for entries in the bibliography together. The distinctions between the two forms are subtle, which is probably the reason that the students with whom I work tend to do their notes incorrectly. Here I will alert you to the four basic differences between the two, differences that are most pronounced in citing books.

BIBLIOGRAPHY ENTRY

> Jarausch, Konrad H., and Michael Geyer. *Shattered Past: Reconstructing German Histories*. Princeton, NJ: Princeton University Press, 2003.

FIRST NOTE

> 4. Konrad H. Jarausch and Michael Geyer, *Shattered Past: Reconstructing German Histories* (Princeton, NJ: Princeton University Press, 2003), 45-46.

- In the bibliography, the name of the first author is inverted because the bibliography is alphabetized according to this name. Since alphabetizing is not an issue in a note, the first author's name appears in its normal form.

- In the bibliography, the major units of the citation are separated by periods. In the note, units are separated by commas.

- In notes that cite books, the facts of publication are enclosed in parentheses. Please, no punctuation immediately before parentheses. In bibliography entries, the facts of publication are simply presented as a separate unit.

- Except in (rare) cases in which a note is citing a complete book, notes end with the number(s) of the pages where you found the material you are citing. Entries in bibliographies for books do not include page numbers since the reference is to the entire book. Inclusive page numbers are given in bibliographic entries for parts of books and for periodicals, where differences between the two forms become less pronounced.

- The bibliography entry is formatted as a hanging indent (first line flush with the left margin, subsequent lines indented one-half inch). If notes are indented, it is the first line only that is indented.

From what I have just said, it should be obvious that, when you are documenting sources in the CMS style for notes & bibliography, you have to pay particularly close attention not only to the placement and mechanics of your citations, but also to using the form appropriate for a note and that appropriate for a bibliography entry.

2. Books

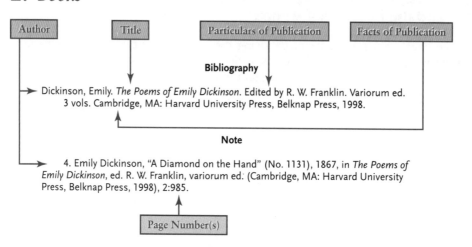

Author

- Entry begins with the name(s) of author(s). In the bibliography, invert the name of the first author, followed by first name (and middle initial). Comma separates last and first names. In the note, author's name is given in its normal order.

- If there is more than one author, in the bibliography invert the name of the first author only. Names of all other authors given in their normal order. Write "and" before the name of the last author. (See example below for editors).

- If entry is for an edited work, give the name(s) of editor(s) in the author position. Follow the guidelines for one author, or for multiple authors. After the last name listed, insert a comma and "ed." for one editor or "eds." for more than one. The example below is for a bibliography entry.

Jacobs, John, ed. *The History of* . . .

Anders, Sally, Nina Wilkerson, and Mona Perkins, eds. *Women* . . .

- If there is no author, begin the entry with the title.

- The author unit in the bibliography ends with a period; in the note, with a comma.

Title

- Give the complete title of the book (including any subtitles) exactly as it appears on the title page of the book. Typically, the main title is separated from the subtitle with a colon.

- Underline (or italicize) the complete title. Capitalize main words; see Section 7.B. Use quotation marks around words in quotation marks in the original. Any words italicized in the original should *not* be italicized.

- End bibliographic unit with a period. In note, add a comma if there are particulars of publication; if title is followed by facts of publication, no punctuation.

Particulars of Publication

- After the title and before the facts of publication, record relevant information about the book that is not provided elsewhere in the entry. Record this information in the order shown below; each item in the list represents a unit. In the bibliography, each unit begins with a capital letter and ends with a period (do not add a period if the final word is an abbreviation). Units in notes are lowercase and separated with a comma.

  - Editor and/or translator when an author is given. In the bibliography, spell out "Edited by" and "Translated by" and capitalize as shown. If a work has both an editor and a translator, each is a separate unit. In notes, use the following abbreviations before names: ed. for editor(s); trans. for translator/translators. Provide first and last names in their normal order.

  - Edition, if not the first. Represent as follows: 2nd ed., 3rd ed., 4th ed., and so on.

  - If multivolume set, number of volumes in the set, or the volume being used (see more below).

  - If a series, the name (and number) of the series.

- Always use arabic numerals (4), not roman numerals (IV).

- If this source was originally published in a year much earlier than the copyright date of the edition you are using, it is helpful to include the original date of publication in your entry. Insert this year after the title of the work.

Facts of Publication

This unit is composed of three pieces of information, punctuated as follows: the city of publication, colon, the publisher, comma, the copyright date, period.

- If more than one city is listed, use only the first. Please note that the place is the *city* in which a publisher has offices, *not the state or country.* The state or country may be *added* if the city, by itself, is not well known or could be confused with another city. Use the Postal Service abbreviations for states in the U.S.

- If the book you are using is a paperback, give the paperback imprint after the names of the publishing house: Random House, Vintage.

- The copyright date is the most recent date next to the copyright symbol © on the reverse side of the title page.

Page Number(s)

In the note, end with the page or pages on which we will find the material you are citing. Use a hyphen to signal inclusive pages (25-30); use commas to list nonconsecutive pages (3, 6, 8, 10). Do *not* use "page" or "p." If you are citing a multivolume work, see my comments in subsection B.3. and examples in Part of a Book, subsection C.3.

ORGANIZATION AS AUTHOR

BIBLIOGRAPHY

United Nations Educational, Scientific, and Cultural Organization, International Institute for Educational Planning. *HIV/AIDS and Education: A Strategic Approach.* New York: UNESCO, 2003. Available online from: http://unesdoc.unesco .org/ ulis/index.html.

National Education Association. *Teaching with Technology.* Washington, DC: NEA, 1999.

NOTE

3. United Nations Educational, Scientific, and Cultural Organization, International Institute for Educational Planning, *HIV/AIDS and Education: A Strategic Approach* (New York: UNESCO, 2003), 45.

5. National Education Association, *Teaching with Technology* (Washington, DC: NEA, 1999), 78-79.

BOOK IN A MULTIVOLUME SET

In citing a book that is part of a multivolume set, the issue is simply to be sure that your reader always knows which volume you are citing! Typically, if you are using a multivolume work, you are citing a discrete part or parts of one or more books. For a full discussion of citing books in a multivolume set, see Section 8.D.4. For more on this issue, see subsection C.3. on citing part of a book.

BIBLIOGRAPHY ENTRY FOR THE COMPLETE SET

Bronson, Bertrand H., ed. *The Traditional Tunes of the Child Ballads with Their Texts, according to the Extant Records of Great Britain and America.* 4 vols. Princeton, NJ: Princeton University Press, 1959-72.

BIBLIOGRAPHY ENTRY FOR ONE VOLUME, SAME TITLE

Bronson, Bertrand H., ed. *The Traditional Tunes of the Child Ballads with Their Texts, according to the Extant Records of Great Britain and America.* Vol. 3. Princeton, NJ: Princeton University Press, 1966.

NOTE FOR ONE VOLUME, SAME TITLE

(See Dickinson example above and examples in subsection C.3.)

BIBLIOGRAPHY ENTRY FOR ONE VOLUME, DIFFERENT TITLE

Caro, Robert A. *Master of the Senate.* Vol. 3 of *The Years of Lyndon Johnson.* New York: Knopf, 2002.

NOTE FOR ONE VOLUME, DIFFERENT TITLE

13. Robert A. Caro, *Master of the Senate,* vol. 3 of *The Years of Lyndon Johnson* (New York: Knopf, 2002), 461-62.

PAMPHLET

BIBLIOGRAPHY

A Brief Wrap on Ethics. Washington, DC: Government Printing Office, 2000.

NOTE

3. *A Brief Wrap on Ethics* (Washington, DC: Government Printing Office, 2000), 15.

3. Part of a book, including reference works

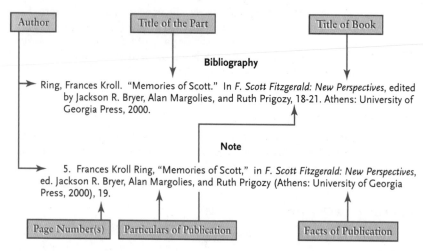

Author

- Entry begins with the name of the person(s) responsible for the part you are citing. In the bibliography, invert the name of the first author, followed by first name (and middle initial). Comma separates last and first names. In the note, author's name is given in its normal order.

- If there is more than one author, in the bibliography invert the name of the first author only. Names of all other authors given in their normal order. Write "and" before the name of the last author.

- If the author of the part of the book is also the editor of the book, list the editor in the author position. It is not necessary to repeat this information in the particulars of publication.

- If the part has no author, begin the entry with the title.

Title of the Part

- Give the full title of the part, including any subtitles. Capitalize main words; see Section 7.B. End with a period in the bibliography, a comma in the note.

- Enclose the title in quotation marks with the following exceptions:

  - Titles of plays are underlined (italicized), as are the titles of other works that were originally published as a book.

- Common units of books—introduction, afterword, preface—are not put in quotation marks (see example below).

- If the title is in quotation marks, the period or comma is placed *inside* the end quotation mark. Any word/words in quotation marks in the original are enclosed in single quotation marks. Underline (italicize) any word(s) in the title that are italicized.

Title of Book

- The title of the book is preceded by the word "in." Capitalize in the bibliography.

- Otherwise, follow guidelines for titles of books (subsection C.2).

Particulars of Publication

- If the book is an anthology or edited collection, give the name(s) of editor(s) immediately after the title of the book. In the bibliography write out "edited by." Abbreviate to "ed." in the note.

- When the book was written by a person whose name has not yet been given, write "by" immediately after the title of the book, separated by a comma.

- If any other information about this book needs to be given, provide it here. See Particulars of Publication for a book (subsection C.2).

Facts of Publication

Follow the guidelines for Facts of Publication of a book (subsection C.2).

Page Numbers

In the note, end with the page(s) you are citing in this note. In the bibliography entry, it is courteous (but not required) to give the inclusive page numbers of the part (the pages on which the part begins and ends) after the name(s) of the editor(s). Provide just the numbers; no p. or pp.

PART AND BOOK BY SAME AUTHOR

BIBLIOGRAPHY

> Wolfe, Tom. "Sorry, but Your Soul Just Died." In *Hooking Up*. New York: Farrar, Giroux, Straus, 2000.

NOTE

> 3. Tom Wolfe, "Sorry, but Your Soul Just Died," in *Hooking Up* (New York: Farrar, Giroux, Straus, 2000), 94.

PART AND BOOK BY DIFFERENT AUTHORS

BIBLIOGRAPHY

> Prida, Dolores. *Botánica*. In *Puro Teatro: A Latina Anthology*, edited by Alberto Sandoval-Sánchez and Nancy Saporta Sternbach, 7-45. Tucson: University of Arizona Press, 2000.

NOTE

> 5. Dolores Prida, *Botánica*, in *Puro Teatro: A Latina Anthology*, ed. Alberto Sandoval-Sánchez and Nancy Saporta Sternbach (Tucson: University of Arizona Press, 2000), 8-9.

INTRODUCTION, AFTERWORD, PREFACE

BIBLIOGRAPHY

> Hollander, Robert. Introduction to *Inferno*, by Dante Alighieri. Translated by Robert and Jean Hollander, xvii-xxxiii. New York: Doubleday, 2000.

NOTE

> 8. Robert Hollander, introduction to *Inferno*, by Dante Alighieri, trans. Robert and Jean Hollander (New York: Doubleday, 2000), xiv.

PART WITH NO AUTHOR, MULTIVOLUME WORK

BIBLIOGRAPHY

> "Robin Hood Rescuing Three Squires" (Child No. 140). In *The Traditional Tunes of the Child Ballads with Their Texts*, edited by Bertrand H. Bronson, 53-57. Vol. 3. Princeton, NJ: Princeton University Press, 1966.

NOTE

> 7. "Robin Hood Rescuing Three Squires" (Child No. 140), in *The Traditional Tunes of the Child Ballads with Their Texts*, ed. Bertrand H. Bronson, vol. 3 (Princeton, NJ: Princeton University Press, 1966), 55-56.

DICTIONARIES, ENCYCLOPEDIAS, AND OTHER REFERENCE WORKS

STANDARD REFERENCE WORK

According to CMS, standard reference works (English dictionaries, *The Encyclopedia Britannica*, *Who's Who*, and the like) are not included in your bibliography. When you cite such a work in your note, use the following form. "S.v." is an abbreviation for a Latin phrase which means "you will find this entry under this word or phrase."

4. *Encyclopedia Americana*, international ed., 1999, s.v., "Folk Music, American" by Bruno Nettl.

7. *Encyclopedia Britannica Online*, s. v., "Pullman Strike," http://www.search .eb.com/eb/article?eu=63450 (accessed August 8, 2003).

10. *Oxford English Dictionary*, 2nd ed., 1989, s.v., "Silly," http://dictionary.oed .com/ (accessed August 15, 2003).

SPECIALIZED DICTIONARIES AND ENCYCLOPEDIAS

It is acceptable, however, to put specialized dictionaries or encyclopedias in your bibliography. If the entry in such a work is signed, is long, and otherwise looks very much like the parts of books I've just been describing, I'd suggest you cite such entries using the form for part of a book.

USING THE CMS FORM FOR REFERENCE WORKS

BIBLIOGRAPHY

The Dictionary of Women Artists, edited by Delia Gaze. 2 vols. London: Fitzroy Dearborn Publishers, 1997.

NOTE

4. *The Dictionary of Women Artists*, ed. Delia Gaze (London: Fitzroy Dearborn Publishers, 1997), s. v. "O'Keeffe, Georgia" by Roxana Robinson.

USING THE CMS FORM FOR PART OF A BOOK

BIBLIOGRAPHY

Haugaard, Mark. "Liberalism." In *Encyclopedia of Nationalism*. Vol. 1, 441-63. San
Diego: Academic Press, 2001.

NOTE

3. Mark Haugaard, "Liberalism," in *Encyclopedia of Nationalism*, vol. 1 (San Diego: Academic Press, 2001), 445-46.

4. Articles from journals and magazines

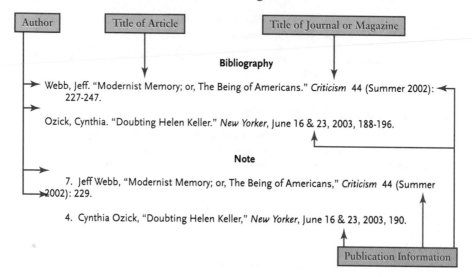

Bibliography

Webb, Jeff. "Modernist Memory; or, The Being of Americans." *Criticism* 44 (Summer 2002): 227-247.

Ozick, Cynthia. "Doubting Helen Keller." *New Yorker*, June 16 & 23, 2003, 188-196.

Note

7. Jeff Webb, "Modernist Memory; or, The Being of Americans," *Criticism* 44 (Summer 2002): 229.

4. Cynthia Ozick, "Doubting Helen Keller," *New Yorker*, June 16 & 23, 2003, 190.

Author

- Entry begins with the name(s) of the author(s) of the article. In the bibliography, invert the name of the first author, followed by first name (and middle initial). Comma separates last and first names. In the note, author's name is given in its normal order.

- If there is more than one author, in the bibliography invert the name of the first author only. Names of all other authors given in their normal order. Write "and" before the name of the last author.

- If the article has no author, begin the entry with the title.

Title of Article

- Give the full title of the article, including any subtitles. Capitalize main words (see Section 7.B). End with a period in the bibliography, a comma in the note.

- Enclose the title in quotation marks. The period (bibliography) or comma (note) is placed *inside* the end quotation mark. Any word/words in quotation marks in the original are enclosed in single quotation marks. Underline (italicize) any word(s) in the title that are italicized.

Title of the Journal or Magazine

Spell out the full title and underline (italicize). Capitalize all main words; ignore any initial article (*a, an* or *the*). Notice that there is no punctuation between the title of a journal and the volume number; otherwise, end with a comma.

Publication Information

- In citing journals, give the volume number immediately after the title. If the journal begins each issue with page 1, also include the issue number. Volume 27, issue number 1 is represented this way: 27, no. 1. In parentheses, give the year of publication; a month or season would be helpful but is not required.

- In the case of magazines, give the date of the issue (month and year, or month, date, and year).

- In the bibliography, end with the inclusive page numbers of the article (the pages on which the article begins and ends). In citations of journals, a colon and a space separate the date from the page numbers. In magazines, commas separate the title from the date, and the date from the page number(s). The note ends with the number(s) of the specific page(s) to which you are referring in your paper.

ALERT!

If you downloaded an article from a database or an online site, you must include this information after your citation of the print version. See subsection C.6., Web Sites and Other Electronic Sources. For more discussion of the issue in general, see Section 8.D.6., Documenting Material Downloaded from Computers.

5. Articles from newspapers

Note: In this section, I am taking some liberties with the CMS style, since CMS recommends not having entries for newspapers in bibliographies, unless they are cited under the name of the newspaper. It prefers that you cite articles only in notes, and would really prefer that the entire citation be given, like a personal communication, fully in your text. In addition, when citations are made, CMS typically does not include page numbers. You'll see here that I modify these recommendations, following the CMS style for popular magazines. If you have qualms about following my advice, check with your instructor.

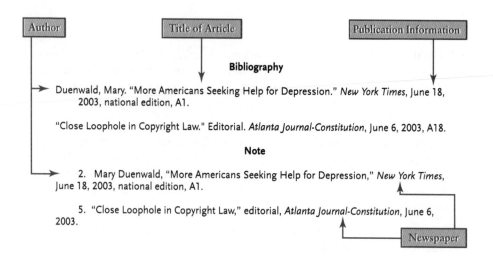

Author

- Begin with the name of the first person listed in the byline. In the bibliography, start with last name, followed by first name (and middle initial). Comma separates last and first names. In the note, author's name is given in its normal order. If there is more than one author, the name of the first author only is inverted in the bibliography.

- If there is no author, begin with the title of the article.

Title of Article

- Give the main headline of the article. Capitalize main words (see Section 7.B). Enclose in quotation marks. The period (bibliography) or comma (note) is placed *inside* the end quotation mark. Any word/words in quotation marks in the original are enclosed in single quotation marks.

- In the case of special types of articles—editorials, letters to the editor, and the like—it is very helpful to include such information. Insert the description between the title of the article and the name of the newspaper. If you are citing a review, check CMS for the appropriate form for reviews.

Newspaper

- Capitalize main words; underline (italicize).

- Typically articles (*the, an, a*) are not included as part of the name of a newspaper.

- If you are citing a local paper whose name does not include the city (or state) of origin, add that information in parentheses:

(Portland) *Oregonian,* Smalltown (OR) *Tribune*

Publication Information

- Immediately following the name of the newspaper, provide the date of the issue; commas before and after.

- If the newspaper comes out in various editions, tell us which edition you used.

- Take care with page numbers in newspapers. Since various sections tend to begin with page 1, you'll need to give us the section letter along with the page number. If an article begins on one page, and is continued on a non-adjacent page, give the number of the first page only.

ALERT!

If you downloaded an article from a database or an online site, you must include this information after your citation of the print version. See subsection C.6, Web Sites and Other Electronic Sources. For more discussion of the issue in general, see Section 8.D.6., Documenting Material Downloaded from Computers.

6. Web sites and other electronic sources

In this section, I'm using the term "electronic source" to cover any material transmitted through a computer; thus, electronic sources include textual material from CD-ROMs and material from any and all online sources, public and restricted, edited and unedited (databases, Web and Internet sites, online journals and magazines, newsgroups, discussion groups, online forums, e-mail messages, and the like).

Although CMS has, at last, developed forms for electronic sources, the information it requires in such citations is sparse; your instructor may ask you to provide more information. Moreover, CMS advises authors to cite material generated solely for a Web site in notes only, and not in the bibliography. Here I am providing a form for a bibliography entry for such material so that you have a model if and when your instructor wants to see this material in your bibliography.

For more detailed discussion of issues related to documentation of electronic sources, read over Section 8.D.6. Information I'm giving here should be sufficient for you to create appropriate entries for electronic sources in CMS notes & bibliography style. If it is not, consult the 15th edition of *The Chicago Manual of Style*, which is the one I am following. Be aware, however, that forms for electronic sources may be updated at any time.

Material from a Web or Internet Site

Bibliography

Swartz, Carl. "Concept Formation and Problem Solving: Understanding and Managing Two
   Key Components of Higher Order Cognition." *All Kinds of Minds*. http://www
   .allkindsofminds.org/articleDisplay.aspx?categoryID=10&articleID=18

Note

   7. Carl Swartz, "Concept Formation and Problem Solving: Understanding and
Managing Two Key Components of Higher Order Cognition," *All Kinds of Minds*,
http://www.allkindsofminds.org/articleDisplay.aspx?categoryID=10&articleID=18

Print Text from a Database

Bibliography

Schminke, Marshall, Maureen L. Ambrose, and Jeffrey A. Miles. "The Impact of Gender and
   Setting on Perceptions of Others' Ethics." *Sex Roles* 48 (2003): 361-76. http://web6
   .infotrac.galegroup.com/

Note

   3. Marshall Schminke, Maureen L. Ambrose, and Jeffrey A. Miles, "The Impact of
Gender and Setting on Perceptions of Others' Ethics," *Sex Roles* 48 (2003), 362,
http://web6 .infotrac.galegroup.com/

Author and Title

- Begin with the name of the author, or the person or organization responsible for the material you are using (see Section 8.D.6. for further discussion
  of this issue). Follow standard CMS form for authors. End with a period. If
  no author is given or discernable, begin the entry with the title.

- Provide the title of the text or document you are citing, or the title of the Web page, following the form that would be appropriate for the type of source if it were published in paper form. In citing the title of a Web page, follow the form for the title of a journal article.

Particulars about the Text or Material

- If the text was originally published in print form, or is available in a print version, provide any information you are given about the print version. Use standard CMS form for a print version of this material.

- If the text is an electronic publication (a book published online, an article in an online journal or magazine), provide all publication information. Follow the standard CMS form for a print version of this type of source.

- For other types of material that have formal copyright dates, I recommend adding the date here.

Where You Located This Text or Material

- If you have already provided "publication" information of the material you are citing (see above), simply add the complete URL at the end of the entry. If and when the material has been taken from a full-text database, it is sufficient to give only the URL that would take your reader to the search page. In cases where the information in the material you are citing is time-sensitive, or you are otherwise required to, provide the date you accessed the material (in parentheses, after the URL). Unless the text you downloaded is in a stable format, you will not be able to use page numbers in your notes; for full discussion of this matter, see Section 8.D.6. If, however, you are citing an online periodical that numbers paragraphs, use the appropriate paragraph number(s).

- If you have given only author and/or title (of a text, for example, posted on a Web site, or simply a Web page itself), add the following:

  - the title of the site or the name of the sponsor of the site; if you have used the sponsor of the site as the author of the material, it is not necessary to repeat this information;

  - the complete URL;

  - in cases where the information in the material you are citing is time-sensitive, or you are otherwise required to, provide the date you accessed the information (in parentheses, after the URL).

MORE EXAMPLES OF A PRINT TEXT FROM A DATABASE

BIBLIOGRAPHY

Bhatt, Shakti. "State Terrorism vs. Jihad in Kashmir." *Journal of Contemporary Asia* 33 (2003): 215-225. http://web9.epnet.com/

Lesesne, Catherine A., Susanna N. Visser, and Carla P. White. "Attention-Deficit/Hyperactivity Disorder in School-Aged Children: Association with Maternal Mental Health and Use of Health Care Resources." *Pediatrics* 111 (May 2003): 1232-1237. http://web9.epnet.com/

NOTE

4. Shakti Bhatt, "State Terrorism vs. Jihad in Kashmir," *Journal of Contemporary Asia* 33 (2003), http://web9.epnet.com/

7. Catherine A. Lesesne, Susanna N. Visser, and Carla P. White, "Attention-Deficit/Hyperactivity Disorder in School-Aged Children: Association with Maternal Mental Health and Use of Health Care Resources," *Pediatrics* 111 (May 2003), 1233, http://web9.epnet.com/

MORE EXAMPLES OF MATERIAL FROM A WEB OR INTERNET SITE

BIBLIOGRAPHY

"U.S.: Libya Taking Lockerbie Blame." August 15, 2003. *CNN.com*. http://www.cnn.com/2003/US/08/15/lockerbie.delay/index.html

The American National Red Cross. "A Brief History of the American Red Cross." 2001. http://www.redcross.org/museum/briefarc.html (accessed June 30, 2003).

World Health Organization. "Case Definitions for Surveillance of Severe Acute Respiratory Syndrome (SARS)." May 1, 2003. http://www.who.int/csr/casedefinition/en/print.html

NOTE

13. "U.S.: Libya Taking Lockerbie Blame," August 15, 2003, *CNN.com*, http://www.cnn.com/2003/US/08/15/lockerbie.delay/index.html.

5. The American National Red Cross, "A Brief History of the American Red Cross," 2001, http://www.redcross.org/museum/briefarc.html (accessed June 30, 2003).

8. World Health Organization, "Case Definitions for Surveillance of Severe Acute Respiratory Syndrome (SARS)," May 1, 2003, http://www.who.int/csr/casedefinition/en/print.html

TEXT FROM AN ONLINE PUBLICATION

BIBLIOGRAPHY

Goldberg, Brian. "Byron, Blake, and Heaven." *Romanticism on the Net*. Issue 27 (August 2002). http://www.erudit.org/revue/ron/2002/v/n27/006561ar.html

NOTE

> 8. Brian Goldberg, "Byron, Blake, and Heaven," *Romanticism on the Net*, issue 27 (August 2002), para. 6, http://www.erudit.org/revue/ron/2002/v/n27/006561ar.html

More examples of citations of electronic sources can be found in subsection C.3 (Part of a Book: Dictionaries, Encyclopedias, and Other Reference Works).

D. The Final Bibliography, including a Sample

You may have noticed that the authors of some books break their bibliographies down into separate categories; a common division is Primary Sources and Secondary Sources. If you think it would help your readers to make such divisions, consult your instructor. Otherwise, plan to put all your sources in the same list.

- If you are citing parts of books, or books in multivolume sets, be sure your notes provide sufficient information to enable the reader to find the appropriate entry in the bibliography.

- For important information about ordering entries on your list, turn back to Section 8.E.2. Follow the guidelines under "The MLA and CMS Notes & Bibliography Styles."

- For information on electronically formatting individual entries on the list, also see Section 8.E.2.

Format for the Final List

- Print (type) on separate sheet or sheets of paper using the same font, font size, and margins as those used in the body of the paper.

- The bibliography will follow immediately after the body of the paper if you have used footnotes, and after the note pages if you have created endnotes. Number all pages consecutively with the body of the paper.

- Head the list "Bibliography." Center this heading one inch from the top of the page. Leave a line of space, and begin your first entry.

- Leave a line of space between entries on the list.

- Format individual entries as hanging indents: first line flush with the left margins; subsequent lines indented one-half inch (or five spaces).

- You may double-space or single-space individual entries. See my discussion of this issue in Section 7.C., then consult your instructor for his/her preferences.

- If your list includes more than one work by the same *primary* author, you may substitute a 3-em dash (three hyphens, no space between them) followed by a period for the author's name in subsequent entries. In using this device, keep in mind that the dash stands for the name of the author (or authors) in the first entry, and only for the name (not roles, such as editor). If you have questions, consult the manual.

Bibliography

Bhatt, Shakti. "State Terrorism vs. Jihad in Kashmir." *Journal of Contemporary Asia* 33 (2003): 215-225. http://web9.epnet.com/

A Brief Wrap on Ethics. Washington, DC: Government Printing Office, 2000.

Caro, Robert A. *Master of the Senate.* Vol. 3 of *The Years of Lyndon Johnson.* New York: Knopf, 2002.

Dickinson, Emily. *The Poems of Emily Dickinson.* Edited by R. W. Franklin. Variorum ed. 3 vols. Cambridge, MA: Harvard University Press, Belknap Press, 1998.

Haugaard, Mark. "Liberalism." In *Encyclopedia of Nationalism.* Vol. 1, 441-63. San Diego: Academic Press, 2001.

Ozick, Cynthia. "Doubting Helen Keller." *New Yorker,* June 16 & 23, 2003, 188-196.

Ring, Frances Kroll. "Memories of Scott." In *F. Scott Fitzgerald: New Perspectives,* edited by Jackson R. Bryer, Alan Margolies, and Ruth Prigozy, 18-21. Athens: University of Georgia Press, 2000.

United Nations Educational, Scientific, and Cultural Organization, International Institute for Educational Planning. *HIV/AIDS and Education: A Strategic Approach.* New York: UNESCO, 2003. Available online from: http://unesdoc.unesco.org/images/0012/ 001286/128657e.pdf

"U.S.: Libya Taking Lockerbie Blame." August 15, 2003. *CNN.com.* http://www.cnn .com/2003/US/08/15/lockerbie.delay/index.html

Webb, Jeff. "Modernist Memory; or, The Being of Americans." *Criticism* 44 (Summer 2002): 227-247.

Wilde, Oscar. *The Picture of Dorian Gray.* New York: Penguin, 2003.

---. *Salome.* Illustrated by Aubrey Beardsley. New York: Three Sirens Press, n. d.

Wolfe, Tom. "Sorry, but Your Soul Just Died." In *Hooking Up.* New York: Farrar, Giroux, Straus, 2000.

World Health Organization. "Case Definitions for Surveillance of Severe Acute Respiratory Syndrome (SARS)." May 1, 2003. http://www.who.int/csr/casedefinition/en/print.html.

C.

The APA Style

A. How the APA Style Works

The APA style is a parenthetical citation system that lists all sources referred to in the text in a final reference list attached at the end of the paper.

A page in the body of your paper (in-text citations noted in boldface)	A separate sheet at the end of the paper
...In the past, individuals with learning differences were "diagnosed" as either mentally deficient or simply lazy **(e.g., Adams & Frey, 1972; Brown, Nunn, & Kettle, 1966).** However, psychologists' views have changed dramatically in the last two decades. **Grey and Jenkins (2005)** note the "major psychological and social damage" that such diagnoses caused such individuals and their families **(p. 45).** Currently there are many models for conceptualizing these differences. According to **Holloway and Wong (2010),** for example, we should think in terms of learning styles. Others connect these differences more specifically to cognitive functions **(e.g., Krull, 2006)** or information processing **(Moreno & Adams, 2004)...**	**References** Adams, H. G., & Frey, Y. L. (1972). *Learning disabilities.* (2nd ed.). New York: Nonesuch. Brown, M. B., Nunn, L. U., & Kettle, K. Q. (1966). Diagnosing learning disabilities. *Journal of Mental Illness, 102,* 56-78. Grey, T. V., & Jenkins, R. W. (2005). Reassessing assessments. In B. J. Howard et al. (Eds.), *Learning differences then and now* (pp. 45-60). New York: Nevernever Press. Holloway, D. L., & Wong, K. H. (2010). Learning difference as learning style. *LD Quarterly, 67,* 155-79. Krull, T. E. (2006). Learning style and cognitive function. In B. L. Pedersen & J. B. Chung (Eds.), *A handbook of cognition* (pp. 234-67). Salem, OR: Beaver State Press. Moreno, U. O., & Adams, Y. O. (2004). Strides in our understanding of information processing. *Journal of Neuropsychology, 103,* 99-132.

To cite a source in the body of your paper, you provide the last name of the **author(s)** of the source and the **date** (the year) when the material was published. The illustration here shows you the various ways in which **reference citations** are made. Notice that, normally, the source as a whole is being cited; page numbers are given only for direct quotations.

The combination of author name(s) and date is the key to the final list, headed **References.** Each entry on this list begins with these two pieces of information; the entry then goes on to provide the rest of the bibliographic information required for the source. Only those sources directly cited in the paper are included on this final list. The list is printed on a separate sheet attached to the end of the paper.

Note that this documentation system will work if, and only if, the reference citation leads directly to an entry on the reference list, and if the citation leads to one, and only one, entry on this list.

> When you are ready to document your sources using the APA style, turn to Section 8.E., where I give you important advice and information regarding this process.
>
> * * *
>
> If you are not familiar with the fundamental principles of documentation and the terminology that goes with it, I'd recommend that you look over the whole of Section 8.

The purpose of this appendix is to provide basic information about how to document a paper using the APA style. Here I am following the style as it is laid out in the *Publication Manual of the American Psychological Association*, 5th ed. (Washington, DC: APA, 2001). If you do not find information you need in this appendix, check the manual.

This appendix is laid out in the following way:

- Subsection B provides information about in-text reference citations.

- Subsection C provides forms for basic types of sources as they will appear on your reference list.

- Subsection D discusses the format for the final reference list and provides a sample list.

Some Particulars of the APA Style

- In the reference list, the **names of all individuals in the author position** are inverted. Initials are used in place of a first name.

  Doe, J. S., Mandel, K. L., & Witherspoon, R. O.

- Most texts in psychology are written by more than one person, and APA has definite conventions for presentation of **multiple authors** in reference citations in the body of the paper; see subsection B.2. Here let me add that in those (rare) cases in which a text has **more than six authors,** list the first six followed by et al. in the reference list, and use the name of the first author plus et al. in all reference citations in the body of the paper.

- In cases where you are referencing a "classic" work that was originally published much earlier than the copyright date of the edition you used, provide this information in parentheses after the publisher in the following form: (Original work published 1928). In citing the work in your paper, use the **original date** and the date in which your work was published: (Freud 1928/1961).

- With the exception of the titles of periodicals, the only words capitalized in **titles** are (1) the first word, (2) the first word after a colon; (3) words that are proper nouns. Titles of articles and parts of books are not placed in quotation marks.

- APA expects you to use **italic type** for the titles of books and periodicals (as well as the volume numbers of scholarly journals). In cases where italic type is called for, you may either underline the relevant words or put them in italics. Ask your instructor for his or her preference. Whichever of these options you select, you must use it consistently throughout the entire paper for each and every instance where italic type is required.

- You will notice that, in entries on the reference list, APA places a number of elements in **parentheses.** Thus, parentheses should be used only for those traditional bibliographic elements. If and when you want to add some explanatory or descriptive information, you will do so in squared brackets.

- The APA has very definite expectations about the **format and appearance of manuscripts** (for example, running heads for pages, inclusion of an abstract, placement of parts of the manuscript, styles for headings within the body of the paper). Check with your instructor to see if you are expected to follow these and other requirements of manuscript style.

- **Explanatory Notes and Appendixes.** If there are certain points you would like to elaborate on but they do not belong in the body of your paper, consider creating an explanatory note. An appendix is just a very long explanatory note. For more details, see Section 8.E.4.

B. In-Text Reference Citations

1. The basic form

The citation consists of the last names of all authors of a specific source, and the year in which that work was published. These two pieces of bibliographic information must always be provided. If you use the names of the authors in your narrative, this information does not need to be repeated in the parenthetical citation. Note, however, that if and when you use the names of authors in your narrative, all names that APA requires for the citation must be given.

> Johnson, Smith, and Johnson (2010) have presented compelling evidence that behavior modification techniques are successful in weight control.

> There is compelling evidence that behavior modification techniques are successful in weight control (Johnson, Smith, & Johnson, 2010).

- Use only the year of publication in the citation, even if the entry on the reference list includes a month or a month and a date.

- As the example illustrates, use an ampersand (&) instead of "and" in parenthetical citations and the reference list. When you use authors' names as part of your narrative, spell out "and."

- In those cases where you spend several sentences summarizing the work of one of your sources, and you have followed the advice I gave in Section 6 about making it absolutely clear that you are still giving material from that source, you need not continue to reference the source. The one exception would be the introduction of a quotation, at which point you will have to provide page number(s).

> Smith and Jones (2008) did a longitudinal study of gender differences in play. Participants were 400 girls and 400 boys, who were observed from the time they were three until the year they reached their fourteenth birthday. Smith and Jones hypothesized that "marked differences in play behavior will be obvious from an early age" (p. 345).

- In cases in which you use author names in your narratives, the year, in parentheses, comes immediately afterward. Otherwise, place citations where they are least obtrusive, especially if the citation is long; at the same time, you must make sure that there is no ambiguity about what material or information is being referenced.

2. Variations of the basic form

Authors with Identical Last Names

If your reference list includes two or more entries that begin with authors with identical last names, even if the years of publication are different always use the authors' initials in citations in your paper.

> The work of A. Jones (2014) indicates that side effects of this drug are negligible, although a number of other researchers have come to very different conclusions (e.g., N. I. Jones & Hemingway, 2013).

Source with Two Authors

Whenever you refer to a work by two authors, always use both names. Even if both authors have the same last name, both names must be repeated.

(Anderson & Wilson, 2007)

Robertson and Robertson (2010) concluded . . .

(Robertson & Robertson, 2010)

Source with Three, Four, Five Authors

In citing works with three, four, and five authors, use all names in the first citation of the work. In the second and subsequent citations, use the last name of the first author and et al., which is an abbreviation of a Latin phrase that means "and others." Thus, in the first citation you list Green, Short, Adams, and Witherspoon, but in the next citation they become Green et al.

Before shortening citations with et al., double-check your reference list to be sure that this citation does not refer your reader to more than one entry on the list, as it would if Green was the first author of two multi-authored works published in 2013: Green, Short, Adams, and Witherspoon; and Green, Andrews, Wong, and Perez. If such is the case, add the name of the second author to all citations; comma before the et al.

(Green, Andrews, et al., 2013)

(Green, Short, et al., 2013)

Source with Six or More Authors

If a source has six or more authors, in your reference list begin the entry with the names of the first six authors, then add et al. All citations in the text will use the name of the primary author followed by et al. If this citation would take readers to more than one entry on the list, add the name of the second author to the citations; place a comma before the et al.

REFERENCE LIST

Kelly, B. M., Wong, K. L., Eggers, H. O., Murphy, L. K., Valdez, R. O., et al. (2008).

CITATION

(Kelly et al., 2008) *or* (Kelly, Wong, et al., 2008)

Source with Group as Author

(National Institute of Mental Health, 2007)

(Educational Testing Service, 2008)

Citation of a Work with No Author

If a text has no author, the entry in the reference list will begin with the title of the text, and the citation will be the first two or three words in the title, ignoring an initial article (*a, an* or *the*). Place these words in quotation marks if the title is the title of an article; if the title is that of a book, italicize.

> ("Depression," 2006)

> (*Overview*, 2009)

Citation That Includes Specific Pages or Sections of a Work

Whenever you quote directly from a source, you must include the page number(s) in the citation.

> The results have been called "poppycock" (Wilson, 2009, p. 70).

> Wilson (2009) has called the results "poppycock" (p. 70).

If you are citing an electronic text that has provided paragraph numbers, give the number(s) after the paragraph symbol.

> (Harper, 2011, ¶ 20)

If you are referring to a specific portion of a book or a specific table or figure in a work, readers would appreciate it if you would include this information in your citation. Use an accepted abbreviation for the part.

> (Smith, 2015, sec. 19.7)

> (Smith, 2015, chap. 12)

> (Smith, 2015, fig. 14)

Be careful about citations of direct quotations from multivolume works in your reference list. If the reference in your list is to several volumes of a work with the same author and title, your citation must include the volume number before the page number(s):

> (Jones, 2011, 2:197)

If, however, your entry is a reference to only one volume of a multivolume set, then, obviously, the volume number is not needed in such citations.

Citation That Refers to More Than One Source

If a citation includes more than one source, separate sources with a semicolon. Order the sources according to the order in which they are listed on the reference list.

> (Heath & Yung, 2013; Pepperdine, Leonard, & Kingston, 2008; Smith, 2009).

When referring to a series of sources by the same author(s), list the dates chronologically from oldest to most recent and separate with commas.

(Winston, 1999, 2003a, 2003b, 2005)

Winston (1999, 2003a, 2003b, 2005) has always contended . . .

At times authors of scholarly papers provide a list of sources intended to be only illustrative. Such a citation says "many researchers have made this point in their work; here are a few examples of such work." You can send this message by using e.g., which is the abbreviation of a Latin phrase that means "for example." (Need I add that any source you list must be a source that you have actually read?)

(e.g., Heath & Yung, 2013; Pepperdine, Leonard, & Kingston, 2008; Smith, 2009).

Citation of Material Found in a Secondary Source

In Section 4.H.3 and again in Section 8.D.7, I talk about the importance of seeking out the original source any time you find mention of a work in one of the sources you are reading. If you have not been able to put your hands on the original, follow this procedure.

- In your reference list, enter the work in which you found the material.

- When you cite the material in the body of your paper, give the author of the original work first, then cite the work that you have listed in your reference list.

REFERENCE LIST

Smith, C. E. (2009). *The mechanism of behavior* . . .

CITATION IN THE PAPER

Johnson (as cited in Smith, 2009) found. . . .

Citation of Interviews and Other Personal Communications

If you have done a primary study that included doing a series of interviews, discuss with your instructor how you will present these interviews in your paper. Otherwise, information given directly to you personally (face-to-face, over the phone, or in an e-mail message) is a "personal communication." In APA, you do not list personal communications in your reference list, but, rather, give necessary information about them in the body of your paper. **NOTE:** It is always helpful to give your reader any and all information about your informant that would increase the authority of that person to speak on the given issue.

Judy Hawk, director of Save the Kids, contends that most street kids do not use drugs (personal communication, Nov. 11, 2005).

The director of a local agency that provides services for street kids told me that most of these kids do not use drugs (personal communication, Nov. 11, 2005).

In an e-mail message sent to me by Judy Hawk, director of Save the Kids, she contends . . . (personal communication, Nov. 14, 2005).

C. Forms for Sources on the Reference List

1. Books

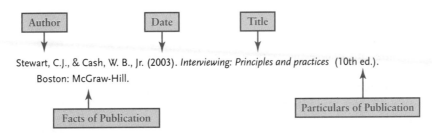

Stewart, C.J., & Cash, W. B., Jr. (2003). *Interviewing: Principles and practices* (10th ed.).
     Boston: McGraw-Hill.

Author

- Open with the last name of the first author, followed by first (and middle) initial. Comma between last name and initials.

- If more than one author, names of *all* authors are inverted. Follow form for one author. Separate authors with commas. Place an ampersand (&) before the last name of the final author listed. End with a period.

- If entry is for an edited work, give the name of the editor(s) in the author position. Follow the form for author(s). After listing name(s), write Ed. (for one editor) or Eds. (more than one). Put in parentheses, followed by a period.

Jacobs, J. K. (Ed.). (2005).

Anderson, S., Wilkerson, T. M., & Perkins, M. L. (Eds.). (2005).

Date

- For the year of publication, use the most recent copyright date (see the reverse side of the title page). Place in parentheses, followed by a period.

- In cases where you are referencing a "classic" work that was originally published much earlier than the copyright date of the edition you used, see "Some Particulars of the APA Style" in subsection A, and examples here and in Part of a Book, C.2.

Title

- Give the complete title of the book (including any subtitles) exactly as it appears on the title page of the book. End with a period. Typically, the main title is separated from the subtitle with a colon.

- Capitalize *only* the first word in the title, the word following a colon, and proper nouns. Italicize the complete title. Use quotation marks around words in quotation marks in the original. Any words italicized in the original should *not* be italicized.

- End with a period.

Particulars of Publication

After the title and before the facts of publication, record relevant information about this book that is not provided elsewhere in the entry. The following list represents units that should be presented in parentheses followed by a period. See examples below and in Part of a Book, C.2.

- Editor and/or translator. List names in their normal order first, followed by the appropriate abbreviation: Ed. for editor, Eds. for editors; Trans. for translator/translators.

- Edition, if not the first. Represent as follows: (2nd ed.), (3rd ed.), (4th ed.), and so on.

- If a multivolume set, information about the volume being used or the number of volumes in the complete set; abbreviate and capitalize: (Vol. 2) or (Vols. 1-4).

- If part of a series, the name of the series.

- Always use arabic numerals (13) rather than roman numerals (XIII).

- You may add any information for the purpose of clarifying the precise nature of this publication *in brackets*. For example:

  Manual for training supervisors [Brochure]. Portland, OR: Street Kids.

Facts of Publication

This unit is composed of the place of publication and the publisher, separated by a colon. The entry ends with a period.

- Please note that the place is the *city* in which a publisher has offices, *not the state or country*. The state or country may be *added* if the city, by itself, is not well known or could be confused with another city. Use the Postal Service abbreviations for states in the U.S.

- If more than one city is listed, use only the first.
- Give the name of the publisher as succinctly as possible.

> **NOTE**
>
> Check all the examples below; some illustrate more than one variable in a citation. Some material here also illustrates forms for electronic sources.

OLDER WORK WITH EDITOR AND TRANSLATOR

Freud, S. (1961). *The future of illusion* (J. Strachey, Ed. & Trans.). New York: Norton. (Original work published 1928).

In-text reference: (Freud 1928/1961).

GROUP AS AUTHOR

U.S. Public Health Service. (2000). *Report of the surgeon general's conference on children's mental health: A national action agenda.* Washington, DC: Department of Health and Human Services.

PAMPHLET

United Nations Educational, Scientific, and Cultural Organization. International Institute for Educational Planning. (2003). *HIV/AIDS and education: A strategic approach.* New York: UNESCO. Retrieved July 28, 2003, from http://unesdoc.unesco.org/images/0012/001286/128657e.pdf

RESEARCH REPORTS

Entries for reports on research should include two types of information about the report: (1) information about the sponsor and/or number of the report; this information should be put in parentheses before the facts of publication; (2) information that would enable the reader to obtain a copy of the report; for example, an NTIS number, or an ERIC number, and/or an online address. This information follows publication information (or replaces it) and is also placed in parentheses (with the exception of the online address).

Bonner, B. L., Walker, C. E., & Berliner, L. (2003). *Children with sexual behavioral problems: Assessment and treatment* (Final Report, Grant No. 90-CA-1469, National Center on Child Abuse and Neglect). Retrieved June 18, 2003, from the Web site of the National Clearinghouse on Child Abuse and Neglect Information: http://www.calib.com/nccanch/pubs/otherpubs/childassessment/index.cfm

Carroll, K. M. (2002). *Cognitive-behavioral approach: Treating cocaine addiction* (Report No. NIH-PUB-02-4308). Bethesda, MD: National Institute on Drug Abuse. (NTIS No. PB 2002-105932).

2. Part of a book, including reference works

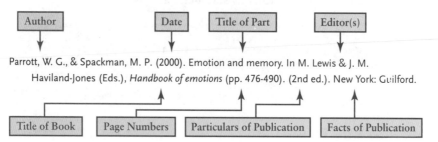

Parrott, W. G., & Spackman, M. P. (2000). Emotion and memory. In M. Lewis & J. M.
    Haviland-Jones (Eds.), *Handbook of emotions* (pp. 476-490). (2nd ed.). New York: Guilford.

Author

- Begin with the name or names of the person(s) responsible for the words or ideas you are using in your paper. Open with the last name of the first author, followed by first (and middle) initial. Comma between last name and initials.

- If more than one author, names of *all* authors are inverted. Follow form for one author. Separate authors with commas. Place an ampersand (&) before the last name of the final author listed. End with a period.

- If author of the part is the editor of the book, editors could be listed in author position. See "Author" in Books, C.1. Otherwise, follow form for referencing a part when part and book are by the same author.

Date

- For the year of publication, use the most recent copyright date of the book (see the reverse side of the title page). Place in parentheses, followed by a period.

- In cases where you are referencing a "classic" work that was originally published much earlier than the copyright date of the edition you used, see "Some Particulars of the APA Style" in subsection A and examples below.

Title of Part

- The title of the part comes next. Give the full title, including any subtitles, ending with a period.

- Use neither quotation marks nor italics. Capitalize only the first word in the title, the first word after a colon, and proper nouns. If words in the original are italicized or in quotation marks, represent accordingly.

Editor(s)

The following unit begins with "In" (capitalized).

- If the author of the part is the author of the book, the title follows.
- If the author of the part is different from the author (or editor) of the book, name(s) of editor(s) follows. Give name(s) in normal order; if more than one, use ampersand (&) instead of "and." After name(s) write Ed. (for one editor) or Eds. (for more than one). Place in parentheses, followed by a comma.

Title of Book

Follow all guidelines for titles of books (subsection C.1). No punctuation at the end.

Page Numbers

In parentheses, give the inclusive page numbers of the part (the pages on which the part begins and ends). End with a period.

Particulars of Publication

If any other information about this book needs to be given, provide it here. See Particulars of Publication for a book (subsection C.1).

Facts of Publication

Follow the guidelines for Facts of Publication of a book (subsection C.1).

For a detailed discussion of documenting parts of books, see Section 8.D.3.

PART AND BOOK BY SAME AUTHOR

> Jung, C. G. (1990). *On the nature of dreams*. In R. F. C. Hull (Trans.), *The basic writings of C. G. Jung* (Vol. 8, pp. 377-94). (Bollingen Series 20). Princeton, NJ: Princeton University Press. (Original work published 1945).

> **In-text Reference:** (Jung 1945/1990).

PART AND BOOK BY DIFFERENT AUTHORS

> Cialdini, R. B., & Trost, M. R. (1998). Social influence: Social norms, conformity, and compliance. In D. T. Gilbert, S. T. Fiske, & G. Lindzey (Eds.), *The handbook of social psychology* (Vol. 2, pp. 151-92). (4th ed.). Boston: McGraw-Hill.

REFERENCE WORKS

> Lind, E. A. (2000). Social justice. In *Encyclopedia of Psychology* (Vol. 7, pp. 346-47). Oxford: Oxford University Press.

3. Articles from journals and magazines

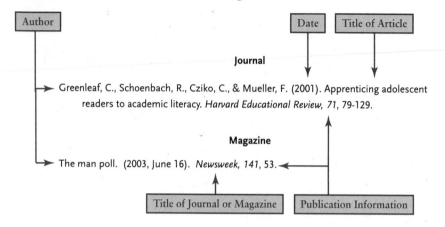

Author

- Open with the last name of the first author, followed by first (and middle) initial. Comma between last name and initials.

- If more than one author, names of *all* authors are inverted. Follow form for one author. Separate authors with commas. Place an ampersand (&) before the last name of the final author listed. End with a period.

- If there is no author, begin the entry with the title. Ignore any initial article (*a, the,* or *an*) when placing on the reference list; alphabetize according to the first main word in the title.

Date

- For scholarly journals, the year of publication is usually sufficient.

- For other types of periodicals, give the year, followed by a comma, and then the season, the month, or the date of the issue you are citing.

- Enclose all in parentheses and end with a period.

Title of Article

- Give the full title of the article, including any subtitles, ending with a period.

- Use neither quotation marks nor italics. Capitalize only the first word in the title, the first word after a colon, and proper nouns. If words in the original are italicized or in quotation marks, represent accordingly.

Title of Journal or Magazine

- Spell out the full title and italicize, followed by a comma.

- Main words in these titles *are* capitalized.

Publication Information

- The number that follows the title of the journal or magazine is the volume number. It is italicized. Comma after title and after volume number.

- If you are citing a journal in which each issue begins with page 1, give the issue number after the volume number in parentheses. It is not italicized, no space between.

  Journal of Disciplines, 76(2), 2-5.

- End with the inclusive page numbers of the article (the numbers of the first and last pages); they are preceded by a comma and a space. End with a period.

ALERT!

If you downloaded an article from a database or an online site, you must include this information after your citation of the print version; see subsection C.5, Web Sites and Other Electronic Sources. For more discussion of the issue in general, see Section 8.D.6., Documenting Material Downloaded from Computers.

---

4. Articles from newspapers

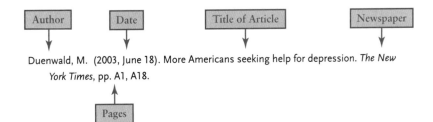

Author

- Open with the last name of the first author, followed by first (and middle) initial. Comma between last name and initials.

- If more than one author, names of *all* authors are inverted. Follow form for one author. Separate authors with commas. Place an ampersand (&) before the last name of the final author listed. End with a period.

- If there is no author, begin the entry with the title of the article. Ignore any initial article (*a, the,* or *an*) when placing on the reference list; alphabetize according to the first main word in the title.

Date

In parentheses, give the year, followed by a comma, and month and date of the issue you are citing; end with a period.

Title of Article

- Give the title of the article or main headline, ending with a period.

- Use neither quotation marks nor italics. Capitalize only the first word in the title and proper nouns. If words in the original are in quotation marks, represent accordingly.

- In the case of special types of articles—reviews, editorials, letters to the editor, and the like—it is very helpful to include such descriptions. Place in square brackets, immediately after the headline, followed by a period.

  Prison not the answer [Letter to the editor]. *The Washington Post*

Newspaper

- Give the name of the newspaper, capitalizing main words and italicizing all. End with a comma.

- If you are citing a local paper whose name does not give the city (or state) of origin, add that information in square brackets after the newspaper name:

  Oregonian [Portland], *The Herald Tribune* [Anywhere, IA].

Pages

- Write p. for one page, pp. for more than one. Be sure to include any section letters along with page numbers.

- If the article is printed on more than one page:

  - put a hyphen between the numbers if the pages are consecutive (pp. B1-B2);

  - put commas between numbers if the pages are discontinuous (pp. A2, A6).

ALERT!

If you downloaded an article from a database or an online site, you must include this information after your citation of the print version; see subsection C.5, Web Sites and Other Electronic Sources. For more discussion of the issue in general, see Section 8.D.6., Documenting Material Downloaded from Computers.

---

5. Web sites and other electronic sources

In this section, I'm using the term "electronic source" to cover any material transmitted through a computer; thus, electronic sources include textual material from CD-ROMs, and material from any and all online sources, public and restricted, edited and unedited (databases, Web and Internet sites, online journals and magazines, newsgroups, discussion groups, online forums, e-mail messages, and the like).

For more detailed discussion of issues related to documentation of electronic sources, read over Section 8.D.6. Information I'm giving here should be sufficient for you to create appropriate entries for such sources in the APA style. If you need more information, however, consult the APA *Publication Manual*. Be aware, however, that forms for electronic sources may be updated at any time.

Material from a Web or Internet Site

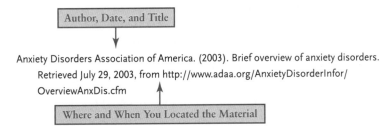

Author, Date, and Title

Anxiety Disorders Association of America. (2003). Brief overview of anxiety disorders. Retrieved July 29, 2003, from http://www.adaa.org/AnxietyDisorderInfor/ OverviewAnxDis.cfm

Where and When You Located the Material

Print Text from a Database

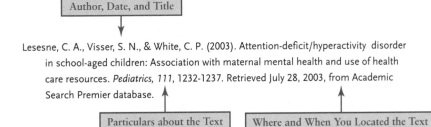

Author, Date, and Title

Lesesne, C. A., Visser, S. N., & White, C. P. (2003). Attention-deficit/hyperactivity disorder in school-aged children: Association with maternal mental health and use of health care resources. *Pediatrics, 111*, 1232-1237. Retrieved July 28, 2003, from Academic Search Premier database.

Particulars about the Text   Where and When You Located the Text

Author, Date, and Title

- Begin with the name of the author(s), or the person or organization responsible for the material you are using (see Section 8.D.6. for further discussion of this issue). Follow standard APA form for authors. End with a period. If no author is given or discernable, begin the entry with the title.

- When the text or material you are citing has a copyright or publication date, provide the date here in standard APA form. If the material you are citing is part of a page of a Web site, the date of the page may be used (the copyright date or the date the page was most recently updated). If the text has no date, put "n. d." (for no date) in parentheses in the date position.

- Then provide the title of the document or material you are citing, using standard APA format for the type of material. If the title is the name of a Web page, follow the form for the title of an article in a journal.

Particulars about the Text

- If the text was originally published in print form, or is available in a print version, provide any information you are given about the print version. Use standard APA form for a print version of this material.

- If the text is an electronic publication (a book published online, an article in an online journal or magazine), provide all publication information. Follow the standard APA form for a print version of this type of source.

Where and When You Located the Text or Material

- As you will see in all the examples in this subsection, APA has a simple formula for indicating where and when you downloaded material from a computer. It is: Retrieved [insert date] from [insert source].

  - The date here is the month, day, and year you downloaded or accessed the material.

  - For the source, you typically will provide the name of the database or, for online sources, the URL. In the case of material from Web sites, if you deem it helpful you may add the sponsor of the site between the accessed date and the URL.

MORE EXAMPLES OF A PRINT TEXT FROM A DATABASE

Paulson, A. (2003, March 6). States grapple with gay rights and definition of the family. *Christian Science Monitor*, p. 2. Retrieved July 29, 2003, from Newspaper Source database.

Schminke, M., Ambrose, M. L., & Miles, J. A. (2003). The impact of gender and setting on perceptions of others' ethics. *Sex Roles, 48*, 361-76. Retrieved July 28, 2003, from Expanded ASAP database.

ANOTHER EXAMPLE OF MATERIAL FROM A WEB OR INTERNET SITE

> Swartz, C. (n. d.). Concept formation and problem solving: Understanding and managing two key components of higher order cognition. Retrieved July 28, 2003, from http://www. allkindsofminds.org/articleDisplay.aspx? categoryID= 10&articleID=18

TEXT FROM AN ONLINE PUBLICATION

> Dudley-Marling, C. (2003, March 7). How school troubles come home: The impact of homework on families of struggling learners. *Current Issues in Education, 6*(4). Retrieved July 28, 2003, from http://cie.ed.asu.edu/volume6/number4/

D. The Final Reference List, including a Sample

- Two central reminders:
  - The author's name (or authors' names) in your text or reference citations must take the reader to one and only one entry on your list.
  - Only those sources cited in the paper may be included on the list.
- For important information about ordering entries on your list, turn back to Section 8.E.2. Follow the guidelines under "Author-Date and Name-Year Styles."
- For information on electronically formatting individual entries on the list, see also Section 8.E.2.

Format for the Final Reference List

- Print (type) on separate sheet or sheets of paper using the same font, font size, and margins as those used in the body of the paper.
- The reference list will follow immediately after the body of the paper, and that will be followed by notes, appendixes and other end material. Number all pages consecutively with the body of the paper.
- Head the list "References." Center this heading one inch from the top of the page. Leave a line of space, and begin your first entry.
- Leave a line of space between entries on the list.
- Format individual entries as hanging indents: first line flush with the left margins; subsequent lines indented one-half inch (five spaces).
- You may double-space or single-space individual entries. See my discussion of this issue in Section 7.C, then consult your instructor for his/her preferences.

References

Anxiety Disorders Association of America. (2003). Brief overview of anxiety disorders. Retrieved July 29, 2003, from http://www.adaa.org/AnxietyDisorderInfor/ OverviewAnxDis.cfm

Dudley-Marling, C. (2003, March 7). How school troubles come home: The impact of homework on families of struggling learners. *Current Issues in Education, 6*(4). Retrieved July 28, 2003, from http://cie.ed.asu.edu/volume6/number4/

Duenwald, M. (2003, June 18). More Americans seeking help for depression. *The New York Times*, pp. A1, A18.

Greenleaf, C., Schoenbach, R., Cziko, C., & Mueller, F. (2001). Apprenticing adolescent readers to academic literacy. *Harvard Educational Review, 71*, 79-129.

Jung, C. G. (1990). *On the nature of dreams*. In R. F. C. Hull (Trans.), *The basic writings of C. G. Jung* (Vol. 8, pp. 377-94). (Bollingen Series 20). Princeton, NJ: Princeton University Press. (Original work published 1945).

Lesesne, C. A., Visser, S. N., & White, C. P. (2003). Attention-deficit/hyperactivity disorder in school-aged children: Association with maternal mental health and use of health care resources. *Pediatrics, 111*, 1232-1237. Retrieved July 28, 2003, from Academic Search Premier database.

The man poll. (2003, June 16). *Newsweek, 141*, 53.

Parrott, W. G., & Spackman, M. P. (2000). Emotion and memory. In M. Lewis & J. M. Haviland-Jones (Eds.), *Handbook of emotions* (pp. 476-490). (2nd ed.). New York: Guilford.

Schminke, M., Ambrose, M. L., & Miles, J. A. (2003). The impact of gender and setting on perceptions of others' ethics. *Sex Roles, 48*, 361-76. Retrieved July 28, 2003, from Expanded ASAP database.

Stewart, C. J., & Cash, W. B., Jr. (2003). *Interviewing: Principles and practices*. (10th ed.). Boston: McGraw-Hill.

APPENDIX

D

Scientific Styles: The CMS Author-Date Style and Two Systems in the CSE Style

A. A General Introduction

The sciences encompass a broad spectrum of disciplines, fields, and subfields. This is true if, by "science," we mean those disciplines typically described as the "hard" sciences (e.g., chemistry, physics, mathematics, the life sciences). If we include areas of the social sciences that take an empirical approach to their subjects (economics, for example, or political science) the territory increases. In their approach to documentation, however, these disparate groups share a number of fundamentals. The sciences can be credited with leading the way in developing streamlined ways of meeting the two basic premises of documentation that I discussed in Section 8. Scientific systems and styles have

- eliminated the intermediate step of notes, common in traditional humanities systems (and still found in the CMS notes & bibliography system; see Appendix B). In scientific systems, bibliographic information about a source is given only once, usually in a list of references collected at the end of the body of the paper.

- cut down on the space required to give such bibliographic information both by abbreviating words in the citation and by using highly elliptical methods of providing publication information, particularly for articles in periodicals.

At the same time, even a casual survey of books and journals published by practicing scientists for their peers reveals quite a bit of variation in the specific ways in which writers acknowledge the sources they have used.

In this appendix, I will be introducing you to three versions of scientific documentation that fit our criteria of being both respected and widely-used in academia. Two of them fall into the category of parenthetical citation systems, but differ in particulars because they have been developed by two different organizations. These styles are the author-date system developed by the publishers of *The Chicago Manual of Style* (hereafter referred to as CMS), and the name-year system developed by the Council of Science Educators (hereafter referred to as CSE). While specifics differ, both these styles fall into the same basic system as that of the MLA and the APA in that parenthetical citations within the text lead readers to entries on a list that comes after the body of the paper. The third version I will introduce to you falls into the category of numbered citations. Unlike the CMS notes & bibliography style, however, the numbers in the CSE citation-sequence system take the reader to a numbered list at the end of the paper. The numbered entry on that list that matches the number in the text gives readers full bibliographic information about the source. Any and all references to a source in the paper are signaled by this same number.

As is always the case, you will consult with your instructor in determining which of these styles (if any) is the one he or she wants you to use in a particular paper. Although the CMS author-date and the CSE name-year systems resemble each other, they have differences because they have been developed by different groups using different criteria. So this appendix has been set up in the following manner: subsection B covers the CMS author-date style; subsection C covers the two systems in the CSE style.

B. The CMS Author-Date Style

1. How the CMS author-date style works

A page in the body of your paper (in-text citations noted in boldface)	A separate sheet at the end of the paper
Several studies done in the past two years suggest that the impact earthquakes could have on the Los Angeles area would be much more severe than had been traditionally thought **(Agnew 2001; Becker and Zeno 2003; Smith, Jones, and Anderson 2003)**. Based on the **Erskine (2000)** model of degrees of vibration, we have accumulated compelling data that a magnitude (M) 6 earthquake ...	**References** Agnew, F. H. 2001. Earthquakes in Los Angeles. *Journal of Earth Sciences* 200: 34-45. Becker, R. K., and T. U. Zeno. 2003. Movers and shakers. *Journal of Seismic Studies* 312: 133-78. Erskine, Y. L. 2000. *A new theory of earthquakes.* New York: Science Press. Smith, E. F., W. A. Jones, and B. S. Anderson. 2003. A study of potential damage in Los Angeles. In *Earthquakes Reconsidered,* ed. G. L. Cookson, 35-70. San Francisco: Nevernever Press.

To cite a source in the body of your paper, you provide the last name of the author(s) of the source and the date (usually only the year) when the material was published. The illustration here shows you the various ways in which text citations are made. Notice that, normally, the text as a whole is being cited; page numbers are given only for direct quotations.

The combination of author name(s) and date is the key to the reference list. Each entry on this list begins with these two pieces of information; the entry then goes on to provide the rest of the bibliographic information required for this source. Only those sources directly cited in the paper are included on this final list. The list is printed on a separate sheet attached to the end of the paper (usually right after the last page of the body of the paper).

Note that this documentation system will work if, and only if, the text citation leads directly to an entry on the list, and if the citation leads to one, and only one, entry on this list.

When you are ready to document your sources using the CMS author-date style, turn to Section 8.E., where I give you important advice and information regarding this process.

* * *

If you are not familiar with the fundamental principles of documentation and the terminology that goes with it, I'd recommend that you look over the whole of Section 8.

The purpose of this appendix is to provide basic information about how to document a paper using the CMS author-date style. Here I am following the style as it is laid out in *The Chicago Manual of Style*, 15th ed. (Chicago: University of Chicago Press, 2003). If you do not find information you need in this appendix, check the CMS. In the manual, specific forms for sources are given in Chapter 17. For appropriate text citations, look for examples marked T; for appropriate forms for entries in the reference list, look for examples marked R. This section of Appendix D is laid out in the following way:

- Subsection B.2 provides information about in-text citations.

- Subsection B.3 provides forms for basic types of sources as they will appear on your reference list.

- Subsection B.4 discusses the format for the final reference list, and provides a sample reference list.

Some Particulars of the CMS Author-Date Style

- In subsection B.3, "Forms for Sources," I have not included newspaper articles because CMS discourages the inclusion of such sources in reference lists. If you have used such articles, see my commentary on this issue in the following subsection (B.2), and consult CMS and your instructor.

- **Shortening reference entries.** CMS recognizes that it is the practice of certain publishers to shorten references in several ways. The two most common are to abbreviate the titles of journals, and to leave out entirely the title of articles in journals. Ask your instructor if you are expected to follow either of these guidelines. If your instructor wants you to abbreviate titles of journals, you might want to look at the CSE manual, which goes into detail on this matter (*Scientific Style and Format: The CBE Manual for Authors, Editors, and Publishers*. 6th ed. Cambridge: Cambridge University Press, 1994, Appendix "Abbreviated Forms of Journal Titles"). If a more current manual is available, use it.

- **Explanatory Notes and Appendixes.** If there are certain points you would like to elaborate on, but they do not belong in the body of your paper, consider creating an explanatory note. An appendix is just a very long explanatory note. For more details, see Section 8.E.4.

- In cases where **italic type** is called for (titles of books and the like) you may either underline the relevant words or put them in italics. Ask your instructor for his or her preference. Whichever options you select, you must use it consistently throughout the entire paper for each and every instance where italic type is required.

- In citations, **always use arabic numerals** (13) rather than roman numerals (XIII) except when page numbers in the source are in roman numerals.

- If the text you are citing was **originally published much earlier** than the copyright date of the edition you are using, you will want to acknowledge this fact. Check CMS under "reprint editions."

2. Text citations

a. The basic form

In your paper, each citation of a source must provide the last name(s) of the author(s) of the source and the date (year) of publication of the source. If you are quoting the words of an author, you must also provide page number(s). In referring to longer texts, you may decide it is helpful in include information about the chapter or the section of the work to which you are referring.

> Wong and Murphy (2011) have used this procedure successfully.

> This procedure has been used successfully (Wong and Murphy 2011).

Note that if you mention the name(s) of author(s) in the sentence you write, all you need to add in parentheses is the year; however, you must always give the names of all authors that would be required in a parenthetical citation. Whenever you use the names of authors in your sentences, years should be added immediately after the name. Otherwise, to prevent citations from becoming obtrusive, place them at the end of a sentence, or, if they must come wi sentences, before points of punctuation.

> Although this procedure has been used successfully (Wong and Murphy 2011), a number of ophthalmologists have raised questions about its value to the patient (Howard, Clark, and Epstein 2011; Chan and Jenkins 2012; Rodriguez et al. 2012).

b. Variations of the basic form

Source with Two or More Authors

In citing sources with two or three authors, use all authors' names in all citations:

> Jones and Welsh (2012) have suggested that . . .
>
> It has been suggested . . . (Jones and Welsh 2012).
>
> In a recent study, Williams, Valdez, and Yamada (2014) found . . .
>
> There is evidence that . . . (Williams, Valdez, and Yamada 2014).

Even if two of the authors of a source have the same last name, both names must be repeated:

> Lee and Lee (2010) reported . . .
>
> (Lee and Lee 2010)

In citing works with four to ten authors, all authors are listed in the entry in the reference list. However, in text citations use the last name of the first author and the Latin abbreviation et al. Thus, Green, Short, Adams, and Witherspoon becomes Green et al. When referring to such studies in your own sentences, it is more graceful to use expressions such as "and others" or "and colleagues."

> (Green et al. 2013)
>
> Green and others (2013) tried a similar . . .

Before shortening citations with et al., double-check your reference list to be sure that this citation does not refer your reader to more than one entry on the list, as it would if Green was the first author of two multi-authored works published in 2013: Green, Short, Adams, and Witherspoon; and Green, Andrews, Wong, and Perez. If such is the case, add the name of the second author to all citations.

> (Green, Andrews, et al. 2013)
>
> (Green, Short, et al. 2013)

Source with an Organization as Author

> (World Health Organization 2009)
>
> (The American National Red Cross 2013)

ımes are long, such citations can get clumsy. Most organ-
...acronyms. CMS allows you to use such an acronym, but
... a cross-list for it in your reference list. Check the manual
...as Author."

...vspaper Article

...ewspaper articles should not be included in reference lists.
Instead, necessaɪy ...iformation about the source should be presented directly in
your paper:

> In a story on the front page of the *Wall Street Journal* (May 24, 2011), Mark Williams
> reported that demand for products made from recycled plastics has risen fifty percent in
> the past ten years.

If your instructor wants newspaper articles listed on your reference list,
simply follow the form for magazines, being careful to use complete page
numbers and appropriate editions. If you downloaded the article from a database, see subsection 3.d., "Web Sites and Other Electronic Sources."

Citation That Includes Specific Pages or Sections of a Work

Whenever you quote directly from a source, you must include the page
number(s) in the citation.

> The results have been called "poppycock" (Wilson 2009, 70).

> Wilson (2009, 70) has called the results "poppycock."

> Wilson (2009) has called the results "poppycock" (70).

Be careful about citations of multivolume works in your reference list. If the
reference in your list is to several volumes of a work with the same author and
title, your citation must include the volume number before the page number(s):

> (Jones 2011, 2:197)

If you are referring to a specific portion of a book or a specific table or figure
in a work, readers would appreciate it if you would include this information in
your citation. Use an accepted abbreviation for the part.

> (Smith 2015, sec. 19.7)

> (Smith 2015, chap. 12)

> (Smith 2015, fig. 14)

Citation That Refers to More Than One Source

If a citation includes more than one source, separate sources with a semicolon.
Order the sources according to relevance (the sources most relevant first), or
alphabetically according to the name of the first author.

> (Heath and Yung 2013; Smith 2009; Pepperdine, Leonard, and Kingston 2008).

When referring to a series of sources by the same author(s), list the years chronologically and separate with commas.

(Winston 1999, 2003a, 2003b, 2005)

Winston (1999, 2003a, 2003b, 2005) has always contended . . .

Citation of Material Found in a Secondary Source

In Section 4.H.3, and again in Section 8.D.7, I talk about the importance of seeking out the original source any time you find mention of a work in one of the sources you are reading. If you have not been able to put your hands on the original, follow this procedure. Cite the original in your text: (Zuckerman 1891). Then list this source in your reference list by first providing all information you have about the original, and then by providing complete information about the source where you found it. Make clear whether you are drawing from a direct quotation ("quoted in"), or a paraphrase or mention by the author of the secondary source ("cited in").

> Zuckerman, I. 1891. *Correspondence of Isaac Zuckerman*. Trans. and ed. M. E. Jones. London: Nonesuch Press. Quoted in H. Green and J. Smith, *Great scientists* (New York: Science, 2000), 87.

Citation of Interviews and Other Personal Communications

There are forms for published interviews (including those given on television or the radio) and unpublished ones that you may come across in libraries. Check the manual. Information given directly to you personally (face-to-face, over the phone, or in an e-mail message) would be considered a "personal communication." In CMS, you do not list personal communications in your reference list, but, rather, give necessary information about them in the body of your paper. Technically, any interviews you conduct would fall into the category of personal communications. But check with your instructor. If he or she wants interviews in your reference list, use the form in the manual for unpublished interviews. **NOTE:** It is always helpful to give your reader any and all information about your informant that would increase the authority of that person to speak on the given issue.

> I had an extended telephone conversation with the CEO of Clean-Up Environments, Judy Hawk, on November 11, 2005. In that conversation, Ms. Hawk . . .

> Judy Hawk, CEO of Clean-Up Environments, contends that mercury is the most threatening toxin in our landfills today (pers. comm., Nov. 11, 2005).

> In an e-mail message sent to me by Judy Hawk, CEO of Clean-Up Environments, Ms. Hawk contends that . . . (pers. comm., Nov. 14, 2005).

3. Forms for sources on the reference list

a. Books

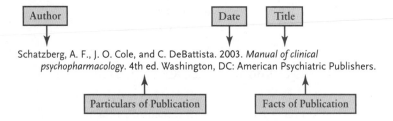

Schatzberg, A. F., J. O. Cole, and C. DeBattista. 2003. *Manual of clinical psychopharmacology.* 4th ed. Washington, DC: American Psychiatric Publishers.

Author

- Begin with the last name of the first author, followed by a comma. Although it is acceptable to spell out first names of authors, preferred use is first (and middle) initials.

- If there is more than one author, invert the name of the *first author only.* Write "and" before name of last author. End with a period.

- If an editor is being entered in the author position, follow style for authors. After the final name listed, put a comma and add "ed." for one editor or "eds." for more than one.

  Jacobs, J. F., ed. 2003. *Invertebrates . . .*

  Anderson, S., N. Wilkerson, and M. Perkins, eds. 2005. *Women in . . .*

Date

Provide the year of publication. Use the most recent year next to the copyright symbol © on the reverse side of the title page. End with a period.

Title

- Give the complete title of the book (including any subtitles) exactly as it appears on the title page. End with a period. Typically, the main title is separated from a subtitle with a colon.

- Underline (or italicize) the complete title.

- The only words to be capitalized are as follows: the first word of the title, the first word after a colon, and any proper nouns.

- Use quotation marks around words in quotation marks in the original. Any words italicized in the original should *not* be underlined (italicized).

- End with a period.

Particulars of Publication

- After the title and before the facts of publication, record relevant information about this book not provided elsewhere in the entry. Record this information in the following order; each of these units is separated from others with a period.

  - editor and/or translator. Use the abbreviation Ed. in front of the name(s) of editor(s); end with period. Use abbreviation Trans. in front of the name(s) of translator(s); end with a period. If the same person performed both roles, combine in one unit.

  - edition, if not the first. Abbreviate as follows: 2nd ed., 3rd ed., 4th ed., and so on.

  - if multivolume set, number of volumes.

  - if a series, the name (and number) of the series.

  - if the text is a research or technical report, provide the sponsoring agency, the report number, and any other information that would enable readers to locate this material.

- Always use arabic numerals (4) rather than roman numerals (IV).

Facts of Publication

This unit is composed of the place of publication and the publisher, separated by a colon. The entry ends with a period.

- If more than one city is listed, use only the first.

- Please note that the place is the *city* in which a publisher has offices, *not the state or country*. The state or country may be *added* if the city, by itself, is not well known or could be confused with another city. Use the Postal Service abbreviations for states in the U.S.

ORGANIZATION AS AUTHOR

United Nations Educational, Scientific, and Cultural Organization. International Institute for Educational Planning. 2003. *HIV/AIDS and education: A strategic approach.* New York: UNESCO.http://unesdoc.unesco.org/images/0012/001286/128657e.pdf

National Human Genome Research Institute. 2001, Nov. 15. *Five-year strategic plan for reducing health disparities.* http://www.genome.gov/1001492 (accessed September 16, 2003).

U.S. Public Health Service. 2000. *Report of the surgeon general's conference on children's mental health: A national action agenda.* Washington, DC: Department of Health and Human Services.

RESEARCH OR TECHNICAL REPORT

CMS does not address the specific issue of research and technical reports. However, information about the report goes a long way toward enabling the reader to locate it, so I would recommend including such information as part of particulars of publication, between the title of the book and the facts of publication.

> Carroll, K. M. 2002. *Cognitive-behavioral approach: Treating cocaine addiction.* NIH-PUB-02-4308. NTIS Order No. PB2002-105932. Bethesda, MD: National Institute on Drug Abuse.

b. Part of a book

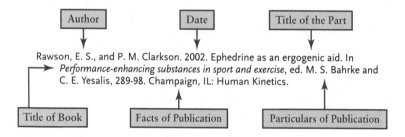

Author

- The author is the person or persons responsible for the words and/or ideas you are citing in your paper. Begin with the last name of the first author, followed by a comma. Although it is acceptable to spell out first names of authors, preferred use is first (and middle) initials.

- If there is more than one author, invert the name of the *first author only*. Write "and" before the name of the last author. End with a period.

Date

Provide the year of publication of the book. Use the most recent year next to the copyright symbol © on the reverse side of the title page. End with a period.

Title of the Part

- Give the title of the part as it appears on the first page of the part. End with a period.

- Use neither quotation marks nor italics. Capitalize only the first word in the title, the first word after a colon, and proper nouns. If words in the original are italicized or in quotation marks, represent accordingly.

Title of Book

- Write the word "In" (capitalized) followed by the complete title of the book (including any subtitles) exactly as it appears on the title page of the book. Typically, the main title is separated from a subtitle with a colon. End this unit with a comma.

- Underline (or italicize) the complete title.

- The only words to be capitalized are as follows: the first word of the title, the first word after a colon, and any proper nouns.

- Use quotation marks around words in quotation marks in the original. Any words italicized in the original should *not* be underlined (italicized).

Particulars of Publication

- If the author of the part is different from the author (editor) of the book, the editors(s) of the book comes next. Write "ed." and then give the name(s) of the editor(s) in normal order; use initials rather than first names. End with period unless you are providing page numbers.

- It is helpful, but not required, to provide the page numbers on which the part begins and ends. Place after the name of the editor, or the title if there is no editor. A comma comes before the numbers.

- End with a period.

- If any other information about this book needs to be given, provide it here. See Particulars of Publication for a book (subsection 3.a).

Facts of Publication

Follow the guidelines for Facts of Publication of a book (subsection 3.a).

For a detailed discussion of documenting parts of books, see Section 8.D.3.

PART AND BOOK BY SAME AUTHOR

> Gould, S. J. 1996. The bare bones of natural selection. In *Full house: The spread of excellence from Plato to Darwin*, 135-46. New York: Three Rivers Press.

PART AND BOOK BY DIFFERENT AUTHORS (EDITED COLLECTION)

> Dingle, H., and M. Holyoak. 2001. The evolutionary ecology of movement. In *Evolutionary ecology: Concepts and case studies*, ed. C. W. Fox, D. A. Roff, and D. J. Fairbairn, 247-61. New York: Oxford University Press.

PART IN A MULTIVOLUME SET

> Lighthill, J. 1995. Fluid mechanics. In *Twentieth century physics*, ed. L. M. Brown, A. Pais, and B. Pippard, 795-912. Vol. 2. New York: American Institute of Physics Press.

CMS advises not listing standard reference works in reference lists, mainly because scholars typically do not make use of such sources. However, specialized dictionaries and encyclopedias can be authoritative sources, and, if you have made use of material in such works, they need to be cited. I'd suggest you cite such entries using the form for part of a book. For more detailed discussion of such sources, see Sections 8.D.1 and 8.D.3.

> Near-earth asteroids (NEAs). 2001. In *Encyclopedia of astronomy and astrophysics*, ed. P. Murdin. Vol. 2. London: Nature Pub. Group.
>
> Nasir, J. 2001. Genetics of Huntington's disease: When more is less. In *Encyclopedia of genetics*, ed. E.C.R. Reeve. London: Fitzroy Dearborn Pub.

c. Articles from journals and magazines

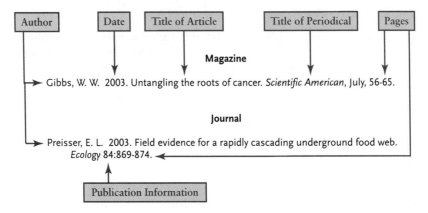

Author

- Begin with the last name of the first author, followed by a comma. Use first (and middle) initials.

- If there is more than one author, invert the name of the *first author only*. Write "and" before the name of the last author. End with a period.

- If there is no author, begin the entry with the title of the article. Use the first main word(s) in the title in both ordering the entry in the reference list and as the citation in the text. The date follows the title.

Date

Give the year of publication, followed by a period.

Title of Article

- Give the title of the article as it appears in the original, ending with a period.

- Use neither quotation marks nor italics. Capitalize only first word in the title, the first word after a colon, and proper nouns. If words in the original are italicized or in quotation marks, represent accordingly.

Title of Periodical

Spell out the full title and underline (italicize). Main words in these titles are capitalized. See notes in subsection B.1 regarding abbreviation of journal titles.

Publication Information

- **Journals.** The number that follows the title of the journal is the volume number (no punctuation). If the journal begins each issue with page 1, also include the issue number. Volume 27, issue number 1 is represented this way: 27, no. 1. Always give these numbers in arabic form; separate from the page numbers with a colon.

- **Magazines.** The title of the magazine is followed by a comma. Then give the season, the month, or the month and date of publication, followed by a comma.

Pages

End with the inclusive page numbers of the article (the numbers of the pages on which the article begins and ends). A period closes the entry. **Note: When and if a volume number (or volume and issue number) is immediately followed by page numbers, there is no space after the colon.**

ALERT!

If you downloaded an article from a database or an online site, you must include this information after your citation of the print version. See subsection B.3.d., Web Sites and Other Electronic Sources. For more discussion of the issue in general, see Section 8.D.6., Documenting Material Downloaded from Computers.

---

d. Web sites and other electronic sources

In this section, I'm using the term "electronic source" to cover any material transmitted through a computer; thus electronic sources include textual material from CD-ROMs, and material from any and all online sources, public and restricted, edited and unedited (databases, Web and Internet sites, online journals and magazines, newsgroups, discussion groups, online forums, e-mail messages, and the like).

Although CMS has, at last, developed forms for electronic sources, the information it requires in such citations is sparse; your instructor may ask you to provide more information. For more detailed discussion of issues related to documentation of electronic sources, read over Section 8.D.6. Information I'm giving here should be sufficient for you to create appropriate entries for electronic sources in the CMS author-date style. If it is not, consult the 15th edition of *The Chicago Manual of Style,* which is the one I am following. Be aware, however, that forms for electronic sources may be updated at any time.

Material from a Web or Internet Site

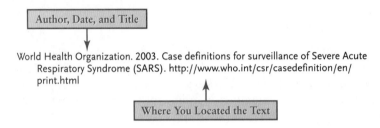

World Health Organization. 2003. Case definitions for surveillance of Severe Acute
    Respiratory Syndrome (SARS). http://www.who.int/csr/casedefinition/en/
    print.html

Print Text from a Database

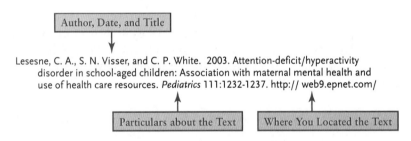

Lesesne, C. A., S. N. Visser, and C. P. White. 2003. Attention-deficit/hyperactivity
    disorder in school-aged children: Association with maternal mental health and
    use of health care resources. *Pediatrics* 111:1232-1237. http:// web9.epnet.com/

Author, Date, and Title

- Begin with the name of the author, or the person or organization responsible for the material you are using (see Section 8.D.6. for further discussion of this issue). Follow standard CMS form for authors. End with a period. If no author is given or discernable, begin the entry with the title; the date will follow the title.

- If the text is a print text you downloaded from a database, or it is an online book or journal article, give the year of publication as you normally would after the name of the author(s). If the document or material does not have a date, omit this element of the citation.

- Then provide the title of the text or document you are citing, or the title of the Web page. Follow the form that would be appropriate for the type of source if it were published in print form. For titles of Web pages, follow the form for the title of a journal article.

Particulars about the Text

- If the text was originally published in print form, or is available in a print version, provide any information you are given about the print version. Use standard CMS form for a print version of this material.

- If the text is an electronic publication (a book published online, an article in an online journal or magazine), provide all publication information. Follow the standard CMS form for a print version of this type of source.

Where You Located the Text

- If you have already provided "publication" information for the material you are citing (see above), simply add the complete URL at the end of the entry. If and when the material has been taken from a full-text datebase, it is sufficient to give the URL that would take your reader to the search page. In cases where the information in the material you are citing is time-sensitive, or you are otherwise required to, provide the date you accessed the material (in parentheses, after the URL).

- If you have given only author, date, and/or title (of a text, for example, posted on a Web site, or simply a Web page itself), add the following:

  - the title of the site or the name of the sponsor of the site; if you have used the sponsor of the site as the author of the material, it is not necessary to repeat this information;

  - the complete URL;

  - in cases where the information in the material you are citing is time-sensitive, or you are otherwise required to, provide the date you accessed the information (in parentheses, after the URL).

ANOTHER EXAMPLE OF A PRINT TEXT FROM A DATABASE

Turner, M. G., S. L. Collins, A. E. Lugo, J. J. Magnuson, T. S. Rupp, F. J. Swanson. 2003. Disturbance dynamics and ecological response: The continuation of long-term ecological research. *Bioscience* 53:46-57. http://web8.epnet.com/

MORE EXAMPLES OF MATERIAL FROM A WEB OR INTERNET SITE

Swartz, C. Concept formation and problem solving: Understanding and managing two key components of higher order cognition. *All Kinds of Minds.* http://www.allkindsofminds.org/articleDisplay.aspx?categoryID=10& articleID=18 (accessed July 28, 2003).

The American National Red Cross. A brief history of the American Red Cross. http://www.redcross.org/museum/briefarc.html (accessed June 30, 2003).

TEXT FROM AN ONLINE PUBLICATION

> Maddala, R., V. N. Reddy, D. L. Epstein, V. Rao. 2003. Growth factor induced activation of
> Rho and Rac GTPases and actin cytoskeletal reorganization in human lens epithe-
> lial cells. *Molecular Vision* 9:329-336. http://www.molvis.org/molvis/v9/a46/

**More examples of citations of electronic sources can be found in subsection 3.a.
(Books).**

4. The final reference list, including a sample

- Two central reminders:
  - The author's name (or authors' names) and dates in your text citations must take the reader to one and only one entry on your list.
  - Only those sources cited in the paper may be included on the list.
- For important information about ordering entries on your list, turn back to Section 8.E.2. Follow the guidelines under "Author-Date and Name-Year Styles."
- For information on electronically formatting individual entries on the list, also see Section 8.E.2.

Format for the Reference List

- Print (type) on a separate sheet or sheets of paper using the same font, font size, and margins as those used in the body of the paper.
- The list will follow immediately after the body of the paper, and will be followed by explanatory notes and appendixes. Number all pages consecutively with the body of the paper.
- Head the list "References." Center this heading one inch from the top of the page. Leave a line of space, and begin your first entry.
- Leave a line of space between entries on the list.
- Format individual entries as hanging indents (first line flush with the left margins; subsequent lines indented one-half inch or five spaces). As for line spacing, you may double- or single-space entries. See my discussion of this issue in Section 7.C, and consult your instructor.
- If your list includes more than one work by the same author(s), you may substitute a 3-em dash (three hyphens, no space between them) followed by a period for the author's name in subsequent entries. In the case of multiple authors, the "same" authors mean the same authors listed in the same order! Also, in using this device, keep in mind that the dash stands for the name(s) of author(s) in the first entry, and only for the name(s)—not roles, such as editor, or dates. If you have questions, consult CMS.

References

Autumn, K., J. Jindrich, D. Denardo, and R. Mueller. 1999. Locomotor performance at low temperature and the evolution of nocturnality in geckos. *Evolution* 53:580-599.

Autumn, K., M. J. Ryan, and D. B. Wake. 2002. Integrating historical and mechanistic biology enhances the study of adaptation. *Quarterly Review of Biology* 77:383-408.

Binford, G. M. 2001a. An analysis of geographic and intersexual chemical variation in venoms of the spider *Tegenaria agresits* (Agelenidae). *Toxicon* 39:955-68.

---.2001b. Differences in venom composition between orb-weaving and wandering Hawaiian *Tetragnatha* (Araneae). *Biological Journal of the Linnean Society* 74:581-95.

Dingle, H., and M. Holyoak. 2001. The evolutionary ecology of movement. In *Evolutionary ecology: Concepts and case studies*, ed. C. W. Fox, D. A. Roff, and D.J. Fairbairn. New York: Oxford University Press.

Fact and fission. 2003. *Economist*, July 19-25, 11-12.

Gibbs, W. W. 2003. Untangling the roots of cancer. *Scientific American*, July, 56-65.

Lighthill, J. 1995. Fluid mechanics. In *Twentieth century physics*, ed. L. M. Brown, A. Pais, and B. Pippard. Vol. 2. New York: American Institute of Physics Press.

Preisser, E. L. 2003. Field evidence for a rapidly cascading underground food web. *Ecology* 84:869-874.

Rawson, E. S., and P. M. Clarkson. 2002. Ephedrine as an ergogenic aid. In *Performance-enhancing substances in sport and exercise*, ed. M. S. Bahrke and C. E. Yesalis, 289-98. Champaign, IL: Human Kinetics.

Schatzberg, A. F., J. O. Cole, and C. DeBattista. 2003. *Manual of clinical psychopharmacology*. 4th ed. Washington, DC: American Psychiatric Publishers.

Turner, M. G., S. L. Collins, A. E. Lugo, J. J. Magnuson, T. S. Rupp, F. J. Swanson. 2003. Disturbance dynamics and ecological response: The continuation of long-term ecological research. *Bioscience* 53:46-57. http://web8.epnet.com/

World Health Organization. 2003. Case definitions for surveillance of Severe Acute Respiratory Syndrome (SARS). http://www.who.int/csr/casedefinition/en/print.html

C. CSE Systems: Name-Year and Citation-Sequence

1. How the CSE systems work

The main difference between Name-Year and Citation–Sequence is the system by which a citation is signaled in the text.

The Name-Year System

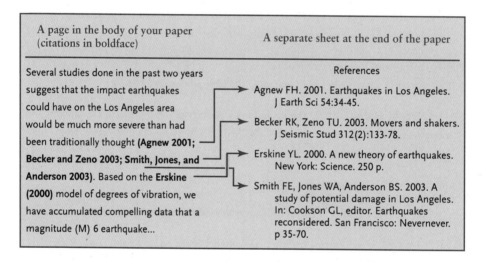

A page in the body of your paper (citations in boldface)	A separate sheet at the end of the paper
Several studies done in the past two years suggest that the impact earthquakes could have on the Los Angeles area would be much more severe than had been traditionally thought **(Agnew 2001; Becker and Zeno 2003; Smith, Jones, and Anderson 2003)**. Based on the **Erskine (2000)** model of degrees of vibration, we have accumulated compelling data that a magnitude (M) 6 earthquake...	References Agnew FH. 2001. Earthquakes in Los Angeles. J Earth Sci 54:34-45. Becker RK, Zeno TU. 2003. Movers and shakers. J Seismic Stud 312(2):133-78. Erskine YL. 2000. A new theory of earthquakes. New York: Science. 250 p. Smith FE, Jones WA, Anderson BS. 2003. A study of potential damage in Los Angeles. In: Cookson GL, editor. Earthquakes reconsidered. San Francisco: Nevernever. p 35-70.

To **cite a source** in the body of your paper, you provide the last **name** of the author(s) of the source and the **year** when the material was published. The illustration here shows you the various ways in which **citations** are made. Notice that, normally, the text as a whole is being cited; page numbers are given only for direct quotations.

The combination of author name(s) and year is the key to the **reference list.** Each entry on this list begins with these two pieces of information; the entry then goes on to provide the rest of the bibliographic information required for this source. Only those sources directly cited in the paper are included on this final list. The list is given at the end of the paper.

Note that this documentation system will work if, and only if, the text citation leads directly to an entry on the list, and if the citation leads to one, and only one, entry on this list.

The Citation-Sequence System

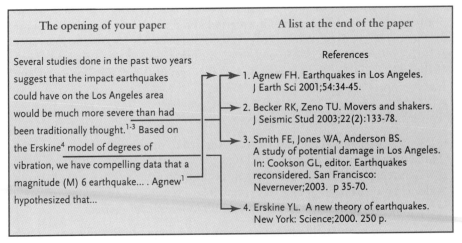

The opening of your paper	A list at the end of the paper
Several studies done in the past two years suggest that the impact earthquakes could have on the Los Angeles area would be much more severe than had been traditionally thought.[1-3] Based on the Erskine[4] model of degrees of vibration, we have compelling data that a magnitude (M) 6 earthquake.... Agnew[1] hypothesized that...	**References** 1. Agnew FH. Earthquakes in Los Angeles. J Earth Sci 2001;54:34-45. 2. Becker RK, Zeno TU. Movers and shakers. J Seismic Stud 2003;22(2):133-78. 3. Smith FE, Jones WA, Anderson BS. A study of potential damage in Los Angeles. In: Cookson GL, editor. Earthquakes reconsidered. San Francisco: Nevernever;2003. p 35-70. 4. Erskine YL. A new theory of earthquakes. New York: Science;2000. 250 p.

To cite a source in the body of your paper using the citation-sequence system, you signal your use of a source with a **number** in the body of the paper. You assign numbers according to the order in which you refer to sources in the body of your paper. Thus, the first source you refer to is assigned the number 1, the second source you refer to is assigned the number 2, and so on. If and when you have occasion to refer to any of these sources again, you simply use the number that you have already assigned to it.

Full bibliographic information about each source is provided in an entry on a list, headed **References,** at the end of the paper. Each entry on the list begins with the number you assigned to the relevant source, and the entries are listed in ascending numerical order (1 comes first, followed by 2, and so on).

When you are ready to document your sources using a CSE system, turn to Section 8.E., where I give you important advice and information regarding this process.

* * *

If you are not familiar with the fundamental principles of documentation and the terminology that goes with it, I'd recommend that you look over the whole of Section 8.

The purpose of this appendix is to provide basic information about how to document a paper using the CSE style. Here I am following the two systems as they are laid out by The Council of Science Educators in *Scientific Style and Format: The CBE Manual for Authors, Editors, and Publishers,* 6th ed., Cambridge, England: Cambridge University Press, 1994. For information about other types of sources, and more extensive information about the sources I cover, check the most recent edition of this manual.

In subsection C.2., I discuss specifics of in-text citations first for the name-year (N-Y) system and then for the citation-sequence (C-S) system. Since forms for presentation of bibliographic information about sources is very similar in the two systems, I have divided subsection C.3, "Forms for Sources on the Reference List," according to types of sources. In each of these categories of sources, you will find the form for both the N-Y and C-S systems. **NOTE:** Technical and research reports are covered in C.3.a., Books.

Some Particulars of the CSE Style

- If your experience in the past has been limited to documentation styles in the humanities, you are going to find that the CSE style is *very* **different** in the way it represents elements of the source (author, titles, etc.). For that reason alone, you will have to pay very, very close attention to all aspects of forms for sources, particularly mechanical and typographical matters.

- The CSE style perfectly illustrates the second premise of documentation: for the sake of saving space, references can be highly compressed, and, at times, truncated. **Truncation** is most obvious in two areas: CSE wants you to shorten the names of publishers, and to abbreviate the titles of scholarly journals. The manual includes handy appendixes which discuss these matters in detail, including a list of standard abbreviations for common words in journal titles.

- **There is no period at the end of abbreviations** in the CSE style. If the abbreviation comes at the end of a unit of the refrence list, a period will be used to mark the end of the unit.

- **Dates** are given in an inverse order; there is no punctuation between the elements and months are abbreviated to three letters: 2004 Apr 30.

- Please notice that references for books are expected to include the **number of pages in the book.** If you fail to make a note of this information when you are using a text, it is usually recorded in the library catalog record of the book.

- **Explanatory Notes and Appendixes.** If there are certain points you would like to elaborate on but they do not belong in the body of your paper, consider creating an explanatory note. An appendix is just a very long explanatory note. For more details, see Section 8.E.4.

2. In-text citations

a. The name-year system

(1) Basic Form

In your paper, each citation of a source must provide the last names of the author(s) of the source and the year of publication of the source. If you are quoting the words of an author, you must also provide page number(s).

Wong and Murphy (2011) have used this procedure successfully.

This procedure has been used successfully (Wong and Murphy 2011).

Note that if you mention the name(s) of an author(s) in the sentence you write, all you need to add in parentheses is the year; however, you must always give the names of all authors that would be required in a parenthetical citation. Whenever you use the names of authors in your sentences, years should be added immediately after the name. Otherwise, place citations so that there is no ambiguity about what information is being referenced.

Although this procedure has been used successfully (Wong and Murphy 2011), a number of ophthalmologists have raised questions about its value to the patient (Howard, Clark, and Epstein 2011; Chan and Jenkins 2012; Rodriguez and others 2012).

(2) Variations of the Basic Form

Source with Two or More Authors

In citing sources with two or three authors, use all authors' names in all citations:

Jones and Welsh (2012) have suggested that . . .

It has been suggested that . . . (Jones and Welsh 2012).

In a recent study, Williams, Valdez, and Yamada (2014) found . . .

There is evidence that . . . (Williams, Valdez, and Yamada 2014).

Even if two of the authors of a source have the same last name, both names must be repeated:

Lee and Lee (2010) reported . . .

(Lee and Lee 2010)

In citing works with three or more authors, use the last name of the first author and the phrase "and others." Thus, Green, Short, Adams, and Witherspoon becomes Green and others.

(Green and others 2013)

Green and others (2013) tried a similar . . .

Before shortening citations with "and others," double-check your reference list to be sure that this citation does not refer your reader to more than one entry on the list, as it would if Green was the primary author of two multiauthored works published in 2013: Green, Short, Yamada, and Witherspoon; and Green, Andrews, Wong, and Perez. If such is the case, add the name of the second author to all citations.

(Green, Andrews, and others 2013)

(Green, Short, and others 2013)

Source with an Organization as Author

(WHO 2009)

(The American National Red Cross 2013)

In order to use acronyms in in-text citations, you must provide the acronym, in brackets, at the beginning of the entry on the reference list, followed by the full name of the organization:

[WHO] World Health Organization. 2009.

Citation That Includes Specific Pages

Whenever you quote directly from a source, you must include the page number(s) in the citation.

The results have been called "poppycock" (Wilson 2009, p 70).

Wilson (2009, p 70) has called the results "poppycock."

Wilson (2009) has called the results "poppycock" (p 70).

Citation That Refers to More Than One Source

If a citation includes more than one source, separate the sources with a semi-colon. Order the sources chronologically, beginning with the oldest and ending with the most recent.

(Heath and Yung 2004; Smith 2009; Pepperdine, Leonard, and Kingston 2013).

When referring to a series of sources by the same author(s), list the years chronologically and separate with commas.

(Winston 1999, 2003a, 2003b, 2005)

Winston (1999, 2003a, 2003b, 2005) has always contended . . .

Citation of Material Found in a Secondary Source

In Section 4.H.3 and again in Section 8.D.7, I talk about the importance of seeking out the original source any time you find mention of a work in one of the sources you are reading. If you have not been able to put your hands on the original, follow this procedure. Cite the original in your text and follow that with the source where you found the material:

(Zuckerman 1891, cited in Green and Smith 2000)

Then list this source in your reference list by first providing all information you have about the original, and then, in parentheses, by providing complete information about the source in which you found it. Make clear whether you are drawing from a direct quotation ("quoted in"), or a paraphrase or mention by the author of the secondary source ("cited in").

> Zuckerman I. 1891. Correspondence of Isaac Zuckerman. Jone ME, translator and editor. London: Nonesuch. Cited in Green H, Smith M. 2000. Great scientists. New York: Science. p 97.

Citation of Personal Communications

Information given directly to you personally (face-to-face, over the phone, or in an e-mail message) would be considered a "personal communication." In CSE, you do not list personal communications in your reference list, but rather, give necessary information about them in the body of your paper. If any information about the source is provided in parentheses, add the phrase "unreferenced" so readers know you are not listing this source with your other references in your final list. **NOTE:** It is always helpful to give your reader any and all information about your informant that would increase the authority of that person to speak on the given issue.

> I had an extended telephone conversation with the CEO of Clean-Up Environments, Judy Hawk, on November 11, 2005. In that conversation Ms. Hawk . . .

> Judy Hawk, CEO of Clean-Up Environments, contends that mercury is the most threatening toxin in our landfills today (telephone conversation with me on 2005 Nov 11; unreferenced).

> In an e-mail message sent to me by Judy Hawk, CEO of Clean-Up Environments, Ms. Hawk contends . . . (2005 14 Nov; unreferenced).

b. In-text citations: The citation-sequence system

I will remind you that citations in the citation-sequence system are numbers in the body of your paper. Numbers are assigned to sources in the order in which you cite them in the body of the paper. If and when you want to cite a source for a second time, you will simply use the number that has already been assigned to that source. See the illustration in subsection C.1.

In the C-S system, you have two basic choices about how you want to represent these citation numbers.
As superscripts:

> Studies on the efficacy of this procedure[4,7,9] have shown mixed results.

Or on the text line in parentheses or brackets:

> Studies on the efficacy of this procedure [4,7,9] have shown mixed results.

The problem with placing citation numbers in parentheses is that they could be confused with other sorts of information you want to provide in parentheses.

Journals avoid this problem by having citations placed in brackets, by boldfacing citation numbers, or otherwise setting them off typographically.

Further Information

- When you are presenting a **continuous sequence** of numbers, separate the first and the last numbers with a hyphen: 3-5. Otherwise, order in numerical sequence; **separate with commas but no spaces.**

- **Place citations** in your paper as close as possible to the material being referenced so that there is no ambiguity about material you have taken from others.

- **Citing material found in a secondary source.** In Section 4.H.3 and again in Section 8.D.7, I talk about the importance of seeking out the original source any time you find mention of a work in one of the sources you are reading. If you have not been able to put your hands on the original, cite the sources as follows: The Zuckerman text (number 12) is the original source, and the Green and Smith text (number 13) is the text in which you found the Zuckerman material.

IN YOUR PAPER

In a letter to Hertz, Zuckerman [12 (cited in 13)] suggested that . . .

IN YOUR REFERENCE LIST

12. Zuckerman I. 1891. Correspondence of Isaac Zuckerman. Jones ME, translator and editor. London: Nonesuch. (Cited in 13, p 87).

13. Green H, Smith M. 2000. Great scientists. New York: Science. 354 p.

- **Citation of Personal Communications.** Information given directly to you personally (face-to-face, over the phone, or in an e-mail message) would be considered a "personal communication." In CSE, you do not list personal communications in your reference list, but, rather, give necessary information about them in the body of your paper. **NOTE:** It is always helpful to give your reader any and all information about your informant that would increase the authority of that person to speak on the given issue.

I had an extended telephone conversation with the CEO of Clean-Up Environments, Judy Hawk, on November 11, 2005. In that conversation Ms. Hawk . . .

In an e-mail message sent to me on Nov. 14, 2005, Judy Hawk, CEO of Clean-Up Environments, contends that . . .

3. Forms for sources on the reference list

a. Books

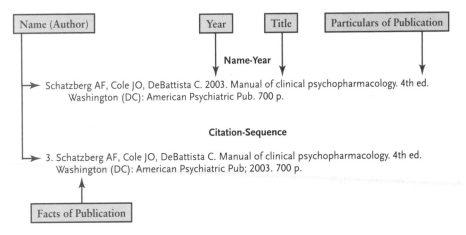

Name (Author)

- In both systems, the names of all authors are inverted. First (and middle) initials only; no space between them. Space between last name and initials, but no punctuation. Separate authors with commas.

- If the name of the author cannot be determined, write [Anonymous].

- If the entry is for an edited work, give name(s) of editor(s) in the author position. Follow the style for author(s). After the final name listed, add a comma and the word "editor" or "editors."

  Jacobs JF, editor. 2005. Invertebrates . . .

  13. Anderson S, Wilkerson NB, and Perkins M, editors. Inorganic . . .

- End unit with a period.

Year

- In both systems, use the most recent year next to the copyright symbol © on the reverse side of the title page.

- In the N-Y system, place the year immediately after the author position, followed by a period.

- In the C-S system, the year is given in the facts of publication (see below).

Title

- Give the complete title of the book (including any subtitles) exactly as it appears on the title page of the book. End with a period.

- Capitalize *only* the first word in the title and proper nouns. Do not underline/italicize. If words in the original are in quotation marks or italics, represent those words accordingly. End with a period.

Particulars of Publication

After the title and before the facts of publication, record any relevant information about this book that is not provided elsewhere in the entry. Such information would include:

- an edition other than the first, given in abbreviated form (2nd, 3rd, 4th, etc.).

- editor(s) (if the work has an author) and/or translator, using the following form:

  . . . Collected letters of Einstein. Howard GB, translator; Smith DW, editor.

- if a multivolume work, or part of a multivolume work, volume number and other information required about title (if different for separate volumes); see examples in subsection 3.b., Part of a Book.

Facts of Publication

This unit is composed of the city of publication, the publisher, and, in the C-S system, the year. In the C-S system, the year comes after the publisher, separated by a semicolon. End the unit with a period. Then provide pagination.

- If more than one city is listed, use only the first.

- Please note that the place is the *city* in which a publisher has offices, *not the state or country*. The state or country may be *added* if the city, by itself, is not well known or could be confused with another city. Use the Postal Service abbreviations for states in the U.S.; place in parentheses.

- The name of the publisher should be shortened. For example, J Wiley for John Wiley & Sons Publishers. A list of appropriate abbreviations can be found in an appendix in the CSE manual.

- Pagination. Give the total number of pages in the body of the book, including the index. Indicate this number in arabic numerals, followed by a p. Close the entry with a period.

ORGANIZATION AS AUTHOR AND PAMPHLET

N-Y

In order to shorten in-text citations, open the reference with the acronym that will be used in the citations; place in brackets. Then spell out the name of the organization.

> [UNESCO.IIEP]. United Nations Educational, Scientific, and Cultural Organization. International Institute for Educational Planning. 2003. HIV/AIDS and education: a strategic approach. New York: UNESCO. 61 p. Available online from: http://undesdoc.unesco.org/images/0012/001286/128657e.pdf. Accessed 2003 Jul 28.

C-S

> 8. United Nations Educational, Scientific, and Cultural Organization. International Institute for Educational Planning. HIV/AIDS and education: a strategic approach. New York: UNESCO; 1 2003. 61 p. Available online from: http://unesdoc.unesco.org/images/0012/001286/128657e.pdf. Accessed 2003 Jul 28.

SCIENTIFIC AND TECHNICAL REPORTS

Follow the form for books through the publisher or publisher/date. When relevant, list the sponsor of the study as the publisher. Then provide the following information, as it applies, in the following order: the report number, the contract number, the total number of pages. At the end, give an availability statement. Here you provide sufficient information that would enable the reader to obtain a copy of this report (for example: Available from: NTIS, Springfield, VA; AD-A555555). If the report is available online, then give the URL instead of a place of publication (see examples below). If and when you downloaded such a report from an online source, end your citation with the date you downloaded it; see subsection C.3.e., Web Sites and Other Electronic Sources.

N-Y

> Unnasch S, Browning L, Kassoy E. 2001 Apr. Refinement of selected fuel-cycle emissions analyses. Volume 1. Final report. Cupertino, CA: California State Air Resources Board, Sacramento, CA. Contract nr. CARB-98-338. 166 p. Available from: NTIS, http://www/ntis.gov;PB2003-100837.

> Carroll, KM. 2002 Apr. Cognitive-behavioral approach: treating cocaine addiction. Bethesda, MD: National Institute on Drug Abuse. Report nr. NIH-PUB-02-4308. 142 p. Available from: NTIS, http://www/ntis.gov/;PB2002-105932. Accessed 2003 Jul 28.

C-S

> 4. Unnasch S, Browning L, Kassoy E. Refinement of selected fuel-cycle emissions analyses. Volume 1. Final report. Cupertino, CA: California State Air Resources Board, Sacramento, CA; 2001 Apr. Contract nr. CARB-98-338. 166 p. Available from: NTIS, http://www/ntis.gov;PB2003-100837.

> 12. Carroll, KM. Cognitive-behavioral approach: treating cocaine addiction. Bethesda, MD: National Institute on Drug Abuse; 2002 Apr. Report nr. NIH-PUB-02-4308. 142 p. Available from: NTIS, http://www/ntis.gov/;PB2002-105932. Accessed 2003 Jul 28.

b. Part of a book

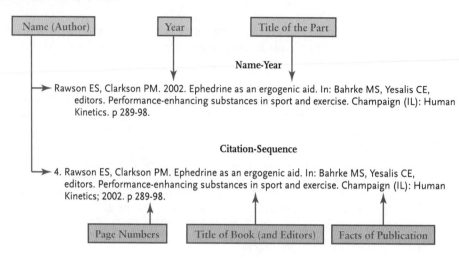

Name (Author)

- The author is the person or persons who wrote this part of the book.

- In both systems, the names of all authors are inverted. First (and middle) initials only; no space between them. Space between last name and initials, but no punctuation. Separate authors with commas.

- If the name of the author cannot be determined, write [Anonymous]. End with a period.

Year

- In both systems, use the most recent year next to the copyright symbol © on the reverse side of the title page.

- In the N-Y system, place the year immediately after the author position, followed by a period.

- In the C-S system, the year is given in the facts of publication (see below).

Title of the Part

- If author(s) of the part and author(s) of the book are different, give the full title of the part here. If the author of the part and the author of the book are the same, the title of the part comes after facts of publication and before page numbers. See example below.

- If the title is excessively long, give only the first, main part. Capitalize *only* the first word in the title and proper nouns. Do not underline/italicize. If words in the original are in quotation marks or italics, represent those words accordingly. End with a period.

Title of Book (and Editors)

- When the part and the book have different authors, follow this style. After the title of the part, write "In," capitalized, followed by a colon. Then give names of editors(s) or author(s) of the book, following the style for authors' names. If these individuals are editors, put a comma after the last set of initials and spell out "editor" or "editors." End with a period. Then give the title of the book, following guidelines for titles of books (see C.3.a.)

- If author(s) of the part and the book are the same, follow the basic style for a book (see subsection C.3.a. and the example below).

- After the title and before the facts of publication, record any necessary information about this book that is not provided elsewhere in the entry. See Particulars of Publication for a book (subsection C.3.a) and the example below for a Part in a Multivolume Set.

Facts of Publication

Follow the style for Facts of Publication for a book (subsection C.3.a.).

Page Numbers

In both systems, the entry ends with the inclusive page numbers of the part (the pages on which the part begins and ends). These numbers are preceded by a "p" and followed by a period.

PART AND BOOK BY SAME AUTHOR(S)

N-Y

> Freeman LW, Lawlis GF. 2001. Mosby's complementary and alternative medicine: a research-based approach. St. Louis: Mosby. Psychoneuroimmunology and conditioning of immune function; p 66-94.

C-S

> 6. Freeman LW, Lawlis GF. Mosby's complementary and alternative medicine: a research-based approach. St. Louis: Mosby; 2001. Psychoneuroimmunology and conditioning of immune function; p 66-94.

PART AND BOOK BY DIFFERENT AUTHORS

N-Y

> Dingle H, Holyoak M. 2001. The evolutionary ecology of movement. In: Fox CW, Roff DA, Fairbairn DJ, editors. Evolutionary ecology: concepts and case studies. New York: Oxford Univ Pr. p 247-61.

C-S

> 7. Dingle H, Holyoak M. The evolutionary ecology of movement. In: Fox CW, Roff DA, Fairbairn DJ, editors. Evolutionary ecology: concepts and case studies. New York: Oxford Univ Pr; 2001. p 247-61.

PART IN A MULTIVOLUME SET

N-Y

> Lighthill J. 1995. Fluid mechanics. In: Brown LM, Pais A, Pippard B, editors. Twentieth century physics. Volume 2. New York: Am Inst of Physics Pr. p 795-912.

C-S

> 8. Lighthill J. Fluid mechanics. In: Brown LM, Pais A, Pippard B, editors. Twentieth century physics. Volume 2. New York: Am Inst of Physics Pr; 1995. p 795-912.

While the CSE manual specifies no particular form for dictionaries and encyclopedias, the form for part of a book should serve for entries in specialized reference works.

N-Y

> [Anonymous]. 2001. Near-earth asteroids (NEAs). In: Murdin P, editor. Encyclopedia of astronomy and astrophysics. Volume 2. London: Nature Pub. Group. p 1794.

C-S

> 4. [Anonymous]. Near-earth asteroids (NEAs). In: Murdin P, editor. Encyclopedia of astronomy and astrophysics. Volume 2. London: Nature Pub. Group; 2001 p 1794.

N-Y

> Nasir J. 2001. Genetics of Huntington's disease: when more is less. In: Reeve ECR, editor. Encyclopedia of genetics. London: Fitzroy Dearborn. p 459-66.

C-S

> 7. Nasir J. 2001. Genetics of Huntington's disease: when more is less. In: Reeve ECR, editor. Encyclopedia of genetics. London: Fitzroy Dearborn. p 459-66.

c. Articles from journals and magazines

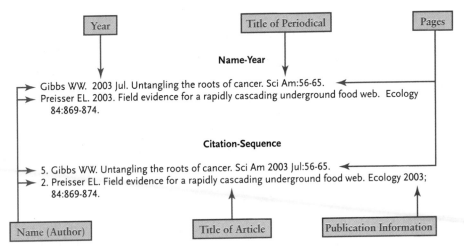

Name (Author)

- In both systems, the names of all authors are inverted. First (and middle) initials only; no space between them. Space between last name and initials, but no punctuation. Separate authors with commas.

- If the article is not signed, write [Anonymous].

- End unit with a period.

Year

N-Y

- The year follows the author's name.

- In the case of magazines, after the year add the month, or the month and date, of the issue. Use a three-letter abbreviation for the month. Example: 2004 Sep 24. If the magazine has an easily discernable volume and issue number, you may use that instead of the specific month/date; indicate only the year at this point in the reference, and add volume and issue number in publication information. End unit with a period.

C-S

The year/date comes with publication information (see below).

Title of Article

If the title is excessively long, give only the first, main part. Use neither quotation marks nor italics. Capitalize *only* the first word in the title and proper nouns. If words in the original are italicized or in quotation marks, represent accordingly. End with a period.

NOTE: If such information would be helpful to readers, add a description of the article in brackets after the title of the article. For example:

We can't stop now [editorial].

Title of Periodical

- Except for titles of only one word, titles of scholarly journals should be abbreviated according to the recommendations in the CSE manual.

- Capitalize main words. Otherwise, do *not* underline (italicize).

Publication Information

N-Y

- In the case of scholarly journals, the title of the journal is followed by the volume; if it is necessary to add an issue number, do so in parentheses. End with a colon. Space only after the journal title.

- In the case of magazines:
  - If you have already provided the complete date with the year of publication, put a colon after the title of the magazine.
  - If you are providing volume and issue number, follow the form for scholarly journals.

    Sci Am 289(1):56-65.

    Ecology 84(4):869-874.

C-S

- In the case of scholarly journals, provide the year of publication following the title of the journal, a space, but no punctuation between. Add a semicolon, then the volume number. If an issue number is required, add in parentheses immediately after the volume, and close with a colon.

- In the case of a magazine, after the year provide the month, or the month and date, of publication. Use a three-letter abbreviation for the month. End with a colon. If the magazine has an easily discernable volume and issue number, you may substitute this information for the month or month and date. Follow the form for a scholarly journal.

    Sci Am 2003;289(1):56-65.

    Ecology 2003;84(4):869-874.

    Time 2010 Aug 24:14.

Pages

In both systems, the reference ends with the inclusive page numbers of the article (the pages on which the article begins and ends). End with a period.

Notes

- For a **more complete discussion** of issues related to documenting periodicals, see Section 8.D.5.

- **Electronic Sources.** If the article you are citing comes from an online magazine or journal, see subsection C.3.e for the appropriate form for citing this material. If the article you are citing is a print article that you found in a database, add an availability notation and then information that would allow your reader to access the same material, or would, at least, provide information about where you found this material. Complete information would also include the date you accessed or downloaded this material.

  Available from: Expanded ASAP database. Accessed 2003 Jul 27.

  Available from: http://xxxxx.org/xxxxxxxx. Accessed 2003 Jul 27.

d. Articles from newspapers

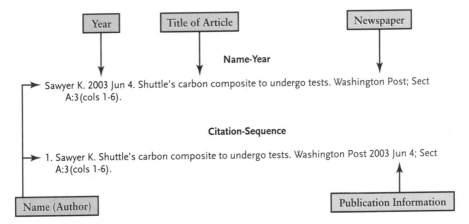

Name (Author)

- In both systems, the names of all authors are inverted. First (and middle) initials only; no space between them. Space between last name and initials, but no punctuation. Separate authors with commas.

- If the article is not signed, write [Anonymous].

- End with a period.

Year

- Give the date in the following format: year, month, date; no punctuation between the elements. The month is abbreviated to three letters.

- In the N-Y system, the date comes immediately after the author's name, followed by a period.

- In the C-S system, the date comes after the name of the newspaper.

Title of Article

Give only the first, main part of the headline. Use neither quotation marks nor italics. Capitalize *only* the first word in the title and proper nouns. If words in the original are in quotation marks, represent accordingly. End with a period.

NOTE: If such information would be helpful to readers, add a description of the article in brackets. For example:

We can't stop now [editorial].

Newspaper

- Articles (*a, the, an*) are not included in the names of newspapers.

- Capitalize main words. Otherwise, do *not* underline (italicize).

- If the name of the newspaper does not make clear its city (and/or state) of origin, add such information after the name, in parentheses:

Oregonian (Portland), Times Tribune (Smalltown IA).

Publication Information

- In the N-Y system, the name of the newspaper is followed by a semicolon. Since most newspapers begin each section of an issue with page one, give section designation with page number as shown (colon between section letter and page number). Finish with the number(s) of the columns on which the story is printed on that page. Columns may be omitted. If the story appears on more than one page, give all pages: Sect A:3-4 (for consecutive pages) or Sect A1,5 (for discontinuous pages).

- In the C-S system, the name of the newspaper is followed by the date. No punctuation between these units; end with a semicolon. Since most newspapers begin each section of the issue with page one, give section designation with page number as shown (colon between section letter and page number). Finish with the number(s) of the columns on which the story is printed on that page. Columns may be omitted. If the story appears on more than one page, give all pages: Sect A:3-4 (for consecutive pages) or Sect A1,5 (for discontinuous pages).

- **Electronic Sources.** If the article you are citing comes form an online newspaper, see C.3.e for the appropriate form for citing this material. If the article you are citing is a print article that you found in a database, add an availability notation and then information that would allow your reader to access the same material, or, at least, that would provide information about where you found this material. Complete information would also include the date you accessed or downloaded this material.

Available from: Expanded ASAP database. Accessed 2003 Jul 27.

Available from: http://xxxxx.org/xxxxxxxx. Accessed 2003 Jul 27.

e. Web sites and other electronic sources

In this section, I'm using the term "electronic source" to cover any material transmitted through a computer; thus, electronic sources include textual material from CD-ROMs, and material from any and all online sources, public and restricted, edited and unedited (databases, Web and Internet sites, online journals and magazines, newsgroups, discussion groups, online forums, e-mail messages, and the like).

For a more detailed discussion of issues related to documentation of electronic sources, read over Section 8.D.6. Information about appropriate forms for citing electronic sources in the CSE style is limited, both because coverage in the 1994 edition of the manual is limited and because that edition, and thus information in it regarding electronic sources, is rather dated. CSE recommends following the documentation style of the National Institute of Health; thus, in this section, I am using a combination of the fundamentals of the CSE style and the NIH style for electronic sources as it is set out in "Guidelines for Citing Internet Publications," which I found on the NIH Web site (http://www.nlm.nih.gov/pub/formats/internet.pdf). For further information about citing electronic sources, first of all check to see if the promised revision of the CSE manual has been published. If not, I would recommend that you consult the NIH Web site and an individual familiar with the CSE style.

For more examples, see Books, C.3.a.

Material from a Web or Internet Site

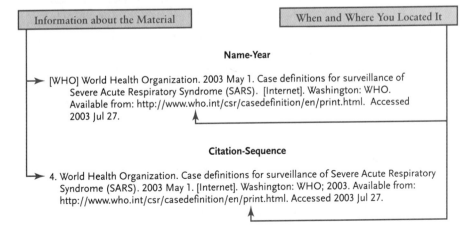

| Information about the Material | When and Where You Located It |

Name-Year

[WHO] World Health Organization. 2003 May 1. Case definitions for surveillance of Severe Acute Respiratory Syndrome (SARS). [Internet]. Washington: WHO. Available from: http://www.who.int/csr/casedefinition/en/print.html. Accessed 2003 Jul 27.

Citation-Sequence

4. World Health Organization. Case definitions for surveillance of Severe Acute Respiratory Syndrome (SARS). 2003 May 1. [Internet]. Washington: WHO; 2003. Available from: http://www.who.int/csr/casedefinition/en/print.html. Accessed 2003 Jul 27.

Article from an Online Journal

When and Where You Located It

Name-Year

Maddala R, Reddy VN, Epstein DL, Rao V. 2003. Growth factor induced activation of Rho and Rac GTPases and actin cytoskeletal reorganization in human lens epithelial cells. Mol Vision [online journal] 9:329-336. Available from: http://www.molvis.org/molvis/v9/a46/ Accessed 2003 Jul 28.

Citation-Sequence

7. Maddala R, Reddy VN, Epstein DL, Rao V. Growth factor induced activation of Rho and Rac GTPases and actin cytoskeletal reorganization in human lens epithelial cells. Mol Vision [online journal] 2003; 9:329-336. Available from: http://www.molvis.org/molvis/v9/a46/ Accessed 2003 Jul 28.

Information about the Publication

Information about the Publication or Material

- For print materials that you found in a database, provide publication information in standard CSE form for print versions of that type of source. Then add an availability notation. I'd suggest simply using the name of the database.

  Available from: LexisNexis Academic Universe database.

- For material from online publications (books published online, articles from online journals), follow the standard CSE form for print versions of that type of source. If and when it is necessary to clarify information you have provided (to be sure your readers know the precise nature of this electronic source), add such clarification in brackets after the relevant point in the citation.

- For material available only through a Web or Internet site, use the standard CSE form for a book or part of a book, substituting information about the site and its sponsor where you would normally give information about the title of the book and its publisher. If and when it is necessary to clarify any information presented, add it in brackets after the relevant point in the citation.

When and Where You Located It

- Type "Available from:" and then paste in the complete URL for the source.

- Type "Accessed" and then give us the date you downloaded this material, using the standard CSE form for dates.

4. The final reference list, including samples for both systems

- For information on electronically formatting individual entries on the list, see Section 8.E.2.

- For those of you using the N-Y system,

    - Remember that the author's name (or authors' names) and years in your in-text citations must take the reader to one and only one entry on your reference list.

    - Also remember that only those sources explicitly referred to in the paper may be included on the list.

    - For important information about ordering entries on your list, turn back to Section 8.E.2. Follow the guidelines under "Author-Date and Name-Year Styles."

Format for the Reference List

The CSE manual recognizes that editors have different requirements for manuscript layout and format. The advice I'm giving here is based on standards for other academic styles. You should, however, check with your instructor before you make any final choices.

- Print (type) on a separate sheet or sheets of paper using the same font, font size, and margins as those used in the body of the paper.

- The list will follow immediately after the body of the paper, and will be followed by explanatory notes and appendixes. Number all pages consecutively with the body of the paper.

- Head the list "References." The heading may be centered, or flush left. Leave a line of space, and begin your first entry.

- Leave a line of space between entries on the list.

- Format individual entries as hanging indents (first line flush with the left margins; subsequent lines indented). In the N-Y system, indent subsequent lines one-half inch or five spaces. In the C-S system, indent subsequent lines so that the numbers stand apart and the content of all notes has the same left margin (see sample list). As for line spacing, you may double- or single-space entries. See my discussion of this issue in Section 7.C, and consult your instructor.

Sample N-Y Reference List

References

[Anonymous]. 2003 Jul 19-25. Fact and fission. Economist: 11-12.

Autumn K, Jindrich J, Denardo D, Mueller R. 1999. Locomotor performance at low temperature and the evolution of nocturnality in geckos. Evolution 53:580-599.

Autumn K, Ryan MJ, Wake DB. 2002. Integrating historical and mechanistic biology enhances the study of adaptation. Quar Rev Biol 77:383-408.

Binford GM. 2001a. An analysis of geographic and intersexual chemical variation in venoms of the spider Tegenaria agrestis (Agelenidae). Toxicon 39:955-68.

---. 2001b. Differences in venom composition between orb-weaving and wandering Hawaiian Tetragnatha (Araneae). Biol J Linnean Soc 74:581-95.

Dingle H, Holyoak M. 2001. The evolutionary ecology of movement. In: Fox CW, Roff DA, Fairbairn DJ, editors. Evolutionary ecology: concepts and case studies. New York: Oxford Univ Pr. p 247-61.

Gibbs WW. 2003 Jul. Untangling the roots of cancer. Sci Am:56-65.

Maddala R, Reddy VN, Epstein DL, Rao V. 2003. Growth factor induced activation of Rho and Rac GTPases and actin cytoskeletal reorganization in human lens epithelial cells. Mol Vision [online journal] 9:329-336. Available from: http://www.molvis .org/molvis/v9/a46/ Accessed 2003 Jul 28.

Preisser EL. 2003. Field evidence for a rapidly cascading underground food web. Ecology 84:869-874.

Schatzberg AF, Cole JO, DeBattista C. 2003. Manual of clinical psychopharmacology. 4th ed. Washington: American Psychiatric Pub. 700 p.

[WHO] World Health Organization. 2003 May 1. Case definitions for surveillance of Severe Acute Respiratory Syndrome (SARS). [Internet]. Washington: WHO. Available from: http://www.who.int/csr/casedefinition/en/print/html. Accessed 2003 Jul 27.

Sample C-S Reference List

References

1. Binford GM. Differences in venom composition between orb-weaving and wandering Hawaiian *Tetragnatha* (Araneae).Biol J Linnean Soc 2001;74:581-95.

2. Dingle H, Holyoak M. The evolutionary ecology of movement. In: Fox CW, Roff DA, Fairbairn DJ, editors. Evolutionary ecology: concepts and case studies. New York: Oxford Univ Pr; 2001. p 247-61.

3. United Nations Educational, Scientific, and Cultural Organization. International Institute for Educational Planning. HIV/AIDS and education: a strategic approach. New York: UNESCO; 2003. 61 p. Available online from: http://unesdoc.unesco.org/images/0012/001286/128657e.pdf

4. Schatzberg AF, Cole JO, DeBattista C. Manual of clinical psychopharmacology. 4th ed. Washington: American Psychiatric Pub; 2003. 700 p.

5. World Health Organization. Case definitions for surveillance of Severe Acute Respiratory Syndrome (SARS). 2003 May 1. [Internet]. Washington: WHO; 2003. Available from: http://www.who.int/csr/casedefinition/en/print/html. Accessed 2003 Jul 27.

6. [Anonymous]. Near-earth asteroids (NEAs). In: Murdin P, editor. Encyclopedia of astronomy and astrophysics. Volume 2. London: Nature Pub. Group; 2001. p 1794.

7. Gibbs WW. Untangling the roots of cancer. Sci Am 2003 Jul:56-65.

8. Preisser EL. Field evidence for a rapidly cascading underground food web. Ecology 2003;84:869-874.

9. [Anonymous]. Fact and fission. Economist 2003 Jul 19-25:11-12.

10. Maddala R, Reddy VN, Epstein DL, Rao V. Growth factor induced activation of Rho and Rac GTPases and actin cytoskeletal reorganization in human lens epithelial cells. Mol Vision [online journal] 2003;9:329-336. Available from: http://www.molvis.org/molvis/v9/a46/ Accessed 2003 Jul 28.

11. Binford GM. An analysis of geographic and intersexual chemical variation in venoms of the spider *Tegenaria agrestis* (Agelenidae). Toxicon 2001;39:955-68.

APPENDIX

E

Interviews

Depending on the type of research project you are involved in and the specific working hypothesis/thesis you have developed, you may decide that potential sources of evidence are people with whom you would talk directly. But interviews involve a great deal more than dropping in on a person for a casual chat about your subject. Effective interviews take prior thinking and planning, just as the whole research process does. If you are considering doing interviews, I'd suggest that you read this appendix in its entirety first; come back to especially relevant parts as you get ready to do your interviews.

The suggestions I give you here are a combination of common sense, my own experience, and the wise words of Leslie Baxter, who has used interviewing extensively in her own research and who has taught interviewing techniques to students for a number of years. These suggestions are divided into four stages: determining what you need, preparing for the interview, the interview itself, and writing up the interview.

A. Determining What You Need

Before I go on, I need to distinguish two different purposes for interviewing. Some research projects rely completely on evidence gathered through interviews; these types of projects fall into the category of primary research projects, often carried out in the social sciences, in which the researcher develops a working hypothesis (for example, "I predict that women use different language than men do in talking about romantic relationships"), then tests this hypothesis by interviewing a random sampling of subjects. The answer to the research question is developed from a systematic analysis of the responses of the interviewees. While the advice I give here applies to such studies, it doesn't go far enough. If I have just described the type of research you are doing, you must work very closely with your instructor in determining whom you will interview and preparing your interview script. In writing this section on interviews, I have had in mind those of you who are thinking of interviews as one of many kinds of sources you will be using in gathering your evidence.

Determining specifically whom you should interview, what kinds of questions to ask—even whether an interview is necessary—will depend on your answer to the question: What do I need to know? So you will start by going back to the Research Strategy section of your Researcher's Notebook. If you are considering interviews, follow these two rules of thumb:

- You do not want to carry out an interview if the information you need can be obtained in other ways.

- Assume that you interview a person because that person is the best and most direct source of a *specific kind of evidence*.

Let us say, for example, that you are contemplating interviews to gather some data about an organization: How many buses does Rose City Transit operate? What are the goals and objectives of the Helping Hand Child Care Center? Before you set up any interviews, especially face-to-face interviews with senior people in the organization, you should do enough homework to know whether this information is available in printed form, or whether it could be obtained through a short telephone interview with a person in the public information office of the organization. Obtaining some facts about an organization may be part of the reason to set up an interview, but I would assume that you want to talk to a person to obtain information about how that person carries out his or her job, or the opinions, perspectives, point of view this person has about your subject. When you set up an interview, you are to some extent imposing on an individual; you certainly use his or her time. For these reasons, set up interviews only when you really need them, and set up the type of interview that meets your need.

If you decide that an interview would be valuable, study your research questions to decide whom you want to interview. If your working thesis has to do with female executives, for example, you will have to decide how you are defining "executive," and you will then need to answer some other questions. How much of a sample do you want? Do you want to talk only with female executives in one company or female executives in one industry or type of business? Or do you want a cross section of female executives involved in a wide variety of organizations? Do you want to interview only the executives themselves, or do you want to talk to people who work for these women? If your working thesis, on the other hand, is focused on one organization or one type of organization, then you'll need to decide how many people to interview and which employees have the information you need (accountants? supervisors? marketing specialists? salespeople?). You can make these decisions only by first knowing precisely what information you want, then doing some research on the organization itself. If this research isn't enough, try calling the personnel office or the public information office and asking who could best answer your questions.

Before you can walk into an interview or even conduct a short interview on the phone, however, you still have preparation to do. Television talk shows make interviewing look easy and spontaneous; as in any endeavor, these interviewers are so skilled in their craft that the work that lies behind it doesn't show. For your part, you cannot assume that all you need to do is ask a question or two, and then wait for your source to reel off a gold mine of evidence into your tape recorder. If you want the interview to be productive, if you want to receive the information that led you to consider interviews in the first place, then you need to have a plan for the interview.

B. Preparing for the Interview

Your preparation for the interview involves four steps:

- educating yourself about the subject matter of the interview;
- preparing an interview script;
- pilot testing the interview;
- contacting potential interviewees.

1. Educating yourself about the subject matter of the interview

By the "subject matter of the interview," I mean first of all the topic that you and the interviewee will be discussing, which is probably embodied in your working thesis and research questions. Second, I mean having a clear idea of the context in which this person operates as an "expert." If you are interviewing someone who works for an organization, for example, you need to know what the organization does, and you should also have a general idea of what your interviewee does in his or her job. Let me repeat: An interview should never be a substitute for other kinds of research. You should not be interviewing the president of Electronics, Inc., to find out what kind of products Electronics makes. Like a good investigative reporter, you will have learned what you could learn from other sources; now you have come to this person because she, and only she, can answer the questions you have. For these reasons, it is wise to conduct your interviews after you have had an opportunity to do some preliminary investigations.

2. Preparing an interview script

You will be walking into the interview with a script, a carefully prepared list of questions that you have developed. The fact that you are going in with a script doesn't mean that the interview is going to resemble an oral exam, with your marching in lockstep from one question to another regardless of the answers you are receiving. But it does mean that you want to be absolutely sure that you get the information you need, and thus you intend to guide the conversation in a certain direction. Interestingly enough, you will find that this script (and the work that goes into it) is the best way to prepare yourself to engage meaning-fully in the conversation you will have; it will allow you to pick up on and pursue relevant points your interviewee raises and to ask questions that may not have been in your original script. And you needn't worry about the interviewee thinking you are too forward or aggressive. This isn't an ordinary conversation. You set up the interview; the interviewee wants and expects you to take charge.

Writing your script involves deciding not only the content of your questions but also the way you will phrase the questions and the order in which you will ask them. In preparing your script, here are some things you will want to keep in mind.

Questions can be thought of as falling along a spectrum from closed questions to open-ended ones. Closed questions are the kind that invite a short, simple answer: How long have you been an accountant? Did Electronics show a profit this year? Open-ended questions invite longer, less restricted, and less directed responses: What are some of your thoughts on X? In preparing your questions, you should be aware that closed questions tend to be questions that are easy to answer, but they restrict the kind of information you receive—and to an extent they may bias it in the sense that they force the interviewee to put himself or herself in a camp or category. Compare the closed question "Do you favor quotas for minorities?" with the open-ended "I'd like to hear what you think about quotas for minorities."

But open-ended questions also have their pitfalls. They can encourage direc-tionless, rambling answers. So when you use open-ended questions, you must also write out a series of follow-up questions, designed to move the interviewee to talk about the specific points you are most interested in. If, for example, your open-ended question was "What do you think about the proposal to put in a light-rail system on the west side of the city?" Some possible follow-up questions might be: What route do you think would be the best? Do you think the plan to build a tunnel under the West Hills is feasible? Desirable? How would you respond to the neighborhood associations that are opposed to the Sunset Corri-dor plan? If the topic of your interview is complex (What makes a businessper-son successful?), it is wise to start with closed questions and move to more open-ended ones.

In this area of open-ended questions, Leslie Baxter called my attention to the problem of the "unanswerable" question. Often, she told me, novices at inter-viewing will go to an interview and ask their major research question, which, as you have already discovered, tends to be general and abstract. In an interview, such a question could stop your interviewee cold as he or she tries to figure out how to approach it or tries to figure out what you want. You can solve that problem by asking for more concrete, specific answers that will reveal the inter-viewee's thinking on the larger question. Let's say, for example, that you want to know what makes a businessperson successful. Instead of asking that question point blank, you say, "Think of the last time you had a feeling of real success on the job. Could you describe that experience for me?" You could elicit similar information by saying, "I'd like you to think of an incident at work in which you felt you failed to achieve what you thought you should have achieved. Could you describe that incident for me?" By listening to these answers and using the paraphrasing technique ("So you believe that making decisions quickly is important to success?"), you will gradually accumulate a rich, clear picture of this person's answer to your big question.

In writing the script for your interview, you must continually return to this major point: What do I want to know? Here are some further guidelines for phrasing and ordering your questions.

- You will probably want to start the interview with a few closed and/or easy questions; questions about the person's exact title and how long he or she has worked for this company or done this sort of work are naturals. You could also ask some questions that confirm information you have already uncovered ("I understand that Helping Hand takes care of 300 children a day; is that correct?"). These questions should be designed to elicit or confirm specific background information that you need about the person or organization; they should set the topic and direction of the interview; and you make them easy in order to build rapport with your interviewee. Since most interviewees are distracted by a tape recorder for the first two or three minutes it is on, you do not want to start the interview with any major questions.

- In general, order your questions from "easy" and/or closed ones to more open-ended and/or probing ones. This ordering is especially important if your topic is complex or sensitive or both.

- Use every strategy you know to be sure the questions in your script are eliciting the kind of information you want, and be sensitive to a series of questions that may either unnecessarily restrict the answers you receive or inadvertently bias them.

- If you use open-ended questions, be sure you put a series of follow-up questions in your script.

- Your last question should always be one that invites the interviewee to express his or her point of view on your topic clearly (and catches anything important you may have missed): Is there anything else you'd like to say that would provide me with a better understanding of X?

3. Pilot testing the interview

Even the most carefully prepared script won't give you a completely clear picture of how the interview will go, so you should always test your script in a trial interview. Find someone whose area of expertise is similar to that of your real interviewee. If you are going to interview business executives, for example, do your trial interview with one of the instructors in the business department; or find a friend of your parents who is in business, or a parent of one of your friends. Go through the whole interview as if it were the real thing. This trial interview has several purposes:

- to develop an accurate estimate of how long the interview will take;

- to be sure your questions are really eliciting the information you want;

- to give you a chance to make any needed adjustments to your script (changing the wording of questions or the ordering of questions, adding or deleting follow-up questions, and the like);

- to test your general performance as an interviewer.

When you make arrangements for the trial interview, be sure to ask the "interviewee" to be prepared to critique the whole interview and your behavior as an interviewer.

When your script is in its final form, memorize it.

4. Contacting potential interviewees

Plan to make you initial contact with interviewees over the phone or in person. *Never* conduct the interview itself in this initial contact. Leslie Baxter advises her students to write what they are going to say in this initial contact so that they are sure they've covered everything and so that they pay close attention to the words they use. In your initial contact, here's what you need to cover.

- Identify yourself (in addition to your name, tell the person that you are a student at X).

- Tell the person how and why you selected him or her for an interview.

- Tell the person the purpose of the interview and how your record of the interview will be used (e.g., "I'm doing a research project on what makes businesspeople successful. The information I gather from you will be used in a paper on this topic that I am writing for X class").

- Settle the issue of confidentiality. Before you make this contact, you will need to decide whether you want to acknowledge your sources by name in your paper, or if you intend to keep the identity of your interviewees confidential, referring to them in your paper only in general terms like "an executive in a large company in Portland." In your initial contact, tell the person you intend to keep his or her identity confidential, or ask permission to acknowledge the person by name in your paper. Unless you have decided to keep all of your sources confidential, keep a written record of those people who have given you permission to use their names and those who wish their identities to be kept confidential.

- Tell the person approximately how long the interview will last; it is crucial that your estimate be accurate.

- Set up a time and place for the interview (and be sure you write it down in your engagement calendar!).

It is a good idea to call the day before the interview to reconfirm.

C. The Interview Itself

When you leave for the interview, be sure you have

- a tape recorder and a blank tape. Before you leave, start the tape, and identify the interview ("This is a record of my interview with John Doe, March 12, 2006"). As you are setting up the tape recorder at the beginning of the interview, you can say, "I prefer to tape this interview so that I can give my full attention to you and what you are saying." Leslie Baxter tells me this statement normally overcomes any qualms an interviewee has about being recorded.

- a clipboard, your script, a pen, and blank paper. During the interview, you are going to check off your questions as you ask them—just another guarantee that you haven't missed anything important. You want to have paper so that you can jot down any follow-up questions that occur to you during the interview, to make a quick note of any part of the interview you particularly want to use, and to take full notes in case your interviewee really doesn't want to be tape-recorded.

Your script and the trial test you've done should give you a fairly clear sense of how the interview *should go*. But here are some further observations and advice.

- Remain flexible, open, and, above all, attentive. Just because you have a script and a tape recorder doesn't mean you can become a passive sponge. You are going to be an active participant in a conversation, and to do that you have to listen closely to what your interviewee is saying. As long as you are getting the type of information you need, you can change the order in which you ask your questions. You can also abandon parts or all of your script if the situation calls for it.

- Throughout the interview, give clear signals, verbal and nonverbal, that you are paying close attention (nod your head, say "That's interesting," or "I see," or give other such "encouraging" cues). Always give positive feedback; never give the impression that what the interviewee said was wrong or beside the point (don't frown, don't say "That's not what I asked" or "Let's move on to the next question"). As often as you can, try to integrate the questions on your script with what the interviewee has said ("A minute ago you mentioned X; I'd like to ask you something more about that").

- Throughout the interview, plan to use paraphrase as feedback. Restate to the interviewee what you heard him or her say: "If I understand correctly, you are saying that . . ." or "So you mean X?" or "You are saying, then, that . . ." It is particularly useful to paraphrase those points that get at the heart of the information you need.

- If you have an interviewee who isn't talking enough, it probably means either that you have not established enough rapport, that the person doesn't understand what the interview is about, or that the questions you are asking are unanswerable. You will have to try to read the situation on the spot and make amends. Try increasing the positive feedback you are giving, and see what happens with a "Could you describe a personal experience you've had with X?" approach.

- If you have a person who is talking too much, you need to regain control of the conversation—in a tactful manner (you don't want your interviewee to shut up completely!). Interrupt the interviewee at a natural speech pause, but don't switch the topic or go on to a new question. Rather, pick up something he or she has said that is relevant or potentially relevant to your interests, and gradually get the conversation back on track ("What you have been saying is very interesting. It brings X to mind. Could you talk a bit more about X?").

- If, during the interview, the person says something that strikes you as very important, feel free to say, "That's very nice. May I quote you on that?" Otherwise, on the issue of permission to quote, at the end of the interview, while the tape is still running, ask, "Is there anything you have said during our conversation that you would not want me to quote or to attribute to you?" Ask this question in such a way that the interviewee will feel free to be honest. On your part, you will have to abide by his or her response.

- You really need to repay the interviewee in some way for his or her time. As you are leaving, offer to send him or her a copy of your final paper. (I hope the person says yes; it is a good incentive for you to do your best on this paper!)

D. Writing Up the Interview

As soon as possible after the interview is over, sit down and freewrite about it in your Researcher's Notebook. If you are doing a series of interviews, you might want to create a special section for them in your Notebook; otherwise, do your freewrite in the Reading section. Don't listen to the tape; write your freewrite from your memory of the interview.

- Try to capture the flavor of the interview; record your general impressions.

- Write about what stands out in your memory about what the interviewee said.

- If the interview had any glitches, write about what went wrong, and give yourself some advice about how to avoid such problems in the future.

At this point, your tape becomes a document, just like a book or a journal article. The rest of my advice follows my general advice for taking notes; you will find more detailed information in Section 4.D through H.

- In your working bibliography, record the following information. If you are doing a number of interviews, I'd recommend keeping these records in a separate file.
  - the full name of the interviewee;
  - his/her official title;
  - the full official name of the company or organization for which this person works;
  - the date of the interview.

Be sure to write the name of the interviewee and the date on the cassette, too.

- After listening to the tape and rereading your interview notes, write a summary (Section 4.G) and make notes on specific information. If you are quoting the interviewee in a note, play back the tape after you've written down the words to be sure they are accurate.
- Plan to keep the tape until your paper is turned in, just in case you need to refer to it while you are writing your drafts.

If you took written notes rather than tape recording the interview, plan to rewrite all your notes in "clean" form as soon as you can after the interview is over. If you have not done so already, put quotation marks around the words you know are the exact words your interviewee used. Your clean notes now become the basic document of the interview, just as a tape recording would be. From these notes you should make a record of the interview, write a summary of it, and take specific notes, following the process outlined above.

When it is time to write your final paper, check the manual of the documentation style you are using to learn how you should cite material you have obtained from an interview.

Several further suggestions:

- If, in your final paper, you will be relying heavily on material you have obtained through interviews, consult with your instructor about the best way for you to document these interviews.
- Keeping in mind what I said in Section 3 about sources and their authority, in the body of your paper give us the sort of information about your interviewee that would indicate such authority: "John Doe, head of marketing for the large retail chain Clothes Unlimited, told me that. . . ."
- You must, of course, abide by confidentiality agreements you have made with your interviewees. In such cases, give us as much information as you can ethically about the source: "In an interview with me last month, an official of a major lumber company, who wishes to remain anonymous, informed me that. . . ."

Four Sample Research Papers

Jennifer Welsh

English 470

Professor Berkson

Willa Cather: Challenging the Canon

The literary canon of American classics of the nineteenth and early twentieth centuries is composed nearly exclusively of works by male writers. The fact that this canon was created by predominantly male writers and critics in a male-dominated world of academia explains this imbalance to a certain extent. Yet this canon has had accepted and unchallenged authority for so long that its sources are rarely questioned. Writers like Melville, Hawthorne, Emerson, and James are considered the "masters," and other writers are often obscured by the years of praise and criticism built up around these "classics." Only recently, nearly a century later, have the criteria of establishing a classic been re-evaluated through a contemporary perspective.

In her article "When We Dead Awaken: Writing as Revision," Adrienne Rich argues the necessity of "looking back, of seeing with fresh eyes, of entering an old text from a new critical direction" (18). The "critical direction" she speaks of is the new basis of feminist theory that has developed over the past few decades. The "fresh eyes" are those that have a clearer vision of how gender functions in today's society and the historical roots of gender-specific roles. Rich promotes this process of "revision" not simply as a new critical approach but as an "act of survival. Until we can understand the assumptions in which we are drenched we cannot know ourselves" (18). The crux of this statement is "assumptions." This is where literature begins to function not solely as an art form but as a reflection of the context of shared values and beliefs that make up the society in which it is written. These assumptions must be explored and questioned when re-evaluating the canon of "classics" of the nineteenth and early twentieth centuries.

Welsh 2

Several important theories have been presented concerning the patterns and common ideals of this body of literature. R. W. B. Lewis presents the archetypal figure of the "American Adam," and compares the perceptions of America found in the literature of the nineteenth century to the biblical Garden of Eden. In this myth the New World discovered and claimed by the pilgrims was seen as a fresh start. The land was wild and untainted by generations of European dominance, and (so the myth goes) the courageous men who came to conquer this land left their roots behind and started over, pitting themselves against the unknown. The "American Adam" was "a figure of heroic innocence and vast potentialities poised at the start of a new history" (Lewis 1). Among the many characteristics of this archetype that Lewis describes, celibacy is an important factor. Exploring the land and facing various adventures, the Adam is free from any restraining ties (i.e., women).

Yet given this myth, which can be identified in the works of Twain, Melville, Emerson, and many others, where does the woman find herself in the literature? In her book The Faces of Eve, Judith Fryer presents four archetypal roles of women found in this male literature: the Temptress, the American Princess, the Great Mother, and the New Woman (24-25). Fryer's descriptions of these roles are interesting if somewhat controversial, yet they each offer undeniably distressing portrayals of women's options. Each archetype defines itself in relation to men. The American Eve is either tempting Adam into sin, depending on Adam for protection of her virtue, striving for power over Adam, or trying to escape Adam by escaping from life itself. For a woman reading this literature these are hardly attractive options with which to identify.

Nina Baym draws on the theory that women are excluded from the canon and forced to identify with its male figures, and goes on to explore the reasons for this situation. In her article "Melodramas of Beset Manhood," she argues that since American literary criticism is based on content, and since the quality of this content cannot be compared to the European traditions from which it is trying to assert its independence, then the evaluation of its quality must lie in its "Americanness" itself. Defining this Americanness presents obvious difficulties. Yet Baym contends that criteria of "Americanness" did form. She states that two conditions must be met: "America as a nation must be the ultimate subject of the work," and the purpose of writing must be to "display, to meditate" on certain aspects of this nation in order to "derive from them certain generalizations and conclusions about the 'American experience'" (127). Baym goes on to argue that women's fiction of the period, although popularly read, was not considered to reflect American experience: "The certainty here that stories about women could not contain the essence of American culture means that the matter of American experience is inherently male" (130). Baym concludes that women are not likely to write successful novels that reflect solely male experience and are therefore excluded from the canon of American authors.

If these theories are what arise from examination of the traditional canon, then Adrienne Rich's call for "re-vision" does indeed seem crucial. How could today's developing feminist literature ever have taken root with such an imbalanced heritage? Obviously we must look outside the sphere of the male classic to find the missing link. We must make use of our present broader, more egalitarian understanding of gender relations to look again at the literature of the past centuries in order to acknowledge and explore the female literary tradition that has been eclipsed for so many generations. The new, revised canon that appears

Welsh 4

under this re-examination includes authors such as Dickinson, Stowe, Alcott, Fuller, Chopin, and Cather. In works of these authors one finds a whole new understanding of American experience as defined by the woman's perspective. For each of these authors the experience of developing and fulfilling themselves as women writers living and working in a patriarchal culture had a profound effect on their literature. Some, such as Louisa May Alcott and Kate Chopin, wrote from within the sphere of conventional society, exploring the repression experienced by women. Others, notably Willa Cather, struggled to create characters who formed their identity outside of the conventions. In creating such characters, Cather has developed an alternative conception of women than that offered by the literature of her male counterparts.

The conventional role of women during the nineteenth century was quite narrow and explicit. Barbara Welter terms this phenomenon the "Cult of True Womanhood" in her book Dimity Convictions: The American Woman in the Nineteenth Century. These conventions were based on the premise that the difference between the sexes was total and innate (4). Women had no place in the men's realm and vice versa. Welter presents four "cardinal virtues" of femininity: piety, purity, submissiveness, and domesticity (21). These ideals were socialized into each generation of women by their mothers and formed the governing rules of their lives. Piety was considered the superior domain of women; not only were they responsible for their own morality but for that of their husbands as well (21). Religion was the sacred interest outside of themselves and one of the few worthy causes for which to use their talent and energies. Purity was the essential virtue and property of the woman, to be guarded until the marriage night at which time it, and therefore the woman herself, would become the property of the man (24). Submissiveness was the key to obtaining all other rewards. The subservience of women to men was "the order of the Universe" itself and not to be tampered with (28). Finally, domesticity was the happy culminating state of a woman's life. All of her childhood and adolescence was geared toward reaching the goal of marriage and only by marrying could she achieve the status that men achieved through education and work (8). All of a wife's efforts and good qualities were put into helping the husband to rise in the world (16). A happy home and husband made a happy woman (10) and provided security from the evils of the outside world (31). The state of being a woman was equated with these virtues to the end that failure in any one category made them, in Welter's words, "semi-woman . . . mental hermaphrodites" (40). Like Judith Fryer's archetypal figures the True Woman derived her identity and satisfaction only from her role in relation to men and rarely sought fulfillment of her own self as a way of achieving womanhood.

Yet Willa Cather, among other emerging writers of her time, challenges this definition of womanhood in her female characters. Cather creates women that form their identities outside of the traditional sphere of the home, choosing instead the land to reflect their ambitions and desires. She creates characters who struggle to evolve outside of the conventional identity of woman as wife and mother, dependent on men for their existence. When Cather does place a woman in a conventional role, she portrays her situation as insecure, dependent, and frustrating. Yet Cather's conception of these characters did not grow out of a serene and certain background of belief in the inherent strength of women. She struggled with her identity both as a woman and a writer and these struggles are often reflected in her characters.

Welsh 6

Willa Cather was born in 1873 in Back Creek, Virginia, and eventually moved with her parents and six younger brothers and sisters to the plains of Nebraska in 1883 and finally to the nearby town of Red Cloud in 1884. Her father, Charles Cather, was a gentle and well-read man who was quite pleased with his daughter and encouraged her intellectual ambitions. His soft-spoken, aesthetic character eventually provided the model for several of her characters, such as Mr. Shimerda and Carl Linstrum, alternatives to the powerful, domineering, masculine stereotype of the time (O'Brien, Willa Cather 14). Both of Willa's grandmothers, Caroline Cather and Rachel Silbert Boak, and one great-aunt, Sidney Cather Gore, were strong women who found ways to express and assert themselves while still remaining within the boundaries set for nineteenth-century women. Willa's mother was a complex personality and may have contributed to Cather's ambiguities about her own femininity.

In her biography of Cather (Willa Cather 39-41), Sharon O'Brien presents Mary Virginia Boak Cather as a beautiful, impeccably dressed product of a boarding-school education. She was well-versed in society's codes and her efforts at socializing Willa into these codes met with a great deal of resistance. On the one hand she was a strong-willed disciplinarian and overshadowed her husband in the home. Yet, O'Brien points out, she didn't seem to exercise much control over her own life. She was often sick, a victim of the classic nineteenth-century woman's disease, hysteria, and relied passively on the care of doctors during these periods. Often her illness followed the birth of a child and one can't help but wonder whether she really wanted seven children. She also allowed Charles to move the family to Nebraska despite her strong objections, and once there sank into even more frequent bouts of illness.

O'Brien suggests that these contradictions within Cather's mother's character contributed to Cather's own ambivalence toward the female role in general (42-46). Cather struggled with her desire for identification and connection with her mother, yet feared losing her own sense of self when faced with her mother's domineering, powerful nature. She also recognized the futility of her mother's strength when she succumbed to her bouts of illness and to the decisions of her husband.

Cather's view of women in this early period of her life was complex to say the least. As an adolescent she declared herself William Cather and took on a male persona in both public and private life. According to O'Brien, socialization into the role of the passive woman was repulsive to Cather and the only way to accommodate her ambitions as an artist was to reject the female identity categorically. By doing so she placed herself at the other end of a socially constructed dichotomy, not resolving the conflict, simply perpetuating it (100-101). Cather dropped her male persona after her first two years at the University of Nebraska but she still saw herself as deviant because of her intimate relationships with other women.

Intimate female relationships were socially condoned during most of the nineteenth century and often known as Boston Marriages. This acceptance was due to the belief that women had no sexual nature and therefore no ability to have sexual relations between themselves (Smith-Rosenberg 8). But with the advent of new psychosexual theories came the tendency to label these relationship deviant by the turn of the century. Cather identifies herself as lesbian, despite the fact that the word didn't exist at the time, by admitting to the "unfortunately deviant" nature of her friendship with Louise Pound (O'Brien, "The Thing Not Named" 580-585). Cather continued to have relationships with other women throughout her life. Phyllis Robinson says of her attachment to Edith

Welsh 8

Lewis, "Their life together was undoubtedly a marriage in every sense. But Willa was too conscious of her ties to home and family, and too much a conservative Midwesterner herself, to live openly with Edith" (208).

In her analysis of Willa Cather's female characters, Susan Rosowski suggests that each woman must struggle to synthesize two selves. The first is the worldy, interactive self exposed to family and friends, while the second is the imaginative and creative inner self. The struggle is against imposed social roles that can trap the woman in one self or the other (261-62). Cather denied seeing herself as a woman for some time in order to see herself as an artist, and she openly scorned women who tried to be both.

One of the factors in Cather's upbringing that contributed to this rejection of female creativity was the body of literature that Cather read as a child. The literature she was exposed to and drawn toward during these crucial formative years of her life had a major impact on her future perception of herself and of the creative process. Not surprisingly, nearly all the authors she encountered were male and she strongly identified with the male adventurer-hero, similar to Lewis' American Adam, of classics such as Treasure Island, Tom Sawyer, Huckleberry Finn, Robinson Crusoe, The Count of Monte Cristo, The Iliad, The Odyssey, and even Pilgrim's Progress and Emerson's writings (O'Brien, Willa Cather 82-84). In her university days in Lincoln, Nebraska, and later, Cather saw creativity as an exclusively male property and publicly scorned women's writing. As Phyllis Robinson states in her biography, "About her own sex Willa was inclined to be uncharitable . . . 'Sometimes I wonder why God ever trusts talent in the hands of women, they usually make such an infernal mess of it,' she wrote. She thought women were sentimental and horribly subjective" (56).

Welsh 9

Sharon O'Brien suggests that Cather's acquaintance with Sarah Orne Jewett provided the key to her resolution of herself as woman and writer. By encouraging Cather to express women's feelings and intimacy in her writing, and through the example of her own work, Jewett fostered a respect for the female voice (O'Brien, Willa Cather 334-350). The development of Cather's female characters often centers around their struggle to emerge as women and creators, to synthesize their two selves, and they often succeed. Yet it is difficult to argue that her characters' successes mark a definite resolution of Cather's own conflicts. Both Alexandra and Thea in O Pioneers! and The Song of the Lark are creators and women, yet My Antonia and A Lost Lady, both written after the previous two books, use a male narrator who is introduced as the creator writing of his muse, the female protagonist. Cather's use of this male narrator seems a step back into the schism between woman and artist.

Cather lead an unconventional life for her time period and it was perhaps the individuality and independence that she developed while struggling with the various conflicts encountered in her own life that allowed her to create such strong and unconventional characters in her literature. Alexandra and Thea are strong, positive alternatives to the limited options offered by the male writers of the period, and Antonia and Marian Forrester portray the struggle and sacrifices that women had to undergo to establish their identities in the face of the limitations society put on them.

In O Pioneers!, Cather relates the history of Alexandra Bergson's struggle to define herself in her own terms and to accomplish her goals in her own way. From the beginning Cather presents Alexandra as a character who challenges female stereotypes. She walks "rapidly and resolutely as if she knew exactly where she was going and what she was going to

Welsh 10

do next" (6). She carries herself not as a woman trying to market herself in a male world but as someone whose body reflects her inner strength: "her body was in an attitude of perfect repose, such as it was apt to take when she was thinking earnestly" (61). When a traveling man exclaims at her "shining mass of hair" (7) she shoots him "a glance of Amazonian fierceness" that makes him feel "cheap and ill-used" (8). This is a definite reversal of the traditional concept of woman as object. Alexandra shows not only "resourcefulness and good judgment" (23), but she has intelligence to mix with it and these qualities encourage her father to pass the responsibility for the farm over to her rather than to her brothers.

Her identity is reflected most strongly in her connection to the land. Unlike her father, who saw the land as a resistant force, an "enigma . . . a horse that no one knows how to harness" (22), Alexandra sees the land as a vast opportunity: "For the first time, perhaps, since that land emerged from the waters of geologic ages, a human face was set toward it with love and yearning. It seemed beautiful to her, rich and strong, and glorious" (65). Yet the ability to take advantage of this opportunity requires not only strength and intelligence but creativity as well: "A pioneer should have imagination, should be able to enjoy the idea of things rather than the things themselves" (48). This ability to create makes Alexandra the active agent of her life. She does not base the quality of her life on the achievements and direction of a husband, or of her brothers. She takes the initiative to form her own wellspring of vitality that both feeds her and is nurtured by her.

This creativity can also be seen as the resolution of Alexandra's second self, to use Rosowski's terms. By putting all her energies into developing the land, Alexandra is nurturing and fulfilling "the otherworldly, imaginative" aspect

Welsh 11

of herself (Rosowski 263) and only when this has been achieved does she feel ready to turn to her relationship with Carl.

This couple appears as a nearly inverted cultural stereotype. Carl is "a thin, frail boy with brooding eyes, very quiet in all his movements. There was a delicate pallor in his thin face, and his mouth was too sensitive for a boy's" (O Pioneers! 10). Alexandra, on the other hand, is tall, strong, and brusque. Cather extends this inversion even further in describing their perspectives: "The eyes of the girl, . . . [looked] with such anguished perplexity into the future: . . . [while] the sombre eyes of the boy . . . seemed already to be looking into the past" (14). The sentimentalism and passivity of "looking into the past" fit the stereotypical image of a woman's preoccupation, while Alexandra is the active, forward thinker of the two. When Carl returns from the East, Alexandra again defies the expectations of her gender by not handing the farm over to her brothers and not accepting a passive role in her relationship with Carl. She instead offers to share what she has with Carl, supporting him through her own means: "Well, suppose I want to take care of him? Whose business is it but my own?" (167). Ironically, it is Carl's inability to accept Alexandra's offer that keeps him from staying on. Pressured by the voices of society, expressed by the Bergson brothers, Carl hasn't the strength to defy convention as Alexandra does. He apologizes to her: "To take what you would give me, I would have to be either a very large man or a very small one, and I am only in the middle class" (182).

This inverted love story is presented against the background of the conventional and tragic story of Emil and Marie. In Marie, Cather presents us with a more traditional female character faced with a traditional temptation. Before their fateful meeting, both Marie and Emil experience an epiphany about their love. Marie discovers that she can bear living the pain as long as no one else is hurt. This is the selfless woman of the nineteenth century, always taking on the burdens of others; she becomes angelic through her sacrifices. Emil resolves to love Marie chastely and maintain his honor and goodness. He will ask nothing of her and leave without the stain of sin. But the imagery Cather uses seems to be working against the two lovers: "Everywhere the grain stood ripe and the hot afternoon was full of the smell of the ripe wheat" (257). The ripe grain, as a symbol of fertility, is the all-pervasive force of nature, and overcomes the lovers' resolutions. The result is the consummation of their love and their violent death at the hands of Frank Shabata.

The contrast between this tragic subplot and the harmonious joining of Carl and Alexandra is striking. While Marie is self-sacrificing, Alexandra is openly generous and giving but still acknowledges her need for Carl as himself. Carl comes to the realization that he too, unlike Emil, will accept Alexandra's offer of himself. They challenge the rules of society yet Cather gives them happiness and success in comparison with the tragedy of Marie and Emil. As Alexandra states, "I think when friends marry they're safe" (308).

In the end Alexandra has fulfilled both the creative and personal aspects of her self in ways that challenge social convention. She is not an accessory to another's life; she is the active agent of her own successful existence. And it is not her value as an object, or ornament, that fulfills her relationship with Carl, but rather her strength and vision in combination with their mutual need for each other.

The character of Thea in The Song of the Lark evolves in an entirely different way than Alexandra does, and yet she shares many of Alexandra's characteristics. Her piano teacher compares her to "a thin glass full of sweet-smelling, sparkling

Moselle wine" (38). The wellspring of life for Thea is not the Nebraska plains but her own inner power. Her story most closely parallels Cather's own realization of her creative power. Thea's struggle is to find the ultimate expression of her inner voice. To achieve this she passes through the hands of a series of mentors only to find that the key to unlocking her power lies ultimately within herself.

Each of the influential characters that interact with Thea during her childhood aid her in developing as a singer. Her mother furnishes her with her own attic room: "The acquisition of this room was the beginning of a new era in Thea's life . . . the clamour about her drowned the voice within herself," but here "she thought things out more clearly" (73). Dr. Archie, Ray Kennedy, and Spanish Johnny instill a sense of uniqueness in Thea. Through them she learns of and yearns for the world. They encourage her special abilities, and Dr. Archie in particular helps to shelter her from conventional expectations of girls by asserting that, because of her talent, she deserves better things. Each of her teachers as well presents her with tools and paths to fulfilling herself but each is painfully aware of his inability to bring her secret out into full bloom.

Early on she has a strong sense of her own inherent power, yet she doesn't see this as truly part of herself for some time: "She knew, of course, that there was something about her that was different. But it was more like a friendly spirit than like anything that was part of herself" (100). She never doubts her potential or her ability and is fully confident that she is equipped for whatever events shall arise: "She lacked nothing. She even felt more compact and confident than usual. She was all there, and something else was there, too— . . . that warm sureness, that sturdy little companion with whom she shared a secret" (199).

Her first real grasp of her own power occurs during her visit to Panther Canyon. This portion of the novel is highly autobiographical and in her biography Sharon O'Brien parallels Thea's experience with the struggle of contradictory forces in Cather's own life. According to O'Brien Cather's perception of creativity for most of her youth was tied exclusively to male violence and virility, making it impossible to synthesize the feminine identity with the creative process (Willa Cather 171). This association of "sword/penis/pen/male/artist" shifts when Cather discovers the pottery left by the ancient Indians in the caves of the canyon. She begins to formulate a new conception of creativity based on the image of the vase that associates "vessel/womb/throat/voice/artist" (171) and therefore makes creativity a female process. Thea experiences this association in a very physical sense. In climbing the trails of Panther Canyon she begins to identify with the ancient women who used those same paths: "It seemed to Thea that . . . certain feelings were transmitted to her. . . . They were not expressible in words, but seemed rather to translate themselves into attitudes of body" (Song of the Lark 376). As she identifies with these ancient artisans she begins to make the connection between the pot that holds the precious but elusive water, and the body that holds the voice: "what was any art but an effort to make a sheath, a mould in which to imprison for a moment that shining, elusive element which is life itself" (378). It is at this point that Thea begins to realize that her power to create lies solely within herself; her own body is the wellspring of her voice. The belief that women can create by their own power and be self-sufficient contradicts the image of the nineteenth-century woman as passive and dependent. It challenges the belief that women's energies must be funneled through husband, child, or church to be valid.

Welsh 15

Thea's discovery of her power is also linked to her flowering relationship to Fred Ottenburg. The dynamics of the two are similar to those of Alexandra and Carl. Although Fred is an extremely virile character, Thea's new-found strength surpasses his endurance in their walks. Her relationship to him is strengthened by her own sense of independence and self-sufficiency; as Thea sees it, "It's waking up every morning with the feeling that your life is your own; that you're all there and there's no sag in you" (394).

As Thea's career explodes she is drawn farther and farther into the professional world but as we meet her again with Dr. Archie and Fred she still has not achieved the final fulfilling expression of herself. She finds this ultimately in the end, when she sings the challenging role of Sieglinde. O'Brien suggests that the opera character herself provides the means for Thea's final fulfillment (Willa Cather 108). Sieglinde is separated at birth from her twin Siegmund and Cather uses their scene of reunion as lovers and siblings for Thea's performance. For Cather, the joining of the male and female siblings could signify the ultimate resolution of the male and female sides of her personality. For Thea, it means the final realization that the "sturdy little companion with whom she shares her secret" (Song of the Lark 199) is an inalienable aspect of herself: "That afternoon nothing new came to Thea Kronborg, no enlightenment, no inspiration. She merely came into full possession of things she had been refining and perfecting for so long" (571).

In My Antonia, the female protagonist is seen through the eyes of Jim Burden, an orphan sent to his grandparents' farm in Nebraska after the death of his parents. In a sense, Antonia is Jim's creation, as reflected in the title and introduction of the book, which sets the story up as his memories of her. Not only does Jim give the male view of a

female character, he also embodies society's own views and
expectations at the same time. Susan Rosowksi suggests that
Jim is the embodiment of the creative self, while Antonia is
the passive muse (265). Yet the vital element of the novel lies
in Antonia's actions, which work against this structure.
Throughout the book, Antonia challenges Jim's perceptions
and expectations of her, refusing to be categorized or molded
to fit into society's limitations.

   Jim's impressions of Antonia when he first meets her are
striking. She is darkly beautiful, foreign, mysterious. She is
drawn and connected to the land from the beginning, sleeping
in a hole dug into the wall of her family's sod house. Despite
Jim's wishes that she conform to social standards she works
as an equal with the men on the farms, developing strong
arms and a sunburned face. She is strong-willed and
opinionated and as soon as she is able to speak English she
openly expresses her thoughts. This leads to Jim's first
resentment of her as a superior, controlling figure. Despite the
fact that she is four years older than he, Jim feels that he "was
a boy and she was a girl and he resented her protecting
manner" (My Antonia 43). This pattern continues in her
protection and proud attitude toward him in the town. She
actively tries to keep Lena Lindgrad from him and tells him
often that "you're not going to sit around here and whittle
store-boxes and tell stories all your life. You are going away to
school and make something of yourself. I'm just awful proud
of you" (224). Jim's perception of Antonia carries overtones
of Fryer's Great Mother archetype, who continually tries to
dominate men through controlling them. Yet Antonia cannot
be described as striving for power over Jim. She protects him
as a mother might, nurturing his abilities and encouraging
him, but she does not see herself as superior to him. When
he kills the rattlesnake, as well as when he makes the

graduation speech, she openly expresses her admiration of his skills.

When Antonia comes to town to work as a housekeeper she starts going to dances with the other hired girls, discovering her emerging sexuality and independence. Jim and others begin to accuse her of transgressing the boundaries of purity and modesty so essential to the nineteenth-century definition of women. Her sexuality definitely holds an allure for Jim, a temptation to sneak out and attend the fireman's balls. Yet she doesn't use it in a manipulative way. One gets the distinct impression that she is simply enjoying herself. When asked by Mrs. Harling what has come over her, she replies, "I don't know . . . something has. . . . A girl like me has got to take her good times when she can. Maybe there won't be any tent next year" (208). She doesn't use her sexuality to tempt Jim, either, and even reprimands him for kissing her with any sort of passion. Her actions are not manipulative, or done for effect; she is simply asserting her right to enjoy the few years of leisure she may have.

While Jim is away at school she falls in love with Larry Donovan. Jim is angry and believes that she is lowering herself by associating with a simple passenger conductor, "a cheap sort of fellow" (304). His expectations of her marrying a "respectable" man and raising a conventional family are simply projections of society's values onto her. Antonia's intentions are honest and open: "I thought if he saw how well I could do for him, he'd want to stay with me" (313). She shows independence, control, and pride in her own life when she refuses to capitulate to society and hide away the child of the man that deserted her. She continues her life with characteristic strength and perseverance and pledges to raise her child to have a better chance than she ever had.

Welsh 18

Antonia's final situation fulfills each side of her life on her
own terms. She is no longer the passive inspiration of Jim's
work. She has become a creator in her own right, of her
children and her orchard. Jim wants her in a specific role,
defined in relation to men: "a sweetheart, a wife, or my
mother or sister—anything that a woman can be to a man"
(321). But she rejects being placed in any one of these
categories, creating her own definition of womanhood that
stands independent of any role defined by men. In the end
she becomes a combination of her greatest talents: a mother
and friend to her children, a ruler of her own household and
orchard, an equal companion to her husband, and a friend to
Jim, "the closest, the realest face, under all the shadows of
women's faces" (322).

In A Lost Lady, Cather presents us with a different type of
character. Marian Forrester is, as Susan Rosowski states, "a
wife, and as such, a woman defined in terms of society" (268).
Here the story does not revolve around a woman's process of
creating her identity, but rather around the effects of imposing
an identity created by society onto a woman. Marian is seen
through the eyes of Neil, a young orphan who is drawn to her
and worships her as he is growing up. Neil not only presents
a male view of Marian but represents also the viewpoint of
conventional society.

Susan Rosowski presents a useful interpretation of
Marian Forrester. She argues that Marian is an object, the
valued possession of her husband (268). Capt. Forrester
brought her from California to complete his idyllic house. As
his guests drive up the lawn they are able to admire all his
property: his poplars, his wide meadows, his stream, and
there on the porch, his wife. She is the incarnation of the
order, happiness, and success of his own life. This is the role

Welsh 19

she must fulfill to maintain her position. In Neil's eyes what is essential is not only her value as a beautiful possession, but her ability to transform the world around her to conform to Neil's idealized and romantic illusion (Rosowski 269). He sees her as an angelic figure: "Her skin had always the fragrant, crystalline whiteness of white lilacs. . . . There could be no negative encounter, however slight, with Mrs. Forrester. . . . One became acutely conscious of her fragility and grace" (<u>A Lost Lady</u> 31). She is an oasis of vitality and aesthetic beauty in a world that threatens Neil's romantic ideals.

Yet just as Antonia challenges Jim's expectations, Marian disillusions Neil. She maintains the facade of the effervescent wife for some time at least, yet Cather shows us flashes of the life she would prefer to live. She loves high society, the dancing, and the parties. She yearns to have an outlet for her explosive energy and tells Neil, "I feel such a power to live in me" (125). As her husband becomes increasingly ill their trips to Denver become impossible and, shut up in the house all winter, she begins to fade. Marian's options are limited. As Jennifer Bailey states in her article "The Dangers of Femininity in Willa Cather's Fiction," "The only method by which Marian can assert her identity and refuse to decline as a symbol of a passing age is to use her powerful sexuality" (402). This is her sole means of power and in using it she destroys the idealistic image Neil has of her and in doing so she destroys his romantic view of the world.

The scene in which Neil overhears Marian and Frank Ellinger in her bedroom is filled with images of burgeoning sexuality: "thickets of wild roses, with flaming buds, just beginning to open. . . . burning rose-colour . . . a dye made of sunlight and morning and moisture, so intense that it cannot possibly last . . . must fade, like ecstasy" (<u>A Lost Lady</u> 82). Neil cuts these roses for Marian, symbolizing his own sexual

Welsh 20

awakening. At this point the idealistic Marian is still intact in his mind; his sexual awareness of her does not necessarily endanger that ideal. Yet when he realizes that she is with Frank in the bedroom, that she has asserted her own sexuality, the ideal is shattered: "It was not a moral scruple that she had outraged but an aesthetic ideal" (84). This aesthetic ideal is the role set up by society that denies women the power over their own sexuality. They are accepted as sexual objects but not as sexual beings. As Barbara Welter argues in her "Cult of True Womanhood," the only action nineteenth-century women were to take with their sexuality was to keep it hidden until the night when they hand it over to their husbands (24). In presenting Marian in a situation where her only way to assert her own identity is by exercising her own sexual power, Cather exposes the dilemma of the conventional role of wife.

When her husband dies, Marian no longer makes any effort to maintain the facade. She creates her own society in the house by inviting young men over for dinner: "they call me the Merry Widow—I rather like it" (A Lost Lady 158). She exchanges her sexuality for Ivy Peters' protection in order to survive. She leaves eventually for California, and out last image of her is as the wife of a "rich, cranky old Englishman" (174), but she is laughing and living the high life once again. As Neil states, "she preferred life on any terms" (172), meaning that she chose to use the power of her sexuality, the one option that lets her live the life she desires. Cather makes the cost of this choice quite apparent, for she is once again the property of another man, attempting to measure up to the expectations of a socially defined role.

Willa Cather grew up in a period dominated by the literature of the male canon. She began to write professionally just after the turn of the century, as ideas were changing but old stereotypes still maintained their hold on society. Yet she,

Welsh 21

among other writers such as Jewett and Chopin, drew on her experience of these stereotypes and the struggle she went through to resolve her perception of herself with that projected onto her by society. Judith Fryer's "American Eve" defines herself solely in relation to Adam, whereas Cather's women define themselves through their experience and their achievements. The idealized woman of the "Cult of True Womanhood" finds her ultimate fulfillment in a happy home and a happy husband, whereas Cather shows the idealized domestic scene as dangerous and costly for a woman. In challenging the social conventions Cather chips away at their validity and authority. She opens a path toward a new conception of women, creating a precedent for a long line of strong female writers and characters to follow. Contemporary feminist literary critics are part of this line and therefore must maintain the tradition of challenging stereotypical conventions of society through their work. Only by chipping away at the validity of the male canon will it lose its exclusive authority. "Re-vision" is the only means to bring such writers as Cather into this canon to correct and balance the expression of American experience.

Welsh 22

Works Cited

Bailey, Jennifer. "The Dangers of Femininity in Willa Cather's
Fiction." Journal of American Studies 16 (1982): 391-406.

Baym, Nina. "Melodramas of Beset Manhood: How Theories
of American Literature Exclude Women Authors."
American Quarterly 33 (1981): 123-139.

Cather, Willa. A Lost Lady. 1923. New York: Knopf, 1973.

---. My Antonia. Boston: Houghton, 1918.

---. O Pioneers! Boston: Houghton, 1913.

---. The Song of the Lark. 1915. Boston: Houghton, 1983.

Fryer, Judith. The Faces of Eve: Women in the Nineteenth-
Century American Novel. Oxford: Oxford UP, 1976.

Lewis, R. W. B. The American Adam: Innocence, Tragedy, and
Tradition in the Nineteenth Century. Chicago: U of
Chicago P, 1955.

O'Brien, Sharon. "The Thing Not Named: Willa Cather as a
Lesbian Writer." Signs 9 (Summer 1984): 576-599.

---. Willa Cather: The Emerging Voice. New York: Oxford UP,
1987.

Rich, Adrienne. "When We Dead Awaken: Writing as Re-
Vision." College English 34 (1972): 18-30.

Robinson, Phyllis C. Willa: The Life of Willa Cather. Garden
City: New York: Doubleday, 1983.

Rosowski, Susan. "Willa Cather's Women." Studies in
American Fiction 9 (Autumn 1981): 261-275.

Smith-Rosenberg, Carol. "The Female World of Love and
Ritual: Relations between Women in Nineteenth-Century
America." Signs 1.1 (1975): 1-29.

Welter, Barbara. Dimity Convictions: The American Woman in
the Nineteenth Century. Athens: Ohio UP, 1976.

Cookson 1

Elizabeth Cookson

Professor David Savage

History 400

The Forgotten Women: British Nurses, VADs,
and Doctors across the Channel during World War I

"The Rose That Grows in No-Man's Land"

> It's the one red rose,
> The soldier knows;
> It's the work of the Master's hand.
> In the war's great curse
> Stood the Red Cross Nurse,
> She's the rose in No-Man's-Land!
>
> Song, 1916[1]

> A woman child. She dream'd the dreams
>   of men.
> Of fiery purposes, and battle's din.
> She left her dolls to play with soldier toys
> And glow'd in enterprise of heroes bold.
> Such child—
> Grown to the kingdom of her woman's heart,
> Goes forth with joy beneath her country's flag.
> Gives her skill to those who call for aid.
> She faces death in many cruel guise,
> Holding life cheap, for honour and her King.
>
> A. M. Johns, 1916[2]

When Great Britain plunged into World War I on August
1, 1914, the British people responded with patriotic
enthusiasm. Men volunteered for active duty by the
thousands, and women were not far behind in their efforts to
help with "The Cause." Responding to the government's pleas
for aid, British women took over traditionally male jobs,
serving as police officers, tram drivers, munitions workers,
and farm laborers.

Cookson 2

One more traditional area which attracted thousands of
women was that of nursing and hospital work. By the time
World War I began, nursing was already a well-organized and
respected profession for women. Professional nurses were
supplemented by the Voluntary Aid Detachment, which had
been developed in 1909. VADs received lectures in first aid
and home nursing.[3] The war, however, created the demand for
thousands of extra nurses and VADs. The *Times* of May
7,1915, noted that

> Every day at Devonshire House a long stream of
> women, varying in age from 23 to 38, are seen by the
> standing committee which has been appointed to deal
> with the application made by the War Office for 3,000
> members of the Voluntary Aid Detachment to help in
> military hospitals in the coming months.[4]

Louise Dalby, in her lecture *The Great War and Women's
Liberation,* noted that most of the VADs were young women
from middle- and upper-class families to whom farm labor
and munitions work was unappealing.[5] Under the orders of
the Joint War Committee, the VADs were to do the cooking,
cleaning, and light nursing tasks in order to relieve the work
load of the professional nurses.

When the war began in August 1914 there were only 463
nurses employed in Queen Alexandra's Imperial Nursing
Service, and on August 12, 1916, The *Times* reported:

> As a result of the appeal made in *The Times* on
> behalf of the British Red Cross Society for nurses for the
> military hospitals, more than 3,000 women have already
> volunteered, but many more are urgently needed.
> Miss Swift, matron-in-chief of the Joint Committee,
> said yesterday that she has vacancies for nurses of one
> or two years' training and also nurses with fever
> experience as staff nurses. New hospitals are being
> opened, and the work is increasing.[6]

Cookson 3

By November 1918 the number of nurses employed in war work had risen to 13,000.[7] The VAD movement grew, too, from 47,000 women in August 1914 to 83,000 by April 1920.[8] During the war, the majority of the nurses and VADs were employed in civilian and military hospitals in Great Britain, but a small percentage served near the combat zones in Belgium, France, Serbia, and elsewhere. In August 1918 there were 2,396 nurses and 2,547 VADs on the Continent with the British Expeditionary Force, and 285 nurses and 657 VADs with the British Red Cross and other independent organizations in France.[9] The *Times* cautioned would-be volunteers that, "It is impossible to stipulate for foreign service as the proportion of nurses needed abroad is comparatively small."[10] Only about 6 percent of the nursing force was required for service overseas.

The British Red Cross Society and the Order of St. John worked together under the title of the Joint War Committee. This committee developed extremely stringent terms for service abroad. VADs, for example, had a one-month probationary period; thereafter they were required to sign a declaration to serve six months. They did not receive a salary, but room, board, and traveling expenses were paid.[11]

In spite of these disadvantages, service in France and elsewhere in Europe was considered to be a thing of great social status and prestige. Perhaps the thought of nursing foreign, as well as British, soldiers added to the appeal. Young women begged to be allowed to cross the Channel. One woman who worked at the headquarters of the British Red Cross remembered, "all day long there came an endless procession of women wanting to help . . . some anxious for adventure and clamouring 'to go to the front at once'."[12]

Women doctors were also anxious to help on the Continent. A few of these women organized and funded groups themselves when they were denied permission to help. After being told to "go home and keep quiet," Dr. Elsie Inglis

Cookson 4

founded the Scottish Women's Hospitals in Russia and
Serbia.[13] The three hospitals were staffed entirely by women.
Dr. Elizabeth Garret Anderson and Dr. Flora Murray were
similarly dismissed, so they offered their services to the
French, who accepted their aid with delight.[14]

A number of the British women who finally made it to the
Continent wrote of their experiences in the zones of battle.
While much attention and scholarly effort has been expended
in analyzing the memoirs, letters, and journals of the British
soldiers, little or no attention has been given to the writings of
the women who worked within a few miles of the actual
fighting. As the war had a profound effect on the men who
fought in the trenches, so it affected the women who heard
the noise of battles and attempted to care for the wounded
the war churned out daily. For the British women who worked
as nurses, VADs, and doctors near the lines of fighting, World
War I proved to be a positive and profound experience which
was, nonetheless, filled with contradictions. The women
experienced times of despair and fear, but also enjoyed the
adventures, challenges, excitement, and companionship which
went with service overseas.

For these women, the adventure began upon receiving
notice of being selected for duty abroad. The overwhelming
reaction of the women was one of excitement. In September
1914 one professional nurse noted, "Proudly they [the
Territorial nurses] went away, clad in military uniform, whilst
those left behind envied them with an almost bitter envy."[15]
When writing of her own efforts to go abroad, the same nurse
said, "Speaking for myself, to want a thing badly means to get
it—if possible. When the Servians [sic] started I went to the
Matron and asked permission to be released from my
services." Finally, she received a telegram: "ten nurses wanted
at once for Antwerp; must be voluntary."[16] She quickly wired
her acceptance, and after weeks of waiting she received a

Cookson 5

telegram to "meet the nine-thirty boat train, Victoria, tonight."
She packed "in delighted excitement" and rushed off to catch
her train.[17]

Nursing Sister Violetta Thurstan could not suppress her
excitement when she was allowed to go to Belgium in the fall
of 1914. Thurstan wrote, "On Monday afternoon I was
interviewing my nurses, saying good-bye to friends—shopping
in between—wildly trying to get everything I wanted at the
eleventh hour . . ."[18]

Vera Brittain, a young VAD, volunteered for duty overseas
in 1916 mainly to escape her parents and her thoughts of her
fiance's death. But despite the saddening causes for her
departure, Vera noted "the exhilaration of that day [of
departure] still lives on in the pages of my diary."[19]

As a volunteer in 1914 for the English Motor Field
Ambulance Corps, May Sinclair noted the frustration and
competition involved in getting to Belgium:

> After the painful births and deaths of I don't know how
> many committees, after six weeks struggling with
> something we imagined to be Red Tape, which proved
> to be the combined egoism of several persons all
> desperately anxious to "get to the Front," and all
> desperately afraid of somebody else getting there too,
> and getting there first, we were actually off.[20]

The few positions for service abroad were greeted with eager
competition by the women of Great Britain. The dreams of
adventure and excitement and the mysterious qualities of
foreign peoples and places must have added greatly to the
mystique of serving overseas.

Once overseas, however, the women were inundated by
the frantic and unceasing work demanded by hospitals near
the Front. During a "push" or special attack, the numbers of
wounded men doubled and trebled from the normal load,
over 300 arriving in a night in some instances.[21] In spite of the

Cookson 6

long, hard hours and back-breaking work, the nurses and
VADs delighted in the challenge. Vera Brittain, rather cynically
looking back on her early days as a VAD, remarked, "Every
task, from the dressing of a dangerous wound to the
scrubbing of a bed-mackintosh, had for us in those early days
a sacred glamour which redeemed it equally from tedium and
disgust."[22] VAD Sarah Macnaughtan concurred, but noted that
"the girls, of course, and very naturally, were all keen about
ward work. No one had come out to Antwerp to wait on or
cook for an English staff, for instance. They must serve
soldiers!"[23]

As soon as work began, though, it seemed to many to be
an unceasing treadmill. One nurse noted, "How those [first]
five weeks passed is just a vague impression of constant work,
conflicting rumours, rush and weariness. I can remember
nothing consecutively."[24] She went on to describe her work in
further detail:

> My friend and I had a large flat containing fourteen
> wards, with seventy men to attend to. We had no
> orderlies. . . . All the patients were gravely wounded;
> they usually required two dressings a day. . . . The meals
> alone were a perfect nightmare to get served, as
> scarcely any patient could feed himself. For the first two
> weeks there were only two of us to do everything.[25]

A young VAD, in a letter to her uncle, wrote:

> I cannot write properly, as I am dog-tired. We had a
> convoy of wounded, 266 on Friday night and 70 on
> Saturday. They came straight from the trenches into the
> wards after a two days' journey, thick with Champagne
> mud and lice and blood. It is trying to cut off clothes
> and dress wounds by candle-light. For two nights and
> three days we did not take our clothes off or our
> hairpins out. Things are better now, but I do forty-one
> dressings every day and work from 7:30 a.m. till 8 p.m.,
> with only one break for lunch.[26]

Cookson 7

This and other VAD reports conflict noticeably with a general report issued by the Joint War Committee after the war. The report stated that "The V.A.D. members were not . . . trained nurses; nor were they entrusted with trained nurses' work except on occasions when the emergency was so great that no other course was open."[27] The reading of VAD accounts would indicate that the realities of war nursing made it expedient for VADs routinely to perform professional nursing duties.

For most of the women who worked in the military hospitals on the Continent, the hours were long, the breaks few, and the work many times overwhelming. But though they wrote of the strains and stresses involved in their jobs, the ability to withstand the rigor and hardships made for a personal triumph of will. One woman, a radiographer in France, writing under the pseudonym of Skia, exulted: "During the battle of the Somme the strain was terrific—physically, psychologically. We were stretched taut, and not a strand of the rope was frayed. We held!"[28]

Though most British women seemed to take the long hours and pressures of work in their stride, the awful reality of brutally wounded men proved to be another matter. To the inexperienced VADs and nurses used to working in civilian hospitals, the sight of hundreds of grossly wounded men had a startling and profound impact.

VAD Lesley Smith wrote about the wounded with stark simplicity. "Day after day," she said,

> we cut down stinking bandages and exposed wounds which destroyed the whole original plan of the body . . . [In surgery] the leg I was holding came off with a jerk and I sat down still clasping the foot. I stuffed the leg in the dressing pail beside the other arms and legs. The marquee grew hotter and hotter and the sweat ran off the surgeons' faces.[29]

Vera Brittain recalled

> . . . standing alone in a newly created circle of hell
> during the "emergency" of March 22nd, 1918, and
> gazing, half hypnotised, at the dishevelled boots and
> piles of muddy khaki, the brown blankets turned back
> from smashed limbs bound to splints by filthy
> bloodstained bandages. Beneath each stinking wad of
> sodden wool and gauze an obscene horror waited me—
> and all the equipment I had .. . was one pair of
> forceps.[30]

Skia remembered a similar experience as "a nightmare of
glaring lights, appalling stenches of ether and chloroform."[31]
Violetta Thurstan made use of the same noun:

> It is a dreadful nightmare to look back at. Blood-stained
> uniforms hastily cut off soldiers were lying on the
> floor—half-open packets of dressings were on every
> locker . . . men were moaning with pain, calling for
> water, begging that their dressings might be done
> again.[32]

One nurse wrote simply:

> It becomes monotonous to tell you again that all the
> hundreds and hundreds of men we nursed were far
> spent—suffering from shock collapse, excessive
> hemorrhage, broken to pieces, all in agony.
>
> * * *
>
> Some were so terribly burned that it was difficult to tell
> where their faces were; how they lived is a marvel to us,
> for no features seemed left to them. We had sometimes
> to force an opening where the mouth had been to insert
> a tube to feed them.[33]

Constant exposure to such grotesque and horrible sights
invariably had a numbing effect on the women. Vera Brittain
described the effect as a shutter which came down and
allowed her to cease thinking.[34] Mary Borden, an English

Cookson 9

nurse who worked in a French hospital, described many of the
sensations in a short story she wrote:

> She [a nurse] is no longer a woman. She is dead already,
> just as I am—really dead, past resurrection. Her heart is
> dead. She killed it. She couldn't bear to feel it jumping
> in her side when Life, the sick animal, choked and
> rattled in her arms. Her ears are deaf; she deafened
> them. She could not bear to hear Life crying and
> mewing. She is blind so that she cannot see the torn
> parts of men she must handle. Blind, deaf, dead—she
> is strong, efficient, fit to consort with gods and
> demons—a machine inhabited by a ghost of a
> woman—soulless, past redeeming, just as I am—just
> as I will be.[35]

Mary Borden's words illustrate the underlying anguish and
helplessness the women must have felt when they were
overwhelmed by the severely and mortally wounded men who
seemed to flood the hospitals.

While caring for the wounded served as a constant
reminder of the war, the British women working on the
Continent were reminded in other ways of their proximity to
the Front. Taubes, German airplanes, often flew over the
military hospitals. One VAD working near Verdun said that she
was soon able, from the sound of the shells, to determine the
size and kind of shells being thrown.[36]

Reactions to the shellings were mixed. Violetta Thurstan
described the shells as making "a most horrible scream before
bursting, like an animal in pain," but noted that she found it
hard to "realize that all this was happening to us. One felt
rather like a disinterested spectator in a far-off dream."[37] Lady
Helena Gleichen, who worked with a mobile X-ray unit in Italy,
treated the whole experience as a joke. The shell, she wrote,
"finally landed with a tremendous bang in the middle of the
road we had at that moment left. . . . And the moral of this
little episode is that it is no use fussing where you are, as

Cookson 10

shells may come anywhere."[38]

One British nurse, however, was understandably upset by the close proximity to her of the falling shells. Her friend thus had to remind her, "Remember we are British women, not emotional continentals. We've got to keep our heads."[39] Sarah Macnaughtan described an incident full of the same stiff-upper-lip attitude. During a prolonged shelling, the nurse and VADs walked through the streets to return to the hospital. It was, she felt, "a matter of honour with us all not to walk too quickly. There is a British obstinacy, of which one saw a great deal during the war, which refuses to hurry for a beastly German shell."[40]

Several women found that the sounds of war were oppressive and served as constant reminders of the carnage and instability of life during a war. Vera Brittain mused that the sounds of war which whispered in the wind created an atmosphere which was always tense and restless, making complete peace impossible.[41] Skia concurred that "the bombing, by night, night after night, when from a crowded hospital full of helpless men one hears the sinister sound beating nearer and nearer, with the sure knowledge that death and destruction are in store for some hapless mortal, is horrible."[42] But it was B. G. Mure, a VAD in France, who realistically noted that "at first the sound was nerve-racking, but the human imagination soon tires, and before long a vague sadness, sometimes merely a sense of irritation at the tragic stupidity of the thing to which we listened, replaced our first emotion."[43]

In spite of the horrors and the tragic nature of the work, the women seemed to find it strangely compelling and were reluctant to leave the zones of action. As units and organizations broke up, or left for the safety of England, many of the women stayed behind to offer their services to other organizations. When Violetta Thurstan's unit was forced to

Cookson 11

leave Belgium under the rapid advance of the German troops, Violetta was seriously ill. She rejoiced at her fever, thinking it would give her a legitimate excuse to stay behind.[44] Dr. Caroline Matthews, serving in Serbia, proclaimed, "I was glad I stayed! Looking back I know it was worth it all."[45] One nurse wrote factually:

> We had come to Belgium to nurse the Belgians; what society we served under was a matter of indifference to us. If our party chose to go home to England, we meant to stay. . . . So we quietly went round to the Belgian Croix Rouge and offered our services. They accepted us with open arms.[46]

In the strangely contradictory nature of war, the women who worked abroad found moments of excitement and adventure during their service. Mrs. St. Clair Stobart, working in hospitals and ambulance units in Serbia and France, thought that the German airplane which flew over the hospital grounds dropping bombs was "an exciting diversion."[47] Helena Gleichen collected shell-cases as souvenirs.[48] B. G. Mure recalled that "there was a certain thrill in the knowledge that we were actually in a country invaded by the enemy."[49]

May Sinclair described the sense of excitement which came from working so close to danger and death:

> It is only a little thrill, so far (for you don't really believe there is any danger), but you can imagine the thing growing, growing steadily until it becomes ecstasy. Not that you imagine anything at the moment. At the moment you are no longer a thinking, reflecting being; you have ceased to be aware of yourself; you exist only in that quiet steady thrill which is so unlike any excitement you have ever known. Presently you get used to it. "What a fool I would have been if I hadn't come. I wouldn't have missed this run for the world."[50]

Cookson 12

Retreating under a German advance, Violetta Thurstan found that

> Danger always adds a spice to every entertainment, and as the wounded were all out and we had nobody but ourselves to think about, we could enjoy our thrilling departure from Lodz under heavy fire to the uttermost. And I must say I have rarely enjoyed anything more. It was simply glorious spinning along in that car.[51]

In another incident, when a Russian regiment began firing on a Taube, Thurstan admitted that she ran a much greater risk "of being killed by a Russian bullet than by the German Taube." But her overwhelming emotion seems to have been regret for her failure to bring along a camera to record the moment.[52]

Another nurse, who rode in a car being shelled by a Taube, noted, "It was great fun! I looked longingly at the fragments falling all over the road, but could not prevail upon the parson [the driver] to pull up whilst we gathered a few bits for presents to our home people."[53] It must be mentioned that this same nurse replied with the true British understatement of "Rather" when she was asked if she cared to eject a shell at the Boches.[54] Perhaps Violetta Thurstan summed up the seductive nature of the joy rides, daring escapes, and bombing activity when she wrote, "The forbidden has always charms."[55]

In spite of a certain devil-may-care attitude toward the danger to themselves, the British women were made fully aware of the effects of the war on the countries in which they resided and their peoples. The sights and sounds of the war were constant reminders of the bloody turmoil and struggle. One young VAD despaired, "Sometimes I wish I could make governments and politicians spend a month or two working with me. Can anyone justify so much blighting of young lives and crippling of young bodies?"[56]

Cookson 13

After watching refugees stream into Brussels, Violetta Thurstan realized for the first time what war entailed. She discerned, "It was not just rival armies fighting battles, it was civilians—men, women, and children—losing their homes, possessions, their country, even their lives."[57]

L. E. Fraser, working in the Serbian unit of the Scottish Women's Hospital, complained that

> The men who go home usually do not tell what they have seen,— they think it unfit for women to hear. Being a woman myself I have no such feelings and when I come home I shall tell every one I can what war really means. I believe that if every one quite realised it we should never have another war again. It is a cruel, senseless waste of life, and no one is finally any better for it.[58]

L. E. Fraser summed up her feelings succinctly. "War," she wrote, "is still the damn'dest piece of silliness the devil ever invented."[59]

Though sharing an abject horror of the war, the British women on the Continent also shared some pleasant memories. The nurses, doctors, and VADs did manage to get some time off duty. They went to teas and dinners, visited other villages, and entertained friends. These little everyday activities seemed to bring some semblance of security to the women. In the spring of 1916, one nurse remembered only the pleasant sights, "the quiet country-fields being plowed, birds building nests, larks soaring in the air."[60] The same woman remembered when she had

> . . . strolled along the banks of the little brooks where forget-me-nots fringed the edges, passed through farmyards where nuns in their quaint costumes sat on three-legged stools milking cows, and soldiers leaned over the gates laughing and chatting. By-the-by the sun sank, a ball of fire, while the mist rose like a veil from the low flat country.[61]

Cookson 14

A VAD who served in France recalled:

> There were bright moments when friends got down
> from the line for a 48-hour leave and with another girl
> as chaperone, as we were never allowed out by
> ourselves, we could bathe—it was the summer of
> 1917—and lunch, with someone near the door to see
> that the Commandant was not about.[62]

Perhaps it was these lighter, more pleasant activities that made
it possible for the British women to continue working. Their life
was not, after all, sheer unadulterated drudgery and despair.
The VADs and nurses were, for the most part, young women.
No doubt a touch of romance and beautiful spring weather
helped to make their work on the hospital wards more bearable.

In the fall of 1918, however, the war finally ended, and the
last of the British nurses, VADs, and doctors could go home
to England. But whether the women left while the war still
continued or held out until the war ended, they were
surprisingly unhappy and sad to leave. Many had found
friends and formed close relationships with their fellow
workers. While serving near the lines of action, the women
had had the satisfaction of knowing that they were directly
participating in the war effort.

One nurse remembered:

> In spite of the contact with suffering, misery and death,
> to us doctors and nurses there was a great share of
> happiness and the joy of life. It is a great thing to feel
> that you are fighting death and saving heroes, besides
> which we were a very happy crowd.[63]

Violetta Thurstan recalled tasting the "joys of companionship
to the full, the taking and giving, and helping and being
helped in a way that would be impossible to conceive in an
ordinary world."[64] One woman remembered the satisfaction of
"real hard work where [I was] . . . really needed."[65] Vera Brittain
was forced by the demands of her parents to leave France to

care for her mother. Once back in England she grieved "for the friendly, exhausting, peril-threatened existence [she] . . . had left behind in Etaples."[66]

Thus, the British women who served in Belgium, France, Italy, Serbia, Russia, and elsewhere had mixed feelings about their World War I experiences. For many, perhaps, the war brought the first taste of freedom; the young women were on their own and out of their parents' houses. The war was, without a doubt, a shocking and eye-opening experience, particularly for the relatively sheltered VADs. The sights of suffering and pain from war injuries had to be seen to be imagined and understood. Into what had been quiet and retiring lives, the war brought danger, excitement, fear, and the sense of participating in and living life to the utmost. Quiet Dr. Caroline Matthews underlined her passionate words, "Life was worth living in those days . . ."[67] Other side products of World War I for these women were the joys of companionship and the challenges and responsibilities of caring for severely wounded men. While the women on the whole felt sickened and saddened by the war debris—the dead, the dying, and the wounded—they invariably regretted leaving when their tenure ended.

One nurse wrote sadly upon her return to London, "life seemed flat after the stirring events through which we had just passed."[68] Vera Brittain recalled that for her the Armistice meant that "already this was a different world from the one I had known during the four long years. . . . And in that brightly lit, alien world I should have no part."[69] But it was Lesley Smith who most acutely discerned that the fun, adventures, exhilaration, despair, the living and participating in life to the fullest had ended. On the ship, returning home to England, Lesley reported with a sad kind of acceptance the question a kind and interested person asked, "I suppose you're going to settle down at home now and buy clothes and do the flowers for mother?"[70] It is significant that Lesley Smith failed to record her own reply.

Cookson 16

Notes

1. Quoted in Ruth Adam, *A Woman's Place, 1910-1975* (London: Chatto and Windus, 1975), 54.

2. Quoted in Dr. Caroline Matthews, *Experiences of a Woman Doctor in Serbia* (London: Mills and Boon, Ltd., 1916), ii.

3. Helen Fraser, *Women and War Work* (New York: G. Arnold Shaw, 1918), 55-56.

4. "Nurses for Military Hospitals," *Times* (London), May 7, 1915, 5c.

5. Louise Elliott Dalby, *The Great War and Women's Liberation*, Skidmore College Faculty Research Lecture (Saratoga Springs, NY: Skidmore College, 1970), 9.

6. "Nurses for Military Hospitals," *Times* (London), August 12,1916, 9c; see also Arthur Marwick, *Women at War, 1914-1918* (London: Fontana Paperbacks in association with the Imperial War Museum, 1977), 84.

7. Marwick, *Women at War*, 167-68.

8. Ibid.

9. Ibid.

10. "Nurses for Military Hospitals," *Times* (London), August 12, 1916, 9c.

11. "Military Hospitals an Urgent V.A.D. Appeal," *Times* (London), April 19, 1917, 9e.

12. Violetta Thurstan, *Field Hospital and Flying Column: Being the Journal of an English Nursing Sister in Belgium and Russia* (London: G. P. Putnam's Sons, 1915), 3.

13. Dalby, *The Great War*, 8.

14. Ibid.

15. *A War Nurse's Diary: Sketches from a Belgian Field Hospital* (New York: Macmillan, 1918), 3.

16. Ibid., 3, 4.

17. Ibid., 51.

18. Thurstan, *Field Hospital*, 6.

19. Vera Brittain, *Testament of Youth* (London: Wideview Books, 1980), 367.

20. May Sinclair, "The War of Liberation: From a Journal," *English Review* 20-21 (June-July 1915): 168.

21. Marwick, *Women at War*, 96.

22. Brittain, *Testament of Youth*, 210.

23. Sarah Macnaughtan, *A Woman's Diary of the War* (London: Thomas Nelson and Sons, n.d.), 27.

24. *A War Nurse's Diary*, 10.

25. Ibid., 10-11.

26. *Letters from a French Hospital* (Boston: Houghton Mifflin, 1917), 12-13.

27. Quoted in Brittain, *Testament of Youth*, 410.

28. Skia, "A Hospital in France," *Blackwood's Magazine*, November 1918, 621.

29. Quoted in David Mitchell, *Monstrous Regiment: The Story of the Women of the First World War* (New York: Macmillan, 1965), 201.

30. Brittain, *Testament of Youth*, 410.

31. Skia, "A Hospital in France," 622.

32. Thurstan, *Field Hospital*, 24.

33. *A War Nurse's Diary*, 20, 62.

34. Brittain, *Testament of Youth,* 380.

35. Mary Borden, *The Forbidden Zone* (London: William Heinemann, Ltd., 1929), 59-60.

36. Thekla Bowser, *Britain's Civilian Volunteers: Authorized Story of British Voluntary Aid Detachment Work in the Great War* (New York: Moffat, Yard and Company, 1917), 219.

37. Thurstan, *Field Hospital,* 136.

38. Helena Gleichen, "A Mobile X-Ray Section on the Italian Front," *Blackwood's Magazine,* July 1918,158.

39. *A War Nurse's Diary,* 22.

40. Macnaughtan, *A Woman's Diary of the War,* 41-42.

41. Brittain, *Testament of Youth,* 372.

42. Skia, "A Hospital in France," 638.

43. B. G. Mure, "A Side Issue of the War," *Blackwood's Magazine,* October 1916, 458.

44. Thurstan, *Field Hospital,* 77.

45. Matthews, *Experiences of a Woman Doctor,* 72.

46. *A War Nurse's Diary,* 38.

47. Mrs. St. Clair Stobart, "A Woman in the Midst of the War: The Remarkable Recital of a Woman Twice Sentenced to Be Shot, and Who Went through the History-Making Scenes of Louvain, Brussels, and Antwerp," *Ladies' Home Journal,* January 1915, 5.

48. Gleichen, "A Mobile X-Ray Section," 175.

49. Mure, "A Side Issue," 446.

50. Sinclair, "The War of Liberation," 170-71.

51. Thurstan, *Field Hospital,* 141-42.

Cookson 19

52. Ibid., 147.

53. *A War Nurse's Diary,* 59.

54. Ibid., 66.

55. Thurstan, *Field Hospital,* 103.

56. *Letters from a French Hospital,* 24.

57. Thurstan, *Field Hospital,* 11-12.

58. L. E. Fraser, "Diary of a Dresser in the Serbian Unit of the Scottish Women's Hospital," *Blackwood's Magazine,* June 1915, 796-97.

59. Ibid., 791.

60. *A War Nurse's Diary,* 94-95.

61. Ibid., 114-15.

62. Quoted in Marwick, *Women at War,* 99-100.

63. *A War Nurse's Diary,* 52-53.

64. Thurstan, *Field Hospital,*174.

65. Quoted in *Women War Workers: Accounts Contributed by Representative Workers of the Work Done by Women in the More Important Branches of War Employment,* ed. Gilbert Stone (New York: Thomas Y. Crowell Company, 1917), 183.

66. Brittain, *Testament of Youth,* 435.

67. Matthews, *Experiences of a Woman Doctor,* 72.

68. *A War Nurse's Diary,* 47-48.

69. Brittain, *Testament of Youth,* 463.

70. Quoted in Mitchell, *Monstrous Regiment,* 202.

Bibliography

Adam, Ruth. *A Woman's Place, 1910-1975*. London: Chatto and
     Windus, 1975.

Borden, Mary. *The Forbidden Zone*. London: William
     Heinemann, Ltd., 1929.

Bowser, Thekla. *Britain's Civilian Volunteers: Authorized Story of
     British Voluntary Aid Detachment Work in the Great War*.
     New York: Moffat, Yard and Company, 1917.

Brittain, Vera. *Testament of Youth*. London: Wideview Books,
     1980. First published 1933 in London by Victor Gollancz,
     Ltd.

Burke, Kathleen. *The White Road to Verdun*. New York: George
     H. Doran Company, 1916.

Dalby, Louise Elliott. *The Great War and Women's Liberation*.
     Skidmore College Faculty Research Lecture. Saratoga
     Springs, NY: Skidmore College, 1970.

Fraser, Helen. *Women and War Work*. New York: G. Arnold
     Shaw, 1918.

Fraser, L. E. "Diary of a Dresser in the Serbian Unit of the
     Scottish Women's Hospital." *Blackwood's Magazine*, June
     1915, 776-797.

Gleichen, Helena. "A Mobile X-Ray Section on the Italian
     Front." *Blackwood's Magazine*, July 1918, 145-177.

Letters from a French Hospital. Boston: Houghton Mifflin, 1917.

Macnaughtan, Sarah. *A Woman's Diary of the War*. London:
     Thomas Nelson and Sons, n.d.

Marwick, Arthur. *Women at War, 1914-1918*. London: Fontana
     Paperbacks in association with the Imperial War
     Museum, 1977.

Matthews, Dr. Caroline. *Experiences of a Woman Doctor in
     Serbia*. London: Mills and Boon, Ltd., 1916.

Cookson 21

McLaren, Barbara. *Women of the War.* New York: George H. Doran Company, 1918.

"Military Hospitals an Urgent V.A.D. Appeal." *Times* (London), April 19, 1917, 9e.

Mitchell, David. *Monstrous Regiment: The Story of the Women of the First World War.* New York: Macmillan, 1965.

Mure, B. G. "A Side Issue of the War." *Blackwood's Magazine,* October 1916, 444-469.

"Nurses for Military Hospitals." *Times* (London), May 7, 1915, 5c.

"Nurses for Military Hospitals." *Times* (London), August 12, 1916, 9c.

Sinclair, May. "The War of Liberation: From a Journal" *English Review* 20-21 (June-July 1915): 168-183, 303-314, 468-476.

Skia. "A Hospital in France." *Blackwood's Magazine,* November 1918, 613-640.

Stobart, Mrs. St. Clair. "A Woman in the Midst of the War: The Remarkable Recital of a Woman Twice Sentenced to Be Shot, and Who Went through the History-Making Scenes of Louvain, Brussels, and Antwerp." *Ladies' Home Journal,* January 1915, 4-5, 43-79.

Stone, Gilbert, ed. *Women War Workers: Accounts Contributed by Representative Workers of the Work Done by Women in the More Important Branches of War Employment.* New York: Thomas Y. Crowell, 1917.

Thurstan, Violetta. *Field Hospital and Flying Column: Being the Journal of an English Nursing Sister in Belgium and Russia.* London: G. P. Putnam's Sons, 1915.

A War Nurse's Diary: Sketches from a Belgian Field Hospital. New York: Macmillan, 1918.

Sorting Leaders and Outcasts   1

Running head: SORTING LEADERS AND OUTCASTS

A Paradigm of Social Sorting Rituals:
Differences between Leaders and Outcasts
Nicholas M. Joyce
Lewis & Clark College

Sorting Leaders and Outcasts   2

Abstract

Children are divided into peer preference groups based upon individual differences and the behaviors that they inspire. Although many researchers have focused upon aggression as the main factor determining a child's social placement, it is a narrow measure that oversimplifies a complex process. Aggression-based theories are useful in identifying children whose behavior indicates that they need help. But, to explain peer preference groups, a theory based upon personality traits is much more effective. Through a series of logical deductions, this theory codes children's differences in terms of the five-factor model of personality and social cognitive ability. The theory states that the prime attributes of social intelligence, neuroticism, and extraversion are found to be the main differentiating factors in children's placement in sociometric groups. The idea that leadership can be predicted through the same theory when it is considered in tandem with conscientiousness is also addressed.

A Paradigm of Social Sorting Rituals:
Differences between Leaders and Outcasts

Looking back at the world of our youth we remember that some children were popular while others were not. How children perceive their peers, and how and why children are sorted into social groups, have been the object of research. Newcomb, Bukowski, and Pattee (1993) acknowledge that most children (60-65%) will be rated as "average." However, psychologists have been mainly interested in children who find themselves in social extremes, children who are perceived as popular, rejected, neglected, or controversial. The interest of psychologists in children in social extremes is understandable; such social standings can have very real effects on a child's social and emotional development, leading some outcast children to have emotional disorders that in some cases will turn into delinquency (Parker & Asher, 1987). However, despite our ability to see the outcomes of this sorting process, the mechanisms responsible for it are debatable. I take issue with the current paradigm and the assumption that children are divided into peer preference groups based upon individual differences and the behaviors that they inspire.

Having read a large body of information on this topic, I have come up with a possible system by which children are socially sorted into peer preference groups. My theory tries to take a broader view of the subject matter, and moves to examine not just the individual, or a single individual difference, but the processes and social tactics that are pervasive in different types of children's attempts to be accepted. From these processes I have theorized factors which may be predictive of future social status. My theory is designed to find a common thread behind the sorting of a child into any of the sociometric classes, and to incorporate leadership into the model, not as a simple individual difference, but rather as an additional dimension within existing social groupings.

A Review of Literature on Social Sorting

The mechanisms that sort children into these groups have been a popular area of study. They have been studied from various angles, but most recent research explores individual differences. Research in this vein has been done in three rather distinct methods. Each method encapsulates a different way of identifying a child's sociometric class, a measurement of a child's social category. The first method is direct observation by the psychologist. This allows for fresh observations to be made, unbiased by prior experience with the children. The second method are self-reports from the children. This method is especially useful because it allows us a first-person perception of the child's social standing, as well as any attributions that the child makes about his or her successes or failures in the social setting. The third and most widely used method is a peer nomination system. In this system children nominate whom they actively like and dislike. This dimension is known as social preference, and measures the relative likeability of each child. In a more recent trend, psychologists have begun to measure a second dimension, social impact (Newcomb et al., 1993). Social impact is a quantifiable measure of how socially visible and noticed the child is. From these sociometric techniques researchers have divided children into four main categories: popular, controversial, rejected, and neglected.

Popular children are a sociometric group that is high in both social preference and impact. Once seen as homogeneous, children who were previously grouped together as popular have now been subdivided into popular-prosocial and popular-antisocial (Rodkin, Fanner, Pearl, & Van Acker,

2000). Popular-prosocial children are characterized by highly developed social skills and academic competence. They might be assertive, but are not overtly aggressive. While children in both peer groupings enjoy popularity with their peers, popular-antisocial children possess highly aggressive temperaments that are not common in popular-prosocial children. They are poorer students than their prosocial counterparts, and often suffer from disciplinary problems. However, these children have sophisticated social skills and usually possess a trait, in most cases athleticism, that makes other children view them as "cool," and allows them to get away with behaviors such as starting fights and being disruptive (Rodkin et al., 2000) that would otherwise be grounds for rejection.

Controversial children are characterized by a very high sociometric rating in social impact, but receive many nominations of both active like and dislike in social preference. These children are often class clowns who display many anti-social behaviors, but have many positive social interactions with their peers. Given their high number of friends, most controversial children are happy with their peer relationships (Newcomb et al., 1993). Because they feel a high degree of acceptance they do not experience greater than average social distress (Crick & Ladd, 1993) and can develop normally in regards to emotional and social skills despite negative behaviors such as inappropriate outbursts. For children this stage is most often temporary, and the controversial child usually moves into an average or popular grouping.

Rejected children have many social problems and fail to fit in. They have high social impact ratings and receive many peer nominations of active dislike. In research by Parker and Asher (1987), children in the rejected category often have a large number of anti-social traits that can contribute to poor school performance and absenteeism. These issues can lead to dropping out and delinquency in early adult life. Also, children who are rejected exhibit a high degree of social stress that may lead to further maladaptive behaviors (Crick & Ladd, 1993). This sociometric category, like that of popular children, has recently been subdivided into two categories: rejected-aggressive and rejected-withdrawn. Rejected-aggressive children, as the term indicates, are highly aggressive. Their social interactions are often perceived as acts of hostility, as they try to force themselves into groups. In addition, they will interpret other children's behaviors as hostile because they perceive themselves to be actively disliked and have come to expect it (Crick & Ladd, 1993). Rejected-withdrawn children are a smaller subgroup that does not exhibit the overt aggression of their counterparts. Instead, being plagued by social anxiety, incompetence, and submissive social tactics, they are highly withdrawn and lonely. Like their counterparts they, too, also misinterpret social cues.

Neglected children, the fourth basic sociometric category, are also highly withdrawn. However, unlike rejected-withdrawn children, they do not suffer from the same social anxieties and will usually be actively liked by at least one peer (Crick & Ladd, 1993). They are characterized by low social impact ratings and neutral ratings of likeability (Newcomb et al., 1993). Though most possess social skills on the level of average children, they lead socially withdrawn lives, satisfied with lower key social standing. However, given their potential for normal interaction most children are in this grouping temporarily (Newcomb et al., 1993).

Though not usually connected with the four aforementioned categories, leadership and social dominance can play a large role in the social life of a child (Pettit, Bakshi,

Sorting Leaders and Outcasts   7

Dodge, & Coie, 1990). Although it would not be accurate to replace one of the four existing sociometric categories with leadership, or even to add a fifth, leadership does add a dimension to existing sociometric classes that allows for more specificity in determining a child's sociometric status. Leaders are often chosen based on their visible competence in a given field (Hogan, Curphy, & Hogan, 1994). This makes the best candidates for leadership popular children and controversial children, as they both receive high social impact scores as well as votes of approval. Neglected children's social skills are not visible enough to warrant being awarded social leadership, and rejected children have too little social competence and are too widely disliked to be considered leadership material. Social competence is an amalgamation of several factors including social cognitive skills, dyadic and group interaction skills, peer group entry skills, and appropriate affective expectancies (Keane, Brown, & Crenshaw, 1990). All of these factors are very important in determining not only qualifications to be in certain peer preference groups but the ability to be an effective social leader.

One of the reasons that leadership is an important factor to consider is that much of the research on the personality factors involved in leadership can be applied to the personality theories of peer preference. In a meta-analysis of the correlation between the big five traits and leadership, Judge, Bono, Ilies, and Gerhardt (2002) found that extraversion and conscientiousness were the two most highly correlated to leadership, at $r = .31$ and $.28$ respectively. They found a negative correlation to neuroticism of $r = .24$. Previous research had described self-confidence as the primary trait involved in leadership. High self-confidence is often correlated with low scores of neuroticism, which supports the data found in the study by Judge et al.

There are many important factors affecting the social status of children; however, many psychologists focus on one trait that they feel is most responsible. A review of the research indicates that aggression tends to be cited as the key mechanism in explaining sociometric differences between children (Newcomb et al., 1993). However, with so many other pieces to the puzzle, it seems to me that relying on one individual difference to explain a whole range of possible outcomes is overly simplistic. Newcomb et al. argue for a multi-factor system using other behaviors such as withdrawal and sociability. I agree that a multi-factor system makes more sense, but I would also argue that, rather than using smaller bandwidth traits measured through behavioral studies, psychologists should use larger personality traits that would be tested separately from behavior. Behaviors can be measured only after the fact, whereas personality traits are relatively stable over time. This makes pre-testing for probable social outcome a possibility. To this end, my theory takes note of children's social tactics and attributions, and uses that data to correlate sociometric grouping with several of the traits in the big five-factors model as presented by McCrae and Costa (1996). Using current data, my theory creates a relatively simple multi-factored approach that narrows down children's personality traits to those that differentiate and predict a child's placement in a sociometric grouping, including leadership positions. My theory postulates that the main personality factors that differentiate one child from another are extraversion, neuroticism, and conscientiousness. Beyond personality traits, my theory proposes that social intelligence is another factor that is highly predictive of a child's peer preference group placement.

Aggression-Based Theories

Although many psychologists have come up with multi-factor models of peer preference groups that involve the common factors of aggression, sociability, and withdrawal (Newcomb et al., 1993), many of them take aggression to be the key factor, the one that is responsible for the most effect. Aggression is most often used to explain the specific mechanism behind rejection. Many psychologists choose to focus only on rejected children and how they get there, because they feel that popular children don't need help and thus do not warrant the further investigation that rejected children have received (Rodkin et al., 2000).

Not only is the idea of aggression as a singular mechanism in rejection overly simplistic, but there is direct evidence that contradicts it. There are two particular examples within existing research that prove to be exceptions to the proposition that overt aggression will be met by rejection in social situations. Both popular anti-social and controversial children have been shown to have high levels of aggression and hostile behavior (Rodkin et al., 2000). Because children in both of these peer groups maintain popularity despite moderate to high levels of aggression, aggression cannot be the primary cause of rejection. Also there is a substantial minority of rejected children whose behaviors are not aggressive. Rejected-withdrawn children suffer from rejection, for example, because of high degrees of withdrawal, and low degrees of sociability.

Even those people who have recommended moving to a more flexible multi-factor construct of the social sorting mechanism still most commonly focus on and study attributes such as aggression, withdrawal, sociability, and cognitive ability (Newcomb et al., 1993). There is a large body of research that is done using the five-factor model of personality. None of the three factors commonly used in sociometric studies have a direct equivalent in the five-factor model. A lot of individual differences research on personality is done using this five-factor model, and so to use different standards when discussing peer preference groups makes comparisons across condition types outside of the immediate body of work difficult.

My Multi-Factor Social Hierarchy Paradigm

Rather than focusing on aggression, which I feel does not account for the entire sorting process, my theory attempts to translate children's described behaviors and their consequences into the five-factor model. I contend that the mechanism for social sorting into peer preference groups is the action taken by a child, and the child acts as she does because of her personality configuration. More specifically, neuroticism and extraversion play the largest roles in differentiating one sociometric group from another. Further I would say that conscientiousness is the key attribute in predicting leadership roles within a peer preference group. Finally, I would say that social intelligence is an important factor in explaining a child's acceptance or rejection.

In the five-factor model, extraversion is defined as "the tendency to be sociable, assertive, active, and to experience positive affects, such as energy and zeal" (Judge et al., 2002, p. 767). Children who lack extraverted tendencies will be more withdrawn than other children. This can lead children to be sorted into neglected and rejected-withdrawn peer groupings. Children who have a high degree of extraversion will go out and try to interact with a peer group. Thus extroversion, in conjunction with varying degrees of neurosis and social intelligence, can explain differentiations in peer preference groupings. In the five-factor model, neuroticism is defined as "the tendency to exhibit poor emotional adjustment and experience negative affects, such as anxiety, insecurity, and hostility" (Judge et al., 2002, p. 767). For children who are neurotic, social anxiety wreaks havoc on their abilities to perform positively in a social setting. It also encourages them to attribute social failures entirely to their own inadequacies (Crick & Ladd, 1993). Many of the attributes outlined in the definition of neurotic are often applied to rejected children of both the aggressive and withdrawn variety (Newcomb et al., 1993).

Although the relationship of intelligence and cognitive ability to sociometric status has been examined (Newcomb et al., 1993), it has mostly been under the guise of academic prowess. The problem with measuring academic intelligence is that there is evidence that academic prowess does not have to exist in popular children, and can be found in intelligent rejected children (Rodkin et al., 2000). For example, children who are popular-antisocial are often not in good academic standing, but are popular and socially gifted. For this reason, academic intelligence does not prove to be a good differentiating factor between groups.

Much more pertinent to the prediction of a child's placement in a social group is social intelligence. Social intelligence is an idea that has been talked about extensively in modern debates about the nature of intelligence. Howard Gardner, in his book entitled *Intelligence Reframed: Multiple Intelligences for the 21st Century* (1999), talks about two specific types of intelligence that are essential to most people's idea of social intelligence. "Interpersonal intelligence," he tells us, "denotes a person's capacity to understand the intentions, motivations, and desires of other people and, consequently, to work effectively with others" (p. 43). This intelligence is crucial to overt dealings with others in a social setting. Children who end up as social leaders will be high in this type of intelligence. The second component to social intelligence is intrapersonal intelligence: "Intrapersonal intelligence involves the capacity to understand oneself—including one's own desires, fears, and capacities— and to use such information effectively in regulating one's life" (p. 43). Someone who had low intrapersonal intelligence would definitely be prone to several of the aspects of neurosis. Conversely, children who possessed high intrapersonal intelligence would know their limits and make realistic attributions about any problems in social interactions.

Although social intelligence does partially overlap with the big five factor of agreeableness, it is not fully captured within its confines. People who are agreeable are described as sympathetic, cooperative, likeable, compliant in a friendly way, and having a need for affiliation (Hogan et al., 1994). The reason that I do not include agreeableness in my model is that it adds unnecessary complications to a model that, while multi-factored, is designed to be as simple and as fluid as possible. I have left out agreeableness, as well as openness to experience, for the reason that they do not sufficiently differentiate one sociometric group from another nor adequately describe a salient difference between groups. On the other hand, though not part of the standard big five, social intelligence is a larger trait that describes the possession of social skills highly important in understanding the division between the socially accepted and rejected.

Finally, the trait of conscientiousness plays heavily into acquisition of leadership roles. Conscientiousness is described as someone's level of achievement and dependability (Judge et al., 2002). As was mentioned earlier, leadership selection studies have shown that people are usually nominated for positions of leadership when they display clear and consistent efficacy in the field of the nomination (Hogan et al., 1994). Other personality traits grouped under conscientiousness include ambition, will to achieve, and need for achievement. These traits, most especially ambition, are highly correlated in most studies with the concept of leadership.

A Synopsis of Sociometric Groupings within My Theory

Rejected-Withdrawn

Children who are rejected-withdrawn have removed themselves from the main parts of social interactions with peers. They are non-sociable and lack active and assertive social tactics. From this description of rejected-withdrawn children, it can be said that they have a low degree of extraversion. Although they are more aware of their social failings than their more aggressive counterparts (Crick & Dodge, 1994), their submissive and inept style of interaction would suggest a low degree of practical social intelligence. They also internalize social failures and suffer from a high degree of anxiety and fear regarding social situations. The degree to which these fears rule over their lives disables them in terms of their ability to break out of their cycle of self-doubt and loneliness. These are the patented marks of someone who is high in neuroticism.

Neglected

Neglected children are characterized by their withdrawn nature, but they have a healthy disposition regarding their solitary state. Because of their withdrawal and their lack of assertive social tactics, it can be said that these children are low in extraversion. However, they do not suffer from the social anxiety that plagues rejected-withdrawn children, and thus they do not have the same sorts of emotional problems. This would tend to suggest a fairly low amount of neuroticism, or conversely a good deal of emotional stability. Longitudinal studies have shown that people of this peer

Sorting Leaders and Outcasts   14

preference group can enter easily into normal social situations later in life, and even their brief interactions while children, even though they are still withdrawn, show signs of competence (Newcomb et al., 1993). These are the signs of people who have a fair amount of social intelligence.

Controversial

Controversial children are highly extraverted. They are characterized as extremely outgoing and sociable. However, these children can alienate some of their peers with their aggressive social tactics, giving them a fair number of votes of active disliking. However, they participate in enough healthy socializing to receive a large number of liking votes as well. This inconsistent behavior speaks to a lack of conscientiousness on the part of the controversial child. He or she is usually rated as sociable and friendly as popular children, despite sometimes disruptive behavior (Newcomb et al., 1993), speaking to a large degree of practical social intelligence. Children who are controversial do not report high degrees of loneliness, anxiety, or social phobias, which would tend to speak to a high ranking in emotional stability.

Popular-Antisocial

Popular-antisocial children are similar in many ways to controversial children. Their behavior can be somewhat disruptive, and yet they are still afforded many peer votes of liking. This, however, is where the similarities stop. Whereas a controversial child is usually similar to a class clown who is sociable and outgoing, children who are popular-antisocial do not have the same degree of sociability. When considering these children in terms of extraversion, one has to be careful. While characterized as active and assertive, they are not described as sociable, despite what might be viewed as Machiavellian social skills. Because of the split nature of their extraversion, it would be rated lower than that of individuals classified as popular-prosocial or controversial. While these children are not highly neurotic, they are not entirely emotionally stable either, and are at times overtly hostile and aggressive. However, these children are high in interpersonal social intelligence, and are able to use it to mask their hostility. But they are low in intrapersonal intelligence, which causes the aggression to begin with. These children are also fairly high in conscientiousness, since they are consistently good at keeping friends and being seen as worthwhile through their exploitation of their athletic abilities.

Rejected-Aggressive

Rejected-aggressive children are extraverted in terms of their assertiveness, but their low degree of social intelligence does not provide them with constructive ways to act on it. For this reason their extroversion is almost always seen as aggressive hostility by other children; rejected children's tactics are met with some disdain. Rejected children will often immediately use high-risk social tactics from the start, thus showing a lack of practical social intelligence. Because these children have an inflated sense of their social skills, they will continue to misinterpret intention cues and will continue to use faulty social tactics (Crick & Ladd, 1993; Keane et al., 1990). Their efforts are often seen as disruptive by peers, they are rejected from the peer group and sometimes ostracized for their previous efforts (Newcomb et al., 1993). The child will internally attribute these social outcomes (Crick & Ladd, 1993) and as a result will suffer a great deal of social anxiety, which correlates with a high degree of neuroticism.

Popular-Prosocial

These children exemplify the features of extraversion, including sociability, positive affect, assertiveness, and activity. Their interactions with children are viewed as healthy and productive. They are socially intelligent, which can be seen in

Sorting Leaders and Outcasts   16

interaction styles that are described as a mix between assertiveness and fairness (Newcomb et al., 1993). When things go wrong they do not unnecessarily internally attribute the problem. They do not suffer from most social anxiety, revealing a very low degree of neuroticism. They are also very conscientious as seen by their high achievement and dependability.

Leadership

In my theory leadership is an additive trait. People have to be consistent, competent, and visible in order to be chosen as leaders (Hogan et al., 1994; Judge et al., 2002). Because child leaders are social leaders, they have to be high in, or at least be perceived as high in, social intelligence. Because of this requirement, the sociometric groups most likely to contain leaders are the popular-prosocial and the popular-antisocial—and the controversial, if only for those who are liked. Neglected children do not have the visibility to be considered leaders. Rejected children are most definitely perceived as having low social skills, which would disqualify them even if they had someone to lead to begin with. Extraversion, in the end, is the most important trait in terms of leadership, as people who are more extraverted are more visibly sociable (Judge et al., 2002).

Conclusions

Aggression-based theories are legitimate in terms of the use to which they are put. It is true that children who have aggression issues can benefit from intervention and help. However, focusing on a single trait or even a set of traits that is designed only to locate those who need help has limited potential as an analytical tool. This is why I feel it is necessary to construct a theory that will help categorize all children from the start, not just when maladaptive behavior starts to manifest in the form of aggression. Personality traits are relatively stable, whereas behavior can change given the context. Children do not start out rejected or alienated from the group. However, once the cycle starts it is very difficult to reverse the situation, as both the child and his/her peers will have expectations of the status quo that are hard to break.

This theory is constructed using logical proofs and is thus subject to criticism on the grounds that it has not been tested. In order to test my hypothesis it would be necessary to do a longitudinal study, starting with personality testing before the children enter into the common social setting. Then after the peer preference groups have formed, data would be collected and correlated with the personality data collected earlier. In terms of prevention, I believe that psychologists must try to head off problems before they become engrained and much more difficult to remove. Children must be reached before their maladaptive personality traits are turned to maladaptive behaviors, and the children are alienated. On a positive note, I feel that it is also important to train children how to be good leaders. My theory is designed to predict a child's placement in any of the sociometric categories. If my theory proves to be a predictive measurement, we would have a test that could pick out both the potential outcasts and leaders before they were unleashed upon their peers, and society would have a chance to head off a fair amount of social angst.

Sorting Leaders and Outcasts   18

References

Crick, N. R., & Dodge, K. A. (1994). A review and reformulation of social information-processing mechanisms in children's social adjustment. *Psychological Bulletin, 115,* 74-101.

Crick, N. R., & Ladd, G. W. (1993). Children's perceptions of their peer experiences: Attributions, loneliness, social anxiety, and social avoidance. *Developmental Psychology, 29,* 244-254.

Gardner, H. (1999). *Intelligence reframed: Multiple intelligences for the 21st century.* New York: Basic Books.

Hogan, R., Curphy, G. J., & Hogan, J. (1994). What we know about leadership: Effectiveness and personality. *American Psychologist, 49,* 493-504.

Judge, T. A., Bono, J. E., Ilies, R., & Gerhardt, M. W. (2002). Personality and leadership: A qualitative and quantitative review. *Journal of Applied Psychology, 87,* 765-780.

Keane, S. P., Brown, K. P., & Crenshaw, T. M. (1990). Children's intention-cue detection as a function of maternal social behavior: Pathways to social rejection. *Developmental Psychology, 26,* 1004-1009.

McCrae, R. R., & Costa, P. T., Jr. (1996). Toward a new generation of personality theories: Theoretical contexts for the five-factor model. In J. S. Wiggins (Ed.), *The five-factor model of personality: Theoretical perspectives* (pp. 51-87). New York: Guilford.

Newcomb, A. F., Bukowski, W. M., & Pattee, L. (1993). Children's peer relations: A meta-analytic review of popular, rejected, neglected, controversial, and average sociometric status. *Psychological Bulletin, 113,* 99-128.

Parker J. G., & Asher, S. R. (1987). Peer relations and later personal adjustment: Are low-accepted children at risk? *Psychological Bulletin, 102,* 357-389.

Sorting Leaders and Outcasts   19

Pettit, G. S., Bakshi, A., Dodge, K. A., & Coie, J. D. (1990). The
emergence of social dominance in young boys' play
groups: Developmental differences and behavioral
correlates. *Developmental Psychology, 26,* 1017-1025.

Rodkin, P. C., Fanner, T. W., Pearl, R., & Van Acker, R. (2000).
Heterogeneity of popular boys: Antisocial and prosocial
configurations. *Developmental Psychology, 36,* 14-24.

An Investigation of Human Diving:
How Do the Ama Avoid Decompression Sickness?

Mary Bricker
Lewis & Clark College
Environmental Physiology
Professor Kellar Autumn

Bricker 1

The ama are professional breath-hold divers in Asia who make frequent, repeated dives to gather marine mollusks and seaweed. This traditional harvesting method dates back nearly 2000 years (Holm and others 1998) and is still practiced, with a few modern innovations, along the coast of Japan and Korea. These divers dive with filled lungs but no external air supply to depths up to 15-20 m (Mohri and others 1995), raising the possibility of decompression sickness due to dissolved nitrogen in the bloodstream. However, decompression illness is not reported as a problem for these divers (Hong and others 1963). In this paper, I will investigate some of the physiological literature on breath-hold divers, to understand if there are physiological adaptations or acclimatizations that allow the ama to perform without being affected by decompression sickness.

Decompression sickness, also known as diver's disease, bends, caisson's disease, or aeroembolism, occurs when a person who has been at depth (generally 20 m or more) returns to the surface. Greater depths and longer times submerged increase the severity of the problems (Schmidt-Nielson 1997). Symptoms, which include joint pain, difficulty breathing, blurred vision, and abdominal pain, happen because the higher pressures (pressure increases rapidly with depth in water) drive nitrogen, which is usually a biologically inert gas, into the bloodstream where it can also saturate tissues. The problem of the bends arises when the subject is returned to normal pressure with the nitrogen still in solution in the blood. The nitrogen returns to gas at the lower pressure, expanding to form bubbles; these can occlude or rupture smaller blood vessels, causing tissue damage and lesions in nerve tissue. This is particularly dangerous when it occurs in the central nervous system (Schmidt-Nielson 1997).

It is most commonly seen in scuba divers, and elaborate tables have been calculated to regulate how long a diver must spend at different depths or pressures to allow for the slow elimination of the nitrogen from the tissues through the blood and the lungs.

It would seem that this problem could arise for any air-breathing animal that regularly dives to depths, such as the marine mammals. However, most of the diving mammals have evolved adaptations that prevent this problem. For instance, most marine mammals, unlike humans, exhale before diving, and do not rely on oxygen in the lung for the duration of their dive. Measurements of the blood nitrogen levels of Weddell seals show that, as they reach depths of about 50 m, their lungs collapse, forcing all of the air that is trapped in the lungs into the trachea and bronchi. These areas are rigid and do not exchange gas with the bloodstream (Falke and others 1985). Because of this, nitrogen is not entering the bloodstream after the lungs are collapsed and, upon surfacing, dissolved nitrogen will not present a problem. Diving mammals have many other adaptations to diving as well, which serve to extend the times that they are able to dive, but which have little or no direct bearing on their absorption of nitrogen (Davis and Kanatous 1999).

However, because humans generally lack these greater oxygen stores and adaptations for efficient diving, they must dive with their lungs inflated. Because of the increased pressure on the lung air at depth, nitrogen passes from the lungs into blood during the entire dive. While in the past it was thought that humans were simply incapable, without supplemental air, of diving to depths great enough, or staying submerged long enough, to develop nitrogen bubbles, several cases in the early 60's showed that this is not the case (Paulev

1965). The Swedish physician P. Paulev, performing escape
practice maneuvers in a navy training tank, developed
symptoms of decompression sickness after spending five
hours doing repetitive breath-hold dives of about two minutes
duration (slightly over a minute at depth, with 40-55 seconds
spent in ascent and descent) to depths of 15-20 m. He rested
for one to two minutes at the surface between dives and made
a total of about 60. Soon after this series of dives, he
developed the classic symptoms of decompression sickness,
including nausea, dizziness, followed by joint pain, severe
chest pain, blurred vision, and numbness in the hands. He was
treated according to Navy treatment tables, spending almost
20 hours in a recompression chamber coming gradually back
to standard pressure. Paulev (1965) also describes several
similar cases which occurred at the same facility.

    This clearly shows that nitrogen poisoning is possible in
breath-hold diving. This leads us back to the ama divers, who
regularly make frequent, consecutive breath-hold dives. Why
do they not suffer the effects of aeroembolism? There are
several possible ways that the ama could avoid decompression sickness while breath-hold diving. There could be
physiological processes or mechanisms that enable them to
dive longer and deeper than would be expected for the
average human without suffering from nitrogen problems.
Alternatively, it is possible that the depths and times that they
dive are not sufficient to move enough nitrogen into the blood
to be problematic upon ascent.

    Physiological investigations indicate that the ama have
many processes that are conditioned to make them more
effective divers, but the direct effects of these adaptations or
acclimatizations on the absorption of nitrogen into the
bloodstream is not very clear.

Bricker 4

Many of the features of the ama physiology are typical of the mammalian diving reflex, which is a set of responses to cold water contacting receptors in the face, and include apnea, bradycardia, and peripheral vasoconstriction (Irving 1963; Song and others 1969). Divers and trained swimmers generally show a heightened dive response (Holm and others 1998). Actively diving ama do show a marked bradycardia and reduction in peripheral blood flow when diving (Radermacher and others 1992), but because their muscles are still active as they work, the muscle tissue remains perfused despite the initial vasoconstriction. Blood flow to the muscles does not decline significantly during actual dives (Radermacher and others 1992). While most of the blood flow adjustment expected from the dive response would defend against cold, it does not necessarily help protect against nitrogen bubble formation. However, if most of the recovery took place with the muscles not well perfused (at rest), this could slow the actual release of nitrogen back into the blood, keeping the overall blood concentration fairly low.

This is similar to the argument used by Falke and others (1985) for Weddell seals; they found that the seals, which collapsed their lungs, actually decreased their blood N_2 level as they dived, as N_2 was deposited in other tissues, particularly muscle and blubber. This allowed for slower elimination of the nitrogen, at a later time, so the blood N_2 level was never very high. A study looking directly at the blood nitrogen level in the ama, during and after shifts of diving (Radermacher and others 1992), found that blood N_2 quickly reached a plateau level of 635 torr (base level being 584 torr) and that it declined much more slowly, starting immediately after the work shift was over.

Bricker 5

Another difference in the ama is that they do have higher lung volumes than non-diving individuals from the same area, and more developed inhalation muscles (Song and others 1963). Furthermore, this study showed that the ama were able, because of the high partial pressure of O_2 at depth, to extract far more oxygen from the air in the lungs than is possible under normal pressure. Again, while this may help them dive for long periods of time, it does not suggest that they would be any less susceptible to nitrogen bubble formation, and would in fact lend support to the idea that N_2 would also be extracted from the air in the lungs.

One of the most significant challenges for the ama is the low temperature of the water they are diving in. The ama are able to tolerate very low body temperatures, and during long dives, their skin temperature can become very close to the temperature of the surrounding water (Kang and others 1963). Another physiological distinction of the ama is a change in metabolic rate, which varies with the seasonal temperature fluctuations of the water they are working in. In the winter, the divers have a significantly higher metabolic rate than non-divers living in the same area (Kang and others 1963). But this is another example of a trait that, though interesting, would actually work toward making it possible for the ama to dive longer, and thus indirectly make them more susceptible to the possibility of nitrogen poisoning.

Since the physiological data do not fully support the idea that the ama are somehow better adapted to avoid nitrogen poisoning than the average human, a closer examination of the actual diver patterns is in order, and a consideration of the work patterns they use, which might also serve to protect them. A comparison of dive profiles from the various populations of ama in these studies reveals that the diving

Bricker 6

Study	Dive Depth	Time at Depth	Dives/ Shift
Paulev 1965	15-20 m	80 s	60
Radermacher and			
others 1992	4-6 m	30-45 s	60-80
Mohri and others 1995			
funado (assisted)	22 m	60 s	25-65
cachido (unassisted)	15-17 m	60 s	80-100
Hong and others 1963	5-7 m	20-40 s	40-50
Holm and others 1998	2-4 m	30-100 s	not reported

Figure 1: Comparison of the dive characteristics of divers who
did (Paulev) and did not (all others listed)
experience symptoms of decompression sickness.

times and depths are variable, with large differences between
groups in different areas (Figure 1). It also shows that though
many of the groups dive as deep as the Swedish physician
who contracted decompression sickness (Paulev 1965), or
stay at depth for as long, or make as many dives, none of
them combine all three of these dive characteristics.

The fact that the cold water limits the time that the divers
can spend at depth may help keep them from being under
high pressure long enough to load enough nitrogen to
become problematic. Especially in areas where local fishing
unions prevent the use of wetsuits (to curtail overharvesting
of mollusks), the work shifts are generally structured around
the temperature of the water at that particular season, and
how quickly they become too chilled to work (Hong and
others 1963). While there is evidence that the female ama, at
least, are more tolerant of cold temperatures than most

Bricker 7

people (Kang and others 1963), they still must stop diving to re-warm. This is notably different from the Swedish case, where the water temperature was "comfortable," and Paulev (1965) was able to continue diving for nearly five hours.

The idea that the work patterns of the ama are more important than the physiological changes is supported by a study of elderly ama males who are still diving, which found that the marked response of bradycardia and lowered peripheral blood flow was not different from that of non-diving persons of the same age, and was significantly lower than that of young divers (Holm and others 1998). Even with a declining dive response, these divers are able to meet the demands of the typical day of diving, and nitrogen poisoning still does not pose a problem.

In conclusion, the ama appear to have a series of acclimatizations to the high pressure, low oxygen, cold atmosphere in which they work. Some of these may help to reduce the instances of nitrogen poisoning, but most of them serve to enhance their ability, relative to other humans, to free dive to significant depths in relatively cold water. The major reason they do not suffer from bends, however, seems to stem from harvest methods and behaviors that prevent them from being at depth long enough to absorb significant amounts of nitrogen into their blood. An interesting comparison could be made between populations of divers in cold and warm water climates. The literature on free divers in warm areas, such as the Caribbean, is much sparser than on the ama; this could be an area of interesting further investigation, as it is possible that if the water were warm enough for divers to spend longer periods submerged, they might experience more problems with nitrogen poisoning, and incidences of decompression sickness would be more common in divers in the tropics.

Bricker 8

Literature Cited

Davis RW, Kanatous SB. 1999. Convective oxygen transport and tissue oxygen consumption in Weddell seals during aerobic dives. J Exp Biol 202:1091-1113.

Falke KJ, Hill RD, Qvist J, Schneider RC, Guppy M, Liggins GC, Hochachka PW, Elliot RE, Zapol WM. 1985. Seal lungs collapse during freediving: evidence from arterial nitrogen tensions. Science 229:556-558.

Holm B, Schagatay E, Kobayashi T, Masuda A, Ohdaira T, Honda Y. 1998. Cardiovascular change in elderly male breath-hold divers (ama) and their socio-economical background at Chikura in Japan. J Physiol Anthropol Appl Human Sci 17(5):181-187.

Hong SK, Rahn H, Kang DH, Song SH, Kang BS. 1963. Diving patterns, lung volumes, and alveolar gas of the Korean diving woman (ama). J App Physiol 18:457-465.

Irving L. 1963. Bradycardia in human divers. J App Physiol 18:489-491.

Kang, BS, Song SH, Suh CS, Hong SK. 1963. Changes in body temperature and basal metabolic rate of the ama. J App Physiol 18:483-488.

Mohri M, Torii R, Nagaya K, Shiraki K, Elsner R, Tekeuchi H, Park YS, Hong SK. 1995. Diving patterns of ama divers of Hegura Island, Japan. Undersea & Hyperbaric Med 22(2):137-143.

Paulev, P. 1965. Decompression sickness following repeated breath-hold dives. J App Physiol 20:1028-31.

Radermacher P, Falke KJ, Park YS, Ahn DW, Hong SK, Qvist J, Zapol WM. 1992. Nitrogen tensions in brachial vein blood of Korean ama divers. J App Physiol 73:2592-2595.

Scmidt-Nielsen, K. 1997. Animal physiology: adaptation and environment. Cambridge: Cambridge Univ Pr.

Bricker 9

Song SH, Kang DH, Kang BS, Hong SK. 1963. Lung volumes and ventilatory responses to high CO_2 and low O_2 in the ama. J App Physiol 18:466-470.

Song SH, Lee WK, Chung YA, Hong SK. 1969. Mechanism of apneic bradycardia in man. J App Physiol 27:323-327.

Index